# Better Homes and Gardens®

# the *ultimate* appetizers book

More than **450** no-fuss nibbles and drinks
Plus simple party planning tips

**WILEY**

John Wiley & Sons, Inc.

For general information on our other products and services or for technical support, please contact our Customer Care Department within the United States at (877) 762–2974, outside the United States at (317) 572–3993 or fax (317) 572–4002.

Wiley also publishes its books in a variety of electronic formats. Some content that appears in print may not be available in electronic books. For more information about Wiley products, visit our web site at www.wiley.com.

Library of Congress Cataloging-in-Publication Data:

The ultimate appetizers book : more than 450 no-fuss nibbles and drinks, plus simple party planning tips.

    p. cm.

  Cover title: At head of title: Better homes and gardens the ultimate appetizers book

  Includes index.

  ISBN 978-0-470-63414-1 (pbk.)

  1. Appetizers. I. Better homes and gardens. II. Title: Better homes and gardens the ultimate appetizers book. III. Title: Better homes and gardens the ultimate appetizers book.

  TX740.U47 2010

  641.8'12--dc22

        2010016418

Printed in the United States of America

10 9 8 7 6 5 4 3 2 1

**Meredith Corporation**

Editor: Jan Miller

Contributing Editor: Lois White

Recipe Development and Testing: Better Homes and Gardens® Test Kitchen

**John Wiley & Sons, Inc.**

Publisher: Natalie Chapman

Associate Publisher: Jessica Goodman

Executive Editor: Anne Ficklen

Editor: Charleen Barila

Production Editor: Jacqueline Beach

Production Director: Diana Cisek

Interior Design: Jill Budden

Layout: Holly Wittenberg

Manufacturing Manager: Tom Hyland

Our seal assures you that every recipe in *The Ultimate Appetizers Book* has been tested in the Better Homes and Gardens® Test Kitchen. This means that each recipe is practical and reliable and meets our high standards of taste appeal. We guarantee your satisfaction with this book for as long as you own it.

Pictured:
Chicken-Spinach Soup,
page 325

**Pictured:**
**Buffalo-Style Chicken**
**Fingers, page 118**

# table of
# contents

Mmmmm . . . awesome party food!

Make food the hit at your next party, whether you're having a few friends over for cocktails and nibbles or hosting a neighborhood fiesta.

No matter what the occasion is—casual, dressy, or just plain fun—the recipes and ideas in this beautifully photographed collection are sure to inspire lively conversation and create the easiest and most enjoyable of gatherings. Wow the crowd with an array of classics, from finger-friendly nachos and ever-popular deviled eggs to jazzed-up meatballs and chicken wings. These crowd-pleasing nibbles never go out of style. Their casual ease—their "everybody-loves-'em" appeal—makes them a hit every time.

When the occasion calls for something more sophisticated, please palates with elegant pastries, cheesy hors d'oeuvres, rich bisques and chowders, or even global-inspired offerings, such as sushi. Round out your menu with stylish cocktails and drinks, guaranteed to go with just about anything.

Short on time? Take advantage of the make-ahead options included with many of the recipes. You'll also discover party menus, tips on tabletop décor, and a rundown of versatile ingredients to keep on hand. With help like this, throwing a party has never been so easy!

Pictured:
**Balsamic Shallot and
Goat Cheese Tart,**
page 168

1

party

bas

If you're new to the scene of at-home entertaining, look here for tantalizing tips on planning and pulling off a feast of appetizers. Our ideas for party-ready ingredients and themed menus will help you entertain friends and family with ease.

ics

# party smart tips

The best parties include an array of "little tastes." Here are helpful tips for planning and prepping the food so you have time to mix and mingle.

## Choose a variety of temptations

Think about colors, textures, and flavors that go together, then select some recipes to present whole, such as Balsamic Shallot and Goat Cheese Tart, page 168, and others to offer as individual pieces, such as Prosciutto–Wrapped Scallops with Roasted Red Pepper Aioli, page 152. Consider both hot and cold appetizers as well. Texture is also key. The crunch of fresh veggies will contrast beautifully with the soft richness of a crab cake. The more variety you offer, the more people will eat, simply because people's appetites are stimulated when they have several dishes to choose from.

## Do the party math

Wondering how many appetizers to serve? We've figured it out for you. For light cocktail parties of the predinner variety, plan to serve about eight hors d'oeuvres per person. For cocktail buffets that may become full meals for your guests, double that amount. For such occasions, a good rule of thumb is to plan to serve something more substantial with the nibbles, such as meatballs or pizza.

## Food for thought

It's always better to have too much food on hand than not enough. At the end of the party, package up any leftovers to give to guests to take home with them to enjoy the next day.

## Take tasty shortcuts

First, know that you don't have to prepare all of the food yourself. Divide and conquer by selecting the recipes and assigning them to your friends or family to bring. Or, if you do want to make the entire menu yourself, be sure to know your limitations of time and skill. No more than 20 percent of the recipes you choose should be new or hard to make. Sixty to 70 percent of the recipes should be easy to prepare or recipes that you can make ahead of time. Then, rely on purchased items to fill out the menu.

Don't try to keep your party beverages cold in the fridge—when it's party time you'll need the space. Instead, offer ice for guests to serve with their drinks. Or present an assortment of drinks in a large ice-filled tin bucket.

## Opt for some make-ahead options

As you plan, weigh practical matters such as how much refrigerator or freezer space is available and how many appetizers you can heat ahead of time. Many party foods can be made in advance, then frozen and heated as the guests arrive. Plan one or two hot appetizers that you can make ahead and heat at the last minute. For the rest of the menu, choose foods you can prepare ahead and chill or ones you can purchase and assemble without last-minute attention.

## When serving, keep it simple

Present all the appetizers on a buffet table, or keep your guests circulating with several food stations throughout the house. A coffee table, desk, large ottoman, even a wide shelf or mantel can stand in as a serving location. Locate your beverage service in an area separate from the food.

## Safe keeping

Have a plan for keeping hot foods hot—140°F to 175°F—and cold foods cold—below 40°F. Be ready with warming trays, chafing dishes, and ice baths.

## Serving wine

Planning on serving wine? Know that one standard-size bottle of wine yields 5 glasses. So, if you're hosting a stand-around-and-chat event, plan on a half bottle per person.

# make some
# buy some

If you're squeezed for time, consider purchasing appetizers in bulk at club or membership warehouses. Pick up any of the following nibbles to round out your menu:

* Prepared dips (spinach and seafood are favorites) and boxes of crackers
* Refrigerated fresh guacamole and/or salsa and bags of tortilla chips
* Crunchy snack mix, dried fruit, and mixed nuts
* Cheese and meat platters
* Trays of assorted cut-up vegetables
* Olives, pickles, and roasted sweet peppers
* Mixed dried fruit, such as apricots and figs
* Cooked shrimp with jars of cocktail sauce
* Mini quiches, chicken wings, meatballs, and more
* Bite-size cheesecakes, mini cream puffs, and cookies

If you're hosting a large gathering, include a few light appetizers. Guests with special dietary needs will be thrilled. Even something as simple as a bowl heaped with assorted fruits can be attractive and offer light appeal.

## party on
## the light side

Here are some luscious, healthier offerings for your appetizer buffet.

✱ Set out lower-fat cheeses—such as mozzarella made with skim milk.

✱ Rather than potato chips, party crackers, and tortilla chips, offer whole grain crackers and toasted whole grain pita chips.

✱ Sprinkle dried fruits, such as raisins, apricots, figs, and dates, amid the cheeses and crackers.

✱ Ditto with walnuts—they'll add heart-healthy omega-3 acids to the menu. Just don't go overboard—1 ounce has about 160 calories.

✱ Serve baked pretzels with flavored mustards.

For even the most casual parties, provide small, sturdy plates instead of paper ones. These hold more food and are easier for guests to handle and set down as they mingle with the crowd.

# stocking the bar

Locate the bar near the entrance. Many guests prefer to begin with a drink and mingle before visiting the food table. If possible, make the bar table accessible from more than one direction for easier self-service.

**glassware:** If you can have only one set of party glasses, make it 9- to 11-ounce stemmed glasses—they're suitable for everything except champagne. Otherwise, the basics include double old-fashioned (rocks) glasses, highball (similar to iced tea) glasses, pilsners (for beer), martini glasses, and some all-purpose wineglasses. If you don't have all of these, start with one or two types and add the others as you host more parties and can afford them.

**equipment:** A jigger, long-handled spoons, napkins, towels, ice bucket, ice tongs, stir-sticks, a blender. Have a couple of coolers nearby to restock ice and to keep bottled beverages cold. Make sure you have plenty of ice for adding to drinks.

**beverages:** A clear liquor (gin or vodka), a dark liquor (whiskey), beer, red wine, and white wine. Also stock up on soft drinks and fruit juices.

**garnishes:** Lemons, limes, oranges, maraschino cherries, cocktail onions, celery stick-stirrers, and stuffed olives.

## drink I.D.eas

Connect guests to their drinks with one of these penny-pinching pitch hitters:

**Hello my name is:** What could be easier than those classic adhesive name tags? Not only do these stickers come without sticker shock, they add a bit of retro, funky fun to your party. Invite guests to personalize their own tags.

**String on a stick:** Put some swizzle into your next party with hand-crafted drink stirrers. Wrap inexpensive wooden frozen dessert sticks with scraps of colorful string or yarn. These striking sticks solve the mystery drink situation and double as cocktail stirrers.

# last-minute magic

Be ready to entertain on a moment's notice. Browse the aisles of your favorite gourmet market for an assortment of cured meats, firm cheeses, and jars of olives, spreads, and other delicacies that keep well in the fridge and the pantry. Then simply open, assemble–and enjoy–when friends come by.

## dried fruit and nut bruschetta

Keep a loaf of French bread in the freezer and your favorite melting cheese in the fridge. Combine them with some dried fruit and nuts for these stylish nibbles.

Cut French bread into 1/2-inch slices; brush one side with olive oil and toast in a toaster oven. Top oiled side with a few slices of a cheese that melts well, such as Monterey Jack, Swiss, Gruyère, or Gouda. Broil until melted. Top with a sprinkling of assorted slivered or diced dried fruit (such as figs, cranberries, apricots, cherries, or golden raisins) and nuts (such as walnuts, almonds, pistachios, or pine nuts). Press toppings into cheese to help them stay in place. Broil about 30 seconds more or until toppings are warm.

## mideast canapés

Freeze pita bread rounds so you'll always have a ready-made base for these clever canapés. The toppings are all items with a long shelf life.

Thaw pita bread rounds, if frozen. Split each pita bread round in half horizontally and brush cut sides with olive oil. Toast until crisp. Slather each pita round with jarred hummus or bean spread. Sprinkle with chopped toppings, such as pitted olives, bottled drained roasted red pepper strips, and/or drained artichoke hearts. Cut rounds into wedges to serve.

## pretty antipasto bowl

Serve the pick of the pantry in one large bowl and let guests assemble their own kabobs.

Toss a variety of hard cheeses, salamis, mixed pitted olives, pickled mushrooms, and pickled pepperoncini peppers with your favorite homemade or purchased vinaigrette. If desired, add fresh herbs and grape tomatoes. Serve in a large glass bowl to show off the colors and textures of the dish, accompanied by wooden toothpicks and small appetizer plates.

## eggplant caviar dip

Traditionally, the salsalike dip known as eggplant caviar calls for roasting a whole fresh eggplant. You can save a step by purchasing marinated eggplant strips.

Drain a jar of marinated eggplant; reserve the marinade. Chop the eggplant finely, then stir in minced garlic and salt and ground black pepper to taste. Stir in enough olive oil (or reserved marinade) to make a moist dip. Serve with crackers or on French bread toasts. Optional stir-ins include crumbled goat cheese, oil-packed dried tomatoes, and any fresh herbs you might have on hand.

## wrap-and-roll basil pinwheels

Tender tortillas with colorful fillings wrapped and rolled into cute little spirals are as easy to serve as they are to eat.

Spread 7- or 8-inch flour tortillas evenly with semisoft cheese with garlic and herbs (if cheese seems crumbly, stir it until smooth). Top cheese with large basil leaves. Arrange bottled roasted red sweet peppers on basil. Top with thinly sliced cooked ham, roast beef, or turkey. Tightly roll up each tortilla; wrap in plastic wrap. Chill for 2 to 4 hours. To serve, trim ends of rolls. Cut rolls into 1-inch slices. If desired, secure each slice with a short skewer and garnish with additional basil leaves.

## cute
## cornichon crackers

When it comes to flavor, few pickles rival the diminutive French sour pickles known as cornichons. Combine them with salami slices for a rich and sprightly bite.

Cut some cornichons into matchsticks. Top a rich, buttery gourmet cracker (about 2 inches in diameter) with a thin slice or two of dry-cured salami. Dab softened butter on top of each salami slice, then press a couple of cornichon slices into the butter. (Butter is a classic accompaniment to cured meats and also helps hold the pickles in place.)

Stock your pantry with an assortment of breadsticks, chips, crackers, and pretzels. They'll come in handy when serving dips or cheese spreads to drop-in guests.

## smoked salmon martinis

Smoked salmon is always a treat for guests—and, conveniently, it has a long shelf life.

In martini glasses or other stylish drink glasses, arrange chunks of smoked salmon with some chopped capers (drained), diced purple onion, and a dollop of sour cream sprinkled with a little dried dillweed. Tuck in a lemon wedge as well as a few round rye crackers for scooping.

# party **pantry**

A well-stocked pantry and refrigerator are the secrets to no-hassle entertaining. With a dozen versatile ingredients on hand, you'll be ready to create something sensational anytime.

- ✔ Chicken Drumettes
- ✔ Peeled and Deveined Large Shrimp
- ✔ Tapenade
- ✔ Prosciutto
- ✔ Pesto
- ✔ Pecans
- ✔ Frozen Chopped Spinach
- ✔ Dried Cherries
- ✔ Brie Cheese
- ✔ Parmigiano-Reggiano Cheese
- ✔ Roasted Red Sweet Peppers
- ✔ Puff Pastry

## toasted ravioli

These versatile mini pillows make a dynamite addition to an appetizer buffet, or serve them as the first course for a sit-down dinner.

Cook one 9-ounce package refrigerated cheese-filled ravioli according to package directions. Drain and cool slightly. Preheat oven to 425°F. Place 1/2 cup Italian-seasoned fine dry bread crumbs in a shallow dish. In another shallow dish using a fork, beat together 1/4 cup milk and 1 egg. Dip cooked ravioli in egg mixture, allowing excess to drip off; dip in bread crumbs to coat.

Place ravioli on a lightly greased baking sheet. Bake for 15 minutes or until crisp and golden. Serve with 1 1/2 cups warmed bottled or refrigerated spaghetti sauce. Makes 10 to 12 servings.

# prosciutto-olive breadsticks

Prosciutto, olives, and bread taste fabulous together.
Why not combine them into one easy-to-manage appetizer?

Finely chop pitted green or ripe olives and pat pieces dry with paper towels (this will help them adhere to the buttered breadstick). For each serving, slather one end of a breadstick with softened butter and press chopped olives into the butter. Wrap a thin slice of prosciutto around the buttered end of the breadstick, allowing a little olive to show.

# cheese, of course

When hosting a big bash, a cheese buffet is the perfect people-pleasing option that allows guests to experiment and get creative with their own cheese pairings. Here are tips for choosing and serving an impressive assortment.

## serving tips

✱ Today's cheeses are texturally interesting, so you'll want to offer whole chunks of different varieties, with their rinds intact when possible.

✱ Pair cheese with complimentary tidbits. For example, fresh goat cheese has a natural affinity to olives. Salt and pungent blue cheese pairs well with something sweet, such as honey, dried figs, or jams. Other flavorful accompaniments include dried fruits, toasted nuts, and compotes.

✱ Serve soft, fresh cheeses slightly chilled, but for peak flavor and aroma, serve all other cheeses at room temperature.

✱ For maximum flavor, bring cheeses out of the refrigerator about 1 hour before you plan to serve your cheese tray. To keep them from drying out, unwrap them just before serving.

✱ Rewrap any leftover cheeses separately with a clean piece of plastic wrap and refrigerate.

### cheese choices

Serve between three and five cheeses that feature different textures (soft or semisoft, semi-hard or sliceable, hard, and blue), types of milk (cow, goat, or sheep), sharpness, and countries of origin—along with any artisan varieties. Not only will you satisfy a wide range of guests, but the range of cheeses makes for a beautiful presentation.

Estimate about 2 ounces of cheese per person.

Manchego

Blue

# the new relish tray

Jazz up the classic with a fun, new look and taste with fresh produce and condiments. Use our tips and hunt through your supermarket for more ideas when it's time to create your own.

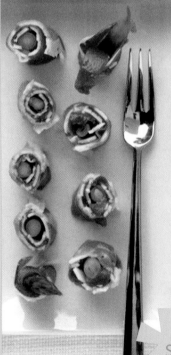

## relish tray pointers
*(clockwise from top left)*

**Start simple** with colorful sweet peppers cut into shapes instead of the usual strips.

**Stuff pitted olives** with blue cheese for a flavor explosion in every bite.

**Skewer pickled** veggies on cocktail picks for mini kabobs. Try baby corn, onions and gherkins. Freshen the lineup with sweet grape tomatoes.

**Put zip** on your relish tray by adding some pickled sweet or hot peppers to the mix.

**Make a quick** cucumber relish by tossing paper-thin cuke slices with a light-colored vinegar such as rice wine vinegar.

**Roll up** thin-sliced Swiss cheese and prosciutto or ham with blanched asparagus or green beans (barely cooked in boiling water). Then, cut them into bite-size pieces for a fresh presentation.

**Make over** your mayo by adding snipped herbs or sea salt to it. Stir in desired amount of seasoning.

Serve small amounts of relishes at a time, swapping out platters and bowls, so the food stays fresh and cold.

# ultimate
# olives

**Cerignola:** The crisp, walnut-size, green variety from Italy adds a sweet-not-salty flavor to appetizer trays.

**Kalamata:** Curing in a red wine vinegar brine gives these Greek olives a salty, rich, fruity, winelike flavor and deep purple color.

**Manzanilla:** A star among table olives for its crisp texture and tangy taste, this brownish-green native of Spain is typically available pitted or stuffed with pimiento. It's also great for cooking.

**Niçoise:** Tree ripened, the little black gem from France has a distinctive flavor and fragrance. It has a larger pit-to-meat ratio than most olives.

**Picholine:** The small, light-green fruit changes to red-black when ripe. Mostly grown in Morocco and processed in France, it has a crunchy texture and delicately tart, nutty flavor, making it ideal for snacks and cocktails.

**Sicilian:** This large, green Italian olive is typically marinated with herbs and stuffed with cheese, garlic, or pimiento. Its crunchy texture and salty, somewhat sour flavor make it a favorite for snacking.

## Marinated Olives

*Fine on their own, olives can also benefit from a good soak with compatible flavors. Try making your own flavorful marinade with this easy recipe, shown above. In a 1-quart jar with a screw-top lid, combine $1/2$ cup olive oil; two 3 x $1/2$-inch strips lemon peel; $1/2$ cup lemon juice; 4 to 6 cloves garlic, sliced; 2 teaspoons snipped fresh oregano; 1 bay leaf; and $1/2$ teaspoon crushed red pepper. Add 2 cups black and/or green olives, rinsed and drained. Cover and shake to coat olives. Marinate in the refrigerator for 2 days up to 2 weeks, shaking jar occasionally. Before serving, let olives stand at room temperature for 1 to 2 hours. Drain olives; discard bay leaf and marinade.*

# dress it up

Now comes the fun part. The secret to making your party stand out is to personalize it. Here are easy, inexpensive ways to bring something new and different to the party scene.

## bottle bouquet

Elaborate floral displays are lovely but expensive. Why drop dollars at the florist when a few grocery store flowers look so perfectly charming in recycled water bottles, mismatched old medicine containers, or even a selection of water glasses or goblets?

What's the most exotic food you're ever tried?

Where is your paradise found?

If they made a movie of your life... Who would play you?

## conversation starters

Jot a few thought-provoking questions on inexpensive beverage napkins. Within minutes, your guests will be chatting away.

Don't limit your serving selection to plates and bowls. Vases or new flowerpots can display bouquets of vegetables. Cream pitchers, sugar bowls, and gravy boats are great for dips. Cutting boards or cooling racks are ideal substitute platters for individual appetizers.

a glass act Stemware offers a surprising range of uses beyond wine. Line up a row of wineglasses filled with party foods. Grapes, cheese cut into sticks, breadsticks wrapped with prosciutto, and skewered tidbits work best. Or use them to hold small amounts of dip with crudités, savory nuts, or snack mixes.

# **pickup** sticks

Skewers and picks make for quick, convenient serving.

* Trim plain bamboo skewers to any length you like; they're good for serving hot or cold foods. For display, insert the skewers into lemon or lime halves or a small head of cabbage or radicchio.

* Slide shrimp or pieces of chicken, pork, or fish onto fresh rosemary sprigs; the rosemary adds flavor during grilling or broiling.

* Use colorful cocktail picks to embellish as they secure mini sandwiches or rolled meats or vegetables. Or attach garnishes to bite-size nibblers with wooden toothpicks.

## name your place

Create a decorative use for wine bottle corks.
When slit with a serrated knife and combined
with bits of scrap paper and card stock, they
become buoyant place cards.

Don't worry if all
your serving trays and
platters don't match.
A variety of patterns,
colors, styles, and
sizes adds vibrant
flair to a buffet table
and showcases
the foods that are
presented on them.
Select a table covering
that ties the color
scheme together.

# tray chic

Even if money were no object, few of
us have enough kitchen space to store
trays and platters that we use just once
or twice a year. Yet our homes are filled
with common utilitarian objects that
are waiting to play exciting new roles.
Allow these unlikely stars—items that
languish in obscurity, tucked away in
cupboards, basements, and garages—
to come out and party. For example, a
trusty muffin pan goes from baking to
the bar, holding an array of garnishes.

mix it up: *Combine two or three kinds of appetizers on a platter or
tray, alternating the shapes for a more interesting look. There's only
one caveat: Don't mix hot and cold foods on the same platter.*

## plate toss

Caterers and buffet specialists add visual interest to tablescapes by presenting food platters at different heights with the use of pricey pedestals and stacking serving pieces. Luckily, a little homegrown ingenuity—like placing plates of appetizers on top of overturned cups and bowls from your own cupboards—provides that same stylish, uptown look, and does so at no cost whatsoever. The snacks themselves can also be stacked for presentation.

# party menus

Whether you're hosting a crowd or inviting a few friends over, make it easy by starting with one of the themed menus on these pages. Recipes are featured throughout the book.

## brunch bites

## game-day chow down

## thai one on

## an antipasto buffet

When the mood is casual, fill large platters and bowls the moment anything comes out of the oven. Then invite guests to serve themselves.

Focus on the glories of the seasonal garden, such as strawberries in the spring and tomatoes in the summer, to bring color and texture to the scene.

## saturday night sushi

## neighborhood fiesta

## cocktails 'n' nibbles

## spring fling

## wine & cheese party

## holiday open house

Surprise is a wonderful ingredient for any party. Choose one of the recipes here for your next bring-a-dish party.

## impromptu get-together

## sweet-as-can-be soiree

dipping

deli

No party is complete without an awesome dip. Grab an assortment of crunchy dunkers: These sweet and savory dips, elegant spreads, and warm, creamy fondues will be the party addiction.

2

ghts

dipping **delights**

*Green and red onion punch up purchased French onion dip, and the fennel lends a slight aniselike flavor.*

# fennel and onion dip

start to finish: 15 minutes  makes: 2¼ cups

1   medium fennel bulb
1   16-ounce container
     dairy sour cream
     French onion–flavor
     dip
2   tablespoons finely
     chopped red onion
2   tablespoons thinly
     sliced green onion
     (1 medium)
     Assorted vegetable
     dippers

**1** Trim feathery leaves from fennel. If desired, snip enough of the leaves to measure 2 tablespoons; set aside. Trim fennel bulb. Chop enough of the bulb to measure 1 cup.

**2** In a medium bowl combine the chopped fennel, onion dip, red onion, and green onion.

**3** Transfer dip to a serving bowl. If desired, sprinkle with the snipped fennel leaves. Serve with vegetable dippers.

nutrition facts per 2 tablespoons: 53 cal., 4 g total fat (2 g sat. fat), 0 mg chol., 178 mg sodium, 4 g carb., 0 g dietary fiber, 1 g protein.

**make-ahead directions:** Prepare as directed through Step 2. Cover and chill for up to 24 hours. Wrap the snipped fennel leaves in plastic wrap and chill separately. Serve as directed in Step 3.

*To change the flavor of this creamy dip for another time, use herbs such as tarragon, basil, or thyme instead of the dill.*

# classic dill dip

prep: 10 minutes  chill: 1 hour  makes: 2 cups

1  8-ounce package
   cream cheese,
   softened*
1  8-ounce carton dairy
   sour cream
2  tablespoons finely
   chopped green
   onion (1 medium)
2  tablespoons snipped
   fresh dill or 2
   teaspoons dried
   dillweed
½  teaspoon seasoned
   salt or salt
1 to 2  tablespoons milk
   (optional)
   Fresh dill sprig
   (optional)
   Assorted vegetable
   dippers (baby
   zucchini, carrots,
   yellow summer
   squash sticks,
   cherry tomatoes,
   radishes, pea pods,
   zucchini slices,
   cauliflower florets,
   and/or jicama or
   red sweet pepper
   strips), chips, or
   crackers

**1** In a medium mixing bowl beat cream cheese, sour cream, green onion, dill, and salt with an electric mixer on low speed until fluffy. Cover and chill for at least 1 hour.

**2** If dip is too thick after chilling, stir in milk. Spoon into a serving bowl. If desired, garnish dip with a dill sprig. Serve with vegetable dippers, chips, and/or crackers.

nutrition facts per 2 tablespoons: 80 cal., 8 g total fat (4 g sat. fat), 22 mg chol., 2 g carb., 0 g dietary fiber, 2 g protein.

*note: To quickly soften cream cheese, heat it, uncovered and unwrapped, in a microwave-safe bowl on 100 percent power (high) for 10 to 20 seconds. Let stand 5 minutes before using.

**make-ahead directions:** Prepare dip as directed in Step 1. Cover and chill for up to 24 hours. Chop vegetable dippers and place in resealable plastic bags; chill for up to 24 hours.

parmesan dip: Prepare Classic Dill Dip as directed, except omit dill and salt. Stir ¼ cup grated Parmesan cheese (2 ounces) and 2 teaspoons dried Italian seasoning into the beaten cream cheese mixture.

*Flecks of artichoke and sweet pepper enhance the color and flavor of this warm, cheesy dip.*

# brie and artichoke dip

start to finish: 25 minutes  makes: 3 cups

2  tablespoons butter
2  tablespoons all-
   purpose flour
1  tablespoon dry
   mustard
1  cup milk
3  4½-ounce rounds
   Brie cheese, rinds
   removed and cut
   into 1-inch cubes
1  6-ounce jar
   marinated artichoke
   hearts, well-drained
   and chopped
¼  cup chopped roasted
   red sweet peppers
   Belgian endive leaves
   or toasted baguette
   slices

**1** In a medium saucepan melt butter over medium heat. Stir in flour and mustard. Stir in milk, whisking until smooth. Cook and stir over medium heat until thickened and bubbly. Gradually add Brie, whisking until smooth. Stir in artichoke hearts and roasted red peppers. Heat through.

**2** Transfer mixture to a serving bowl. Serve with endive leaves.

nutrition facts per ¼ cup: 153 cal., 12 g total fat (7 g sat. fat), 39 mg chol., 267 mg sodium, 4 g carb., 0 g dietary fiber, 8 g protein.

*Pick up a loaf of focaccia or flatbread from your favorite bakery to serve alongside this peppery dip.*

# tuscan bean dip

prep: 15 minutes   chill: 3 hours   makes: 1⅓ cups

| | |
|---|---|
| 1 | 15-ounce can navy beans, rinsed and drained |
| 2 | tablespoons chopped onion |
| 2 | tablespoons purchased basil pesto |
| 1 | tablespoon vinegar |
| 1 | clove garlic, minced |
| ½ | to 1 teaspoon finely chopped fresh red or green chile pepper (see note, page 52) |
| ¼ | teaspoon salt |

In a food processor or blender combine beans, onion, pesto, vinegar, garlic, chile pepper, and salt. Cover and process or blend until nearly smooth. Cover and chill at least 3 hours or overnight.

nutrition facts per tablespoon: 34 cal., 1 g total fat (0 g sat. fat), 0 mg chol., 130 mg sodium, 5 g carb., 1 g dietary fiber, 2 g protein.

*Plan ahead so you'll have perfectly ripe avocados. If you purchase firm, heavy avocados, you'll need to place them in a paper bag for 2 to 4 days or until they yield to gentle palm pressure.*

# guacamole

prep: 15 minutes   chill: Up to 24 hours   makes: 2 cups

| | |
|---|---|
| 2 | medium very ripe avocados, halved, pitted, peeled, and chopped |
| ¼ | of a small onion, chopped |
| 1 | tablespoon snipped cilantro or parsley |
| 1 | tablespoon lime juice |
| 1 | clove garlic, minced |
| ¼ | teaspoon salt |
| ⅔ | cup finely chopped, seeded, peeled tomato (1 medium; optional) |
| | Tortilla chips |

1 In a food processor or blender combine avocado, onion, cilantro, lime juice, garlic, and salt. Cover and process or blend until smooth, scraping sides as necessary.

2 Transfer to a serving bowl. If desired, stir in tomato. Serve immediately or cover and chill up to 24 hours. Serve with chips.

nutrition facts per 2 tablespoons: 37 cal., 3 g total fat (0 g sat. fat), 0 mg chol., 38 mg sodium, 2 g carb., 1 g dietary fiber, 0 g protein.

spicy guacamole: Prepare as directed, except add 2 fresh jalapeño chile peppers, seeded and chopped (see note, page 52); ½ of a 4-ounce can (¼ cup) diced green chile peppers, drained; or several drops of bottled hot pepper sauce.

*If there's extra of this hummus-style dip, spread it on a toasted bagel.*

# dried tomato and white bean dip

start to finish: 30 minutes  makes: 2½ cups

2 15-ounce cans cannellini beans (white kidney beans), rinsed and drained
2 tablespoons lemon juice
1 tablespoon olive oil
1 cup sliced green onion
3 cloves garlic, minced
¼ cup bottled oil-packed dried tomato, drained and finely chopped
¼ cup water
1 tablespoon snipped fresh oregano or ½ teaspoon dried oregano, crushed
½ teaspoon salt
½ teaspoon ground cumin
Several dashes bottled hot pepper sauce
Assorted crackers

**1** In a food processor or blender combine one can of the beans and the lemon juice. Cover and process or blend until nearly smooth; set aside.

**2** In a large skillet heat oil over medium heat. Cook green onion and garlic in hot oil just until tender. Stir in pureed beans, the remaining can whole beans, the dried tomato, the water, oregano, salt, cumin, and hot pepper sauce. Heat through. Serve with crackers.

nutrition facts per ¼ cup: 72 cal., 2 g total fat (0 g sat. fat), 0 mg, chol., 258 mg sodium, 13 g carb., 4 g dietary fiber, 5 g protein.

*From the refried beans and salsa base to the colorful tomato topper, these luscious layers will delight all the Mexican-food lovers in your party crowd.*

# mexican **seven-layer** dip

prep: 20 minutes   chill: 4 to 24 hours   makes: 16 servings

1   16-ounce can refried beans
½   cup bottled salsa
½   of a 14-ounce package refrigerated guacamole
1   8-ounce carton dairy sour cream
1   cup shredded cheddar or taco cheese (4 ounces)
¼   cup sliced green onion (2)
¼   cup sliced pitted ripe olives
1   cup chopped, seeded tomato (1 large)
8   cups tortilla chips or crackers

**1** In a medium bowl combine refried beans and salsa. Spread onto a 12-inch platter or in a 2-quart rectangular baking dish. Carefully layer guacamole and sour cream over bean mixture. Top with cheese, green onion, and olives. Cover and chill for 4 to 24 hours.

**2** Before serving, sprinkle with chopped tomato. Serve with tortilla chips.

nutrition facts per ¼ cup dip and ½ cup chips: 179 cal., 11 g total fat (4 g sat. fat), 15 mg chol., 340 mg sodium, 16 g carb., 3 g dietary fiber, 5 g protein.

*Purchased hummus makes this an easy dip to prepare. Look for containers of hummus near the gourmet cheeses in supermarkets.*

# greek layer dip

start to finish: 20 minutes  makes: 10 (¼-cup) servings

1   6-ounce carton plain yogurt
¼   cup coarsely shredded unpeeled cucumber plus more for topping (optional)
1   tablespoon finely chopped onion
1   teaspoon snipped fresh mint
1   8-ounce container plain hummus (¾ cup)
½   cup chopped, seeded tomato
½   cup crumbled feta cheese (2 ounces)
3   large white and/or whole wheat pita bread rounds

**1** In a small bowl combine yogurt, cucumber, onion, and mint. Spread hummus in the bottom of a 10-inch shallow dish or 9-inch pie plate. Spread yogurt mixture over hummus. Sprinkle with tomato and feta cheese. If desired, top with additional cucumber.

**2** Split each pita bread round in half horizontally. Cut each round into 8 wedges. For crisper wedges, bake in a 350°F oven about 10 minutes; cool. Serve dip with pita wedges.

nutrition facts per ¼ cup: 120 cal., 4 g total fat (1 g sat. fat), 6 mg chol., 231 mg sodium, 17 g carb., 2 g dietary fiber, 5 g protein.

**make-ahead directions:** Prepare the baked pita bread wedges and store in an airtight container in a cool, dry place for up to 2 days.

*Using already cooked bacon pieces makes this dip especially quick to stir together.*

# horseradish-bacon dip

start to finish: 15 minutes  makes: 1¼ cups

1¼  cups finely shredded
    cheddar cheese
    (5 ounces)
½   cup dairy sour cream
1   3-ounce package
    cream cheese,
    softened
3   to 4 teaspoons
    prepared
    horseradish
¼   cup cooked bacon
    pieces
1   tablespoon snipped
    fresh chives
    Assorted crackers

**1** In a medium mixing bowl combine 1 cup of the shredded cheese, the sour cream, cream cheese, and horseradish. Beat with an electric mixer on medium speed until nearly smooth. Spread mixture in a microwave-safe 9-inch pie plate.

**2** Microwave, uncovered, on 100 percent power (high) for 1 minute. Stir mixture and spread in an even layer in the pie plate. Sprinkle with the remaining ¼ cup cheese and the bacon. Microwave for 1 to 2 minutes more or until cheese is melted, turning once. Sprinkle with chives. Serve with assorted crackers.

nutrition facts per tablespoon: 55 cal., 5 g total fat (3 g sat. fat), 14 mg chol., 71 mg sodium, 0 g carb., 0 g dietary fiber, 2 g protein.

*Hummus is a traditional Middle Eastern spread based on chickpeas. Find tahini, a ground sesame paste that adds a lively boost of flavor, in the condiment aisle or the ethnic foods section of the store.*

# hummus

start to finish: 15 minutes  makes: about 1³/₄ cups

1   15-ounce can chickpeas (garbanzo beans), rinsed and drained
1   clove garlic, minced
¼   cup tahini (sesame seed paste)
¼   cup lemon juice
¼   cup olive oil
½   teaspoon salt
¼   teaspoon paprika
1   tablespoon snipped fresh parsley
2   to 3 teaspoons olive oil (optional)
2   tablespoons pine nuts, toasted (optional)
    Toasted pita wedges and/or assorted vegetable dippers

**1** In a food processor or blender combine chickpeas, garlic, tahini, lemon juice, ¼ cup oil, salt, and paprika. Cover and process or blend until smooth, scraping sides as necessary.

**2** Spoon the hummus onto a serving platter. Sprinkle with parsley. If desired, drizzle with oil and garnish with pine nuts. Serve with pita wedges and/or vegetable dippers.

nutrition facts per 2 tablespoons: 97 cal., 6 g total fat (1 g sat. fat), 0 mg chol., 176 mg sodium, 8 g carb., 2 g dietary fiber, 2 g protein.

*Full-flavor dried tomatoes make this cheesy spread impossible to resist.*

# creamy dried-tomato spread

prep: 25 minutes  chill: 2 hours  stand: 10 minutes  makes: 10 (2-tablespoon) servings

⅓  cup dried tomato (not oil packed)
    Boiling water
4  ounces soft goat cheese (chèvre)
½  of an 8-ounce package reduced-fat cream cheese (Neufchâtel), softened
¼  cup snipped fresh basil or 2 teaspoons dried basil, crushed
3  cloves garlic, minced
⅛  teaspoon ground black pepper
2  to 3 tablespoons fat-free milk
    Miniature toasts and/or reduced-fat crackers

**1** In small bowl cover dried tomato with boiling water. Cover and let stand for 10 minutes. Drain tomato, discarding liquid. Finely snip tomato.

**2** In medium bowl combine tomato, goat cheese, cream cheese, basil, garlic, and pepper. Stir in enough of the milk to reach spreading consistency. Cover and chill for 2 to 8 hours. Serve spread with toasts.

nutrition facts per 2 tablespoons: 67 cal., 5 g total fat (3 g sat. fat), 14 mg chol., 126mg sodium, 2 g carb., 0 g dietary fiber, 4 g protein.

*Just a little super-spicy chipotle pepper gives this dip a nice touch of heat. If you're feeling extra spicy, add a full teaspoon.*

# triple-smoked
# salmon-pepper dip

prep: 20 minutes  bake: 25 minutes  broil: 10 minutes  stand: 15 minutes
oven: 350°F  makes: 3 cups

1   large green sweet
    pepper
1   8-ounce package
    reduced-fat cream
    cheese (Neufchâtel),
    softened
½   cup light dairy sour
    cream
2   tablespoons fat-free
    milk
½   cup thinly sliced
    green onion (4 to 6)
2   cloves garlic, minced
½   teaspoon smoked
    paprika or paprika
½   to 1 teaspoon finely
    chopped chipotle
    chile pepper in
    adobo sauce (see
    note, page 52)
4   ounces hot-style
    smoked salmon,
    flaked, skin and
    bones removed
Toasted baguette-style
    French bread slices,
    carrot sticks, and/or
    cucumber slices

**1** Preheat the broiler. Line a baking sheet with foil; set aside. Cut sweet pepper into quarters, removing stem, seeds, and membranes. Place pepper quarters, skin sides up, on prepared baking sheet. Broil 4 to 5 inches from the heat for 10 to 15 minutes or until pepper skins are charred. Wrap pepper quarters in the foil; let stand for 15 to 20 minutes or until cool enough to handle. Peel off skin and discard. Chop pepper.

**2** Preheat oven to 350°F. In a large mixing bowl beat cream cheese with an electric mixer on medium speed until smooth. Beat in sour cream and milk until smooth. Stir ¼ cup of the green onion, the garlic, paprika, and chipotle pepper into cream cheese mixture. Gently fold in salmon and chopped roasted pepper. Spread in the bottom of a 1-quart gratin dish.

**3** Bake for 25 minutes or until heated through, stirring once halfway through baking. Sprinkle with the remaining ¼ cup green onion. Serve warm with baguette slices, carrot sticks, and/or cucumber slices.

nutrition facts per ¼ cup: 81 cal., 6 g total fat (3 g sat. fat), 24 mg chol., 192 mg sodium, 3 g carb., 0 g dietary fiber, 4 g protein.

**make-ahead directions:** Prepare as directed through Step 2. Cover and store dip and remaining green onion in the refrigerator for up to 24 hours. Preheat oven to 350°F. Bake for 30 to 35 minutes or until dip is heated through, stirring once halfway through baking. Serve as directed in Step 3.

*Smoked paprika is ground from sweet red peppers that have been smoked over wood for flavor, then dried.*

# spinach, artichoke, and bacon dip
## with smoked paprika pita chips

start to finish: 40 minutes  makes: 32 servings

2   10-ounce packages
    frozen chopped
    spinach, thawed
    and well-drained
12  slices bacon
1   medium shallot,
    finely chopped
6   cloves garlic, minced
1   6-ounce jar marinated
    artichoke hearts,
    drained and
    coarsely chopped
1   8-ounce carton light
    dairy sour cream
½   cup light mayonnaise
½   teaspoon freshly
    ground black
    pepper
1   recipe Smoked
    Paprika Pita Chips

**1** Press spinach with clean paper towels to remove as much liquid as much as possible; set aside.

**2** In a large skillet cook bacon over medium heat, 6 slices at a time, until crisp. Drain on paper towels, reserving 1 tablespoon drippings in skillet. Crumble bacon.

**3** Add shallot to skillet. Cook and stir until it just begins to brown. Add garlic. Cook for 1 minute. Stir in spinach and artichoke hearts. Add sour cream, mayonnaise, and pepper. Cook and stir just until heated through. Stir in bacon. Serve warm with Smoked Paprika Pita Chips.

nutrition facts per serving: 73 cal., 5 g total fat (1 g sat. fat), 7 mg chol., 161 mg sodium, 5 g carb., 1 g dietary fiber, 3 g protein.

smoked paprika pita chips: Preheat oven to 350°F. Split one 6- to 7-ounce bag of miniature pita bread rounds in half horizontally. Arrange halves, cut sides up, in two 15×10×1-inch baking pans. Spray rounds lightly with nonstick cooking spray, then sprinkle lightly with smoked paprika. Bake for 16 minutes or until lightly browned, rotating baking pans once. Cool on wire racks.

**make-ahead directions:**
Prepare dip as directed, stirring in bacon but not heating through. Cover and chill for up to 2 days. Prepared pita chips as directed; store in covered container at room temperature for up to 2 days. To serve, transfer dip to a skillet; heat through. Serve with pita chips.

*A little bit nutty, a little bit spicy, this intriguing Indian-inspired recipe journeys off the well-beaten chip-and-dip path. Choose a chutney to suit your taste—some are sweeter, others are hot.*

# curry-chutney dip

prep: 10 minutes   chill: 2 hours   makes: 1¼ cups

¼   cup mango chutney
½   of an 8-ounce package reduced-fat cream cheese (Neufchâtel), softened
⅔   cup light dairy sour cream
1   teaspoon curry powder
¼   cup chopped dry-roasted or honey-roasted cashews
    Crisp breadsticks and/or assorted vegetable dippers

**1** Snip any large mango pieces in chutney. In a small bowl combine cream cheese, sour cream, and curry powder. Stir in chutney. Cover and chill for 2 to 48 hours.

**2** Before serving, sprinkle the dip with cashews. Serve with breadsticks and/or vegetables.

nutrition facts per 1 tablespoon: 92 cal., 6 g total fat (3 g sat. fat), 14 mg chol., 84 mg sodium, 8 g carb., 0 g dietary fiber, 3 g protein.

*Lemongrass gives this protein-packed hummus a terrific Thai taste. If your supermarket doesn't carry lemongrass, look for it at Asian specialty stores.*

# edamame-lemongrass
# hummus

start to finish: 25 minutes  makes: 2½ cups

2   green onions
1   10-ounce package
    frozen sweet
    soybeans (edamame;
    2 cups)
½   cup fresh Italian
    parsley sprigs
½   cup water
2   tablespoons lemon
    juice
1   tablespoon chopped
    fresh lemongrass or
    ½ teaspoon finely
    shredded lemon
    peel
1   tablespoon canola oil
2   cloves garlic,
    quartered
1   teaspoon finely
    chopped fresh
    ginger or ¼ teaspoon
    ground ginger
¾   teaspoon salt
¼   teaspoon crushed red
    pepper (optional)
    Assorted vegetable
    dippers (radishes,
    red sweet pepper
    strips, Belgian
    endive leaves, and/
    or peeled jicama
    sticks)

**1** Thinly slice green onions, keeping green tops separate from white bottoms; set aside. Cook edamame according to package directions, except omit salt. Drain; rinse with cold water. Drain well.

**2** In food processor combine cooked edamame, white green onion bottoms, parsley, the water, lemon juice, lemongrass, oil, garlic, ginger, salt, and, crushed red pepper (if desired). Cover and process until nearly smooth. Transfer to serving bowl and stir in green onion tops. Serve with vegetable dippers.

nutrition facts per ¼ cup: 47 cal., 3 g total fat (0 g sat. fat), 0 mg chol., 179 mg sodium, 3 g carb., 2 g dietary fiber, 3 g protein.

**make-ahead directions:** Prepare as directed, except cover and store in the refrigerator for up to 24 hours.

*Sprinkling coarse colored sugar on top adds sparkle and makes this taste all the sweeter. Pictured opposite.*

# creamy fruit dip

prep: 15 minutes   chill: 1 hour   makes: 2 cups

1   8-ounce package
    cream cheese,
    softened
1   8-ounce carton dairy
    sour cream
¼   cup packed brown
    sugar
1   teaspoon vanilla
2   to 3 tablespoons milk
    Assorted fruit
    (pineapple wedges,
    sliced apples or
    kiwi, kumquats,
    and/or blueberries)

**1** In a small mixing bowl beat cream cheese with an electric mixer on low speed until smooth. Gradually add sour cream, beating until combined.

**2** Add brown sugar and vanilla. Beat just until combined. Stir in enough of the milk to reach dipping consistency. Cover and chill for at least 1 hour before serving. Serve with assorted fruit.

nutrition facts per 2 tablespoons: 95 cal., 8 g total fat (5 g sat. fat), 22 mg chol., 52 mg sodium, 5 g carb., 0 g dietary fiber, 2 g protein.

# strawberries
## with citrus dip

start to finish: 15 minutes   makes: 8 (2-tablespoon) servings

1   6-ounce carton plain
    low-fat yogurt
⅓   cup frozen light
    whipped dessert
    topping, thawed
2   tablespoons
    powdered sugar
2   teaspoons finely
    shredded lime,
    orange, and/or
    lemon peel
1   tablespoon orange
    juice
3   cups small
    strawberries

**1** In small bowl combine yogurt, whipped dessert topping, powdered sugar, citrus peel, and orange juice.

**2** Wash strawberries but do not remove stems. Drain on several layers of paper towels. Serve dip with berries.

nutrition facts per 2 tablespoons: 46 cal., 1 g total fat (1 g sat. fat), 1 mg chol., 15 mg sodium, 9 g carb., 1 g dietary fiber, 1 g protein.

*A lively pepper paste, made by rehydrating and processing dried ancho chiles, adds a sweet, smoky flavor and just the right hotness.*

# tunisian **bean dip**

prep: 15 minutes  stand: 20 minutes  makes: 2½ cups

| | |
|---|---|
| 4 | dried ancho and/ or pasilla chile peppers, stems and seeds removed* |
| 1 | cup boiling water |
| 1 | tablespoon olive oil |
| 1 | tablespoon lemon juice |
| ¾ | teaspoon caraway seeds, finely crushed |
| ½ | teaspoon salt |
| 1 | clove garlic, halved |
| ¼ | teaspoon ground coriander |
| ⅛ | teaspoon ground cumin |
| ⅛ | teaspoon ground black pepper |
| 1 | 15-ounce can garbanzo beans (chickpeas), rinsed and drained |
| 1 | 15-ounce can cannellini beans (white kidney beans), rinsed and drained |
| | Toasted whole wheat pita wedges |

**1** Place peppers in bowl. Add boiling water. Cover; let stand for 20 minutes or until softened. Drain, reserving liquid.

**2** In a food processor combine peppers, olive oil, lemon juice, caraway seeds, salt, garlic, coriander, cumin, and black pepper. Cover and process until smooth, adding 2 to 3 tablespoons of the drained pepper liquid to make a thin paste. Remove 2 tablespoons paste; set aside. Add garbanzo and cannellini beans to remaining paste in food processor. Cover; process until smooth, adding about ½ cup reserved liquid to reach dipping consistency. Transfer bean mixture to a serving bowl.

**3** Swirl reserved paste into the top of the bean mixture. Serve with pita wedges.

nutrition facts per ¼ cup: 64 cal., 2 g total fat (0 g sat. fat), 0 mg chol., 333 mg sodium, 12 g carb., 4 g dietary fiber, 5 g protein.

*note: Because chile peppers contain oils that can burn your skin and eyes, avoid direct contact with them as much as possible. When working with chile peppers, wear rubber or plastic gloves. If your bare hands do touch the peppers, wash your hands and nails well with soap and warm water.

**make-ahead directions:** Prepare as directed through Step 2. Cover and chill mixture in serving bowl and reserved paste for up to 24 hours. Continue as directed in Step 3.

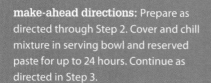

*Oven-roasted shallots and garlic introduce mellow nutty flavors and sweetness that come through in this refreshing sour cream dip.*

# roasted shallot dip

prep: 15 minutes  bake: 40 minutes  cool: 15 minutes  oven: 400°F
makes: about 2⅓ cups

2 shallots, peeled
4 cloves garlic, peeled
1 tablespoon olive oil
1 cup light mayonnaise
½ cup light dairy sour cream
¼ cup chopped bottled roasted red sweet pepper
2 tablespoons red wine vinegar
1 teaspoon snipped fresh tarragon or ¼ teaspoon dried tarragon, crushed
¼ teaspoon coarsely ground black pepper
1 tablespoon drained capers
Chopped bottled roasted red sweet pepper and/or snipped fresh tarragon (optional)
Assorted dippers (trimmed green onions, blanched asparagus spears and/or green beans, roasted fennel wedges and/or broccoli florets, flatbread, and/or assorted crackers)

**1** Preheat oven to 400°F. Cut each shallot and garlic clove in half lengthwise and place in a 10-ounce custard cup or a small baking dish. Drizzle with olive oil. Cover and bake for about 40 minutes or until very tender. Cool for 15 minutes.

**2** In a food processor combine shallots, garlic, mayonnaise, sour cream, the ¼ cup sweet pepper, vinegar, the 1 teaspoon tarragon, and the black pepper. Cover and process until combined. Transfer to a serving bowl. Top with capers. If desired, sprinkle with additional chopped sweet pepper and/or fresh tarragon. Serve with dippers.

nutrition facts per 2 tablespoons: 59 cal., 5 g total fat (1 g sat. fat), 6 mg chol., 99 mg sodium, 3 g carb., 0 g dietary fiber, 0 g protein.

**make-ahead directions:** Prepare dip in food processor as directed. Cover and chill for up to 24 hours. Garnish dip and serve as directed.

*Oven roasting coaxes wonderful flavor from veggies with high sugar content, such as carrots, red sweet peppers, and shallots. Pureed into a dip with balsamic vinegar and rosemary, they taste even more extraordinary.*

# roasted vegetable dip

prep: 20 minutes  roast: 40 minutes  oven: 425°F  makes: 2 cups

4  medium carrots, cut into 1-inch pieces
2  large red sweet peppers, seeded and cut into 1-inch pieces
2  medium shallots, halved
3  cloves garlic
1  tablespoon olive oil
½  teaspoon freshly ground black pepper
¼  teaspoon salt
2  tablespoons balsamic vinegar
1  teaspoon snipped fresh rosemary
   Fresh rosemary sprigs (optional)
   Assorted crackers and/or assorted vegetable dippers (broccoli florets, cauliflower florets, and/or zucchini sticks)

**1** Preheat oven to 425°F. Line a shallow roasting pan with foil. Place carrots, sweet peppers, shallots, and garlic in prepared pan. Drizzle with olive oil and sprinkle with black pepper and salt. Cover with foil.

**2** Roast for 20 minutes. Uncover and stir vegetables. Roast, uncovered, for 20 to 25 minutes more or until vegetables are tender and lightly browned. Cool slightly on a wire rack.

**3** Transfer vegetable mixture to a food processor. Add vinegar and snipped rosemary. Cover and process until smooth. If desired, garnish with rosemary sprigs. Serve with crackers and/or vegetable dippers.

nutrition facts per ¼ cup: 49 cal., 2 g total fat (0 g sat. fat), 0 mg chol., 97 mg sodium, 7 g carb., 2 g dietary fiber, 1 g protein.

*As a flavorful acidic ingredient, beer helps keep the fondue creamy and smooth and prevents it from scorching. To create visual interest, place the fondue pot on a large platter and arrange the items for dipping around the pot.*

# beer and cheddar fondue

start to finish: 20 minutes  makes: 6 to 8 (¼-cup) servings

1 clove garlic, halved
1 cup light beer
½ teaspoon instant chicken bouillon granules
2 tablespoons cornstarch
2 tablespoons cold water
1 cup shredded American cheese (4 ounces)
2 cups shredded sharp cheddar cheese (8 ounces)
  Assorted items for dipping (French or Italian bread cubes, soft pretzels, breadsticks, red sweet pepper pieces, broccoli florets, and/or precooked baby sunburst squash)

**1** Rub the bottom and sides of a heavy metal fondue pot with the garlic halves.* Discard garlic. In the fondue pot combine beer and bouillon granules. Bring to boiling over medium-high heat.

**2** In a small bowl stir together cornstarch and the cold water. Add cornstarch mixture in a steady stream to beer mixture while stirring with a heat-resistant rubber spatula or wooden spoon. Cook and stir until thickened and bubbly. Reduce heat to medium low. Gradually stir in shredded cheeses, stirring after each addition until cheese melts.

**3** Keep mixture warm over a fondue burner. Serve with dippers. Spear dipper with a fondue fork or wooden skewer. Dip into cheese mixture, swirling to coat. (Fondue will thicken as it sits over the burner.)

nutrition facts per ¼ cup: 258 cal., 18 g total fat (12 g sat. fat), 57 mg chol., 580 mg sodium, 6 g carb., 0 g dietary fiber, 14 g protein.

*note: If you want to use a ceramic fondue pot, use a medium saucepan to prepare as directed through Step 2. Transfer cheese mixture to ceramic fondue pot and continue as directed in Step 3.

*When serving this delightfully sweet-savory dip, rub each pear slice with a little lemon juice to prevent browning through oxidation.*

# caramelized onion–blue cheese dip

prep: 15 minutes   cook: about 20 minutes   makes: 2 cups

1   tablespoon olive oil
1   large sweet onion, halved and cut into thin slivers
8   ounces cremini mushrooms, chopped
½   of an 8-ounce package reduced-fat cream cheese (Neufchâtel), softened
⅓   cup crumbled blue cheese
¼   cup fat-free milk
1   teaspoon snipped fresh thyme or sage
⅛   teaspoon salt
⅛   teaspoon ground black pepper
    Pear slices, melba toast, and/or whole grain crackers

**1** In a large nonstick skillet heat oil over medium heat. Add onion. Cover and cook in hot oil for 10 minutes, stirring occasionally. Uncover and add mushrooms. Cook, uncovered, for 8 to 10 minutes or until mushrooms are tender and onion is golden brown, stirring occasionally.

**2** Add cream cheese, blue cheese, milk, thyme, salt, and pepper. Cook and stir over low heat until mixture melts. Serve warm with pear slices, melba toast, and/or whole grain crackers.

nutrition facts per ¼ cup: 99 cal., 7 g total fat (3 g sat. fat), 15 mg chol., 172 mg sodium, 6 g carb., 1 g dietary fiber, 4 g protein.

*This popular Tex-Mex dip is a breeze, calling for just a handful of ingredients and taking less than 30 minutes to whip together. If you prefer more spiciness but not too much heat, try the variation using roasted poblano peppers.*

# chili con queso

prep: 10 minutes  cook: 15 minutes  makes: 2⅔ cups

1   tablespoon butter
½   cup finely chopped onion (1 medium)
1⅓  cups chopped, seeded tomato (about 2 medium)
1   4-ounce can diced green chile peppers, undrained
½   teaspoon ground cumin
2   ounces Monterey Jack cheese with jalapeño peppers, shredded (½ cup)
1   teaspoon cornstarch
1   8-ounce package cream cheese, cubed
    Tortilla chips or corn chips

**1** In a medium saucepan melt butter over low heat. Cook onion in hot butter for 5 minutes or until tender. Stir in tomato, peppers, and cumin. Heat to boiling; reduce heat. Simmer, uncovered, for 10 minutes, stirring occasionally.

**2** Toss shredded Monterey Jack cheese with cornstarch. Gradually add cheese mixture to saucepan, stirring until cheese melts. Gradually add the cream cheese, stirring until cheese melts and mixture is smooth. Heat through. Serve with chips.

nutrition facts per 2 tablespoons: 58 cal., 5 g total fat (3 g sat. fat), 16 mg chol., 79 mg sodium, 5 g carb., 0 g dietary fiber, 2 g protein.

**slow-cooker directions:** Prepare as above. Transfer chili to a 1½- or 2-quart slow cooker. Keep warm on low heat setting, if available, up to 2 hours, stirring occasionally.

roasted poblano chili con queso: Preheat oven to 425°F. Line a baking sheet with foil; set aside. Cut 2 fresh poblano chili peppers lengthwise into quarters, removing stems, seeds, and membranes (see note, page 52). Place pepper quarters, skin sides up, on prepared baking sheet. Bake for 20 to 25 minutes or until skins are blistered and dark. Bring foil up around peppers to enclose. Let stand for about 15 minutes or until cool. Using a sharp knife, loosen edges of the skins; gently pull off the skin in strips and discard. Finely chop peppers. Prepare Chili con Queso as above, except substitute the finely chopped poblano peppers for the canned diced green chile peppers.

*Although Asiago cheese originally hails from Italy, American cheese makers have perfected their own versions, which are widely available. Try it in this dip—you'll love the way the dip stays warm in a slow cooker during a party. Pictured on page 34.*

# asiago cheese dip

prep: 25 minutes  cook: 3 hours (low) or 1½ hours (high)  makes: 7 cups

1  cup chicken broth or water
4  ounces dried tomato (not oil packed)
2  16-ounce cartons dairy sour cream
1½  cups finely shredded Asiago cheese (6 ounces)
1¼  cups mayonnaise
½  of an 8-ounce package cream cheese, cut up
1  cup sliced fresh mushrooms or 1 ounce rehydrated dried mushrooms (such as porcini, shiitake, chanterelle, and/or oyster)*
1  cup thinly sliced green onion
   Thinly sliced green onion
   Baguette-style French bread slices, topped with finely shredded Asiago cheese and toasted

**1** In a small saucepan bring broth to boiling. Remove from heat. Add dried tomato. Cover and let stand for 5 minutes. Drain, discarding liquid. Chop tomato (you should have about 1¼ cups).

**2** Meanwhile, in a 3½- or 4-quart slow cooker combine sour cream, Asiago cheese, mayonnaise, cream cheese, mushrooms, and green onion. Stir in chopped tomato.

**3** Cover and cook on low heat setting for 3 to 4 hours or on high heat setting for 1½ to 2 hours.

**4** Stir well before serving. If desired, keep warm in the slow cooker on low heat setting for up to 2 hours. Sprinkle dip with additional green onions and serve with bread slices.

nutrition facts per ¼ cup: 196 cal., 19 g total fat (8 g sat. fat), 29 mg chol., 269 mg sodium, 4 g carb., 1 g dietary fiber, 4 g protein.

*note: To rehydrate dried mushrooms, place the dried mushrooms in a small bowl. Add enough boiling water to cover; let stand for 30 minutes. Drain mushrooms, squeezing out any excess liquid. Coarsely chop mushrooms.

*Hot enough for your taste? Turn up the heat by using spicy salsa or Monterey Jack cheese with jalapeño peppers.*

# rio grande dip

prep: 20 minutes   cook: 3 hours (low) or 1½ hours (high)   makes: 8 cups

8   ounces bulk Italian sausage
1   small onion, finely chopped
2   15-ounce cans refried black beans
1½   cups shredded Monterey Jack cheese (6 ounces)
1½   cups bottled salsa
1   4-ounce can diced green chile peppers, undrained
    Shredded Monterey Jack cheese (optional)
    Scoop-shape tortilla chips and/or corn chips

**1** In a large skillet cook sausage and onion over medium-high heat until meat is brown. Drain off fat. Transfer meat mixture to a 3½- or 4-quart slow cooker. Stir in refried beans, the 1½ cups cheese, the salsa, and chile peppers.

**2** Cover and cook on low heat setting for 3 to 4 hours or on high heat setting for 1½ to 2 hours.

**3** Stir well before serving. If desired, keep warm in the slow cooker on low heat setting for up to 2 hours. If desired, sprinkle with additional cheese. Serve with tortilla and/or corn chips.

nutrition facts per ¼ cup: 70 cal., 4 g total fat (2 g sat. fat), 10 mg chol., 279 mg sodium, 5 g carb., 1 g dietary fiber, 4 g protein.

*Hot artichoke dip always gets plenty of oohs and aahs. Ours garners even more thanks to banana peppers, very mild chiles with a sweet and fruity flavor.*

# hot artichoke
## and banana pepper dip

prep: 25 minutes  bake: 25 minutes  oven: 400°F  makes: 5½ cups

3   9-ounce packages frozen artichoke hearts, cooked, drained, and coarsely chopped
2   cups finely shredded Parmigiano-Reggiano or Parmesan cheese (8 ounces)
1½  cups light mayonnaise
1   large red, yellow, or green sweet pepper, finely chopped
1   medium fresh banana chile pepper, sliced crosswise and seeded (see note, page 52), or ½ cup bottled banana peppers, drained
6   cloves garlic, minced
2   teaspoons ground cumin
1   recipe Pita Crisps

**1** Preheat oven to 400°F. In a large bowl combine artichokes, Parmigiano-Reggiano cheese, mayonnaise, sweet pepper, banana pepper, garlic, and cumin. Transfer mixture to a 1½-quart baking dish.

**2** Bake for 25 to 30 minutes or until mixture is heated through and top is golden brown. Serve with Pita Crisps.

nutrition facts per ¼ cup: 101 cal., 8 g total fat (2 g sat. fat), 11 mg chol., 251 mg sodium, 5 g carb., 2 g dietary fiber, 4 g protein.

**make-ahead directions:** Prepare Pita Crisps as directed. Store in an airtight container at room temperature for up to 1 week.

pita crisps: Preheat oven to 350°F. Split 3 pita bread rounds in half horizontally, separating each into 2 rounds. Cut rounds into 1-inch-wide strips. In a small bowl stir together 3 tablespoons olive oil, ½ teaspoon chili powder, and ¼ teaspoon garlic salt. Brush oil mixture lightly over rough surfaces of pita strips. Arrange strips, brushed sides up, in a single layer on baking sheets. Bake for 10 to 12 minutes or until crisp. Cool.

*The licoricelike tones of fennel combine with blue cheese and bacon for one unbelievably good party dip.*

# baked fennel–
## blue cheese dip

prep: 35 minutes  bake: 15 minutes  oven: 400°F  makes: 4 cups

4 slices bacon

3 medium fennel bulbs, halved lengthwise, cored, and thinly sliced*

2 cloves garlic, minced

1 8-ounce jar mayonnaise

1 8-ounce carton dairy sour cream

1 4-ounce package crumbled blue cheese (1 cup)

20 black or pink peppercorns, crushed

2 tablespoons finely shredded Parmesan cheese

2 tablespoons fine dry breadcrumbs
Assorted vegetable dippers (Belgian endive leaves and/ or jicama sticks)

**1** Preheat oven to 400°F. In a large skillet cook bacon over medium heat until crisp. Drain bacon on paper towels, reserving 1 tablespoon drippings in skillet. Crumble bacon.

**2** Add fennel and garlic to reserved drippings. Cook over medium heat for about 10 minutes or just until fennel is tender and starts to brown, stirring occasionally. Remove from heat. Add bacon, mayonnaise, sour cream, blue cheese, and peppercorns to fennel mixture. Stir to combine. Divide mixture between two 16-ounce ovenproof crocks, soufflé dishes, or gratin dishes. In a small bowl combine Parmesan cheese and breadcrumbs; sprinkle over fennel mixture.

**3** Bake, uncovered, for about 15 minutes or just until mixture is heated through and tops are lightly browned (do not overbake). Serve with vegetable dippers.

nutrition facts per ¼ cup: 212 cal., 21 g total fat (7 g sat. fat), 24 mg chol., 287 mg sodium, 3 g carb., 1 g dietary fiber, 4 g protein.

*note: You may substitute 4½ cups shredded cabbage or 3½ cups chopped cauliflower for the fennel. Cook as directed.

*Elevate the spiciness of this quick, convenient cheese fondue by adjusting the heat level from 1 to 2 canned chipotle chile peppers.*

# smoky chipotle fondue

start to finish: 15 minutes  makes: 1 cup

8  ounces American cheese, cubed
2  tablespoons dry white wine
2  teaspoons Dijon-style mustard
½  teaspoon Worcestershire sauce
1  to 2 canned chipotle chile peppers in adobo sauce, chopped (see note, page 52)
2  to 4 tablespoons milk
   Assorted dippers (crusty French bread cubes and/or tortilla chips)

**1** In a heavy medium saucepan combine cheese, wine, mustard, Worcestershire sauce, and chipotle peppers. Cook and stir over medium-low heat until melted and smooth. Stir in enough of the milk to reach desired consistency. Transfer cheese mixture to a fondue pot. Keep mixture warm over a fondue burner.

**2** Serve with dippers. If mixture becomes too thick, stir in a little warm milk to reach desired consistency.

nutrition facts per ¼ cup: 114 cal., 9 g total fat (6 g sat. fat), 27 mg chol., 427 mg sodium, 1 g carb., 0 g dietary fiber, 6 g protein.

dipping **delights**

*French Comté is a wonderful melting cheese for this rich, sherry-flavored fondue. Tossing a little flour with the cheese prevents clumping and helps thicken the fondue to a creamy consistency.*

# fondue comté

start to finish: 45 minutes  makes: 12 (¼-cup) servings

1¼ pounds Comté cheese or Gruyère cheese, rind removed and shredded (5 cups)

3 tablespoons all-purpose flour

1½ cups dry white wine

¼ cup milk

2 tablespoons dry sherry

⅛ teaspoon ground nutmeg

⅛ teaspoon ground white pepper

Assorted dippers (French bread cut into 1-inch cubes and toasted,* pretzel rods, apple slices, and/or pear slices)

**1** Bring shredded cheese to room temperature. Toss with flour.

**2** In a large saucepan heat wine over medium heat until small bubbles rise to the surface. Just before wine boils, reduce heat to low and stir in the cheese mixture, a little at a time, stirring constantly. Make sure the cheese is melted before adding more. Stir until mixture bubbles gently.

**3** Stir in milk, sherry, nutmeg, and pepper. Transfer cheese mixture to a fondue pot. Keep mixture bubbling gently over a fondue burner. Serve with dippers. If mixture becomes too thick, stir in a little warm milk to reach desired consistency.

nutrition facts per serving: 233 cal., 15 g total fat (9 g sat. fat), 52 mg chol., 162 mg sodium, 3 g carb., 0 g dietary fiber, 14 g protein.

*note: To toast bread, place cubes on a baking sheet. Toast in a 350°F oven for 5 to 7 minutes or until crisp and toasted.

*This is it! A rich, wine-laced, Swiss-style recipe for the fondue purist, featuring smooth-melting Gruyère and classic nutty-sweet Emmentaler.*

# swiss fondue

start to finish: 65 minutes   oven: 350°F   makes: 16 (¼-cup) servings

1¼  pounds Gruyère, Emmentaler, and/ or Swiss cheese, shredded (5 cups)
1   clove garlic, halved
3   tablespoons all-purpose flour
3   to 4 ounces French bread, herb bread, or rye bread, cut into 1-inch cubes, and/or 4 cups vegetable dippers (broccoli florets, cauliflower florets, tiny new potatoes, and/or cherry tomatoes)
1½  cups dry white wine
¼   cup milk
1   tablespoon Cognac or brandy (optional)
1   teaspoon Dijon-style mustard
⅛   teaspoon ground nutmeg

**1** Let shredded cheeses stand at room temperature for 30 minutes. Meanwhile, rub inside of a fondue pot with garlic. Discard garlic; set pan aside. Toss cheeses with flour; set aside.

**2** Preheat the oven to 350°F. Place bread cubes on a baking sheet and bake for 5 to 7 minutes or until crisp and toasted; set aside.

**3** In a large saucepan bring a small amount of water to boiling; add broccoli or cauliflower florets. Simmer, covered, for about 3 minutes or until crisp-tender. Drain; rinse with cold water. Drain well; set aside. To cook potatoes, simmer, covered, for 10 to 12 minutes or until tender.

**4** In a large saucepan heat wine over medium heat until small bubbles rise to the surface. Just before wine boils, reduce heat to medium low and stir in the cheese mixture, a little at a time, whisking constantly. Make sure the cheese is melted before adding more. Gradually stir in milk. Cook and stir until bubbles begin to form.

**5** Stir in Cognac (if desired), mustard, and nutmeg. Transfer cheese mixture to a fondue pot. Keep mixture bubbling gently over a fondue burner. Serve with toasted bread cubes and/or vegetables. If mixture becomes too thick, stir in a little warm milk to reach desired consistency.

nutrition facts per serving: 188 cal., 12 g total fat (7 g sat. fat), 39 mg chol., 164 mg sodium, 5 g carb., 0 g dietary fiber, 11 g protein.

*Here's a yummy change of pace for traditional chocolate fondue. Cinnamon adds an unexpected flavor twist and marshmallow cream adds ooey-gooey richness.*

# s'mores fondue

start to finish: 20 minutes  makes: 3½ cups

⅓ cup unsweetened cocoa powder
¼ cup sugar
2 tablespoons cornstarch
¼ teaspoon ground cinnamon
2½ cups low-fat milk
⅔ cup marshmallow crème
Low-fat milk
Graham cracker sticks and/or assorted fruit dippers (strawberries, banana chunks, and/or apple wedges)

**1** In a medium saucepan combine cocoa powder, sugar, cornstarch, and cinnamon. Gradually whisk in the 2½ cups milk. Cook and stir over medium heat until thickened and bubbly; reduce heat to low. Cook and stir for 2 minutes more. Remove from heat. Add marshmallow crème, whisking until well combined.

**2** Transfer chocolate mixture to a 1- or 1½-quart slow cooker or a fondue pot. Keep warm for up to 2 hours on low heat. Stir occasionally and add additional milk to thin as needed. Serve warm with graham cracker sticks and/or fruit dippers.

nutrition facts per ¼ cup: 54 cal., 1 g total fat (0 g sat. fat), 2 mg chol., 23 mg sodium, 11 g carb., 1 g dietary fiber, 2 g protein.

*Serve this dessert fondue year-round; just vary the fruits and other dippers to suit the season. Even leftover fondue creates sweet decadence when reheated and drizzled over ice cream.*

# chocolate–peanut butter fondue

start to finish: 15 minutes   makes: 1¼ cups

1   11½-ounce package milk chocolate pieces
¼   cup milk
1   tablespoon crunchy peanut butter
Milk
Assorted dippers (orange sections, whole strawberries, pear slices, banana slices, and/or apple chunks; angel cake or pound cake cubes; thin butter cookies)

**1** In a heavy small saucepan (or the top of a double boiler placed over gently simmering water) combine chocolate pieces and the ¼ cup milk. Cook, stirring constantly, over low heat until chocolate melts and is smooth. Stir in peanut butter. Cook and stir until heated through. Stir in additional milk, 1 tablespoon at a time, to reach desired consistency.

**2** Transfer mixture to a fondue pot. Keep mixture warm over a fondue burner. Serve with dippers. If mixture becomes too thick, stir in additional milk, 1 tablespoon at a time, to reach desired consistency.

nutrition facts per ¼ cup: 374 cal., 21 g total fat (11 g sat. fat), 12 mg chol., 61 mg sodium, 40 g carb., 0 g dietary fiber, 6 g protein.

flaming caramel-pecan fondue: Prepare as directed in Step 1, except omit peanut butter. Stir in 2 tablespoons caramel ice cream topping. Cook and stir until heated through. Pour mixture into a fondue pot. Keep warm over a fondue burner. Slowly pour 1 tablespoon rum into fondue pot. Ignite rum by touching lighted match to edge of pot. (Cooking or flambéing with an open flame should be done with great care. It will take about 1½ minutes for the flame to burn down.) After the flame burns down, sprinkle 1 tablespoon finely chopped pecans over the top. Do not stir.

nutrition facts per ¼ cup: 392 cal., 21 g total fat (11 g sat. fat), 12 mg chol., 78 mg sodium, 45 g carb., 0 g dietary fiber, 5 g protein.

3

meatballs 'n'

slid

Roly-poly meatballs and juicy, bite-size burgers are cute, fun, and easy ways to wow a crowd. Set out a buffet of these people-pleasing possibilities. (Bet your guests can't eat just one.)

ers

*Use prepared meatballs for convenience and you won't spend much time in the kitchen. Even the fruity sauce that glazes these takes just a handful of ingredients.*

# sweet, hot, and sour
## meatballs

prep: 10 minutes  bake: 20 minutes  oven: 350°F  makes: 10 servings

1  **16-ounce package frozen cooked plain meatballs (32)**
⅓  **cup apple jelly**
3  **tablespoons spicy brown mustard**
3  **tablespoons whiskey or apple juice**
½  **teaspoon Worcestershire sauce**
  **Few dashes bottled hot pepper sauce**

**1** Preheat oven to 350°F. Place frozen meatballs in a single layer in a shallow baking pan. Bake for about 20 minutes or until heated through.

**2** Meanwhile, in a large saucepan stir together jelly, mustard, whiskey, Worcestershire sauce, and hot pepper sauce over medium heat. Cook and stir until jelly melts and mixture is bubbly.

**3** Using a slotted spoon, transfer meatballs to jelly mixture. Stir gently to coat. Return to boiling; reduce heat. Simmer, uncovered, for 3 to 5 minutes or until sauce thickens, stirring occasionally. Serve meatballs with short skewers or toothpicks. If desired, keep warm in a slow cooker on warm or low heat setting for up to 2 hours.

nutrition facts per serving: 183 cal., 12 g total fat (5 g sat. fat), 16 mg chol., 425 mg sodium, 11 g carb., 1 g dietary fiber, 6 g protein.

*The beer and stone-ground mustard sauce tastes extraordinary when combined with bacon-enhanced meatballs. When choosing a beer, keep in mind, the darker the brew, the stronger the flavor. For really bold taste, use a dark malty ale such as stout.*

# beer-braised meatballs

prep: 35 minutes  bake: 18 minutes  start to finish: 400°F
makes: 24 meatballs

| | |
|---|---|
| 2 | eggs, lightly beaten |
| 1 | cup soft breadcrumbs |
| 4 | slices bacon, crisp cooked and crumbled |
| ½ | cup chopped fresh parsley |
| 2 | tablespoons chopped onion |
| 1 | clove garlic, minced |
| 1 | teaspoon dried thyme, crushed |
| 1 | teaspoon black pepper |
| 1 | pound lean ground beef |
| 2 | tablespoons butter |
| 2 | tablespoons chopped onion |
| ⅓ | cup beer |
| 1 | tablespoon stone-ground mustard |
| 1½ | cups beef broth |
| 2 | tablespoons cornstarch |
| 1 | tablespoon honey |

1 Preheat oven to 400°F. In a large bowl combine eggs, breadcrumbs, bacon, parsley, 2 tablespoons onion, garlic, thyme, and pepper. Add beef; mix well. Shape mixture into 24 meatballs.

2 Arrange meatballs in a single layer in a 15×10×1-inch baking pan. Bake, uncovered, for about 25 minutes or until cooked through (160°F), checking with an instant-read thermometer.

3 In a large skillet melt butter over medium heat. Cook 2 tablespoons onion in melted butter for 5 minutes or until onion is tender. Add beer and mustard. In a medium bowl combine beef broth and cornstarch. Add to skillet. Cook and stir until sauce thickens and is bubbly. Cook and stir for 2 minutes more. Stir in honey. Add meatballs; heat through.

4 Serve meatballs with short skewers or toothpicks. If desired, keep warm in a slow cooker on warm or low heat setting for up to 2 hours.

nutrition facts per meatball: 68 cal., 4 g total fat (2 g sat. fat), 34 mg chol., 137 mg sodium, 3 g carb., 0 g dietary fiber, 5 g protein.

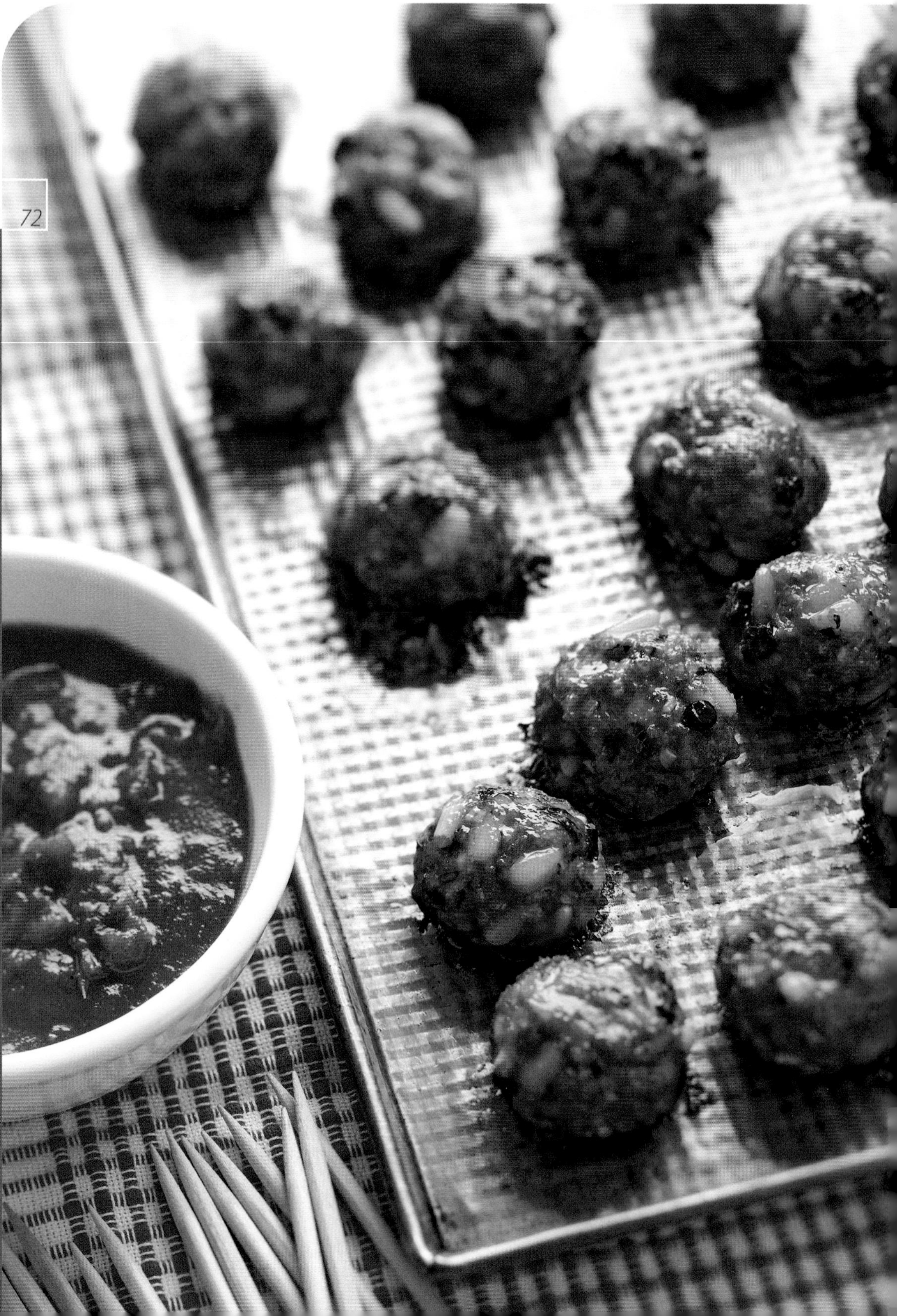

*Italian sausage comes in "sweet" and "hot" versions. Sweet Italian sausage is not actually "sweet," but rather seasoned with fennel and garlic, while the "hot" version also contains crushed red pepper flakes.*

# oven-baked
# sicilian meatballs

prep: 20 minutes  bake: 25 minutes  oven: 350°F  makes: 24 meatballs

⅔   cup soft breadcrumbs
3   tablespoons milk
1   egg, lightly beaten
⅓   cup grated Parmesan
     cheese
¼   cup finely chopped
     onion
¼   cup snipped fresh
     basil
3   tablespoons pine
     nuts, toasted
3   tablespoons dried
     currants
½   teaspoon salt
1   clove garlic, minced
¼   teaspoon freshly
     ground black
     pepper
1   pound bulk sweet
     Italian sausage
     Bottled pasta sauce,
     warmed (optional)

**1** Preheat oven to 350°F. In a large bowl combine breadcrumbs and milk. Let stand for 5 minutes. Stir in egg, Parmesan cheese, onion, basil, pine nuts, currants, salt, garlic, and pepper. Add sausage; mix well. Shape mixture into 24 meatballs.

**2** Arrange meatballs in a single layer in a 15×10×1-inch baking pan. Bake, uncovered, for 25 to 30 minutes or until cooked through (160°F), checking with an instant-read thermometer. Drain off fat.

**3** Serve meatballs with short skewers or toothpicks. If desired, serve with pasta sauce for dipping. If desired, keep warm in a slow cooker on warm or low heat setting for up to 2 hours.

nutrition facts per meatball: 58 cal., 3 g total fat (1 g sat. fat), 16 mg chol., 199 mg sodium, 3 g carb., 0 g dietary fiber, 4 g protein.

*In Mexico, meatballs are most commonly found in soups, but your guests will love eating them on top of tortilla chips.*

# appetizer albondigas

prep: 30 minutes   bake: 15 minutes   oven: 425°F   makes: 32 meatballs

1   egg, lightly beaten
½   cup finely chopped onion
3   tablespoons yellow cornmeal
2   tablespoons snipped fresh cilantro
1   tablespoon finely chopped chipotle chile peppers in adobo sauce (see note, page 52)
¾   teaspoon dried oregano, crushed
½   teaspoon ground cumin
¼   teaspoon salt
12   ounces ground beef
12   ounces ground pork
½   cup shredded Mexican-style four-cheese blend
32   tortilla chips
     Fresh salsa

**1** Preheat oven to 425°F. In a large bowl combine egg, onion, cornmeal, cilantro, chipotle peppers, oregano, cumin, and salt. Add beef and pork; mix well. Shape mixture into 32 meatballs.

**2** Arrange meatballs ½ inch apart in a 15×10×1-inch baking pan. Bake, uncovered, for 12 to 15 minutes or until cooked through (160°F), checking with an instant-read thermometer.

**3** Remove pan from oven. Using a spatula, push meatballs together so they are touching on all sides. Sprinkle with cheese. Bake for 2 to 3 minutes more or until cheese melts.

**4** To serve, place each meatball on a tortilla chip. Serve with salsa.

nutrition facts per meatball: 83 cal., 6 g total fat (2 g sat. fat), 23 mg chol., 86 mg sodium, 3 g carb., 0 g dietary fiber, 5 g protein.

*These fun mini meatballs are on skewers, so they're perfect party fare. For easier skewering, pour boiling water over the mushrooms and drain.*

# fontina-stuffed
# meatball kabobs

prep: 30 minutes  grill: 10 minutes  makes: 16 servings

1  egg, lightly beaten
⅓  cup grated Parmesan cheese
2  cloves garlic, minced
1  teaspoon dried Italian seasoning
½  teaspoon salt
⅛  teaspoon ground black pepper
1½  pounds lean ground beef
2  ounces very thinly sliced prosciutto, chopped
1½  ounces fontina cheese cubes
8  canned artichoke hearts, drained and halved
1  6- to 8-ounce package fresh cremini mushrooms
1  pint grape tomatoes
1  recipe Balsamic Glaze
   Fresh basil (optional)

**1** Preheat the grill. In a large bowl combine egg, Parmesan cheese, garlic, Italian seasoning, salt, and pepper. Add beef and prosciutto; mix well.

**2** Divide mixture into 16 portions. Shape into balls around cheese cubes. Thread meatballs, artichoke halves, mushrooms, and tomatoes on sixteen 8- to-10-inch skewers, leaving ¼ inch between pieces. (If using wooden skewers, soak them in water for at least 30 minutes before threading with food to prevent burning when grilling.) Prepare Balsamic Glaze; set aside.

**3** For a charcoal grill, place skewers on the greased rack of an uncovered grill directly over medium coals. Grill for 10 to 12 minutes or until meat is no longer pink (160°F), checking with an instant-read thermometer. Turn meatballs and brush with half of the glaze halfway through grilling. (For a gas grill, preheat grill. Reduce heat to medium. Place skewers on a greased grill rack over heat. Cover and grill as above.) To serve, drizzle with remaining glaze. Sprinkle with fresh basil, if desired.

nutrition facts per serving: 135 cal., 8 g total fat (3 g sat. fat), 46 mg chol., 337 mg sodium, 4 g carb., 1 g dietary fiber, 12 g protein.

balsamic glaze: In a small saucepan combine ⅓ cup balsamic vinegar; 2 teaspoons olive oil; 1 clove garlic, minced; ¼ teaspoon salt; ¼ teaspoon dried Italian seasoning; and ⅛ teaspoon ground black pepper. Bring to boiling; reduce heat. Simmer uncovered for 4 minutes or until slightly thickened and reduced to ¼ cup. Divide in half.

*The fresh version of these mushrooms are difficult to find in the United States. Luckily, the dehydrated ones do a great job of infusing the meatballs with their aromatic woodsy flavor.*

# porcini-herb meatballs

prep: 30 minutes   cook: 30 minutes   stand: 30 minutes   makes: 18 meatballs

2½   ounces dried porcini
       mushrooms
       Boiling water
1   egg, lightly beaten
1   cup finely chopped
       onion
¼   cup fine dry
       breadcrumbs
1   tablespoon dry red
       wine
2   teaspoons snipped
       fresh thyme
2   cloves garlic, minced
½   teaspoon salt
1   pound lean ground
       beef or ground veal
3   tablespoons olive oil
1   cup dry red wine
2   tablespoons snipped
       fresh parsley
2   tablespoons snipped
       fresh thyme
1   teaspoon sugar
¼   teaspoon ground
       black pepper
1   to 2 tablespoons dry
       red wine

**1** In a bowl combine mushrooms and enough boiling water to cover. Let stand for 30 minutes. Drain, squeezing out any excess liquid. Reserve ½ cup of the mushrooms; finely chop remaining mushrooms.

**2** Combine egg, ¾ cup of the onion, breadcrumbs, 1 tablespoon wine, 2 teaspoons thyme, garlic, salt, and finely chopped mushrooms. Add ground beef; mix well. Shape mixture into 18 meatballs.

**3** In a skillet heat oil over medium-high heat. Cook meatballs in for hot oil for about 8 minutes or until brown, turning occasionally. Remove meatballs from skillet. Drain off fat.

**4** In the skillet combine 1 cup wine, remaining onion, the parsley, the 2 tablespoons thyme, the sugar, pepper, and the reserved ½ cup mushrooms. Bring to boiling; reduce heat. Stir in meatballs. Simmer, uncovered, for about 30 minutes or until cooked through (160°F), checking with an instant-read thermometer, and sauce reaches desired consistency. Gently stir mixture occasionally to keep meatballs moistened. Before serving, stir in the 1 to 2 tablespoons wine.

**5** Serve meatballs with short skewers or toothpicks. If desired, keep warm in a slow cooker on warm or low heat setting for up to 2 hours.

nutrition facts per meatball: 108 cal., 6 g total fat (3 g sat. fat), 28 mg chol., 130 mg sodium, 6 g carb., 0 g dietary fiber, 6 g protein.

*Here's a hearty crowd-pleasing appetizer that takes just three ingredients.*

# sweet and sassy
# meatballs

start to finish: 30 minutes  makes: 64 meatballs

1  16-ounce can jellied cranberry sauce
1  18-ounce bottle barbecue sauce
2  16-ounce packages frozen cooked meatballs (32), thawed

**1** In a large skillet combine cranberry sauce and barbecue sauce over medium heat. Cook until cranberry sauce melts, stirring occasionally.

**2** Add meatballs to skillet. Cook, uncovered, for 10 minutes or until meatballs are heated through, stirring occasionally. Serve meatballs with short skewers or wooden toothpicks. Keep warm in a slow cooker on warm or low heat setting for up to 2 hours.

nutrition facts per 4 meatballs: 60 cal., 4 g total fat (2 g sat. fat), 5 mg chol., 177 mg sodium, 5 g carb., 1 g dietary fiber, 2 g protein.

**make-ahead directions:** Prepare as directed in Step 1. Stir in frozen or thawed meatballs. Cover and chill for up to 24 hours. Heat meatballs and sauce in a large skillet over medium heat until heated through, stirring occasionally.

chipotle sauce: Prepare sauce as directed, except substitute one 12-ounce bottle chili sauce for the barbecue sauce and stir in 3 to 4 tablespoons finely chopped canned chipotle chile pepper in adobo sauce.

hawaiian sauce: Prepare sauce as directed, except substitute one 8-ounce can crushed pineapple for the cranberry sauce.

*Almonds accentuate the robust taste of sage in these meatballs, while pecans will make them taste slightly sweeter.*

# sage and bacon meatballs

prep: 40 minutes  bake: 25 minutes  broil: 4 minutes  cool: 15 minutes
oven: 350°F  makes: 8 servings

12  slices bacon
1  egg, lightly beaten
1  cup whipping cream
¾  cup finely chopped
    red onion
¼  cup ground toasted
    pecans or almonds
3  tablespoons snipped
    fresh sage or 1½
    teaspoons dried
    sage, crushed
⅛  teaspoon salt
⅛  teaspoon ground
    black pepper
1  pound ground pork
1  clove garlic, minced
    Fresh sage leaves
    (optional)

**1** Preheat oven to 350°F. In a large skillet cook 4 slices of the bacon over medium heat until crisp. Drain on paper towels. Cook remaining bacon for 4 to 5 minutes or just until beginning to brown, turning once. Drain on paper towels, reserving 1 tablespoon drippings in skillet. Finely chop the 4 strips crisp bacon; set aside.

**2** In a large bowl combine egg, 2 tablespoons of the whipping cream, ½ cup of the onion, the pecans, 2 tablespoons of the snipped sage, the salt, and pepper. Add pork and three-quarters of the finely chopped bacon; mix well. Shape mixture into 16 meatballs.

**3** Arrange meatballs in a single layer in a 15×10×1-inch baking pan. Bake, uncovered, for about 25 minutes or until cooked through (160°F), checking with an instant-read thermometer. Cool for 15 minutes.

**4** Thread 2 meatballs and 1 slice of the partially cooked bacon onto a 4-inch skewer, weaving bacon around meatballs. Repeat with remaining meatballs and bacon slices. Place on the unheated rack of a broiler pan. Broil 3 to 4 inches from the heat for 4 to 5 minutes or until bacon is crisp, turning once.

**5** Meanwhile, for sauce, cook the remaining ¼ cup onion and the garlic in the reserved drippings until tender. Stir in the remaining whipping cream and the remaining 1 tablespoon snipped sage. Bring to boiling; reduce heat. Simmer for 5 minutes or until sauce thickens. Stir in the remaining finely chopped bacon.

**6** Arrange meatball kabobs on a platter. If desired, garnish with sage leaves. Serve with sauce.

nutrition facts per serving: 370 cal., 33 g total fat (14 g sat. fat), 123 mg chol., 369 mg sodium, 3 g carb., 1 g dietary fiber, 16 g protein.

*Here's a slick trick for uniformly shaped meatballs: Pat the meat mixture into a 6×5-inch rectangle on a piece of waxed paper. Cut the mixture into 1-inch cubes, then use your hands to roll each cube into a ball.*

# apricot-glazed **ham balls**

prep: 20 minutes  bake: 20 minutes  cook: 4 to 5 hours (low) or 1½ to 2 hours (high)
oven: 350°F  makes: 30 meatballs

1 egg, beaten
½ cup graham cracker crumbs
2 tablespoons unsweetened pineapple juice
1 teaspoon dry mustard
¼ teaspoon salt
8 ounces ground cooked ham
8 ounces ground pork
½ cup snipped dried apricots
1 18-ounce jar apricot preserves
⅓ cup unsweetened pineapple juice
1 tablespoon cider vinegar
½ teaspoon ground ginger

**1** Preheat oven to 350°F. In a large bowl combine egg, cracker crumbs, 2 tablespoons pineapple juice, dry mustard, and salt. Add ham, pork, and snipped apricots; mix well. Shape mixture into 30 meatballs.

**2** Arrange meatballs in a single layer in a 15×10×1-inch baking pan. Bake, uncovered, about 20 minutes or until cooked through (160°F), checking with an instant-read thermometer. Drain off fat.

**3** Place cooked meatballs in a 3½- or 4-quart slow cooker. In a small bowl combine apricot preserves, ⅓ cup pineapple juice, vinegar, and ginger. Pour over meatballs in cooker.

**4** Cover and cook on low heat setting for 4 to 5 hours or on high heat setting for 1½ to 2 hours. Gently stir just before serving. Serve with short skewers or toothpicks. If desired, keep warm on warm or low heat setting for up to 2 hours.

nutrition facts per meatball: 97 cal., 3 g total fat (1 g sat. fat), 17 mg chol., 151 mg sodium, 15 g carb., 0 g dietary fiber, 3 g protein.

**make-ahead directions:** Prepare meatballs as directed in Step 1. Cover and chill unbaked meatballs for up to 24 hours.

*If you are unable to find pancetta, feel free to substitute an equal amount of bacon.*

# pork meatballs
## and fig sauce

prep: 45 minutes   cook: 20 minutes   makes: 40 meatballs

2½ cups port
8 dried Mission figs, stemmed and chopped
2 sprigs fresh rosemary
2 3-inch sticks cinnamon
1 tablespoon honey
2 tablespoons butter
   Salt
   Ground black pepper
4 ounces thinly sliced pancetta (about 12 slices)
1 egg, lightly beaten
2 cups sourdough breadcrumbs
⅓ cup buttermilk
1 tablespoon olive oil
1 teaspoon snipped fresh rosemary
1 clove garlic, minced
⅛ teaspoon ground black pepper
1 pound ground pork

**1** For sauce, in a medium saucepan combine port, figs, rosemary sprigs, cinnamon, and honey. Bring to boiling, stirring to dissolve honey. Reduce heat and boil gently, uncovered, for about 30 minutes or until reduced to 1¼ cups. Discard cinnamon and rosemary sprigs. Cool sauce slightly. Transfer to a blender or food processor. Cover and blend or process until smooth. Return to saucepan. Add butter and heat through. Season to taste with salt and pepper.

**2** Meanwhile, in a very large skillet cook pancetta over medium heat until crisp. Drain on paper towels, reserving drippings in skillet. Crumble pancetta.

**3** In a large bowl combine egg, breadcrumbs, buttermilk, olive oil, snipped rosemary, garlic, and the ⅛ teaspoon pepper. Add pork and pancetta; mix well. Shape mixture into 40 meatballs.

**4** Heat pancetta drippings in the skillet over medium heat. Cook meatballs, half at a time, in the hot drippings for 10 minutes or until cooked through (160°F), checking with an instant-read thermometer. Gently turn meatballs during cooking to brown evenly. Serve meatballs, using short skewers or toothpicks, with fig sauce. If desired, keep meatballs warm in a slow cooker on warm or low heat setting for up to 2 hours.

nutrition facts per meatball: 89 cal., 4 g total fat (2 g sat. fat), 17 mg chol., 98 mg sodium, 6 g carb., 0 g dietary fiber, 3 g protein.

*Although this recipe calls for a package of 16 frozen meatballs, various brands contain different numbers of meatballs. You can easily substitute a package that contains 35 smaller meatballs.*

# plum-good
# sausage and
# meatballs

prep: 10 minutes   cook: 5 hours (low) or 2½ hours (high)   makes: 16 servings

1   10- to 12- ounce
    jar plum jam or
    preserves
1   18-ounce bottle
    barbecue sauce
1   16-ounce link cooked
    jalapeño smoked
    sausage or smoked
    sausage, sliced into
    bite-size pieces
1   16- to 18-ounce
    package Italian-
    style or original
    flavor frozen cooked
    meatballs (16),
    thawed

In a 3½- or 4-quart slow cooker combine the jam and barbecue sauce. Add the sausage and thawed meatballs. Cover and cook on low heat setting for 5 to 6 hours or on high heat setting for 2½ to 3 hours. Serve meatballs with short skewers or toothpicks. If desired, keep warm in a slow cooker on warm or low heat setting for up to 2 hours.

nutrition facts per serving: 267 cal., 16 g total fat (6 g sat. fat), 38 mg chol., 19 g carb., 2 g dietary fiber, 12 g protein.

*Lamb and mint give these meatballs an enticing North African flavor.*

# lamb meatballs
## with cranberry drizzle

prep: 35 minutes  bake: 15 minutes  oven: 300°F  makes: 32 meatballs

1   egg, lightly beaten
1   cup panko (Japanese-
     style breadcrumbs)
¼   cup snipped fresh
     mint
3   cloves garlic, minced
½   teaspoon salt
¼   teaspoon ground
     black pepper
1   pound ground lamb
1   pound lean ground
     beef
1   16-ounce bottle
     cranberry juice
1   tablespoon packed
     brown sugar
3   tablespoons olive oil
1   recipe Toasted Pita
     Wedges (optional)
     Fresh mint leaves
     (optional)

**1** Preheat oven to 300°F. In a large bowl combine egg, panko, the ¼ cup mint, the garlic, salt, and pepper. Add lamb and beef; mix well. Shape into 32 meatballs; set aside.

**2** In a medium saucepan bring cranberry juice to boiling; reduce heat. Simmer for 25 to 30 minutes or until reduced to ½ cup. Add brown sugar. Stir until sugar dissolves.

**3** Meanwhile, in a 12-inch skillet heat oil over medium heat. Brown half of the meatballs at a time in hot oil, turning to brown evenly.

**4** Arrange meatballs in a single layer in a 15×10×1-inch baking pan. Bake, uncovered, for 15 to 20 minutes or until cooked through (160°F), checking with an instant-read thermometer.

**5** Add cranberry mixture to the 12-inch skillet. Bring to boiling; reduce heat. Simmer for 3 to 5 minutes or until mixture thickens to a syrupy consistency. Add meatballs and stir to coat.

**6** To serve, arrange meatballs on a serving plate. Drizzle with cranberry sauce. If desired, serve with Toasted Pita Wedges and sprinkle with mint leaves.

nutrition facts per meatball: 101 cal., 7 g total fat (3 g sat. fat), 27 mg chol., 62 mg sodium, 4 g carb., 0 g dietary fiber, 5 g protein.

toasted pita wedges: Preheat oven to 350°F. Cut a pita bread round into 6 wedges and split each wedge in half horizontally. Brush wedges with 1 tablespoon olive oil and sprinkle with salt and ground black pepper. Place wedges on a baking sheet and bake for 5 to 8 minutes or until golden brown.

*Serve these fun little nibbles when you want to offer your guests an intriguing Mediterranean-inspired appetizer.*

# lamb meatballs
## with cucumber-yogurt sauce

**prep:** 25 minutes   **bake:** 20 minutes   **oven:** 350°F   **makes:** 36 meatballs

2  teaspoons olive oil
¼  cup finely chopped onion
2  cloves garlic, minced
1  egg, slightly beaten
¼  cup fine dry breadcrumbs
⅓  cup chopped toasted pine nuts
2  teaspoons finely snipped fresh mint
½  teaspoon salt
¼  teaspoon ground allspice
⅛  teaspoon ground cinnamon
⅛  teaspoon ground black pepper
1  pound ground lamb or ground beef
1  recipe Minted Cucumber-Yogurt Sauce

**1** Preheat oven to 350°F. In a small skillet heat oil over medium heat. Cook and stir onion and garlic in hot oil for about 3 minutes or until tender but not brown. Remove from heat.

**2** In a large bowl combine onion mixture, egg, breadcrumbs, pine nuts, mint, salt, allspice, cinnamon, and pepper. Add lamb; mix well. Shape mixture into 36 meatballs.

**3** Arrange meatballs in a 15×10×1-inch baking pan. Bake, uncovered, for 20 minutes. Drain off fat. Using a metal spatula, transfer meatballs to a serving dish. Serve with Minted Cucumber-Yogurt Sauce.

nutrition facts per meatball: 56 cal., 4 g total fat (1 g sat. fat), 15 mg chol., 60 mg sodium, 1 g carb., 0 g dietary fiber, 3 g protein.

minted cucumber-yogurt sauce: In a small bowl stir together one 8-ounce carton plain yogurt; ¼ cup coarsely shredded unpeeled cucumber, drained; 1 clove garlic, minced; 1 tablespoon finely snipped fresh mint; ⅛ teaspoon salt; and a dash of ground black pepper. Cover and chill for up to 24 hours. Stir before serving.

*These Scandinavian meatballs, called* kjottkaker *in Norway, are made even richer with the addition of half-and-half before shaping. Coffee and nutmeg create a bold-flavored sauce that contrasts nicely with the meatballs.*

# rich **norwegian** meatballs

prep: 40 minutes  chill: 2 hours  cook: 24 minutes  makes: 72 meatballs

1½  cups soft
      breadcrumbs
½   cup half-and-half or
      light cream
¼   cup strong coffee
2   eggs, lightly beaten
1   medium onion, finely
      chopped
¼   cup finely snipped
      fresh Italian parsley
1   teaspoon salt
1   teaspoon freshly
      grated nutmeg
¼   teaspoon ground
      black pepper
1   pound lean ground
      beef
½   pound ground turkey
      breast and/or lean
      ground pork
¼   cup butter
¼   cup all-purpose flour
1   cup beef broth
1   cup strong coffee
1   teaspoon freshly
      grated nutmeg
½   teaspoon salt

**1** In a large bowl combine breadcrumbs, half-and-half, and the ¼ cup coffee. Let stand until mixture is evenly moist.

**2** Add eggs, onion, parsley, the 1 teaspoon salt, the 1 teaspoon nutmeg, and the pepper. Add beef and turkey; mix well. Cover and chill for 2 hours. Using moistened hands, shape mixture into 72 meatballs.

**3** In a 12-inch skillet melt 2 tablespoons of the butter over medium heat. Cook half of the meatballs in hot butter for about 12 minutes or until cooked through (165°F), checking with an instant-read thermometer. Carefully turn meatballs during cooking to brown evenly. Using a slotted spoon, transfer meatballs to a platter. Add remaining butter to skillet and repeat with remaining meatballs. Remove meatballs from skillet to platter.

**4** Stir flour into pan drippings until smooth. Add broth, the 1 cup coffee, the 1 teaspoon nutmeg, and the ½ teaspoon salt. Cook and stir over medium heat until thickened and bubbly. Return all meatballs to skillet. Heat through, stirring gently occasionally.

**5** Serve meatballs with short skewers or toothpicks. If desired, keep warm in a slow cooker on warm or low heat setting for up to 2 hours.

nutrition facts per meatball: 30 cal., 2 g total fat (1 g sat. fat), 14 mg chol., 80 mg sodium, 1 g carb., 0 g dietary fiber, 2 g protein.

*Although this mixture will hold together and the meatballs will taste great if prepared with super-lean ground turkey breast, they will be juicier if the less-expensive dark meat ground turkey is used.*

# gingered turkey
## meatballs

prep: 30 minutes  bake: 15 minutes  oven: 425°F  makes: 28 meatballs

1  egg, lightly beaten
1  cup panko (Japanese-style breadcrumbs)
½  cup canned sliced water chestnuts, drained and finely chopped
½  cup finely snipped fresh cilantro
1  tablespoon grated fresh ginger
1  tablespoon reduced-sodium soy sauce
1  tablespoon sesame oil
2  cloves garlic, minced
½  teaspoon salt
¼  teaspoon cayenne pepper
1½  pounds ground turkey
1  cup sliced almonds, finely chopped
1  recipe Sesame-Lime Sauce

**1** Preheat oven to 425°F. In a large bowl combine egg, panko, water chestnuts, cilantro, ginger, soy sauce, sesame oil, garlic, salt, and cayenne pepper. Add turkey; mix well. Shape mixture into 28 meatballs.

**2** Roll meatballs in almonds. Arrange meatballs in a single layer in a 15×10×1-inch baking pan.

**3** Bake, uncovered, for 15 to 20 minutes or until cooked through (165°F), checking with an instant-read thermometer. Serve meatballs, using short skewers or toothpicks, with Sesame-Lime Sauce. If desired, keep warm on warm or low heat setting for up to 2 hours.

nutrition facts per meatball: 78 cal., 5 g total fat (1 g sat. fat), 27 mg chol., 177 mg sodium, 3 g carb., 1 g dietary fiber, 6 g protein.

sesame-lime sauce: In a small bowl combine ¼ cup reduced-sodium soy sauce, ¼ cup water, 2 tablespoons lime juice, 2 teaspoons sesame oil, and 2 teaspoons sugar. Stir until sugar dissolves.

*For super-saucy meatballs, double the sauce. Ancho chile powder adds a pleasing sweet and spicy bite to the sauce.*

# saucy apricot
## 'n' spice meatballs

prep: 25 minutes  bake: 15 minutes  oven: 350°F  makes: 24 meatballs

½   cup soft breadcrumbs
2   tablespoons milk
1   egg white
¼   cup finely chopped onion
¼   cup finely snipped dried apricots
1   clove garlic, minced
¼   teaspoon ancho chile powder or chili powder
6   ounces lean ground pork
6   ounces ground turkey breast
1   recipe Spiced Apricot Sauce

1 Preheat oven to 350°F. Line a 15×10×1-inch baking pan with foil; lightly grease foil. In a bowl combine breadcrumbs and milk. Let stand for 5 minutes. Stir in egg white, onion, dried apricots, garlic, chili powder, and ½ teaspoon *salt*. Add ground pork and turkey; mix well. Shape mixture into 24 meatballs.

2 Arrange meatballs in prepared baking pan. Bake, uncovered, for 15 to 20 minutes or until cooked through (160°F). Drain off fat.

3 Place meatballs in a 1½-quart slow cooker. Add Spiced Apricot Sauce. Toss gently to coat. Serve meatballs with skewers or toothpicks. If desired, keep warm in a slow cooker on warm or low heat setting for up to 2 hours.

nutrition facts per meatball: 38 cal., 2 g total fat (1 g sat. fat), 8 mg chol., 78 mg sodium, 3 g carb., 0 g dietary fiber, 3 g protein.

spiced apricot sauce: In saucepan combine ½ cup apricot nectar, 1 teaspoon cornstarch, ¼ teaspoon ancho chile powder or chili powder, ⅛ teaspoon salt, and ⅛ teaspoon ground nutmeg. Cook and stir over medium heat until thickened and bubbly. Cook and stir 1 minute more. Makes about ½ cup.

**make-ahead directions:** Prepare meatballs as directed through Step 2. Cool. Store in airtight container in refrigerator for up to 24 hours. Prepare sauce as directed. Store in airtight container in refrigerator for up to 2 days. Proceed as directed in Step 3, cooking on low heat setting for 2½ to 3 hours or until heated through. Turn to warm setting or leave on low heat setting; keep warm for up to 2 hours.

*These appetizers make throwing a party easy. Four ingredients and two hours—that's all you need.*

# italian cocktail
## meatballs

prep: 10 minutes   cook: 4 hours (low) or 2 hours (high)   makes: 12 meatballs

1   12-ounce package
    refrigerated or
    frozen cooked turkey
    meatballs (12)
½   cup bottled roasted
    red and/or yellow
    sweet peppers,
    drained and cut into
    1-inch pieces
⅛   teaspoon crushed red
    pepper
1   cup purchased onion-
    garlic pasta sauce

**1** Thaw meatballs, if frozen. In a 1½- or 2-quart slow cooker combine meatballs and roasted peppers. Sprinkle with crushed red pepper. Pour pasta sauce over meatball mixture in cooker.

**2** Cover and cook on low heat setting for 4 to 5 hours or on high heat setting for 2 to 2½ hours. If no heat setting is available, cook for 4 to 5 hours. Skim fat from sauce, if necessary. Stir gently before serving. Serve with short skewers or toothpicks. If desired, keep warm on warm or low heat setting for up to 2 hours.

nutrition facts per meatball: 79 cal., 4 g total fat (1 g sat. fat), 22 mg chol., 304 mg sodium, 6 g carb., 2 g dietary fiber, 5 g protein.

*Garlic and New Orleans–style seasoning are the secrets to the rich, robust flavor in these exquisite meatballs.*

# creole turkey meatballs

prep: 25 minutes  bake: 25 minutes  oven: 375°F  makes: 30 meatballs

1   egg, lightly beaten
1   medium sweet
    pepper, finely
    chopped
½   cup quick-cooking
    rolled oats
1   medium onion,
    chopped
2   tablespoons milk
1   teaspoon dried Italian
    seasoning, crushed
1   teaspoon salt-free
    garlic and herb
    seasoning blend
1   teaspoon Creole
    seasoning
2   cloves garlic, minced
1   pound ground turkey
    or chicken

**1** Preheat oven to 375°F. Lightly grease a 15×10×1-inch baking pan. In a large bowl combine egg, pepper, oats, onion, milk, Italian seasoning, salt-free seasoning, Creole seasoning, and garlic. Add turkey; mix well. Shape mixture into 30 meatballs.

**2** Arrange meatballs in a single layer in prepared baking pan.

**3** Bake, uncovered, for about 25 minutes or until cooked through (165°F), checking with an instant-read thermometer.

**4** Serve meatballs with short skewers or toothpicks. If desired, keep warm in a slow cooker on warm or low heat setting for up to 2 hours.

nutrition facts per meatball: 33 cal., 2 g total fat (0 g sat. fat), 19 mg chol., 37 mg sodium, 2 g carb., 0 g dietary fiber, 3 g protein.

**make-ahead directions:** Prepare as directed through Step 2. Cover and chill for up to 24 hours. Uncover and bake as directed in Step 3.

*Pureed canned peaches make a wonderful sauce base for turkey meatballs. For an unusual twist, stir in ketchup, ginger, and dried cherries.*

# turkey meatballs
## in peach sauce

prep: 35 minutes   cook: 22 minutes   makes: 24 meatballs

1   egg, beaten
¼   cup fine dry
     breadcrumbs
¼   cup finely chopped
     shallot
1   teaspoon grated fresh
     ginger
⅛   teaspoon salt
1   pound ground turkey
1   tablespoon cooking
     oil
1   15- to 16-ounce can
     peach slices (juice
     packed)
¼   cup ketchup
2   tablespoons soy
     sauce
2   tablespoons butter,
     melted
¼   cup dried tart
     cherries

**1** In a large mixing bowl combine egg, breadcrumbs, shallot, ½ teaspoon of the ginger, and the salt. Add turkey; mix well. Shape mixture into 24 meatballs.

**2** In a 12-inch skillet heat oil over medium heat. Cook meatballs in hot oil for 18 to 20 minutes or until brown and no longer pink (165°F), checking with an instant-read thermometer. Turn meatballs occasionally during cooking to brown evenly. Drain off fat.

**3** Meanwhile, drain peaches, reserving ¼ cup of the juice. In a blender or food processor combine drained peaches, reserved juice, ketchup, soy sauce, melted butter, and the remaining ½ teaspoon ginger. Cover and blend or process until smooth. Add peach mixture and cherries to skillet. Bring to boiling. Reduce heat and simmer, uncovered, for 1 to 2 minutes or until heated through, stirring gently to coat the meatballs.

**4** Serve meatballs, using short skewers or toothpicks, with sauce. If desired, keep warm in a slow cooker on warm or low heat setting for up to 2 hours.

nutrition facts per meatball: 66 cal., 4 g total fat (1 g sat. fat), 26 mg chol., 158 mg sodium, 5 g carb., 0 g dietary fiber, 4 g protein.

*Cocktail meatballs are always a hit at holiday gatherings. This variation heads to the Southwest for its inspiration of chipotle peppers and chili sauce.*

# chipotle chicken
## meatballs

prep: 30 minutes  bake: 10 minutes  cook: 10 minutes  oven: 350°F
makes: 48 meatballs

1   egg, lightly beaten
¼   cup fine dry
     breadcrumbs
¼   cup finely chopped
     onion
2   to 3 tablespoons
     finely chopped
     canned chipotle
     chile peppers in
     adobo sauce
2   cloves garlic, minced
¼   teaspoon salt
1   pound ground
     chicken or turkey
½   of a 16-ounce can
     jellied cranberry
     sauce
1   cup bottled chili
     sauce

**1** Preheat oven to 350°F. Lightly coat a 15×10×1-inch baking pan with cooking spray. In a large bowl combine egg, breadcrumbs, onion, 1 tablespoon of the chipotle peppers, the garlic, and salt. Add ground chicken; mix well. Shape mixture into 48 meatballs.

**2** Arrange meatballs in a single layer in prepared pan. Bake, uncovered, for 10 to 15 minutes or until no longer pink (165°F), checking with an instant-read thermometer. Drain off fat.

**3** For sauce, in a large skillet stir together cranberry sauce, chili sauce, and the remaining 1 to 2 tablespoons chipotle peppers. Cook and stir over medium heat until cranberry sauce melts.

**4** Add cooked meatballs to sauce. Cook, uncovered, for about 10 minutes or until heated through, stirring occasionally. Serve with short skewers or toothpicks. If desired, keep warm in a slow cooker on warm or low heat setting for up to 2 hours.

nutrition facts per 4 meatballs: 31 cal., 1 g total fat (0 g sat. fat), 13 mg chol., 104 mg sodium, 4 g carb., 0 g dietary fiber, 2 g protein.

**make-ahead directions:** Prepare meatballs as directed in Step 1. Cover and chill unbaked meatballs for up to 24 hours. Continue as directed.

*Use a light hand when forming the meatballs. This ensures less compacted meat, resulting in tender, juicy bites.*

# sloppy joe
# meatball minis

prep: 35 minutes  bake: 25 minutes  cook: 5 minutes  oven: 350°F
makes: 21 servings

1 egg, beaten
½ cup finely chopped onion
¼ cup fine dry breadcrumbs
¼ teaspoon dried oregano, crushed
¼ teaspoon salt
1 pound lean ground beef
1 tablespoon vegetable oil
½ cup chopped green sweet pepper
1 15-ounce can tomato sauce
2 tablespoons packed brown sugar
1 tablespoon yellow mustard
1 teaspoon chili powder
¼ teaspoon garlic salt
¼ teaspoon ground black pepper
Dash bottled hot pepper sauce (optional)
21 baby spinach leaves
21 2- to 2½-inch cocktail rolls, buttered and toasted

**1** Preheat oven to 350°F. In a large bowl combine egg, ¼ cup of the onion, the breadcrumbs, oregano, and salt. Add beef; mix well. Shape into 21 meatballs.

**2** Arrange meatballs in a single layer in a 15×10×1-inch baking pan. Bake, uncovered, for about 25 minutes or until cooked through (160°F), checking with an instant-read thermometer. Drain off fat.

**3** Meanwhile, in a large saucepan heat the oil over medium heat. Cook the remaining ¼ cup onion and the sweet pepper in hot oil until tender. Stir in tomato sauce, brown sugar, mustard, chili powder, garlic salt, black pepper, and hot pepper sauce (if desired). Bring to boiling; reduce heat. Simmer for 5 minutes. Add meatballs to sauce and heat through.

**4** Place a baby spinach leaf on each roll bottom. Top each with a meatball and some sauce. Cover with roll tops.

nutrition facts per serving: 196 cal., 10 g total fat (4 g sat. fat), 36 mg chol., 362 mg sodium, 19 g carb., 1 g dietary fiber, 8 g protein.

*While the potatoes roast in the oven, you'll have plenty of time to prepare the burgers. The fun part will be assembling these mini-size party bites.*

# burger-potato bites

prep: 15 minutes  bake: 18 minutes  cook: 5 minutes  broil: 1 to 2 minutes
oven: 400°F  makes: 16 servings

16  large frozen French-fried waffle-cut potatoes (⅓ of a 22-ounce package)
1   pound ground beef or turkey
2   to 3 teaspoons grilling seasoning blend
4   slices cheddar cheese, cut into quarters (4 ounces)
4   cherry tomatoes, sliced
    Mustard, ketchup, dairy sour cream, small red onion slices, and/or dill pickle slices

**1** Preheat oven to 400°F. Line a baking sheet with foil. Evenly space potatoes on baking sheet. Bake potatoes for 18 to 20 minutes or until crisp and lightly browned. Remove from oven; set aside. Adjust oven racks and preheat broiler.

**2** Meanwhile, in a medium bowl combine beef and seasoning. Form into sixteen 1-ounce mini burgers (about 2 tablespoons each). In a 12-inch skillet cook burgers, uncovered, over medium-high heat for 5 minutes or until cooked through (160°F), checking with an instant-read thermometer. Turn burgers over halfway through cooking. Drain off fat.

**3** Top each potato with a burger, cheese quarter, and tomato slice. Broil 4 to 5 inches from heat for 1 to 2 minutes or until cheese melts and tomato begins to brown. Serve with mustard, ketchup, sour cream, onion slices, and/or pickles.

nutrition facts per serving: 121 cal., 9 g total fat (4 g sat. fat), 28 mg chol., 152 mg sodium, 3 g carb., 0 g dietary fiber, 7 g protein.

*Arugula's peppery bite romances the sweet-tart flavor of the cranberry chutney that's spooned on top of each burger.*

# hamburger sliders

prep: 25 minutes   grill: 4 minutes per batch for covered indoor grill or 8 minutes per batch for uncovered indoor grill or grill pan   makes: 12 sliders

| | |
|---|---|
| 1 | tablespoon vegetable oil |
| ½ | cup chopped Granny Smith apple |
| ½ | cup chopped red onion |
| 1 | cup canned whole cranberry sauce |
| 2 | tablespoons prepared horseradish |
| 1 | tablespoon lemon juice |
| 1½ | pounds ground beef |
| 2 | tablespoons snipped fresh Italian parsley |
| 1 | teaspoon salt |
| ¼ | teaspoon freshly ground black pepper |
| 12 | cloverleaf rolls, split and toasted |
| 2 | cups baby arugula leaves |

**1** In a large skillet heat oil over medium heat. Cook apple and onion in hot oil for about 5 minutes or until tender. Cool. In a medium bowl stir together apple-onion mixture, cranberry sauce, horseradish, and lemon juice.

**2** In a large bowl combine beef, parsley, salt, and pepper; mix well. Shape mixture into 12 patties slightly larger than the rolls.

**3** Lightly grease the rack of an indoor electric grill or a grill pan. Preheat grill to medium. Place patties on the grill rack, half of them at a time if necessary. If using a grill with a cover, close the lid. Grill for 4 to 5 minutes for a covered grill or 8 to 10 minutes for an uncovered grill or grill pan or until cooked through (160°F), checking with an instant-read thermometer. If using an uncovered grill or grill pan, turn once halfway through grilling time.

**4** Serve in rolls with arugula leaves and cranberry chutney.

nutrition facts per slider: 275 cal., 14 g total fat (5 g sat. fat), 40 mg chol., 384 mg sodium, 25 g carb., 1 g dietary fiber, 13 g protein.

*Caramelizing onions is the simple process of heating them until their natural sugars brown and caramelize, giving them an intense, mellow flavor.*

# cheeseburger bites

prep: 35 minutes  grill: 8 minutes  makes: 12 servings

1 egg, lightly beaten
¾ cup soft breadcrumbs
1 teaspoon steak
  seasoning
1½ pounds lean ground
  beef
  Salt
  Ground black pepper
2 tablespoons butter
2 large sweet onions,
  cut into thin
  wedges
1 teaspoon snipped
  fresh thyme
¼ teaspoon ground
  black pepper
2 ounces smoked
  Gouda cheese,
  shredded (½ cup)
12 2- to 2½-inch sesame
  seed, herb, cheese-
  topped, and/or plain
  cocktail rolls, split
  and toasted

**1** In a large bowl combine egg, breadcrumbs, and steak seasoning. Add beef; mix well. Shape mixture into 12 small patties. Season patties with salt and pepper.

**2** Lightly grease the rack of an indoor electric grill or grill pan. Preheat grill to medium. Place patties on the grill rack. If using a grill with a cover, close the lid. Grill for 8 to 10 minutes or until fully cooked (160°F), checking with an instant-read thermometer. If using an uncovered grill or a grill pan, turn patties once halfway through grilling.

**3** Meanwhile, in a large skillet melt butter over medium-low heat. Add onions, thyme, and ¼ teaspoon pepper. Cover and cook for 13 to 15 minutes or until onion is tender, stirring occasionally. Uncover. Cook and stir over medium-high heat for 3 to 5 minutes more or until onion is golden. Stir in Gouda cheese until melted.

**4** Place patties on roll bottoms. Top with onion mixture. Cover with roll tops.

nutrition facts per serving: 300 cal., 14 g total fat (6 g sat. fat), 65 mg chol., 490 mg sodium, 26 g carb., 1 g dietary fiber, 17 g protein.

*Broccoli-apple slaw adds color, crunch, and flavor to these mini sandwiches. Another time, substitute walnuts for the pecans.*

# nutty pork sliders

start to finish: 35 minutes  grill: 8 minutes  makes: 12 sliders

1¼  pounds pork tenderloin, sliced crosswise into 12 pieces
     Ground black pepper
⅓   cup honey mustard
1½  cups pecans, finely chopped
2   tablespoons vegetable oil
2¼  cups packaged shredded broccoli (broccoli slaw mix)
1   medium Granny Smith apple, cored and coarsely shredded
⅓   cup mayonnaise
2   tablespoons honey
12  small sourdough rolls, split

**1** Using the palm of your hand or the flat side of a meat mallet, flatten each tenderloin piece to about ¼-inch thickness. Sprinkle both sides of each piece with pepper. Brush both sides of each piece with honey mustard. Dip pieces in pecans, turning and pressing to coat evenly.

**2** In a 12-inch skillet heat oil over medium to medium-high heat. Cook pork pieces in hot oil for 8 to 10 minutes or until golden and just slightly pink in center, gently turning once halfway through cooking time. If pork browns too quickly, reduce heat to medium.

**3** Meanwhile, for slaw, in a large bowl combine shredded broccoli, apple, mayonnaise, and honey. Season to taste with additional pepper.

**4** Serve pork in rolls with any remaining nut mixture from skillet and the slaw.

nutrition facts per slider: 320 cal., 18 g total fat (2 g sat. fat), 33 mg chol., 285 mg sodium, 25 g carb., 3 g dietary fiber, 15 g protein.

*To ensure that these sliders are juicy and moist, be sure to use a blend of white and dark turkey meat. The remoulade sauce that tops the sliders is full of distinctive flavors from mayonnaise spiked with capers, mustard, and hot pepper sauce.*

# cajun turkey sliders

prep: 25 minutes   cook: 18 minutes   makes: 12 sliders

| | |
|---|---|
| 2 | tablespoons vegetable oil |
| 1 | medium red sweet pepper, seeded and cut into thin strips |
| 1 | medium yellow sweet pepper, seeded and cut into thin strips |
| 1 | medium onion, cut into thin wedges |
| 1½ | pounds ground turkey |
| ¼ | cup chopped green onion |
| 2 | teaspoons Cajun seasoning |
| 1 | teaspoon bottled hot pepper sauce |
| ½ | teaspoon salt |
| ¼ | teaspoon ground black pepper |
| 2 | tablespoons Old Bay seasoning |
| 12 | whole wheat cocktail buns, split and toasted |
| 1 | recipe Spicy Remoulade |

**1** In a large skillet heat 1 tablespoon of the oil over medium-low heat. Cook sweet peppers and onion in hot oil for about 10 minutes or until very soft and tender. Remove from skillet; keep warm.

**2** In a large bowl combine turkey, green onion, Cajun seasoning, hot pepper sauce, salt, and black pepper; mix well. Form into 12 patties slightly larger than the buns. Sprinkle both sides of each patty generously with Old Bay seasoning.

**3** In the same skillet heat the remaining 1 tablespoon oil over medium heat. Add patties. Cook in hot oil for about 8 minutes or until cooked through (165°F), checking with an instant-read thermometer. Turn once halfway through cooking time.

**4** Serve in buns with sweet pepper mixture and Spicy Remoulade.

nutrition facts per slider: 334 cal., 23 g total fat (4 g sat. fat), 52 mg chol., 878 mg sodium, 20 g carb., 3 g dietary fiber, 13 g protein.

**★test kitchen tip:** The internal color of a burger is not a reliable doneness indicator. A poultry patty cooked to 165°F is safe, regardless of color. To measure the doneness of a patty, insert an instant-read thermometer through the side of the patty into the center of the patty.

spicy remoulade: In a medium bowl combine 1 cup mayonnaise or salad dressing, ¼ cup pickle relish, 2 tablespoons drained capers, 1 tablespoon Creole or spicy brown mustard, 1 tablespoon snipped fresh parsley, 2 teaspoons bottled hot pepper sauce, and 1 teaspoon lemon juice. Makes 1¼ cups.

*Adding wasabi to the creamy coleslaw that tops these meatless sliders throws a party for your taste buds; using packaged coleslaw mix saves time and effort.*

# veggie burger sliders

prep: 30 minutes  grill: 4 minutes per batch for covered indoor grill or 8 minutes per batch for uncovered indoor grill or grill pan  stand: 30 minutes  makes: 12 sliders

½  cup bulgur
1  cup boiling water
   Dash salt
1  15- to 16-ounce can pinto beans, rinsed and drained
¾  cup fine dry breadcrumbs
½  cup chopped green onion
1  medium carrot, coarsely shredded
1  egg, lightly beaten
2  tablespoons bottled tahini
1  tablespoon soy sauce
½  teaspoon garlic powder
¼  teaspoon salt
¼  teaspoon cayenne pepper
1  tablespoon olive oil
3  whole wheat pita bread rounds, quartered and warmed
1  recipe Wasabi Coleslaw

**1** In a medium bowl combine bulgur, boiling water, and the dash salt. Cover bowl and let stand for about 30 minutes or until bulgur is tender but still chewy. Pour into a fine-mesh sieve to drain, pressing firmly to remove excess liquid. Return bulgur to bowl.

**2** Add beans to bulgur. Using a potato masher, mash beans and bulgur together until well mixed. Add breadcrumbs, green onion, carrot, egg, tahini, soy sauce, garlic powder, the ¼ teaspoon salt, and the cayenne pepper; mix well. Divide mixture into 12 portions.

**3** Using clean moistened hands, shape mixture into ¾-inch-thick patties (2 to 2½ inches in diameter). Brush both sides of each patty with olive oil.

**4** Lightly grease the rack of an indoor electric grill or a grill pan. Preheat grill to medium. Place patties on the grill rack, half at a time if necessary. If using a grill with a cover, close the lid. Grill for about 4 minutes for a covered grill or about 8 minutes for an uncovered grill or grill pan or until browned and heated through. If using an uncovered grill or grill pan, turn once halfway through grilling time.

**5** Serve patties in pita bread with Wasabi Coleslaw.

nutrition facts per slider: 218 cal., 9 g total fat (1 g sat. fat), 20 mg chol., 450 mg sodium, 30 g carb., 5 g dietary fiber, 7 g protein.

wasabi coleslaw: In a large bowl combine 3 cups packaged shredded cabbage with carrot (coleslaw mix), ½ cup finely chopped red onion, ⅓ cup mayonnaise or salad dressing, 2 tablespoons rice vinegar, 2 tablespoons honey, 1½ teaspoons prepared wasabi paste, and 1 teaspoon yellow mustard; mix well. Serve immediately for maximum crispness. Makes 3 cups.

wings 'n' thi

Hot wings, riblets,
and other hearty bites
drenched in a bevy
of sauces make for
great party fare. Kick
the flavor up a notch
with special twists that
will be gobbled up in
no time.

*Purchased hoisin sauce and canned plums make this Asian appetizer extra easy. Fire up the sauce by adding ¼ teaspoon cayenne pepper to the plum mixture before cooking.*

# plum-sauced wings

prep: 25 minutes  broil: 14 minutes  makes: 8 servings

1   15- to 16-ounce can whole unpitted purple plums
2   tablespoons bottled hoisin sauce
1   tablespoon frozen orange juice concentrate, thawed
1   tablespoon soy sauce
1   teaspoon grated fresh ginger
¼   teaspoon ground black pepper
16   chicken drummettes (2 pounds)
2   teaspoons sesame seeds, toasted (optional)

1 Preheat the broiler. For sauce, drain plums, reserving liquid. Pit plums. In a food processor or blender combine pitted plums, reserved plum liquid, hoisin sauce, orange juice concentrate, soy sauce, ginger, and pepper. Cover and process or blend until nearly smooth.

2 Transfer plum mixture to a saucepan. Bring to boiling; reduce heat. Simmer, uncovered, for about 15 minutes or until slightly thickened, stirring occasionally.

3 Place drummettes in a single layer on the rack of an unheated broiler pan. Broil 5 to 6 inches from the heat for 8 minutes. Brush with sauce. Turn and brush again. Broil for 6 to 8 minutes or until tender and no longer pink.

4 In a small saucepan bring remaining sauce to boiling. Transfer to a small bowl. Arrange drummettes on a serving plate. If desired, sprinkle drummettes with sesame seeds. Serve drummettes with sauce.

nutrition facts per serving: 182 cal., 10 g total fat (3 g sat. fat), 47 mg chol., 213 mg sodium, 11 g carb., 1 g dietary fiber, 12 g protein.

**make-ahead directions:** Cover and chill plum sauce for up to 3 days before using.

*Cooks along the West Coast were among the first to bring Southeast Asian flavors to American dining. Here a taste of Thailand imbues the ever-popular appetizer wing.*

# thai chicken wings
## with peanut sauce

prep: 25 minutes  bake: 20 minutes  cook: 5 minutes  oven: 400°F
makes: 12 servings

20   chicken drummettes
       (2¼ pounds)
½   cup bottled salsa
2   tablespoons creamy
       peanut butter
1   tablespoon lime juice
2   teaspoons soy sauce
2   teaspoons grated
       fresh ginger
¼   cup sugar
¼   cup creamy peanut
       butter
3   tablespoons soy
       sauce
3   tablespoons water
2   cloves garlic, minced
       Shredded bok choy
       (optional)
     Lime wedges
       (optional)

**1** Preheat oven to 400°F. Place drummettes in a large bowl. Combine salsa, the 2 tablespoons peanut butter, the lime juice, the 2 teaspoons soy sauce, and the ginger. Pour over drummettes. Toss to coat.

**2** Line a 15×10×1-inch baking pan or roasting pan with foil. Place drummettes in a single layer in prepared baking pan. Bake drummettes for about 20 minutes or until tender and no longer pink.

**3** Meanwhile, for the peanut sauce, in a small saucepan combine sugar, the ¼ cup peanut butter, the 3 tablespoons soy sauce, the water, and garlic. Cook over medium-low heat until sugar dissolves and mixture is smooth (mixture will thicken as it stands). Serve drummettes with peanut sauce and, if desired, bok choy and lime wedges.

nutrition facts per serving: 189 cal., 13 g total fat (3 g sat. fat), 58 mg chol., 392 mg sodium, 6 g carb., 1 g dietary fiber, 12 g protein.

*Perfect for a spirited afternoon gathering, these succulent, crispy wings deliver a flavor kick.*

## hot and sassy
# chicken wings

prep: 25 minutes  marinate: 2 hours  bake: 40 minutes  oven: 375°F
makes: 8 to 10 servings

10 chicken wings
   (about 2 pounds)
1 cup white wine
   vinegar
¼ cup packed brown
   sugar
¼ cup honey
2 teaspoons garlic
   powder
2 to 3 teaspoons
   bottled hot pepper
   sauce
1 teaspoon salt
1 teaspoon dried
   thyme, crushed
½ to 1 teaspoon
   cayenne pepper

**1** Cut off and discard tips from wings. Cut each wing at the joint to make 2 pieces. Place chicken in a large resealable plastic bag.

**2** For marinade, in a small bowl whisk vinegar, brown sugar, honey, garlic powder, hot pepper sauce, salt, thyme, and cayenne pepper. Pour over chicken; seal bag. Marinate in the refrigerator for 2 to 4 hours, turning bag occasionally.

**3** Preheat oven to 375°F. Line a 15×10×1-inch baking pan with foil. Lightly coat a large roasting rack with nonstick cooking spray; set rack in prepared pan. Drain chicken, reserving marinade. Place chicken on roasting rack; set aside.

**4** Transfer marinade to a medium saucepan. Bring to boiling over medium-high heat. Boil gently, uncovered, for about 10 minutes or until marinade is reduced to about ½ cup and is thick and slightly syrupy, stirring occasionally.

**5** Brush wing pieces on both sides with some of the reduced marinade. Bake for 30 minutes. Turn wing pieces over. Brush with remaining marinade. Bake for about 10 minutes or until chicken is no longer pink.

nutrition facts per serving: 205 cal., 10 g total fat (3 g sat. fat), 47 mg chol., 339 mg sodium, 16 g carb., 0 g dietary fiber, 11 g protein.

*The marinade makes these little chicks sweet and spicy ginger favorites. Use plain toasted sesame seeds or a combination of plain and black for color contrast.*

# korean-style wings

prep: 15 minutes   marinate: 2 hours   broil: 14 minutes   makes: 6 servings

12  chicken wing
    drummettes
    (1½ pounds)
¼   cup finely chopped
    green onion
¼   cup soy sauce
2   tablespoons packed
    brown sugar
1   tablespoon toasted
    sesame oil
1   tablespoon grated
    fresh ginger
2   large cloves garlic,
    minced
1   tablespoon sesame
    seeds, toasted*
    Finely chopped green
    onion

**1** Place drummettes in a large resealable plastic bag set in a shallow dish. For marinade, combine the ¼ cup green onion, soy sauce, brown sugar, oil, ginger, and garlic. Pour marinade over drummettes; seal bag. Marinate in the refrigerator for 2 to 24 hours, turning bag occasionally. Drain drummettes, discarding marinade.

**2** Place drummettes on the unheated rack of a broiler pan. Broil 5 to 6 inches from the heat for about 8 minutes or until lightly browned. Turn drummettes. Broil for about 6 minutes more or until chicken is tender and no longer pink. Sprinkle with sesame seeds and additional green onion.

nutrition facts per serving: 268 cal., 20 g total fat (4 g sat. fat), 116 mg chol., 328 mg sodium, 3 g carb., 0 g dietary fiber, 20 g protein.

*note: To toast sesame seeds, spread seeds in a single layer in a shallow baking pan. Bake in a 350°F oven for about 5 minutes or until golden brown, stirring and checking to make sure seeds don't turn too brown.

*Serve these saucy little morsels right from the slow cooker.*
*Or transfer them to a plate and add a garnish of orange wedges.*

# five-spice
# chicken drummies

prep: 20 minutes   bake: 20 minutes   cook: 4 to 5 hours (low) or 2 to 2½ hours (high)
oven: 375°F   makes: 16 servings

3   pounds chicken
    drummettes or
    chicken wings
1   cup bottled plum
    sauce
2   tablespoons butter,
    melted
1   teaspoon five-spice
    powder

**1** Preheat oven to 375°F. If using chicken wings, cut off and discard tips from wings. Line a 15×10×1-inch baking pan with foil. Place chicken in a single layer in prepared baking pan. Bake for 20 minutes; drain well.

**2** For sauce, in a 3½- or 4-quart slow cooker combine plum sauce, melted butter, and five-spice powder. Add chicken, stirring to coat with sauce.

**3** Cover and cook on low heat setting for 4 to 5 hours or on high heat setting for 2 to 2½ hours. Serve immediately or keep warm on low heat setting for up to 2 hours.

nutrition facts per serving: 176 cal., 13 g total fat (3 g sat. fat), 70 mg chol., 82 mg sodium, 6 g carb., 0 g dietary fiber, 12 g protein.

kentucky chicken drummies: Prepare chicken as directed in Step 1. For sauce, in a slow cooker, combine ½ cup maple syrup, ½ cup whiskey, and 2 tablespoons melted butter. Add chicken, stirring to coat with sauce. Continue as directed in Step 3.

buffalo-style chicken drummies (pictured on page 98): Prepare chicken as directed in Step 1. For sauce, in a slow cooker, combine 1½ cups hot-style barbecue sauce, 2 tablespoons melted butter, and 1 to 2 teaspoons bottled hot pepper sauce. Add chicken, stirring to coat with sauce. Continue as directed in Step 3. Serve with bottled blue cheese or ranch salad dressing.

*Distilled from fermented grain, bourbon adds deep undertones to these kicky wings.*

# bourbon-molasses glazed
# chicken wings

prep: 30 minutes  marinate: 1 hour  bake: 50 minutes  oven: 375°F
makes: 24 pieces

12  chicken wings
    (2 pounds)
3  tablespoons cider
    vinegar
3  tablespoons molasses
2  tablespoons Asian
    chili sauce
½  cup Dijon-style
    mustard
½  cup maple syrup
2  tablespoons bourbon
2  teaspoons soy sauce
    Kosher salt
    Ground black pepper

1 Cut off and discard tips from wings. Cut each wing at the joint to make 2 pieces. Place chicken in a resealable plastic bag set in a shallow dish.

2 In a bowl combine vinegar, molasses, chili sauce, mustard, maple syrup, bourbon, and soy sauce. Pour marinade over chicken; seal bag. Marinate in the refrigerator for 1 to 4 hours, turning bag occasionally. Drain chicken, reserving marinade.

3 Preheat oven to 375°F. Line a shallow roasting pan with foil; lightly coat with cooking spray. Place wing pieces in a single layer in prepared baking pan. Sprinkle with salt and pepper. Bake for 30 minutes, spooning marinade over wings twice. Turn wings over. Spoon on marinade. Bake for 20 minutes, spooning over marinade after 10 minutes. Serve warm.

nutrition facts per serving: 59 cal., 2 g total fat (1 g sat. fat), 12 mg chol., 143 mg sodium, 5 g carb., 0 g dietary fiber, 3 g protein.

*Serve these sports bar favorites when friends gather to watch a televised football game. Cold beer, celery sticks, and plenty of napkins are the only other items you need.*

# buffalo wings

prep: 20 minutes   marinate: 30 minutes   broil: 20 minutes
makes: 12 servings

12   chicken wings (about 2 pounds)
2   tablespoons butter, melted
3   tablespoons bottled hot pepper sauce
2   teaspoons paprika
¼   teaspoon salt
¼   teaspoon cayenne pepper
1   recipe Blue Cheese Dip
    Carrot sticks, celery sticks, and fennel wedges (optional)

**1** Cut off and discard tips from wings. Cut each wing at the joint to make 2 pieces. Place chicken in a resealable plastic bag set in a shallow dish.

**2** For marinade, stir together melted butter, hot pepper sauce, paprika, salt, and cayenne pepper. Pour over chicken; seal bag. Marinate at room temperature for 30 minutes. Drain chicken, discarding marinade.

**3** Place wing pieces in a single layer on the unheated rack of a broiler pan. Broil 4 to 5 inches from the heat for about 10 minutes or until lightly browned. Turn wing pieces. Broil for 10 to 15 minutes more or until chicken is tender and no longer pink. Serve with Blue Cheese Dip and vegetables, if desired.

nutrition facts per serving: 221 cal., 19 g total fat (6 g sat. fat), 47 mg chol., 258 mg sodium, 1 g carb., 0 g dietary fiber, 11 g protein.

blue cheese dip: In a blender or food processor combine ½ cup dairy sour cream, ½ cup mayonnaise, ½ cup crumbled blue cheese, 1 tablespoon white wine vinegar or white vinegar, and 1 clove garlic, minced. Cover and blend or process until smooth. Cover and chill for up to 1 week. If desired, top with additional crumbled blue cheese before serving. Makes 1¼ cups.

*Jamaican jerk seasoning and cayenne pepper lend a bit of heat, while a crisp coconut and peanut coating adds sweetness and a delightful crunch.*

# twice-cooked
# coconut chicken wings

prep: 25 minutes   bake: 35 minutes   oven: 375°F/425°F   makes: 24 servings

12   chicken wings
      (about 3 pounds)
2    teaspoons Jamaican
      jerk seasoning
½    teaspoon salt
½    teaspoon cayenne
      pepper
3    tablespoons peanut
      oil
1    teaspoon finely
      shredded lime peel
1    tablespoon lime juice
¾    cup flaked coconut
⅓    cup peanuts
      Lime wedges

**1** Preheat oven to 375°F. Line a 15×10×1-inch baking pan with foil.

**2** Cut off and discard tips from wings. Cut each wing at the joint to make 2 pieces. In a small bowl combine jerk seasoning, salt, and cayenne pepper. Sprinkle over wing pieces and rub in with fingers. Place chicken in a single layer in the prepared pan.

**3** Bake, uncovered, for 25 minutes. Remove from pan. Cool slightly. Meanwhile, replace foil in pan with clean foil.

**4** Increase oven temperature to 425°F. In a small bowl whisk together peanut oil, lime peel, and lime juice. In food processor combine coconut and peanuts. Cover and pulse until finely chopped. Transfer to shallow dish. Brush chicken with lime-oil mixture and roll in coconut mixture, pressing to coat. Arrange in foil-lined baking pan. Bake for 10 minutes more or until coating is crunchy and wings are heated through. Serve with lime wedges.

nutrition facts per serving: 169 cal., 13 g total fat (4 g sat. fat), 43 mg chol., 141 mg sodium, 1 g carb., .3 g dietary fiber, 11 g protein.

*If you're planning for a crowd, make a double batch of this lip-smacking recipe. Don't let the cola throw you. Combined with hot pepper sauce and garlic, it makes a fabulous marinade and sauce.*

# hot sauce and cola
## chicken wings

prep: 20 minutes  marinate: 5 hours  roast: 20 minutes  oven: 450°F
makes: 12 servings

24  chicken wings
    (about 4½ pounds)
 1  12-ounce can cola
 1  2-ounce bottle hot
    pepper sauce
 2  tablespoons olive oil
 3  garlic cloves, minced
 ¼  cup cola
 1  tablespoon butter
 1  recipe Avocado Salsa

**1** Cut off and discard tips from wings. Place wings in a large resealable plastic bag set in a shallow dish. Pour the 12-ounce can of cola over wings; seal bag. Marinate in the refrigerator for 1 to 4 hours, turning bag occasionally. Drain wings, discarding marinade. Return wings to bag. Pour hot pepper sauce over wings. Close bag. Marinate in the refrigerator for 4 to 24 hours, turning bag occasionally. Drain chicken, discarding marinade.

**2** Preheat oven to 450°F. Line a large shallow roasting pan with foil; grease well. In a very large skillet heat the oil over medium-high heat. Cook 12 wing pieces in hot oil until brown on all sides. Remove from skillet. Place chicken in a single layer in prepared roasting pan. Repeat with remaining wings, adding more oil if necessary. Reserve the pan drippings. Bake wings for 20 minutes or until tender and no longer pink.

**3** For sauce, in the same skillet cook and stir garlic in reserved drippings over medium heat for 1 minute. Add the ¼ cup cola. Bring to boiling; reduce heat. Simmer, stirring occasionally, for 1 minute or until liquid reduces to about 2 tablespoons. Whisk in butter until melted and sauce thickens.

**4** Transfer chicken wings to a serving platter. Drizzle sauce over the wings. Serve with Avocado Salsa.

avocado salsa: In a medium bowl combine 2 medium avocados, halved, pitted, peeled, and finely chopped; 1 large tomato, finely chopped; 4 green onions, finely chopped; ¼ cup snipped fresh cilantro; 3 tablespoons rice vinegar; 2 tablespoons lime juice; 2 cloves garlic, minced; ¼ to ½ teaspoon crushed red pepper; and ⅛ teaspoon salt. Cover and chill for 1 to 2 hours. Makes about 2½ cups.

nutrition facts per serving: 212 cal., 17 g total fat (4 g sat. fat), 60 mg chol., 90 mg sodium, 5 g carb., 2 g dietary fiber, 10 g protein.

*An intriguing Asian-style sauce gives an unexpected flavor to chicken wings. Serve them hot or cold for finger-licking-good snacks.*

# asian chicken wings

prep: 25 minutes   cook: 20 minutes   makes: 12 servings

12  chicken wings
(about 2 pounds)
1½  cups water
⅔  cup soy sauce
½  cup sliced leek
(1 medium)
4  slices fresh ginger
1  tablespoon sugar
1  tablespoon vinegar
2  or 3 dried red chile
peppers
½  teaspoon five-spice
powder
2  cloves garlic, minced
Bottled teriyaki sauce
(optional)

1 Cut off and discard tips from wings. Cut each wing at the joint to make 2 pieces.

2 For sauce, in a 4-quart Dutch oven combine the water, soy sauce, leek, ginger, sugar, vinegar, chile peppers, five-spice powder, and garlic. Bring to boiling. Add chicken. Return to boiling; reduce heat. Cover and simmer for 20 to 25 minutes or until chicken is no longer pink.

3 Using a slotted spoon, remove chicken wings from the Dutch oven. If desired, serve wings with bottled teriyaki sauce.

nutrition facts per serving: 123 cal., 9 g total fat (2 g sat. fat), 58 mg chol., 204 mg sodium, 0 g carb., 0 g dietary fiber, 10 g protein.

*Tandoori refers to the superhot clay oven used to cook Indian breads and meats. You can replicate the effect by cooking the chicken directly under the broiler.*

# tandoori chicken wings

prep: 45 minutes  marinate: 4 hours  bake: 25 minutes  broil: 6 minutes
oven: 400°F  makes: 16 servings

50  chicken drummettes*
    (about 5 pounds)
1   medium onion, cut
    into wedges
1   8-ounce can tomato
    sauce
1   6-ounce carton plain
    fat-free yogurt
1   tablespoon ground
    coriander
4   cloves garlic, coarsely
    chopped
2   teaspoons chopped
    fresh ginger
1½  teaspoons salt
1   teaspoon cumin seeds
1   teaspoon garam
    masala
½   to 1 teaspoon
    cayenne pepper
    (optional)
¼   to ½ teaspoon red
    food coloring
2   whole cloves

**1** Place the chicken drummettes in a 3-quart rectangular baking dish; set aside.

**2** For the tandoori masala, in a blender or food processor combine onion, tomato sauce, yogurt, coriander, garlic, ginger, salt, cumin seeds, garam masala, cayenne pepper (if desired), red food coloring, and whole cloves. Blend or process to a very smooth paste. (The color should be deep red.)

**3** Pour the tandoori masala over the drummettes. Turn drummettes to coat. Cover and marinate in the refrigerator for 4 to 24 hours.

**4** Preheat oven to 400°F. Drain chicken, discarding marinade. Place as many drummettes on the unheated rack of a broiler pan as will fit in a single layer. Bake for 25 minutes. Turn oven to broil. Broil chicken 4 to 5 inches from heat for 6 to 8 minutes or until chicken is no longer pink and pieces just start to blacken, turning once halfway through broiling.

**5** Transfer drummettes to a serving platter. Repeat baking and broiling with remaining chicken drummettes. If desired, serve with lemon wedges and red onion wedges.

nutrition facts per serving: 119 cal., 4 g total fat (1 g sat. fat), 62 mg chol., 363 mg sodium, 3 g carb., 0 g dietary fiber, 16 g protein.

*note: If you cannot find chicken drummettes, use 25 chicken wings. Cut off and discard tips of chicken wings. Cut wings at joints to form 50 pieces.

*Two tablespoons of red curry paste make these saucy wings succulently spicy; three tablespoons add lip-tingling boldness.*

# red curry chicken wings

prep: 30 minutes  broil: 10 minutes  cook: 3 to 4 hours (low) or 1½ to 2 hours (high)  makes: 16 servings

16  chicken wings (about 3 pounds)
¾  cup unsweetened coconut milk
3  tablespoons fish sauce
2  to 3 tablespoons red curry paste
⅓  cup finely chopped onion
2  tablespoons cornstarch
2  tablespoons cold water
¼  cup finely shredded fresh basil (optional)

1 Preheat broiler. Cut off and discard tips from wings. Cut each wing at the joint to make 2 pieces. Place wing pieces in a single layer on the unheated rack of a foil-lined broiler pan. Broil 4 to 5 inches from the heat for 10 to 12 minutes or until chicken is brown, turning once. Drain off fat.

2 Meanwhile, in a 3½- or 4-quart slow cooker combine coconut milk, fish sauce, and curry paste. Add wing pieces and onion, stirring to coat with curry mixture. Cover and cook on low heat setting for 3 to 4 hours or on high heat setting for 1½ to 2 hours.

3 Using a slotted spoon, remove chicken from cooker. Cover with foil to keep warm. Skim fat from curry mixture.

4 For sauce, in a medium saucepan combine cornstarch and the water over medium heat. Stir in curry mixture. Cook and stir until thickened and bubbly. Cook and stir for 2 minutes more. If desired, stir in basil. Serve chicken wings with sauce.

nutrition facts per serving: 183 cal., 14 g total fat (5 g sat. fat), 47 mg chol., 488 mg sodium, 3 g carb., 0 g dietary fiber, 12 g protein.

*Savor the cool, sweet fruitiness of the salsa with the spiciness of the wings. If you mix this up the night before your barbecue, you'll be ready to go straight to the grill.*

# jamaican jerk
## chicken wings

prep: 25 minutes   marinate: 4 hours   grill: 20 minutes   makes: 12 servings

12   chicken wings
     (about 2 pounds)
¼   to ½ cup Jamaican
     jerk seasoning
¼   cup cider vinegar
¼   cup orange juice
2   tablespoons lime
     juice
2   tablespoons olive oil
2   tablespoons soy
     sauce
1   recipe Mango Salsa

**1** Cut off and discard tips from wings. Cut each wing at the joint to make 2 pieces. Place chicken in a resealable plastic bag set in a shallow dish.

**2** For marinade, in a small bowl stir together jerk seasoning, vinegar, orange juice, lime juice, oil, and soy sauce. Pour marinade over chicken; seal bag. Marinate in the refrigerator for 4 to 24 hours, turning bag occasionally. Drain chicken, discarding marinade.

**3** For a charcoal grill, place chicken on the rack of an uncovered grill directly over medium coals. Grill for about 20 minutes or until chicken is no longer pink, turning once halfway through grilling. Serve with Mango Salsa.

nutrition facts per serving: 141 cal., 9 g total fat (2 g sat. fat), 38 mg chol., 256 mg sodium, 6 g carb., 1 g dietary fiber, 9 g protein.

**to broil:** Preheat broiler. Place chicken wings on the unheated rack of a broiler pan. Broil 5 to 6 inches from the heat for 16 to 18 minutes or until chicken is no longer pink, once halfway through broiling.

mango salsa: In medium bowl combine 2 cups chopped peeled and seeded mangoes (2 medium); ½ cup finely chopped red sweet pepper; 1 fresh jalapeño chile pepper, seeded and finely chopped (see note, page 52); 4½ teaspoons snipped fresh basil; 2 teaspoons lime juice; 1½ teaspoons red wine vinegar; and ½ teaspoon sugar. Cover and chill for 2 to 24 hours. Let stand at room temperature for 30 minutes before serving. Makes 2½ cups.

*Asked to bring an appetizer to a party? A combo of chicken wings and meatballs glazed with a tangy-sweet sauce is a sure winner.*

# cherry-ginger
# sticks and stones

prep: 20 minutes   cook: 3 to 4 hours (low) or 1½ to 2 hours (high)
broil: 12 minutes   makes: 20 servings

| | |
|---|---|
| 12 | chicken wings (2 pounds) |
| 1½ | cups frozen pitted tart red cherries, thawed |
| ½ | cup ketchup |
| ¼ | cup packed brown sugar |
| 2 | teaspoons ground ginger |
| ½ | teaspoon ground allspice |
| ½ | teaspoon salt |
| ¼ | teaspoon ground black pepper |
| 1 | 12-ounce package frozen cooked Swedish-style meatballs |

1 Cut off and discard tips from wings. Cut each wing at the joint to make 2 pieces. Place chicken pieces on the unheated rack of a broiler pan. Broil 4 to 5 inches from the heat for 12 to 15 minutes or until chicken is no longer pink, turning once.

2 In a blender or food processor combine cherries, ketchup, brown sugar, ginger, allspice, salt, and pepper. Cover and blend or process until smooth.

3 Place wings and meatballs in a 3½- or 4-quart slow cooker. Top with cherry mixture. Stir to coat.

4 Cover and cook on low heat setting for 3 to 4 hours or on high heat setting for 1½ to 2 hours.

nutrition facts per serving: 100 cal., 5 g total fat (2 g sat. fat), 24 mg chol., 205 mg sodium, 8 g carb., 1 g dietary fiber, 6 g protein.

*Oven-frying crisps and browns the nutty coating on the chicken.*

# pecan-crusted drummettes
## with dried cherry salsa

prep: 30 minutes   bake: 30 minutes   stand: 30 minutes   oven: 400°F
makes: 10 to 12 servings

2   cups ground pecans
½   cup all-purpose flour
2   tablespoons yellow
    cornmeal
½   teaspoon salt
½   teaspoon ground
    black pepper
1   2½-pound package
    individually
    frozen chicken
    drummettes, thawed
    and patted dry with
    paper towels (about
    22 pieces)
¼   cup butter, melted
1   recipe Dried Cherry
    Salsa

**1** Preheat oven to 400°F. Grease a shallow baking pan. In a large resealable plastic bag combine pecans, flour, cornmeal, salt, and pepper.

**2** Place drummettes, a few at a time, in the mixture in the plastic bag. Seal and shake to coat. Arrange in prepared baking pan. Drizzle drummettes with butter. Bake for 30 to 35 minutes or until golden and chicken is no longer pink. Serve hot with Dried Cherry Salsa.

nutrition facts per serving: 417 cal., 30 g total fat (6 g sat. fat), 75 mg chol., 309 mg sodium, 25 g carb., 3 g dietary fiber, 13 g protein.

**make-ahead directions:** Prepare Dried Cherry Salsa as directed. Cover and chill for up to 24 hours.

dried cherry salsa: In a food processor combine ½ cup dried cherries;* ½ cup cherry jam; 2 tablespoons red wine vinegar; 1 green onion, sliced; ½ of a fresh jalapeño chile pepper, seeded and chopped (see note, page 52); and 1 teaspoon finely shredded lime peel. Cover and pulse until nearly smooth. Allow to stand at room temperature for 30 minutes. Makes about 1 cup.

*note: If you have other dried fruits on hand, such as raisins and dried cranberries, add them to this salsa. Just use ½ cup dried fruit total.

*Mojo is the do-it-all mixture of Latin cuisine—used as a dipping sauce, marinade, salad dressing condiment, and barbecue sauce. Here it does double duty as marinade and base for the sauce to be served alongside the wings.*

# mojo chicken wings
## with mango sauce

prep: 20 minutes   bake: 25 minutes   oven: 450°F   makes: 12 servings

1 cup mango nectar
½ cup lemon juice
½ cup orange juice
½ cup snipped fresh parsley
¼ cup red wine vinegar
¼ cup olive oil
6 cloves garlic, minced
1 or 2 fresh jalapeño chile peppers, seeded and finely chopped (see note, page 52)
1 teaspoon salt
½ teaspoon ground cumin
24 chicken drummettes (about 2½ pounds)
1 mango, seeded, peeled, and chopped
⅓ cup chopped onion
¼ cup snipped fresh cilantro

1 For marinade, in a medium bowl whisk together mango nectar, lemon juice, orange juice, parsley, vinegar, oil, garlic, jalapeño pepper, salt, and cumin. Reserve ½ cup of the marinade for sauce. Cover and chill until needed.

2 Place drummettes in a resealable plastic bag set in a shallow dish. Pour remaining marinade over drummettes; seal bag. Marinate in the refrigerator for 2 hours or overnight, turning bag occasionally. Drain chicken, discarding marinade.

3 Preheat oven to 450°F. Line a 15×10×1-inch baking pan with foil. Place drummettes in a single layer in prepared pan. Bake for about 25 minutes or until chicken is tender and no longer pink.

4 Meanwhile, for sauce, in a blender combine the reserved marinade, mango, onion, and cilantro. Cover and blend until smooth. Serve drummettes with sauce.

nutrition facts per serving: 278 cal., 20 g total fat (4 g sat. fat), 97 mg chol., 283 mg sodium, 9 g carb., 1 g dietary fiber, 17 g protein.

*Line the roasting pan with foil for the easiest cleanup possible.*

## mandarin apricot
# chicken wings

prep: 15 minutes   bake: 25 minutes   oven: 400°F   makes: 8 servings

16   chicken wing
       drummettes
       (2 pounds)
⅔   cup bottled sweet-
       and-sour sauce
½   cup snipped dried
       apricots
⅓   cup bottled hoisin
       sauce
¼   cup soy sauce
2   tablespoons honey
2   cloves garlic, minced
¼   teaspoon ground
       ginger
¼   teaspoon five-spice
       powder
1   tablespoon sesame
       seeds, toasted*
       Chopped green onion
       (optional)
       Dried apricot halves
       (optional)

**1** Preheat oven to 400°F. Line a shallow baking or roasting pan with foil; lightly coat with cooking spray. Place drummettes in a single layer in prepared pan. Bake drummettes for 20 minutes.

**2** Meanwhile, in a small saucepan stir together sweet-and-sour sauce, the snipped apricots, the hoisin sauce, soy sauce, honey, garlic, ginger, and five-spice powder. Bring to boiling; reduce heat. Simmer, uncovered, for 5 minutes. Remove from heat.

**3** Brush about ¼ cup of the sauce mixture over drummettes. Sprinkle with sesame seeds. Bake for about 5 minutes or until drummettes are no longer pink. Serve drummettes with remaining sauce. If desired, garnish with green onion and serve with dried apricot halves.

nutrition facts per serving: 129 cal., 8 g total fat (2 g sat. fat), 44 mg chol., 411 mg sodium, 11 g carb., 0 g dietary fiber, 8 g protein.

*note: See note, page 103.

**make-ahead directions:** Prepare sauce as directed. Cool. Cover and chill for up to 24 hours before using.

*This baked quesadilla recipe is easy to prepare, and you can fill them with other favorite meats, such as cooked chicken or pork, and cheeses, such as Monterey Jack, for an array of options.*

# spicy turkey quesadillas

start to finish: 35 minutes  oven: 400°F  makes: 9 (2-wedge) servings

1   turkey breast tenderloin, cut into thin strips (about 12 ounces)
1   tablespoon chili powder
¼   teaspoon ground black pepper
⅛   teaspoon salt
1   tablespoon olive oil
½   of a 15-ounce can (¾ cup) no-salt-added black beans, rinsed and drained
2   tablespoons lime juice
6   8-inch whole wheat tortillas
½   cup bottled salsa
½   cup shredded reduced-fat cheddar cheese (2 ounces)
½   cup snipped fresh cilantro
1   medium fresh serrano chile pepper, finely chopped (see note, page 52)
½   teaspoon lime juice
1   recipe Lime Sour Cream (optional)

**1** Preheat oven to 400°F. In a large bowl toss together turkey strips, 2 teaspoons of the chili powder, the black pepper, and salt. In a large skillet heat oil over medium heat. Cook and stir turkey strips in hot oil for 10 to 12 minutes or until turkey is no longer pink. Remove from heat and cool slightly. Coarsely chop turkey.

**2** Meanwhile, in a food processor combine the remaining 1 teaspoon chili powder, beans, and the 2 tablespoons lime juice. Cover and process until nearly smooth.

**3** Arrange three of the tortillas on a large baking sheet (do not overlap). Spread some of the black bean mixture evenly over each tortilla. Spoon salsa evenly over bean mixture. Top with chopped turkey; sprinkle with cheese. Place the remaining three tortillas on top. Bake for 12 to 15 minutes or until tortillas are brown and crisp.

**4** Meanwhile, in a small bowl combine cilantro, serrano pepper, and the ½ teaspoon lime juice.

**5** To serve, cut each quesadilla into six wedges; sprinkle with cilantro mixture. If desired, serve with Lime Sour Cream.

nutrition facts per serving: 189 cal., 5 g total fat (1 g sat. fat), 24 mg chol., 411 mg sodium, 21 g carb., 3 g dietary fiber, 15 g protein.

lime sour cream: In a small bowl combine ½ cup light dairy sour cream and 1 tablespoon lime juice. Makes ½ cup.

*Since the first spicy wings flew from Buffalo to parties across the country, countless variations have appeared. We think you'll like this neat-to-eat chicken breast version.*

## buffalo-style
# chicken fingers

prep: 25 minutes  bake: 18 minutes  oven: 425°F  makes: 12 servings

2   cups crushed
    cornflakes
2   tablespoons finely
    snipped fresh
    parsley
½   teaspoon salt
1   pound skinless,
    boneless chicken
    breast halves
⅓   cup bottled blue
    cheese salad
    dressing
2   teaspoons water
1   to 2 teaspoons
    bottled hot pepper
    sauce
    Celery sticks
    Bottled blue cheese
    salad dressing

**1** Preheat oven to 425°F. In a shallow bowl or pie plate combine cornflakes, parsley, and salt. Cut chicken breasts into strips about ³⁄₄ inch wide and 3 inches long. In a large mixing bowl combine ⅓ cup dressing, the water, and hot pepper sauce. Add chicken. Stir to coat. Roll chicken pieces individually in crumb mixture to coat.

**2** Lightly grease a 15×10×1-inch baking pan. Place chicken strips in a single layer. Bake for 18 to 20 minutes or until chicken is no longer pink and crumbs are golden. Serve warm with celery sticks and additional blue cheese dressing for dipping.

nutrition facts per serving: 184 cal., 12 g total fat (2 g sat. fat), 26 mg chol., 408 mg sodium, 9 g carb., 0 g dietary fiber, 11 g protein.

**make-ahead directions:** Prepare as directed through Step 1. Line a baking sheet with foil. Place coated chicken strips on prepared baking sheet. Freeze for about 2 hours or until firm. Place frozen strips in a freezer container. Cover and freeze for up to 1 month. To serve, bake as directed in Step 2.

*These savory slices are filled with a lively mix of Italian flavors—prosciutto, goat cheese, dried tomatoes, and pine nuts. Coating with breadcrumbs just before baking enhances the flavor.*

# mediterranean
# chicken pinwheels

prep: 45 minutes  bake: 25 minutes  cool: 15 minutes  oven: 400° F
makes: about 20 servings

4   skinless, boneless
     chicken breast
     halves (about
     1½ pounds)
     Ground black pepper
4   ounces sliced
     prosciutto
3   ounces goat cheese
     (chèvre), crumbled
¼   cup snipped fresh
     basil
¼   cup oil-packed dried
     tomato, drained and
     chopped
2   tablespoons pine
     nuts, toasted and
     chopped
1   tablespoon olive oil
⅔   cup Italian-style
     panko (Japanese-
     style breadcrumbs)
     Pitted olives, drained
     marinated artichoke
     hearts, crackers,
     and/or toasted
     baguette slices
     (optional)
1   recipe Lemon-Garlic
     Mayonnaise

1 Preheat oven to 400°F. Place chicken breast halves between sheets of plastic wrap. Pound with the flat side of a meat mallet to about ¼ inch thick. Remove top sheet of plastic wrap. Sprinkle chicken lightly with pepper. Place chicken with a short side facing you. Divide prosciutto among breast halves to within ½ inch of edges. Sprinkle with cheese, basil, tomato, and pine nuts. Roll up from a short side; secure with wooden toothpicks.

2 Brush chicken rolls with oil. Place breadcrumbs in a shallow dish. Coat chicken rolls with bread crumbs; place in a 9×9×2-inch pan. Bake, uncovered, for 25 to 30 minutes or until done (170°F). Cool for 15 minutes. Slice into ½-inch-thick slices.

3 Serve pinwheels with olives, artichoke hearts, crackers, and/or baguette slices and Lemon-Garlic Mayonnaise.

nutrition facts per serving: 137 cal., 8 g total fat (2 g sat. fat), 29 mg chol., 392 mg sodium, 4 g carb., 1 g dietary fiber, 12 g protein.

lemon-garlic mayonnaise: In a medium bowl stir together ½ cup mayonnaise, 1 teaspoon lemon or lime juice, and 2 cloves garlic, minced. Cover and chill. Makes ½ cup.

*Aioli (aye-OH-lee) is a garlic dressing that garlic-lovers will adore. You can make a cheater's version by stirring several tablespoons of pureed garlic into ½ cup of mayonnaise.*

# coffee-marinated
# beef skewers

prep: 40 minutes   marinate: 2 hours   broil: 4 minutes   makes: 12 servings

wings 'n' **things**

1 pound boneless beef
   sirloin steak, cut
   1 inch thick
¼ cup strong brewed
   coffee
¼ cup dry red wine
¾ teaspoon ground
   black pepper
½ teaspoon salt
⅛ teaspoon cayenne
   pepper
1 recipe Aioli

**1** Cut steak across the grain into long, thin strips. Place strips in a resealable plastic bag set in a shallow dish.

**2** For marinade, stir together coffee, wine, black pepper, salt, and cayenne pepper; pour over meat; seal bag. Marinate in refrigerator for 2 to 4 hours, turning bag occasionally. Drain meat, discarding marinade.

**3** Thread beef strips accordion-style onto 6-inch skewers. Place skewers on the unheated rack of a broiler pan. Broil 3 to 4 inches from heat for 4 to 6 minutes or until desired doneness, turning once.

**4** To serve, arrange beef skewers on a serving platter. Serve with Aioli.

nutrition facts per serving: 202 cal., 18 g total fat (4 g sat. fat), 18 mg chol., 127 mg sodium, 1 g carb., 0 g dietary fiber, 8 g protein.

aioli: Combine 4 to 6 cloves garlic, minced; ¼ cup refrigerated or frozen egg product, thawed; 2 tablespoons lemon juice; and ¼ teaspoon salt in a blender or food processor. Cover and blend or process for 5 seconds or until smooth. With blender or food processor running, gradually add ¾ cup olive oil in a thin, steady stream. When necessary, stop machine and use rubber scraper to scrape sides. Transfer to a storage container and chill for up to 3 days. Makes 1⅓ cups.

*These tasty pork and vegetable skewers are wonderful with the simple maple syrup glaze. You'll find many imitation or maple-flavored products on the market, but the real syrup is worth the price for the rich, sweet taste.*

# mini maple
# pork kabobs

prep: 20 minutes  broil: 10 minutes  makes: 24 servings

8  ounces pork tenderloin, cut into ¾-inch cubes

24  small cremini mushrooms (about 6 ounces), stems removed

1  small red sweet pepper, cut into ¾-inch squares

4  green onions, cut into 1-inch pieces

¼  teaspoon salt

⅛  teaspoon cayenne pepper (optional)

¼  cup pure maple syrup
Snipped fresh parsley (optional)

**1** Preheat broiler. Thread one pork cube, mushroom, sweet pepper square, and green onion piece on each of twenty-four 6-inch wooden skewers, leaving about 1 inch at bottom for holding. Sprinkle with salt and cayenne pepper, if desired.

**2** Place kabobs in single layer on the unheated rack of a broiler pan. Brush with maple syrup. Broil 3 to 4 inches from the heat for about 10 minutes or until meat is slightly pink in the center, turning and brushing with remaining syrup halfway through broiling. If desired, sprinkle with parsley before serving.

nutrition facts per serving: 23 cal., 0 g total fat (0 g sat. fat), 6 mg chol., 30 mg sodium, 3 g carb., 0 g dietary fiber, 2 g protein.

✱note: Soak wooden skewers in enough water to cover for at least 30 minutes before broiling.

*Party hearty with these ribs. They're perfect for an open-house appetizer party. They stay warm in the honey-sweetened picante sauce, so no one needs to go away hungry.*

# hot honeyed spareribs

prep: 20 minutes   broil: 10 minutes   cook: 6 to 7 hours (low) or 3 to 3½ hours (high)
makes: 10 to 12 servings

3½   to 4 pounds pork
      baby back ribs, cut
      into 1-rib portions
2   cups bottled picante
      sauce or salsa
½   cup honey
1   tablespoon quick-
      cooking tapioca
1   teaspoon ground
      ginger

**1** Preheat broiler. Place ribs on the unheated rack of a broiler pan. Broil 6 inches from the heat for about 10 minutes or until brown, turning once. Transfer ribs to a 3½- to 6-quart slow cooker.

**2** In a medium bowl combine picante sauce, honey, tapioca, and ginger. Pour sauce over ribs.

**3** Cover and cook on low heat setting for 6 to 7 hours or on high heat setting for 3 to 3 ½ hours. If desired skim off fat from sauce. Serve sauce with ribs.

nutrition facts per serving: 215 cal., 6 g total fat (2 g sat. fat), 43 mg chol., 246 mg sodium, 18 g carb., 0 g dietary fiber, 20 g protein.

*A ripe mango will have a sweet, resinous scent. If you smell nothing, you will taste nothing.*

# caribbean **riblets**

prep: 25 minutes  bake: 1½ hours  oven: 350°F  makes: 12 to 16 servings

1   tablespoon packed
    brown sugar
1   teaspoon dried
    thyme, crushed
1   teaspoon ground
    allspice
1   teaspoon ground
    black pepper
½   teaspoon salt
½   teaspoon garlic
    powder
½   teaspoon cayenne
    pepper
¼   teaspoon ground
    nutmeg
⅛   teaspoon ground
    cloves
3   pounds meaty pork
    loin back ribs, cut
    into 1- to 2-rib
    portions*
2   tablespoons
    vegetable oil
2   medium onions,
    chopped
2   medium fresh
    mangoes, seeded,
    peeled, and chopped
⅔   cup lime juice
½   cup honey
¼   cup rum
2   tablespoons soy
    sauce
2   teaspoons dry
    mustard
1   teaspoon Jamaican
    jerk seasoning

**1** Preheat oven to 350°F. For rub, in a small bowl combine brown sugar, thyme, allspice, black pepper, salt, garlic powder, cayenne pepper, nutmeg, and cloves. Place ribs in a very large bowl. Add spice mixture; toss to coat ribs evenly.

**2** Place the ribs, bone side down, in a large shallow roasting pan. Bake, covered, for 1 hour. Carefully drain off fat.

**3** Meanwhile, in a medium saucepan heat oil over medium heat. Cook onions in hot oil for 4 minutes or until tender. Stir in mangoes. Cook and stir for 2 minutes more. Stir in lime juice, honey, rum, soy sauce, mustard, and jerk seasoning. Bring to boiling; reduce heat. Simmer for about 20 minutes or until thickened, stirring occasionally.

**4** Remove ribs from oven. Spoon some of the mango mixture over ribs. Bake, uncovered, for 30 minutes more or until ribs are tender. Pass remaining mango mixture with ribs.

nutrition facts per serving: 314 cal., 19 g total fat (6 g sat. fat), 57 mg chol., 347 mg sodium, 22 g carb., 1 g dietary fiber, 12 g protein.

*note: For appetizer-size portions, have your butcher cut the ribs in half crosswise across the bone.

*To make the ribs easier to eat, ask your butcher to cut the ribs in half crosswise (across the bones) to make smaller portions.*

# flamin' cajun riblets

prep: 20 minutes   cook: 5 to 6 hours (low) or 2½ to 3 hours (high)
makes: 12 servings

3 pounds pork loin back ribs

1 tablespoon Cajun seasoning

1 cup bottled chili sauce

1 medium onion, finely chopped

1 fresh serrano chile pepper, seeded and finely chopped (see note, page 52)

2 tablespoons quick-cooking tapioca, crushed

1 teaspoon finely shredded lemon peel

1 tablespoon lemon juice

1 to 2 teaspoons bottled hot pepper sauce

Snipped fresh parsley (optional)

**1** Sprinkle ribs with Cajun seasoning; rub in with your fingers. Cut ribs into single rib portions. Place ribs in a 3½- or 4-quart slow cooker.

**2** In a medium bowl combine chili sauce, onion, serrano pepper, tapioca, lemon peel, lemon juice, and hot pepper sauce. Pour sauce over ribs.

**3** Cover and cook on low heat setting for 5 to 6 hours or on high heat setting for 2½ to 3 hours. Serve immediately or keep covered on warm or low heat setting for up to 2 hours. (Remove any bones without meat.) If desired, sprinkle with parsley.

nutrition facts per serving: 231 cal., 17 g total fat (6 g sat. fat), 57 mg chol., 369 mg sodium, 7 g carb., 1 g dietary fiber, 12 g protein.

*Have plenty of cocktail napkins handy when serving these saucy sweet-and-sour glazed ribs.*

# ginger-glazed
# cocktail ribs

prep: 20 minutes  roast: 1¼ hours  oven: 350°F  makes: about 30 servings

2½  to 3 pounds meaty
      pork loin back ribs
      or spareribs*
     Salt
     Ground black pepper
2   teaspoons olive oil or
      cooking oil
¼   cup finely chopped
      onion
1   clove garlic, minced
⅓   cup bottled chili
      sauce
⅓   cup apricot or peach
      preserves
1   tablespoon soy sauce
1   teaspoon grated
      fresh ginger or
      ¼ teaspoon ground
      ginger

1 Preheat oven to 350°F. Cut ribs into single-rib portions. Sprinkle ribs with salt and pepper. Arrange ribs, meaty side up, in a shallow roasting pan. Roast for about 1 hour or until tender.

2 Meanwhile, for glaze, in a small saucepan heat oil over medium heat. Cook and stir onion and garlic in hot oil for about 3 minutes or until onion is tender. Stir in chili sauce, preserves, soy sauce, and ginger. Heat and stir until bubbly. Remove from heat.

3 Brush ribs generously with glaze. Roast ribs for 15 minutes more, brushing once or twice with glaze during roasting time.

nutrition facts per serving: 54 cal., 2 g total fat (1 g sat. fat), 11 mg chol., 95 mg sodium, 3 g carb., 0 g dietary fiber, 5 g protein.

**make-ahead directions:** Prepare the ribs as directed through Step 3. Cool and place in an airtight container. Cover and chill for up to 3 days. To serve, preheat oven to 350°F. Place ribs in a large baking pan and bake for about 5 minutes or until heated through.

*These bites practically explode with sweet-salty flavor.*

# sugared bacon-wrapped
# smokies

prep: 35 minutes   bake: 30 minutes   oven: 350°F   makes: about 45 servings

1   16-ounce package
    small cooked
    smoked sausage
    links
15  slices bacon, each
    cut crosswise into
    thirds
¾   cup packed brown
    sugar

**1** Preheat oven to 350°F. Line a 15×10×1-inch baking pan with foil; lightly coat with cooking spray. Set aside.

**2** Wrap each sausage link with a bacon piece, overlapping the bacon piece at the end. Press the end of the bacon piece to seal or secure it with a wooden toothpick.

**3** Place brown sugar in a large resealable plastic bag. Add several bacon-wrapped sausages to bag and seal. Shake bag gently to coat sausages with brown sugar. Place sausages in prepared pan. Repeat with remaining bacon-wrapped sausages and brown sugar.

**4** Bake for about 30 minutes or until the bacon browns. Serve immediately.

nutrition facts per serving: 102 cal., 8 g total fat (3 g sat. fat), 15 mg chol., 210 mg sodium, 4 g carb., 0 g dietary fiber, 3 g protein.

**make-ahead directions:** Prepare as directed through Step 3. Cover and store in the refrigerator for up to 24 hours. To serve, uncover and bake as directed in Step 4.

*Hot appetizers like this one, cooked and served in a slow cooker, eliminate much of the stress and last-minute hassle of party hosting.*

# caribbean
# cocktail sausages

prep: 15 minutes  cook: 4 hours (low)  makes: 12 servings

1  1-pound package cocktail wieners or small, cooked smoked sausage links
1  12-ounce jar pineapple preserves
½  teaspoon finely shredded lime peel
1  tablespoon lime juice
1  teaspoon Jamaican jerk seasoning
1  teaspoon ground ginger
2  cloves garlic, minced
Few dashes bottled hot pepper sauce

In a 1½-quart slow cooker combine wieners, pineapple preserves, lime peel, lime juice, jerk seasoning, ginger, garlic, and hot pepper sauce. Cover and cook on low heat setting for 4 hours. Serve immediately or keep covered for up to 2 hours. Serve with wooden toothpicks.

nutrition facts per serving: 194 cal., 10 g total fat (4 g sat. fat), 24 mg chol., 421 mg sodium, 21 g carb., 0 g dietary fiber, 5 g protein.

**increasing the recipe:** Use two 16-ounce packages of cocktail sausages and place in a 3½- or 4-quart slow cooker. Cover and cook for 4 hours on low heat setting or 2 hours on high heat setting.

*This appetizer holds well for up to an hour—but it's so good, the bites will likely be long gone by then!*

# turkey kielbasa bites

prep: 10 minutes  cook: 2½ to 3 hours  makes: 10 to 12 servings

1  1-pound package cooked turkey kielbasa, cut in 1-inch pieces
1  12-ounce carton cranberry-orange or cranberry-raspberry crushed fruit
1  tablespoon Dijon-style mustard
¼  teaspoon crushed red pepper

1 In a 1½-quart slow cooker combine kielbasa, cranberry-orange crushed fruit, Dijon mustard, and crushed red pepper.
2 Cover and cook on low heat setting for 2½ to 3 hours. Serve immediately or keep warm for up to 1 hour. Serve kielbasa with wooden toothpicks.

nutrition facts per serving: 126 cal., 4 g total fat (1 g sat. fat), 28 mg chol., 441 mg sodium, 15 g carb., 0 g dietary fiber, 7 g protein.

5

Bite-size, versatile, and always a hit with guests, succulent shrimp is an easy grab-and-go-nibble. Guests will also get hooked on smoked salmon, sprightly seasoned crab cakes, sizzling scallops, and more.

seafood

sam

pler

*Delicious, attractive, and easy—that's the perfect description for these tidbits. Leave tails on shrimp to give guests a handle to hold on to for eating.*

# spinach bruschetta
## with pesto-coated shrimp

prep: 30 minutes  broil: 5 minutes  makes: 24 servings

24  frozen peeled, deveined cooked large shrimp
¼  cup refrigerated basil pesto
24  ½-inch-thick slices baguette-style French bread
1  10-ounce package frozen chopped spinach, thawed and well drained
½  of an 8-ounce package cream cheese, softened
⅓  cup grated Parmesan cheese
⅓  cup finely chopped onion
⅓  cup mayonnaise

1 Thaw shrimp. Butterfly shrimp, cutting along the back of each shrimp, though not through to the other side. In a large bowl combine shrimp and pesto. Cover and set aside.

2 Preheat broiler. Place bread slices on the unheated rack of a broiler pan. Broil 3 to 4 inches from heat for about 2 minutes or until toasted, turning once.

3 In a medium bowl stir together spinach, cream cheese, Parmesan cheese, onion, and mayonnaise. Spread mixture over toasted bread slices. Broil 3 to 4 inches from the heat for about 3 minutes or until spinach mixture is hot and bubbly. To serve, place a cooked shrimp on each bread slice. Serve immediately.

nutrition facts per serving: 101 cal., 6 g total fat (2 g sat. fat), 45 mg chol., 164 mg sodium, 4 g carb., 1 g dietary fiber, 6 g protein.

make-ahead directions: Toast bread slices as directed in Step 2. Place in an airtight container. Cover and store at room temperature for up to 24 hours.

*Guests will love the flavorful pairing of nutty sesame-flavored shrimp with a dipping sauce that combines a host of salty, sweet, and spicy ingredients.*

# shrimp with
# asian cocktail sauce

start to finish: 30 minutes makes: 6 servings

1 pound fresh or frozen jumbo shrimp in shells

⅛ teaspoon salt

1 teaspoon sesame seeds, toasted

1 8-ounce can no-salt-added tomato sauce

2 tablespoons finely chopped red onion

2 tablespoons bottled plum sauce

2 tablespoons bottled chili sauce

1 tablespoon rice vinegar

2 teaspoons reduced-sodium soy sauce

½ teaspoon finely shredded orange peel

**1** Thaw shrimp, if frozen. Peel and devein shrimp, leaving tails intact. Rinse shrimp; pat dry with paper towels. Sprinkle shrimp with salt.

**2** Lightly coat a grill pan or a large skillet with cooking spray; heat over medium-high heat. Cook shrimp for 6 to 8 minutes or until shrimp are opaque, turning once. Sprinkle with sesame seeds.

**3** Meanwhile, for sauce, in a small bowl combine tomato sauce, red onion, plum sauce, chili sauce, vinegar, soy sauce, and orange peel. Serve shrimp with sauce.

nutrition facts per serving: 107 cal., 1 g total fat (0 g sat. fat), 86 mg chol., 406 mg sodium, 10 g carb., 1 g dietary fiber, 12 g protein.

make-ahead directions: Prepare sauce as directed; cover and chill for up to 5 days.

## shrimp: sizeable differences

*Use this list as a handy reference for market names and average numbers of shrimp per pound (unshelled).*

- jumbo: *23 pieces per pound*
- large: *33 pieces per pound*
- medium: *45 pieces per pound*
- small: *55 pieces per pound*

*Guests will delight in this sunny Caribbean-style appetizer. Purchasing already cooked shrimp and canned cut-up fruit makes this super easy.*

# jamaican jerk shrimp
## with papaya and pineapple

start to finish: 30 minutes  makes: 12 servings

**1** Thaw shrimp. Place shrimp in a resealable plastic bag. Add jerk seasoning and oil; seal bag. Turn to coat shrimp. Chill for 30 minutes.

**2** Meanwhile, in a medium bowl combine papaya, pineapple, peppers, sliced green onion, lime peel, lime juice, and garlic. Cover and chill until serving time.

**3** To serve, gently stir together shrimp and fruit mixture. If desired, garnish with whole green onions.

2 pounds frozen peeled, deveined cooked large shrimp (with tails)

1 tablespoon Jamaican jerk seasoning*

1 tablespoon cooking oil

½ of a 24- to 26-ounce jar refrigerated sliced papaya, drained and coarsely chopped (1¼ cups)

1 8-ounce can pineapple tidbits, drained and chopped

¼ cup chopped bottled roasted red sweet peppers

¼ cup sliced green onion

1 teaspoon finely shredded lime peel

2 tablespoons lime juice

2 cloves garlic, minced
Green onions (optional)

nutrition facts per serving: 107 cal., 2 g total fat (0 g sat. fat), 147 mg chol., 246 mg sodium, 6 g carb., 1 g dietary fiber, 16 g protein.

*note: Look for jerk seasoning in the herb and spice section of a large supermarket. To make homemade jerk seasoning, in a small bowl combine 1½ teaspoons dried crushed thyme, ½ teaspoon ground allspice, ½ teaspoon black pepper, ⅛ teaspoon salt, ⅛ teaspoon ground cinnamon, and ⅛ teaspoon cayenne pepper.

## buying shrimp

- *The price of shrimp usually depends on the size of shrimp you are purchasing—as a general rule, the bigger the shrimp, the higher the price and the fewer per pound.*

- *Look for firm, juicy shrimp with translucent, moist shells and without black spots (unless you are purchasing black tiger shrimp).*

*Known as bocconcini, the small fresh mozzarella balls featured in this recipe are Italy on a stick when paired with shrimp and tomatoes brushed with a pesto vinaigrette.*

# pesto shrimp
# caprese skewers

prep: 30 minutes   chill: 1 hour   makes: 20 servings

20   fresh or frozen
        medium shrimp in
        shells
1    tablespoon olive oil
¼    cup purchased basil
        pesto
20   bocconcini or 1-inch
        chunks of fresh
        mozzarella cheese
20   grape tomatoes
        Purchased basil pesto
2    tablespoons bottled
        balsamic vinaigrette
        salad dressing
        Ground black pepper
        (optional)

**1** Thaw shrimp, if frozen. Peel and devein shrimp, leaving tails intact. Rinse shrimp; pat dry with paper towels.

**2** In a large skillet heat oil over medium heat. Cook shrimp in hot oil for 2 to 4 minutes or until opaque. Spread shrimp in a single layer on a baking sheet. Cover and chill for at least 1 hour. In a medium bowl combine shrimp and ¼ cup pesto. Toss to coat.

**3** On each of twenty 4-inch skewers thread 1 shrimp, 1 bocconcini, and 1 grape tomato. Serve immediately or cover and chill for up to 4 hours. To serve, brush with additional pesto and balsamic vinaigrette. If desired, sprinkle with pepper.

nutrition facts per serving: 125 cal., 9 g total fat (5 g sat. fat), 47 mg chol., 156 mg sodium, 1 g carb., 0 g dietary fiber, 9 g protein.

make-ahead directions: Cover and chill cooked shrimp and pesto mixture for up to 24 hours before serving. Thread onto skewers as directed.

*This shrimp recipe will win rave reviews for its crispy coconut coating and curry-mango sauce. If you don't own a food processor, finely chop the coconut and cashews.*

# curry-coconut shrimp
## with mango dipping sauce

prep: 30 minutes   cook: 3 minutes per batch   oven: 200°F
makes: 10 to 12 servings

24  fresh or frozen jumbo shrimp in shells
1   teaspoon curry powder
2   cups shredded coconut
½   cup chopped cashews
⅓   cup all-purpose flour
½   teaspoon salt
¼   teaspoon ground black pepper
2   eggs, lightly beaten
1   tablespoon lime juice
    Cooking oil for deep-fat frying
1   recipe Mango Dipping Sauce

1 Thaw shrimp, if frozen. Peel and devein shrimp, leaving tails intact. Rinse shrimp; pat dry with paper towels. Preheat oven to 200°F. Sprinkle shrimp with ½ teaspoon of the curry powder.

2 In a food processor combine coconut and cashews. Cover and pulse until finely chopped. Place mixture in a shallow bowl.

3 In another shallow bowl combine the remaining ½ teaspoon curry powder, the flour, salt, and pepper. In another shallow bowl combine the eggs and lime juice.

4 Dip each shrimp, one at a time, into the flour mixture, shaking off any excess. Dip into egg mixture, then into coconut mixture to coat. Pat coconut mixture in place as necessary to adhere.

5 In a large saucepan heat 1½ inches of cooking oil to 350°F. Fry shrimp, four to six at a time, in hot oil for about 3 minutes or until golden brown. Drain on paper towels. Keep warm on a baking sheet in the oven while frying remaining shrimp. Carefully skim and discard any coconut that falls in oil between batches.

6 Serve warm with Mango Dipping Sauce.

mango dipping sauce: In a small bowl combine ½ cup mango chutney (snip any large pieces), ½ cup dairy sour cream, and ½ teaspoon curry powder. Makes 1 cup.

nutrition facts per serving: 148 cal., 11 g total fat (4 g sat. fat), 48 mg chol., 125 mg sodium, 7 g carb., 1 g dietary fiber, 5 g protein.

make-ahead directions: Place peeled and deveined shrimp on ice. Cover. Chill for up to 24 hours before using. Place cashew mixture in an airtight container. Cover. Store at room temperature for up to 1 week. Cover and chill Mango Dipping Sauce for up to 24 hours before serving.

*It's easier than it looks to present two sauces in the same bowl. Tilt the bowl slightly and put the cocktail sauce in one side. Then tilt the bowl the opposite way and add the sour cream sauce.*

## double-quick
# shrimp cocktail

start to finish: 15 minutes  makes: about 40 servings

1½  pounds frozen peeled, deveined cooked medium shrimp with tails

1  8-ounce carton dairy sour cream

¼  cup prepared horseradish

2  tablespoons snipped fresh chives or thinly sliced green onion tops

1  tablespoon lemon juice

1  12-ounce jar seafood cocktail sauce or chili sauce

Fresh chives and/ or lemon slices or wedges

**1** Thaw shrimp. In a small bowl combine sour cream, horseradish, the snipped chives, and the lemon juice. Place half of the sour cream mixture in one side of a 4-cup shallow serving bowl. Spoon half of the cocktail sauce into bowl next to sour cream mixture. Spoon the rest of the sour cream mixture over the sour cream mixture in bowl, and the rest of the cocktail sauce over the cocktail sauce in bowl. If desired, cover and chill for up to 4 hours before serving.

**2** To serve, place bowl containing dip mixture on a platter. Arrange shrimp around bowl. Garnish with chives and/or lemon slices or wedges.

nutrition facts per serving: 37 cal., 1 g total fat (1 g sat. fat), 36 mg chol., 119 mg sodium, 2 g carb., 0 g dietary fiber, 4 g protein.

*thawing shrimp: Most of the shrimp offered at supermarkets have been previously frozen. If the shrimp you purchase are frozen, place them in a sealed container and thaw overnight in the refrigerator.

### mango salsa

*Serve this refreshing combo with shrimp or the Curried Crab Cakes on page 144. In a medium bowl combine 1½ cups chopped peeled and seeded mangoes or peaches; 1 medium red sweet pepper, finely chopped; ¼ cup thinly sliced green onion; 1 fresh jalapeño chile pepper, seeded and finely chopped (see note, page 52); ½ teaspoon finely shredded lime peel; 1 tablespoon lime juice; 1 tablespoon olive oil; 1 tablespoon cider vinegar; ½ teaspoon salt; and ¼ teaspoon ground black pepper. Makes 2 cups.*

*Citrus-marinated shrimp get an Asian twist, thanks to ginger and fresh pea pods. Use leftover fresh ginger to add sweet, spicy accents to everyday dishes.*

# ginger shrimp skewers

prep: 30 minutes   marinate: 1 to 2 hours   makes: 8 servings

12   ounces fresh or frozen large shrimp in shells
1½   cups water
1   teaspoon finely shredded orange peel
3   tablespoons orange juice
1   tablespoon white wine vinegar
1   teaspoon toasted sesame oil or olive oil
1   teaspoon grated fresh ginger or ½ teaspoon ground ginger
1   clove garlic
⅛   teaspoon salt
⅛   teaspoon cayenne pepper
16   fresh pea pods
2   to 3 oranges, peeled and sectioned and/or 16 fresh pineapple chunks
    Reduced-sodium soy sauce (optional)

1 Thaw shrimp, if frozen. Peel and devein shrimp, leaving tails intact. Rinse shrimp. In a large saucepan bring the water to boiling. Add shrimp. Cover and simmer for 1 to 3 minutes or until shrimp are opaque. Drain; rinse shrimp with cold water. Drain well.

2 Place shrimp in a resealable plastic bag set in a shallow bowl. Add orange peel, orange juice, vinegar, oil, ginger, garlic, salt, and cayenne pepper to bag; seal bag. Toss gently to coat shrimp. Marinate in the refrigerator for 1 to 2 hours.

3 Place pea pods in a steamer basket over boiling water. Cover and steam for 2 to 3 minutes or until just tender. Rinse with cold water. Drain well.

4 Drain shrimp, discarding marinade. On each of eight 6-inch skewers thread shrimp, pea pods, and fruit. If desired, serve with soy sauce.

nutrition facts per serving: 72 cal., 1 g total fat (0 g sat. fat), 65 mg chol., 100 mg sodium, 5 g carb., 1 g dietary fiber, 10 g protein.

make-ahead directions: Prepare as directed in Step 1. Place shrimp in an airtight container. Cover and chill for up to 24 hours. Continue as directed in Step 2.

*It's a double seafood delight when a creamy mixture of lump crabmeat becomes the centerpiece of butterflied shrimp.*

# crab-topped shrimp

prep: 35 minutes  bake: 10 minutes  oven: 425°F  makes: 16 servings

16 fresh or frozen large shrimp in shells
1 ounce cream cheese (2 tablespoons), softened
2 tablespoons mayonnaise
1 teaspoon Dijon-style mustard
⅛ teaspoon salt
1 6.5-ounce can lump crabmeat, drained and flaked
2 tablespoons finely chopped green onion
2 tablespoons finely chopped bottled roasted red sweet pepper

1 Thaw shrimp, if frozen. Peel and devein shrimp, leaving tails intact. Rinse shrimp; pat dry with paper towels. Preheat oven to 425°F. Line a 15×10×1-inch baking pan with foil; set aside.

2 In a medium mixing bowl beat cream cheese with an electric mixer on medium speed until smooth. Beat in mayonnaise, mustard, and salt. Stir in crabmeat, green onion, and pepper until combined.

3 Butterfly shrimp, cutting through the back of each shrimp, though not through to the other side. Open shrimp and lay flat, cut side down, in prepared baking pan. Divide crab mixture among shrimp, shaping the mixture into a mound. Bring shrimp tails up and over the crab mixture.

4 Bake for about 10 minutes or until shrimp are opaque. Serve warm.

nutrition facts per serving: 38 cal., 2 g total fat (1 g sat. fat), 23 mg chol., 90 mg sodium, 0 g carb., 0 g dietary fiber, 4 g protein.

*Juicy, succulent shrimp wrapped in crisp, salty bacon—what's not to like? When choosing bacon, look for pieces that appear to be half fat and half lean.*

# grilled bacon-wrapped
# shrimp

prep: 20 minutes   grill: 8 minutes   makes: 16 servings

1  pound fresh large
    shrimp in shells
    (16 shrimp)
8  slices bacon, halved
    crosswise
    Barbecue sauce,
    heated (optional)

1 Peel and devein shrimp, leaving tails intact. Rinse shrimp; pat dry with paper towels. Wrap each shrimp in a piece of bacon, securing bacon with a wooden skewer or toothpick and skewering shrimp neck to tail in a half-moon shape.

2 For a charcoal grill, place the shrimp on the lightly greased rack of an uncovered grill directly over medium coals for 8 to 10 minutes or until bacon is crisp and shrimp turn opaque, turning once. (For a gas grill, preheat grill. Reduce heat to medium. Add shrimp to grill rack; cover and grill as above.)

3 If desired, serve with barbecue sauce.

nutrition facts per serving: 44 cal., 2 g total fat (1 g sat. fat), 37 mg chol., 119 mg sodium, 0 g carb., 0 g dietary fiber, 6 g protein.

*A fragrant garlic, ginger, and lemon marinade lends fabulous flavor to the cooked shrimp. Be sure to use a serving plate with sides about ½ inch deep, as the shrimp will release some liquid.*

# upside-down
## marinated shrimp bowl

prep: 25 minutes    chill: 12 to 24 hours    cook: 1 minute    makes: 20 servings

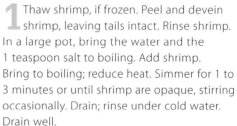

5 pounds fresh or frozen large shrimp in shells
5 quarts water
1 teaspoon salt
½ cup olive oil
½ cup white or red wine vinegar
1½ teaspoons finely shredded lemon peel
¼ cup lemon juice
2 tablespoons tomato paste
1 tablespoon honey
3 cloves garlic, minced
2 teaspoons grated fresh ginger
½ teaspoon salt
¼ teaspoon cayenne pepper
 Thinly sliced cucumber ribbons (optional)
 Thinly sliced red onion (optional)

1 Thaw shrimp, if frozen. Peel and devein shrimp, leaving tails intact. Rinse shrimp. In a large pot, bring the water and the 1 teaspoon salt to boiling. Add shrimp. Bring to boiling; reduce heat. Simmer for 1 to 3 minutes or until shrimp are opaque, stirring occasionally. Drain; rinse under cold water. Drain well.

2 In a glass bowl that is 7 to 8 inches in diameter and about 4 inches deep, arrange the shrimp, tails toward the center, in a circle to make 1 flat layer. (Only the backs of shrimp should be visible from the outside of the bowl.) Repeat layers, pressing down every couple of layers with the bottom of a plate small enough to fit inside the bowl. When bowl is full, press down with plate once again.

3 For marinade, in a screw-top jar combine oil, vinegar, lemon peel, lemon juice, tomato paste, honey, garlic, ginger, the ½ teaspoon salt, and cayenne pepper. Cover and shake well.

4 Pour marinade over shrimp in bowl. Cover and marinate in the refrigerator for 12 to 24 hours, occasionally placing a flat plate larger than the bowl tightly over the bowl and inverting it to redistribute marinade.

5 Before serving, invert the plate off-center on top of the bowl. Invert bowl slightly to drain off marinade. Repeat inverting and draining until all marinade is drained. Discard marinade. Place serving platter over bowl; carefully invert bowl to unmold.

6 If desired, arrange cucumber and red onion around shrimp.

nutrition facts per serving: 176 cal., 7 g total fat (1 g sat. fat), 172 mg chol., 257 mg sodium, 3 g carb., 0 g dietary fiber, 23 g protein.

seafood **sampler**

*Shrimp cocktail has a modern appeal with grape tomatoes and herb sauce.*

# herbed **shrimp** and tomatoes

prep: 20 minutes  marinate: 10 minutes  cook: 4 minutes  makes: 8 servings

2 pounds fresh or frozen jumbo shrimp in shells
2 tablespoons snipped fresh basil or oregano
1 tablespoon lemon juice
¾ teaspoon salt
¼ teaspoon ground black pepper
2 tablespoons extra virgin olive oil
2 cups grape or cherry tomatoes
1 recipe Basil Dipping Sauce
Lemon wedges (optional)
Snipped fresh basil (optional)

**1** Thaw shrimp, if frozen. Peel and devein shrimp, removing tails. Rinse shrimp; pat dry with paper towels. Set aside. In a large bowl combine the 2 tablespoons snipped basil, the lemon juice, salt, and pepper. Add shrimp. Toss to coat. Cover and marinate in refrigerator for 10 to 30 minutes.

**2** In a large skillet heat oil over medium-high heat. Cook shrimp, half at a time, for 2 to 3 minutes or until shrimp are opaque, stirring often to cook evenly. Transfer to serving platter.

**3** Add tomatoes to shrimp, tossing gently to combine. Serve warm or chill until serving time. Serve with Basil Dipping Sauce and, if desired, lemon wedges and snipped basil.

nutrition facts per serving: 162 cal., 5 g total fat (1 g sat. fat), 172 mg chol., 389 mg sodium, 4 g carb., 1 g dietary fiber, 24 g protein.

make-ahead directions: Thaw frozen shrimp. Peel and devein shrimp. Cover and chill for up to 24 hours. Two hours before serving, finish preparing recipe as directed. Cover and chill until serving.

basil dipping sauce: In a small bowl combine 1 cup mayonnaise; 1 tablespoon snipped fresh basil; 2 cloves garlic, minced; 1 teaspoon lemon juice; 1 teaspoon Dijon-style mustard; and ⅛ teaspoon cayenne pepper. Makes 1 cup.

*A martini glass makes an interesting serving dish for this first-course appetizer. Snip a couple more sprigs of parsley and sprinkle on top. Pictured on page 129.*

# sherried shrimp
## with garlic

start to finish: 20 minutes   makes: 6 servings

1 pound fresh or frozen large shrimp in shells

¼ cup sherry or orange juice

2 tablespoons orange juice

½ cup bottled roasted red sweet peppers, cut into thin strips

10 pitted ripe olives, halved (⅓ cup)

2 tablespoons snipped fresh parsley

3 cloves garlic, minced

2 teaspoons capers, drained

2 teaspoons tomato paste

⅛ teaspoon ground black pepper

1 teaspoon olive oil

**1** Thaw shrimp, if frozen. Peel and devein shrimp, leaving tails intact. Rinse shrimp; pat dry with paper towels. Set aside.

**2** In a large skillet combine sherry, orange juice, sweet peppers, olives, parsley, garlic, capers, tomato paste, and black pepper. Bring to boiling. Add shrimp. Cook and stir for 1 to 3 minutes or until shrimp turn opaque. Remove from heat. Stir in olive oil. Serve in small dishes or glasses.

nutrition facts per serving: 101 cal., 3 g total fat (0 g sat. fat), 86 mg chol., 179 mg sodium, 4 g carb., 1 g dietary fiber, 12 g protein.

make-ahead directions: Prepare and cool shrimp mixture as directed. Transfer to an airtight container. Cover and chill for up to 2 days. Let stand for 30 minutes before serving.

*No doubt about it, shrimp is one of the best cocktail nibblers around. This versatile recipe includes Mexican and Cajun flavor variations.*

# mediterranean shrimp

prep: 25 minutes  marinate: 2 hours  makes: 8 servings

1 pound frozen peeled, deveined cooked large shrimp (with tails)
¼ cup olive oil or salad oil
3 tablespoons white wine vinegar
2 tablespoons finely chopped shallot
2 tablespoons snipped fresh oregano
1 teaspoon finely shredded lemon peel
1 tablespoon lemon juice
1 clove garlic, minced
½ teaspoon salt
4 ounces smoked provolone cheese, cut into ½-inch cubes, or crumbled feta cheese (1 cup)
1½ cups grape tomatoes and/or yellow pear-shaped tomatoes
½ cup drained capers

**1** Thaw shrimp. In a large resealable plastic bag combine oil, vinegar, shallot, oregano, lemon peel, lemon juice, garlic, and salt; seal bag. Mix well. Set bag in a large bowl. Add shrimp, cheese, tomatoes, and capers; seal bag. Marinate in the refrigerator for 2 to 6 hours, turning bag occasionally.

**2** Chill eight small glass serving dishes in the refrigerator until ready to use. To serve, spoon into chilled glasses.

nutrition facts per serving: 179 cal., 11 g total fat (4 g sat. fat), 120 mg chol., 654 mg sodium, 3 g carb., 1 g dietary fiber, 16 g protein.

cajun shrimp: Prepare as directed, except omit provolone cheese and capers. For marinade, in a large resealable bag combine ¼ cup lemon juice; ¼ cup salad oil; 2 cloves garlic, minced; and 1½ teaspoons Cajun seasoning. Add 1 cup chopped red, yellow, and/or green sweet pepper and ¾ cup sliced celery to the marinade mixture.

tequila shrimp: Prepare as directed, except omit provolone cheese and capers. For marinade, in a large resealable bag combine ¼ cup olive oil; ¼ cup lime juice; ¼ cup tequila; 2 cloves garlic, minced; 2 tablespoons snipped fresh cilantro; and ⅛ teaspoon salt. Add 1 cup of ¾-inch pieces of red, yellow and/or green sweet pepper to the shrimp mixture. After spooning into glasses top with 1 avocado that has been halved, pitted, peeled, and cut into 8 wedges.

*A splash of dry white wine intensifies the flavor in this shrimp scampi.*

# marinated
## shrimp scampi

prep: 35 minutes  marinate: 1 hour  broil: 4 minutes
makes: 10 to 12 servings

2    pounds fresh or
      frozen extra-jumbo
      shrimp in shells
      (30 to 40)
¼   cup olive oil
¼   cup dry white wine
6    cloves garlic, minced
      (1 tablespoon)
2    teaspoons finely
      shredded lemon
      peel
½   teaspoon crushed red
      pepper
½   teaspoon salt
2    tablespoons snipped
      fresh Italian parsley
      Lemon wedges

**1** Thaw shrimp, if frozen. Peel and devein shrimp, leaving tails intact. Rinse shrimp; pat dry with paper towels. Place shrimp in a large resealable plastic bag set in a shallow bowl.

**2** In a small bowl combine oil, wine, garlic, lemon peel, crushed red pepper, and salt. Pour over shrimp; seal bag. Toss gently to coat. Marinate in the refrigerator for 1 hour.

**3** Remove shrimp from marinade, reserving marinade. Arrange shrimp on unheated broiler pan. Broil 4 to 5 inches from heat for 2 minutes. Turn shrimp and brush with reserved marinade. Broil for 2 to 4 minutes or until shrimp turn opaque.

**4** To serve, mound shrimp on platter; sprinkle with parsley and squeeze lemon wedges over shrimp.

nutrition facts per serving: 126 cal., 4 g total fat (1 g sat. fat), 138 mg chol., 193 mg sodium, 2 g carb., 1 g dietary fiber, 19 g protein.

make-ahead directions: Prepare marinade up to 24 hours before using. Add shrimp and marinate as directed.

*Mango salsa adds the perfect sweet-heat note to the mustard- and curry-flavored crab cakes. Find a recipe for Mango Salsa on page 135. To make nice round cakes with crisp crusts, turn the patties only once.*

# curried crab cakes

prep: 30 minutes   cook: 6 minutes per batch   oven: 300°F   makes: 12 servings

2    eggs, lightly beaten
½    cup mayonnaise
1    tablespoon curry powder
1    tablespoon Worcestershire sauce
1    teaspoon stone-ground mustard
¾    cup panko (Japanese-style breadcrumbs)
¼    cup finely chopped red sweet pepper
¼    cup finely chopped green sweet pepper
¼    cup finely chopped red onion
¼    cup thinly sliced green onion
2    tablespoons snipped fresh parsley
1    pound cooked lump crabmeat, flaked, or three 6-ounce cans crabmeat, drained, flaked, and cartilage removed (about 3 cups)
2    tablespoons olive oil or cooking oil

**1** Preheat oven to 300°F. In a large bowl combine eggs, mayonnaise, curry powder, Worcestershire sauce, and mustard. Stir in breadcrumbs, red and green sweet pepper, red onion, green onion, and parsley. Add crabmeat; mix well. Using moistened hands, shape crab mixture into twelve ½-inch-thick patties.

**2** In a very large skillet heat oil over medium heat. Cook half of the crab cakes in hot oil for about 6 minutes or until golden brown and heated through, turning once. If cakes brown too quickly, reduce heat to medium low. Keep warm in the oven while cooking the remaining crab cakes (add additional oil, if necessary). If desired, serve crab cakes with Mango Salsa, recipe page 135.

nutrition facts per serving: 157 cal., 11 g total fat (2 g sat. fat), 77 mg chol., 201 mg sodium, 4 g carb., 1 g dietary fiber, 10 g protein.

make-ahead directions: Prepare as directed in Step 1. Cover and chill for up to 24 hours. Continue as directed.

*What's the secret behind these delicious mouthwatering cakes? Using a sprightly seasoned crumb mixture and cooking them until golden crisp without burning. Pulse the bread in a food processor until fine crumbs form.*

# creole crab cakes

prep: 30 minutes   cook: 6 minutes per batch   oven: 300°F   makes: 12 servings

1   tablespoon olive oil
½   cup finely chopped celery
⅓   cup finely chopped onion
1   egg, lightly beaten
¼   cup mayonnaise
½   teaspoon dry mustard
¼   teaspoon garlic powder
¼   teaspoon onion powder
¼   teaspoon cayenne pepper
1½  cups soft French breadcrumbs
8   ounces cooked lump crabmeat, flaked, or canned crabmeat, drained, flaked, and cartilage removed (about 1½ cups)
3   tablespoons finely chopped red sweet pepper
3   tablespoons finely chopped green sweet pepper
3   tablespoons olive oil
1   recipe Remoulade

1 Preheat oven to 300°F. In a medium skillet heat the 1 tablespoon oil over medium heat. Cook celery and onion in hot oil until tender. Cool slightly.

2 In a medium bowl combine egg, mayonnaise, dry mustard, garlic powder, onion powder, and cayenne pepper. Add celery mixture, breadcrumbs, crabmeat, and sweet peppers; mix well. Using moistened hands, shape crab mixture into twelve ½-inch-thick patties.

3 In a very large skillet heat the 3 tablespoons oil over medium heat. Cook half of the crab cakes in hot oil for about 6 minutes or until golden brown and heated through, turning once. If cakes brown too quickly, reduce heat to medium low. Keep warm in the oven while cooking the remaining crab cakes. Serve crab cakes with Remoulade.

nutrition facts per serving: 219 cal., 20 g total fat (3 g sat. fat), 34 mg chol., 377 mg sodium, 4 g carb., 0 g dietary fiber, 5 g protein.

make-ahead directions: Prepare crab cakes as directed through Step 2. Place crab cakes on a baking sheet lined with plastic wrap. Cover and chill for up to 4 hours. Cook as directed in Step 3.

remoulade: In a medium bowl combine ¾ cup mayonnaise, 1 tablespoon thinly sliced green onion, 1 tablespoon snipped fresh parsley, 1 tablespoon finely chopped red sweet pepper, 1 tablespoon Creole or brown mustard, 1 tablespoon lemon juice, 1 teaspoon drained capers, ½ teaspoon paprika, and ½ teaspoon bottled hot pepper sauce. Makes 1 cup.

*This is a perfect light and healthy appetizer—and a nice way to use up part of that bumper crop of zucchini that comes around every summer.*

# zucchini **crab cakes**

prep: 25 minutes   cook: 6 minutes   makes: 8 servings

2 teaspoons cooking oil
1 cup coarsely shredded zucchini
¼ cup thinly sliced green onion
1 egg, lightly beaten
⅓ cup seasoned fine dry breadcrumbs
1 tablespoon Dijon-style mustard
1 teaspoon snipped fresh lemon thyme or thyme
⅛ to ¼ teaspoon cayenne pepper
6 ounces cooked lump crabmeat, flaked, or one 6-ounce can crabmeat, drained, flaked, and cartilage removed (about 1 cup)
Cooking oil
8 ¼-inch-thick slices red and/or yellow tomatoes
1 recipe Tomato–Sour Cream Sauce
Thinly sliced green onion (optional)

1 In a medium skillet heat the 2 teaspoons oil over medium-high heat. Cook zucchini and the ¼ cup green onion in hot oil for 3 to 5 minutes or just until vegetables are tender and liquid evaporates. Cool slightly.

2 In a medium bowl combine egg, breadcrumbs, mustard, thyme, and cayenne pepper. Add zucchini mixture and crabmeat; mix well. Using moistened hands, shape crab mixture into eight ½-inch-thick patties.

3 Lightly brush a grill pan with additional oil; heat over medium heat. Cook crab cakes for about 6 minutes or until golden brown and heated through, turning once. If cakes brown too quickly, reduce heat to medium low.

4 To serve, arrange crab cakes on top of tomato slices. Top with Tomato–Sour Cream Sauce and, if desired, sprinkle with additional green onion.

nutrition facts per serving: 98 cal., 5 g total fat (2 g sat. fat), 44 mg chol., 371 mg sodium, 6 g carb., 1 g dietary fiber, 7 g protein.

tomato–sour cream sauce: In a small bowl stir together ½ cup dairy sour cream, 3 tablespoons finely chopped yellow tomato, 1 to 2 tablespoons lemon juice or lime juice, and ⅛ teaspoon seasoned salt. Makes ¾ cup.

*Panko crumbs have a light and flaky texture and create a nice change from traditional, heavier breadcrumbs. Pressing the crumbs into the patties and cooking them in a butter-oil mixture gives them a pretty golden color.*

# mini crab cakes
## with orange aioli

prep: 25 minutes   cook: 8 minutes per batch   oven: 300°F
makes: 12 servings

1   egg, lightly beaten
⅓   cup chopped green onion
¼   cup chopped red sweet pepper
¼   cup mayonnaise
1   tablespoon Worcestershire-style marinade for chicken
2   teaspoons Dijon-style mustard
1   teaspoon Old Bay seasoning
½   teaspoon lemon-pepper seasoning
18   ounces cooked crabmeat or three 6-ounce cans lump crabmeat, drained and cartilage removed
¾   cup panko (Japanese-style breadcrumbs)
2   tablespoons butter
2   tablespoons vegetable oil
    Spinach leaves (optional)
1   recipe Orange Aioli

1 Preheat oven to 300°F. In a large bowl combine egg, green onion, pepper, mayonnaise, Worcestershire-style marinade, mustard, Old Bay seasoning, and lemon-pepper seasoning. Add crabmeat; mix well. Shape into twelve 2-inch patties. Press panko onto both sides of each patty.

2 In a large skillet heat 1 tablespoon of the butter and 1 tablespoon of the oil over medium heat. Cook half the patties for 8 to 10 minutes or until golden and heated through, turning once. Transfer crab cakes to a baking sheet. Keep warm in the oven. Repeat with remaining butter, oil, and patties.

3 If desired, serve on a bed of spinach. Serve with Orange Aioli.

nutrition facts per serving: 220 cal., 18 g total fat (4 g sat. fat), 75 mg chol., 337 mg sodium, 4 g carb., 0 g dietary fiber, 10 g protein.

orange aioli: In a small bowl stir together ½ cup mayonnaise or salad dressing, ½ cup sour cream, ½ teaspoon finely shredded orange peel, 2 tablespoons orange juice, 2 tablespoons snipped fresh chives, and ½ teaspoon ground coriander. Makes 1 cup.

*While fresh crabmeat will give you the best flavor, canned crabmeat works equally well. To remove the metallic taste from canned crabmeat, soak the crabmeat in ice water for 10 minutes, then drain and pat dry with paper towels.*

# maryland crab cakes

prep: 30 minutes   cook: 6 minutes per batch   oven: 300°F   makes: 12 servings

1 egg, lightly beaten
2 tablespoons mayonnaise
1 tablespoon snipped fresh parsley
2 teaspoons Old Bay seasoning
1½ teaspoons snipped fresh thyme
2 slices soft white bread
1 pound cooked lump crabmeat or three 6-ounce cans crabmeat, drained and cartilage removed
1 tablespoon peanut oil or cooking oil
Bottled tartar sauce (optional)

**1** Preheat oven to 300°F. In a large bowl combine egg, mayonnaise, parsley, Old Bay seasoning, and thyme. Remove and discard crusts from bread. Tear bread into very small pieces. Stir bread pieces into egg mixture. Add crabmeat. Mix gently with your hands, keeping crab pieces whole. Shape crab mixture into twelve ½-inch-thick patties.

**2** In a large nonstick skillet heat oil over medium heat. Cook half of the crab cakes in hot oil for about 6 minutes or until golden brown and heated through, turning once. If cakes brown too quickly, reduce heat to medium low. Keep warm in the oven while cooking the remaining crab cakes (add additional oil, if necessary). If desired, serve crab cakes with tartar sauce.

nutrition facts per serving: 82 cal., 4 g total fat (1 g sat. fat), 56 mg chol., 263 mg sodium, 2 g carb., 0 g dietary fiber, 9 g protein.

## crab varieties

- blue: *Known for the color of their claws and shell (though the color changes to red when cooked), they're considered a delicacy. Also delicious in the soft-shell stage.*
- dungeness: *Weighing up to 4 pounds, they're commonly found in the waters of the Pacific from Alaska to Mexico.*
- king: *Also known as Alaskan king crab, they're known for their foot-long legs and can weigh up to 25 pounds.*
- rock: *These spiderlike crustaceans live among rocks in deep ocean waters.*
- stone: *Found in waters surrounding Florida, stone crabs have large, lobsterlike claws that are prized for their meatiness.*

*Serve the crispy clams with a delightfully tangy homemade tartar sauce. Keep leftover sauce for up to 2 weeks and serve with baked or grilled fish.*

# batter-dipped fried clams

prep: 10 minutes   cook: 1½ minutes per batch   oven: 300°F
makes: 8 servings

½   cup milk
1   egg yolk
1   tablespoon butter,
      melted and cooled
¼   teaspoon salt
½   cup all-purpose flour
1   egg white
      Cooking oil for
      deep-fat frying
1   pint shucked clams,
      rinsed and well
      drained
1   recipe Tartar Sauce

**1** Preheat oven to 300°F. In a medium bowl combine milk, egg yolk, melted butter, and salt. Sift flour over milk mixture. Stir until smooth. In a small mixing bowl beat egg white with an electric mixer until soft peaks form (tips curl over). Fold beaten egg white into milk mixture.

**2** In a deep-fat fryer or saucepan heat oil to 375°F. Using a fork to spear clams, dip clams into batter. Fry, a few at a time, for about 1½ minutes or until golden brown, turning once. Using a slotted spoon, remove clams. Drain on paper towels. Keep warm in the oven while frying remaining clams. Serve with Tartar Sauce.

nutrition facts per serving: 219 cal., 17 g total fat (3 g sat. fat), 51 mg chol., 135 mg sodium, 8 g carb., 0 g dietary fiber, 9 g protein.

tartar sauce: In a small bowl stir together 1 cup mayonnaise or salad dressing, ¼ cup finely chopped sweet pickle relish, 1 tablespoon finely chopped onion, 1 tablespoon snipped fresh parsley, 1 tablespoon diced pimiento, and 1 teaspoon lemon juice. Makes 2 cups.

*Here are all the things you love about crab Louis salad—the opulent crabmeat, the piquant dressing—on one easy-to-manage toast. During prep, be sure to pick gently through the crabmeat to find and discard any bits of shell.*

# crab louis canapés

prep: 25 minutes   chill: 1 hour   makes: 40 servings

1   large avocado, halved, pitted, peeled, and chopped
¼   cup mayonnaise
2   green onions, finely chopped
2   tablespoons whipping cream
1   tablespoon prepared horseradish
¼   teaspoon salt
⅛   teaspoon white pepper
1   pound cooked crabmeat, cut into bite-size pieces
¼   cup cocktail sauce
1   tablespoons lime juice
1   teaspoon Worcestershire sauce
40   slices baguette-style French bread, toasted

**1** In a food processor combine avocado, mayonnaise, green onions, whipping cream, horseradish, salt, and pepper. Cover and process until smooth. Transfer mixture to a large bowl. Gently fold in crabmeat with a spatula. Cover and chill for at least 1 hour.

**2** In a small bowl combine cocktail sauce, lime juice, and Worcestershire sauce. Spoon crab mixture onto toasted baguette slices. Drizzle each with cocktail sauce mixture.

nutrition facts per serving: 80 cal., 3 g total fat (1 g sat. fat), 13 mg chol., 176 mg sodium, 10 g carb., 1 g dietary fiber, 4 g protein.

*Sautéed shrimp get a Cajun-style makeover when Worcestershire sauce and paprika pair up with sherry and fresh herbs.*

# new orleans–style
# bbq shrimp

start to finish: 30 minutes   makes: 8 servings

| | |
|---|---|
| 1 | pound fresh or frozen large shrimp in shells |
| ¼ | cup olive oil |
| ¼ | cup butter |
| 12 | cloves garlic, smashed and peeled |
| 2 | bay leaves |
| 4 | sprigs fresh thyme |
| 3 | tablespoons dry sherry |
| 1 | tablespoon paprika |
| 1 | teaspoon Worcestershire sauce |
| ½ | teaspoon kosher salt Lemon wedges Crusty French bread slices |

**1** Thaw shrimp, if frozen. Peel and devein shrimp, leaving tails intact. Rinse shrimp; pat dry with paper towels. Set aside.

**2** In a large skillet combine olive oil, butter, garlic, bay leaves, and thyme. Cook and stir over medium heat until butter melts. In a medium bowl combine sherry, paprika, Worcestershire sauce, and kosher salt. Add shrimp. Toss to combine. Add shrimp mixture to the hot skillet. Cook and stir shrimp for 3 to 5 minutes or until shrimp are opaque.

**3** To serve, transfer shrimp mixture to a serving dish. Serve with lemon wedges and French bread slices.

nutrition facts per serving: 177 cal., 15 g total fat (5 g sat. fat), 81 mg chol., 185 mg sodium, 3 g carb., 0 g dietary fiber, 9 g protein.

# prosciutto-wrapped scallops with roasted red pepper aioli

prep: 35 minutes   broil: 4 minutes per batch   makes: 20 servings

10  fresh or frozen extra-
    large sea scallops
10  very thin slices
    prosciutto (6 to
    7 ounces), halved
    lengthwise
20  medium fresh basil
    leaves
    Ground black pepper
1   recipe Roasted Red
    Pepper Aioli
    Small fresh basil
    leaves (optional)

1 Thaw scallops, if frozen. Halve scallops. Soak twenty 6-inch wooden skewers in water for 30 minutes; drain.

2 Meanwhile, preheat broiler. Rinse scallops; pat dry with paper towels.

3 Lay prosciutto strips on a large cutting board. Top each prosciutto strip with a medium basil leaf; add a scallop half. Starting from a short end, roll up each prosciutto strip around scallop. Thread each appetizer onto a skewer. Sprinkle with pepper.

4 Place half of the skewers on the lightly greased unheated rack of a broiler pan. Broil 4 to 5 inches from the heat for 4 to 6 minutes or until scallops are opaque, turning once. Repeat with the remaining skewers.

5 Serve skewers with Roasted Red Pepper Aioli for dipping. If desired, garnish aioli with small basil leaves.

nutrition facts per serving: 79 cal., 6 g total fat (1 g sat. fat), 6 mg chol., 208 mg sodium, 1 g carb., 0 g dietary fiber, 5 g protein.

roasted red pepper aioli: In a blender or food processor combine $1/2$ cup bottled roasted red sweet peppers, drained, and 2 cloves garlic, chopped. Cover and blend or process until nearly smooth. Add $1/3$ cup mayonnaise. Cover and blend or process until smooth. With the blender or processor running, gradually add 2 tablespoons olive oil through the opening in lid or the feed tube, blending or processing until smooth. Transfer aioli to a small bowl. Season with $1/8$ teaspoon salt and dash black pepper. Cover and chill for up to 2 days. Makes about 1 cup.

*If you like seafood, you'll fall in love with these melt-in-your-mouth scallops, which are cooked in bacon drippings, topped with a sweet onion relish, and presented on baguette slices.*

# seared scallops
## over tropical relish

prep: 15 minutes  cook: 18 minutes  makes: 20 servings

10  large fresh or frozen
    sea scallops
 1  tablespoon olive oil
 1  tablespoon butter
 1  large red onion, thinly
    sliced
 2  tablespoons packed
    brown sugar
 2  tablespoons
    pineapple preserves
 1  teaspoon finely
    shredded orange
    peel
 1  cup orange juice
 1  7-ounce package
    tropical blend
    mixed dried fruit
    bits (1¼ cups)
 3  tablespoons
    raspberry vinegar
    Salt
    Ground black pepper
 3  slices bacon
20  baguette slices,
    toasted

**1** Thaw scallops if frozen. Rinse scallops; pat dry with paper towels. Cut scallops in half horizontally. Set aside.

**2** In a large skillet heat olive oil and butter over medium heat. Cook onion for about 5 minutes or until very tender. Stir in brown sugar and pineapple preserves. Cook and stir over medium heat for about 5 minutes more or until onion caramelizes. Stir in orange peel, orange juice, dried fruit, and vinegar. Heat to boiling; reduce heat. Simmer, uncovered, for 5 to 7 minutes or until desired consistency. Remove from heat. Season to taste with salt and pepper. Cool slightly.

**3** In a 12-inch skillet cook bacon over medium heat until crisp. Remove bacon, reserving 2 tablespoons drippings in skillet. Drain bacon on paper towels. Crumble bacon. Stir into the fruit mixture. Cook scallops in the reserved bacon drippings over medium heat for 2 to 3 minutes or until scallops turn opaque, turning once. To serve, spoon about 1 tablespoon of the fruit mixture on each baguette slice. Top with a scallop half.

nutrition facts per serving: 135 cal., 3 g total fat (1 g sat. fat), 13 mg chol., 220 mg sodium, 19 g carb., 0 g dietary fiber, 7 g protein.

*Serve the lively citrus-flavored relish and sautéed oysters in half shells for a tempting presentation and easy pickup.*

# oysters with
# tomato-fennel relish

prep: 30 minutes  cook: 2 minutes  makes: 8 servings

⅔ cup finely chopped, seeded roma tomato
⅓ cup finely chopped fresh fennel
½ teaspoon finely shredded orange peel
1 tablespoon orange juice
2 teaspoons olive oil
1½ teaspoon snipped fresh chives
⅛ teaspoon salt
16 fresh oysters in shells
1 tablespoon butter
2 cloves garlic, minced

1 For relish, in a small bowl stir together tomato, fennel, orange peel, orange juice, oil, chives, and salt. Cover and chill for up to 24 hours.

2 Thoroughly wash oysters. Using an oyster knife or other blunt-tip knife, open shells. Remove oysters and dry. Discard flat top shells; wash deep bottom shells.

3 Before serving, stir relish. Spoon about 1 tablespoon relish into each bottom shell. Arrange shells on a platter.

4 In a large skillet melt butter. Cook oysters and garlic in hot butter for 2 to 3 minutes or until edges of oysters curl and the surfaces of the oysters begin to brown. Place one cooked oyster on relish in each shell. Serve immediately.

nutrition facts per serving: 48 cal., 3 g total fat (1 g sat. fat), 19 mg chol., 109 mg sodium, 2 g carb., 0 g dietary fiber, 2 g protein.

make-ahead directions: Prepare relish and remove oysters from shells. Place the relish, oysters, and bottom shells in separate airtight containers. Cover and chill for up to 24 hours.

*The simple flavors of lemon and dill bring out the taste of luscious smoked salmon in these elegant and easy canapés. Be sure to try out the shrimp variation as well!*

# smoked salmon–
## cucumber rounds

start to finish: 20 minutes  makes: 20 to 24 rounds

1   medium cucumber
6   to 8 ounces thinly
     sliced lox-style
     smoked salmon
⅓   cup mayonnaise
1   tablespoon snipped
     fresh dill
1   teaspoon finely
     shredded lemon
     peel
1   teaspoon lemon juice
     Fresh dill sprigs

**1** If desired, score cucumber by drawing the tip of a teaspoon or vegetable peeler lengthwise down cucumber at ½-inch intervals. Cut cucumber into ¼-inch-thick slices. Arrange slices on a serving platter.

**2** Cut salmon into pieces to fit cucumber slices. Place a piece of salmon on top of each cucumber slice.

**3** In a small bowl combine mayonnaise, snipped dill, lemon peel, and lemon juice. Spoon ½ teaspoon of the mayonnaise mixture onto each piece of salmon. Garnish with dill sprigs.

nutrition facts per round: 39 cal., 3 g total fat (0 g sat. fat), 5 mg chol., 193 mg sodium, 1 g carb., 0 g dietary fiber, 2 g protein.

make-ahead directions: Cover and chill for up to 1 hour before serving.

shrimp-cucumber rounds: Prepare as directed, except substitute 12 ounces peeled and deveined cooked medium shrimp for the salmon. Spoon mayonnaise mixture onto each cucumber slice, then top each with a shrimp.

nutrition facts per round: 46 cal., 3 g total fat (0 g sat. fat), 36 mg chol., 61 mg sodium, 1 g carb., 0 g dietary fiber, 4 g protein.

*Spread and top these tiny sandwiches ahead of time, or set out the makings and let your guests fix their own.*

# smoked trout bites

start to finish: 15 minutes   makes: 16 servings

¼ cup dairy sour cream
2 ounces cream cheese
  (¼ cup)
1 teaspoon prepared
  horseradish
4 ounces smoked trout
  or smoked salmon,
  flaked
4 to 6 slices marbled
  rye bread
  Sprouts or greens

**1** In a small bowl mix together sour cream, cream cheese, and horseradish until smooth. Stir in trout.

**2** Cut each bread slice into 2×1½-inch rectangles. Spread each rectangle with about 1½ teaspoons of the sour cream mixture. Top with sprouts.

nutrition facts per serving: 51 cal., 3 g total fat (1 g sat. fat), 14 mg chol., 93 mg sodium, 5 g carb., 1 g dietary fiber, 2 g protein.

make-ahead directions: Prepare as directed in Step 1. Cover and chill for up to 24 hours. To serve, let stand at room temperature for 15 minutes. Assemble as directed in Step 2.

*Capers are flower buds pickled in brine. It's a good idea to rinse capers before using them to remove the excess salt. Their piquant flavor perfectly accents salmon.*

# smoked salmon–
## avocado stacks

prep: 20 minutes   chill: 2 hour   makes: 12 servings

1   large ripe avocado, halved, pitted, and peeled
1   tablespoon capers, drained
2   teaspoons lemon juice or lime juice
1   clove garlic, minced
24  cracked pepper or sesame water crackers
4   to 6 ounces thinly sliced lox-style smoked salmon
1   cup watercress
½   cup quartered thinly sliced red onion

**1** For avocado spread, in a small bowl mash avocado. Stir in capers, lemon juice, and garlic. Cover and chill for up to 2 hours.

**2** Spread crackers with avocado spread. Top each cracker with smoked salmon, watercress, and onion.

nutrition facts per serving: 66 cal., 3 g total fat (0 g sat. fat), 2 mg chol., 253 mg sodium, 7 g carb., 1 g dietary fiber, 3 g protein.

6

fanciful

pas

Delicate layers of flaky pastry provide the perfect starting point for savory morsels. Many of the elegant but supremely easy recipes call for purchased phyllo sheets or puff pastry, leaving you more time to whip up mouthwatering fillings and toppings.

# tries

*Mild, nutty Gouda cheese adds a creamy richness to the pastry. Place the cheese in the freezer for 15 minutes so it's nice and firm and easier to shred.*

## olives wrapped in
# cheese pastry

prep: 35 minutes  bake: 25 minutes  oven: 375°F  makes: 24 servings

1　cup all-purpose flour
1　teaspoon baking powder
3　ounces Gouda cheese, finely shredded (¾ cup)
⅓　cup butter, cut in small pieces
2　tablespoons grated Parmesan cheese
1　tablespoon lemon juice
24　medium pimento-stuffed green olives
1　egg yolk, beaten

**1** Preheat oven to 375°F. Line a baking sheet with parchment paper; set aside. In food processor combine flour and baking powder. Cover and process briefly to mix. Add Gouda cheese, butter, and Parmesan cheese. Cover and process to mix thoroughly. With food processor running, add lemon juice, processing until dough just forms a ball. Transfer dough to a clean surface. Divide dough into 24 equal portions.

**2** Drain and rinse olives. Pat dry with paper towels. Pat each portion of dough into a 2-inch circle. Place an olive in the center of each circle. Bring dough up around olives; pat seams to seal. Place olive bundles about ½ inch apart on prepared baking sheet.

**3** Brush olive bundles with egg yolk. Bake for about 25 minutes or until golden brown. Serve warm or at room temperature.

nutrition facts per serving: 64 cal., 4 g total fat (2 g sat. fat), 20 mg chol., 123 mg sodium, 4 g carb., 0 g dietary fiber, 2 g protein.

**make-ahead directions:** Prepare as directed through Step 2. Cover and chill for up to 4 hours. (Or freeze for about 1 hour or until firm. Transfer olive bundles to a freezer container. Seal and freeze for up to 1 month.)

*Goat cheese comes in many shapes. If the goat cheese you find is a round shape, use damp hands to shape it into a log.*

# goat cheese
## pastry rounds

prep: 25 minutes  bake: 20 minutes  stand: 15 minutes  oven: 400°F
makes: 12 appetizers

½  of a 17.3-ounce
  package frozen puff
  pastry (1 sheet),
  thawed
3  tablespoons tomato
  preserves or
  favorite fruit
  preserves*
3  2- to 2½-inch diameter
  logs goat cheese
  (chèvre; 3 to 4
  ounces each)
1  egg, lightly beaten
  Fresh figs or grapes
  (optional)

**1** Preheat oven to 400°F. Line a baking sheet with parchment paper or foil; lightly grease foil. Set aside.

**2** On a lightly floured surface unfold pastry. Roll into a 12-inch square. Cut pastry into four 6-inch squares. Place 1 tablespoon preserves in center of three of the pastry squares. Arrange goat cheese over preserves. Bring corners of pastry together on top of filling; pinch to seal. Trim excess pastry. Place pastries, seam sides down, on prepared baking sheet. Brush with egg. Using a sharp knife, cut slits in pastry for steam to escape. Using a small leaf-shape cutter, cut remaining pastry square into leaves; arrange on top of pastry; brush with egg.

**3** Bake for 20 to 22 minutes or until pastry is puffed and golden. Let stand for 15 to 20 minutes before serving. To serve, cut each pastry round into four wedges. If desired, serve with fresh figs.

nutrition facts per appetizer: 166 cal., 11 g total fat (3 g sat. fat), 27 mg chol., 162 mg sodium, 11 g carb., 0 g dietary fiber, 5 g protein.

*note: For best results, use thick preserves. Thin-bodied preserves ooze through pastry when baking.

**make-ahead directions:** Cover and freeze unbaked pastries in an airtight container for up to 1 month. Thaw pastries in refrigerator for about 4 hours. Bake as directed.

*If you're expecting a large gathering, double the recipe and use the entire package of puff pastry to make the cheese-filled pastry strips.*

# parmesan cheese straws
## with olive tapenade

prep: 20 minutes   bake: 9 minutes per batch   oven: 400°F   makes: 24 straws

2   ounces Parmigiano-
      Reggiano cheese,
      grated
½   teaspoon dried basil,
      crushed
¼   teaspoon garlic
      powder
½   of a 17.3-ounce
      package frozen puff
      pastry (1 sheet),
      thawed
1   egg
1   tablespoon water
1   8-ounce jar olive
      tapenade

**1** Preheat oven to 400°F. In a small bowl combine Parmigiano-Reggiano cheese, dried basil, and garlic powder. Set aside.

**2** On a lightly floured surface unfold pastry. Roll pastry sheet into a 14×12-inch rectangle. Cut rectangle in half crosswise to form two 12×7-inch rectangles. In a small bowl whisk together egg and the water. Brush both pastry rectangles lightly with egg mixture.

**3** Sprinkle cheese mixture over one of the rectangles. Top with the other rectangle, brushed side down. Using your fingers, firmly press rectangles together, forcing out air pockets and sealing the edges. Brush top with egg mixture.

**4** Using a pastry wheel or sharp knife, cut pastry crosswise into ½-inch-wide strips. Arrange strips 1 inch apart on ungreased baking sheets. Holding both ends, twist each strip, pressing ends into baking sheet to secure.

**5** Bake for 9 to 11 minutes or until golden and crisp. Cool slightly. Serve with olive tapenade for dipping.

nutrition facts per straw: 111 cal., 10 g total fat (1 g sat. fat), 11 mg chol., 336 mg sodium, 4 g carb., 0 g dietary fiber, 2 g protein.

**make-ahead directions:** Arrange baked straws in a single layer in an airtight container. Cover. Freeze for up to 1 month. To reheat, preheat oven to 350°F. Place frozen straws on a baking sheets in a single layer. Bake for 5 to 10 minutes or until warm and crisp.

*Even if you didn't make and freeze these cheese-filled pastries, you can still have them ready in about 45 minutes. Purchase a couple packages of preformed phyllo shells instead of making your own.*

# blue cheese–pecan
## phyllo bites

prep: 45 minutes   bake: 7 minutes   oven: 350°F   makes: 30 appetizers

1   8-ounce package cream cheese, softened
1   recipe Homemade Phyllo Shells or two 2.1-ounce packages baked miniature phyllo dough shells (30 shells)
4   ounces blue cheese, crumbled
⅓   cup dried tart cherries, snipped
1   recipe Sugared Pecans
     Honey (optional)

In a medium bowl stir the cream cheese until smooth. Spoon cream cheese evenly into the Homemade Phyllo Shells. Top with blue cheese and cherries. Sprinkle with Sugared Pecans. If desired, drizzle with honey.

nutrition facts per appetizer: 77 cal., 6 g total fat (2 g sat. fat), 11 mg chol., 104 mg sodium, 4 g carb., 0 g dietary fiber, 2 g protein.

**make-ahead directions:**
Prepare Homemade Phyllo Shells as directed. Place in a single layer in an airtight container. Freeze for up to 1 month. Thaw shells before filling. Freeze the Sugared Pecans in an airtight container for up to 1 month. Thaw pecans for 15 minutes at room temperature before using.

homemade phyllo shells: Preheat oven to 350°F. Coat fifteen 1³/₄-inch muffin cups with nonstick cooking spray; set aside. You need four sheets of frozen phyllo dough (14x9-inch rectangles), thawed, and about 2 tablespoons melted butter. Keep phyllo dough covered with plastic wrap to prevent it from drying out, removing sheets as you need them. Lay one sheet of phyllo on a flat work surface. Lightly brush with some of the butter. Top with another phyllo sheet, brushing top with melted butter. Cut phyllo stack lengthwise into three 14-inch-long strips. Cut each strip crosswise into five rectangles. Press each rectangle into a prepared cup, pleating as needed to fit. Bake for 7 to 9 minutes or until cups are golden brown. Carefully transfer cups to a wire rack to cool completely. Cool muffin cups between batches. Repeat with remaining phyllo and butter to make 30 shells.

sugared pecans: Spread ¹/₃ cup chopped pecans in the bottom of a medium skillet. Sprinkle with 1 tablespoon sugar and ¹/₄ teaspoon salt. Cook, without stirring, over medium heat. When sugar begins to melt, turn heat to medium low. Gently stir pecans until all sugar is melted and pecans are lightly coated. Transfer pecans to a foil-lined baking sheet. Cool. To serve, break apart.

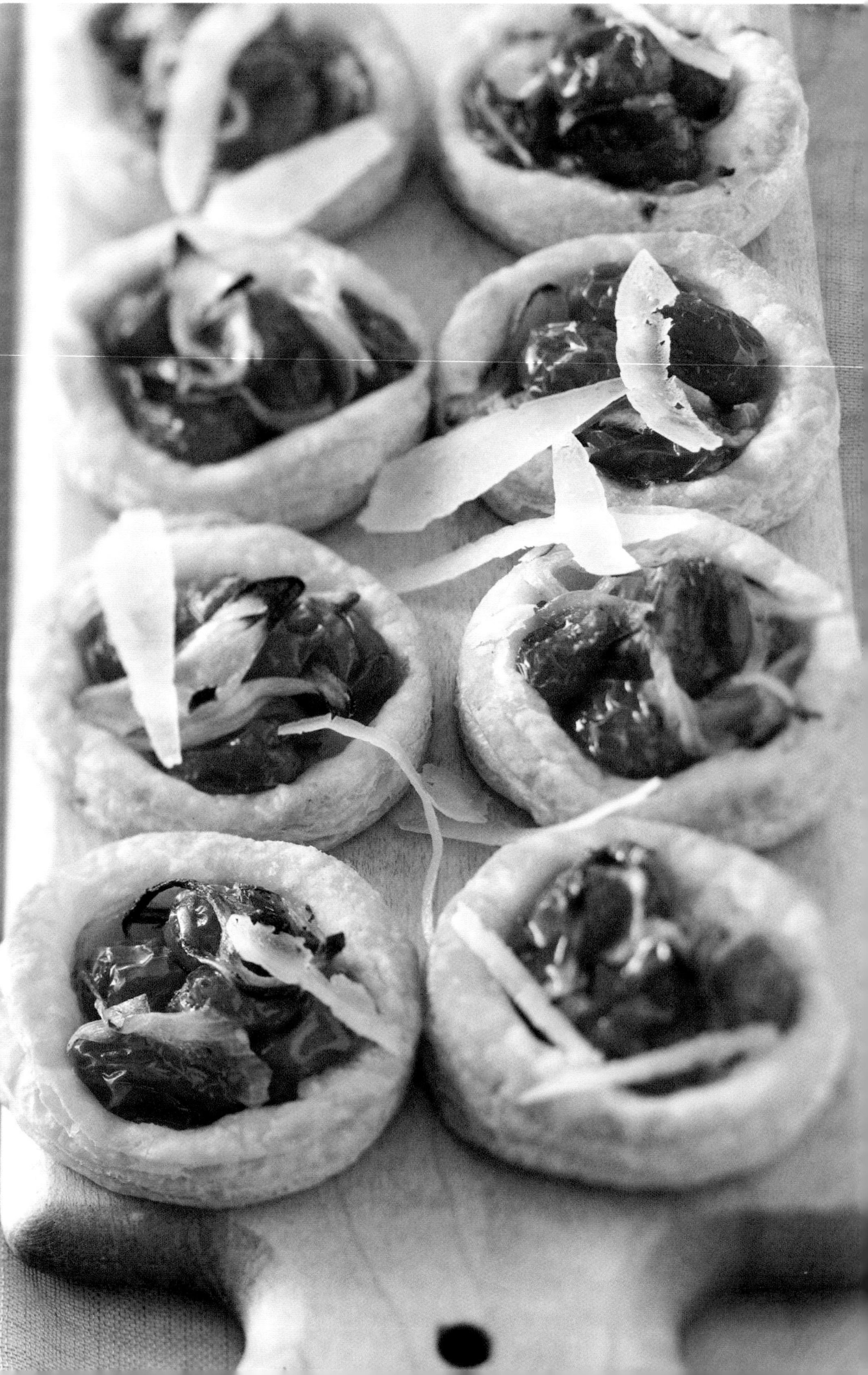

*Store-bought grape tomatoes are tasty all year long. Roasting them with a bit of olive oil and seasonings makes them extra sweet and juicy. For another flavor sensation, use crumbled feta cheese and fresh mint as the garnish.*

# sweet onion—
## tomato tartlets

prep: 30 minutes  bake: 15 minutes  roast: 25 minutes  stand: 5 minutes
oven: 400°F  makes: about 18 tartlets

3    cups grape tomatoes
1    sweet onion,
        quartered and
        thinly sliced (about
        2 cups)
2    tablespoons olive oil
1    tablespoon snipped
        fresh rosemary
½    teaspoon salt
½    teaspoon ground
        black pepper
1    tablespoon sherry
        vinegar
1    17.3-ounce package
        frozen puff pastry
        sheets (2 sheets),
        thawed
     Manchego or
     Parmigiano-
     Reggiano cheese
     shavings

**1** Preheat oven to 400°F. Prick tomatoes with a fork or the tip of a sharp knife. In an ungreased 15×10×1-inch baking pan combine tomatoes, onion, oil, rosemary, salt, and pepper. Roast for 25 to 30 minutes or until onion is tender. Remove from oven. Sprinkle with vinegar. Cool.

**2** Meanwhile, line a large baking sheet with parchment paper or foil. On a lightly floured surface unfold pastry. Using a 3-inch round cookie cutter, cut pastry into rounds. Place rounds on the prepared baking sheet.

**3** Spoon about 2 tablespoons of the roasted tomato mixture onto each pastry round. Bake for 15 to 20 minutes or until edges are puffed and golden brown. Let stand on baking sheet for 5 minutes before serving. Garnish with Manchego cheese.

nutrition facts per tartlet: 154 cal., 11 g total fat (0 g sat. fat), 1 mg chol., 196 mg sodium, 13 g carb., 1 g dietary fiber, 2 g protein.

### thawing pastry dough

- puff pastry: *Thaw only the number of pastry sheets needed (wrap remaining sheets tightly and store in the freezer). An entire package of pastry thaws in the refrigerator in about 6 hours. Individual pastry sheets, covered with plastic wrap, take about 4 hours to thaw in the refrigerator and 30 minutes at room temperature.*

- phyllo dough: *Thaw dough in the refrigerator overnight. Let the dough come to room temperature before using.*

*Tender layers of puff pastry make these irresistible bites the perfect pick-up-and-mingle addition to your party platter.*

# parmesan pastry spirals

prep: 10 minutes  freeze: 30 minutes  bake: 12 minutes  oven: 350°F
makes: about 24 spirals

½ of a 17.3-ounce package frozen puff pastry (1 sheet), thawed
1 tablespoon milk
⅓ cup grated Parmesan cheese
½ teaspoon cracked black pepper

**1** On a lightly floured surface unfold pastry. Roll pastry sheet into a 14×10-inch rectangle. Brush pastry with some of the milk. Sprinkle with Parmesan cheese and pepper. Starting at a short side, loosely roll up into a spiral, stopping at the center. Repeat rolling up, starting at the other short side. Wrap in plastic wrap; freeze for 30 minutes.

**2** Preheat oven to 350°F. Line baking sheets with parchment paper or foil; set aside. Unwrap roll and place on a cutting board. Brush with remaining milk. Using a serrated knife and a sawing motion, cut pastry roll crosswise into $3/8$-inch-thick slices. Place slices 1 inch apart on prepared baking sheets, reshaping as necessary.

**3** Bake for 12 to 14 minutes or until crisp and golden. Transfer to a wire rack. Cool slightly. Serve warm.

nutrition facts per spiral: 50 cal., 4 g total fat (0 g sat. fat), 1 mg chol., 59 mg sodium, 4 g carb., 0 g dietary fiber, 1 g protein.

**make-ahead directions:** Prepare as directed through Step 1. Freeze for up to 1 month. Unwrap, cut, and bake as directed. (If roll is too hard to slice while frozen, let stand at room temperature until easy to slice.)

*Get a taste of the bayou with these buttery crawfish tarts.*
*They're delicious when made with shrimp too.*

# mini cajun
# mushroom tarts

prep: 25 minutes  bake: 15 minutes  oven: 350°F  makes: 30 tarts

4  ounces fresh or
    frozen peeled
    cooked crawfish
    tails or shrimp
2  tablespoons butter
1½  cups chopped fresh
    mushrooms
1  teaspoon Cajun
    seasoning
½  teaspoon lemon juice
¼  teaspoon ground
    black pepper
1  5.2-ounce package
    semisoft cheese
    with garlic and herb
    for (about ⅓ cup)
1  egg, lightly beaten
1  tablespoon milk
2  tablespoons snipped
    fresh parsley
2  2.1-ounce packages
    baked miniature
    phyllo dough shells
    (30 shells)

**1** Preheat oven to 350°F. Coarsely chop crawfish tails; set aside.

**2** In a large skillet melt butter. Cook mushrooms in hot butter for about 4 minutes or until tender and liquid evaporates. Add Cajun seasoning, lemon juice, and pepper. Cook for 1 minute. Cool slightly.

**3** In a medium mixing bowl place cheese, egg, and milk. Beat with an electric mixer on low speed until combined. Stir in mushroom mixture, crawfish, and parsley.

**4** Place phyllo shells in a 15×10×1-inch baking pan. Spoon cheese mixture into phyllo shells. Bake for about 15 minutes or until filling sets. Serve warm.

nutrition facts per tart: 55 cal., 4 g total fat (2 g sat. fat), 16 mg chol., 29 mg sodium, 3 g carb., 0 g dietary fiber, 2 g protein.

**make-ahead directions:** Layer baked and cooled tarts between pieces of waxed paper in an airtight container. Cover and freeze for up to 1 month. To reheat, thaw tarts in the refrigerator for about 4 hours. Transfer tarts to a shallow baking pan. Preheat oven to 400°F. Bake for about 10 minutes or until heated through.

Spend a day or two stocking the freezer with flaky pastries, and you'll be ready for any party opportunity.

*Shallots cooked in a balsamic reduction give a sweet-tart contrast to the creamy, sharp goat cheese in this easy, elegant appetizer.*

# balsamic shallot and goat cheese tart

prep: 15 minutes  bake: 33 minutes  stand: 5 minutes  oven: 400°F
makes: 16 servings

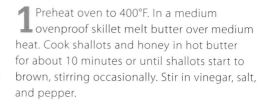

3   tablespoons butter
8   small shallots,
       quartered lengthwise
3   tablespoons honey
3   tablespoons balsamic
       vinegar
½   teaspoon salt
½   teaspoon ground
       black pepper
½   of a 17.3-ounce
       package frozen
       puff pastry sheets
       (1 sheet), thawed
1   egg yolk
2   teaspoons water
4   ounces goat cheese
       (chèvre), broken
       into small chunks
2   teaspoons snipped
       fresh parsley

**1** Preheat oven to 400°F. In a medium ovenproof skillet melt butter over medium heat. Cook shallots and honey in hot butter for about 10 minutes or until shallots start to brown, stirring occasionally. Stir in vinegar, salt, and pepper.

**2** Transfer skillet to oven. Bake for 15 to 20 minutes or until shallots are tender and liquid is syrupy. Remove from oven; set aside.

**3** Meanwhile, on a large baking sheet unfold pastry. Trim a ½-inch-wide strip from each side of pastry sheet. In a small bowl combine egg yolk and the water. Lightly brush edges of the pastry sheet with egg yolk mixture. Place the pastry strips on the edges of the pastry sheet to form a ridge, trimming any excess pastry. Lightly brush ridge with egg yolk mixture. Using a fork, generously prick pastry base.

**4** Bake for 15 to 20 minutes or until pastry is puffed and golden brown. Spread shallot mixture over bottom of pastry (pastry will sink when topped with the shallot mixture). Top with cheese. Bake for 3 to 5 minutes or until cheese softens.

**5** Transfer to a wire rack. Sprinkle with parsley. Let stand for 5 minutes before serving.

nutrition facts per serving: 132 cal., 9 g total fat (3 g sat. fat), 22 mg chol., 174 mg sodium, 11 g carb., 0 g dietary fiber, 2 g protein.

*This recipe remains a favorite because of its ease. Believe it or not, this elegant (and outstandingly delicious) tart starts with something as simple as a refrigerated pizza crust.*

# herbed leek tarts

prep: 25 minutes  bake: 15 minutes  stand: 5 minutes  oven: 425°F
makes: 24 servings

1   13.8-ounce package refrigerated pizza dough
2   tablespoons olive oil
6   medium leeks, thinly sliced (2 cups; white and light green parts only)
3   cloves garlic, minced
4   teaspoons snipped fresh savory, marjoram, and/or thyme
3   tablespoons creamy Dijon-style mustard blend
1   cup shredded Gruyère or Swiss cheese (4 ounces)
¼   cup pine nuts or chopped almonds, toasted
    Fresh savory sprigs (optional)

1 Preheat oven to 425°F. Grease a large baking sheet. Unroll pizza dough onto prepared baking sheet. Press to form a 13×9-inch rectangle. Cut rectangle in half lengthwise to form two 13×4½-inch rectangles. Separate rectangles on baking sheet so edges are at least 1 inch apart. Bake for 7 minutes.

2 Meanwhile, in a large skillet heat oil over medium heat. Cook leeks and garlic in hot oil about 5 minutes or until tender. Remove from heat. Stir in snipped savory. Spread mustard blend over prebaked crusts. Top each evenly with leek mixture, Gruyère cheese, and nuts.

3 Bake for 8 to 10 minutes more or until cheese melts and crust turns golden brown. Let stand for 5 minutes before serving. Cut each rectangle into 12 pieces. If desired, garnish with savory sprigs.

nutrition facts per serving: 82 cal., 5 g total fat (1 g sat. fat), 5 mg chol., 96 mg sodium, 8 g carb., 0 g dietary fiber, 3 g protein.

*If you're looking for a robust olive flavor, top this tart with kalamata olives. If you prefer milder flavor, use ripe black olives instead.*

# leek and olive tart with brie

prep: 45 minutes  bake: 17 minutes  stand: 5 minutes  oven: 400°F
makes: 12 servings

5   large leeks
2   tablespoons olive oil
1   tablespoon butter
¼   teaspoon salt
    Dash cayenne pepper
1   teaspoon snipped
      fresh thyme
½   of a 17.3-ounce
      package frozen
      puff pastry sheets
      (1 sheet), thawed
1   egg, lightly beaten
1   tablespoon water
¼   cup grated Parmesan
      cheese
1   4½-ounce round Brie
      or Camembert
      cheese, thinly sliced
¼   cup pitted kalamata
      olives, coarsely
      chopped

**1** Line a large baking sheet with parchment paper or foil; set aside. Cut off and discard dark green ends of leeks. Halve white portions of leeks lengthwise. Cut into ¼-inch-thick pieces (you should have about 4 cups).

**2** In a large skillet heat oil and butter over medium heat. Cook leeks, salt, and cayenne pepper for 5 minutes, stirring occasionally. Reduce heat to medium low. Cover and cook for about 15 minutes or until leeks are tender but not brown, stirring occasionally. Remove from heat. Stir in thyme.

**3** Preheat oven to 400°F. On a lightly floured surface unfold pastry. Cut off one-third of pastry sheet at the fold; set aside. Roll the remaining pastry into a 14×7-inch rectangle. Place rectangle on the prepared baking sheet. Cut small leaf shapes from the reserved pastry.

**4** In a small bowl combine egg and the water. Lightly brush pastry rectangle with egg mixture. Fold edges over to create a ³⁄₄-inch ridge; lightly brush ridge with egg mixture. Gently press leaves onto ridge. Lightly brush leaves with egg mixture. Sprinkle pastry base with Parmesan cheese.

**5** Bake for 12 minutes. Spread leek mixture over pastry base (if puffed, pastry will sink when topped with the leek mixture). Bake for about 5 minutes or until edges turn golden brown.

**6** Immediately place Brie cheese on top of tart and sprinkle with olives. Let stand for 5 minutes before serving.

nutrition facts per serving: 195 cal., 14 g total fat (3 g sat. fat), 32 mg chol., 270 mg sodium, 13 g carb., 1 g dietary fiber, 5 g protein.

**make-ahead directions:**
Prepare as directed through Step 4. Cover and chill for up to 30 minutes. Bake as directed.

*A sweet, tangy, and spicy chutney-cream sauce deliciously sets off the chunky sweet potatoes in the wonton filling.*

# sweet potato wontons

prep: 25 minutes   bake: 10 minutes   oven: 350°F   makes: 24 servings

24  wonton wrappers
2  tablespoons butter, melted
3  tablespoons mango chutney
2  tablespoons butter
⅓  cup finely chopped onion
2  teaspoons curry powder
1  teaspoon minced fresh ginger
1  clove garlic, minced
1  tablespoon all-purpose flour
1½  cups chopped cooked sweet potato*
⅓  cup whipping cream
Carrots, cut into thin bite-size strips and sautéed (optional)

**1** Preheat oven to 350°F. Brush wonton wrappers with the 2 tablespoons melted butter. Press wrappers, buttered sides down, into twenty-four 1³/₄-inch muffin cups, pleating as necessary. Bake for about 10 minutes or until golden brown.

**2** Meanwhile, snip any large mango pieces in chutney; set aside. In a large heavy skillet melt the 2 tablespoons butter over medium heat. Cook onion, curry powder, ginger, and garlic in hot butter until onion is tender. Stir in flour. Stir in cooked sweet potato, whipping cream, and chutney. Cook and stir until thickened. Cook and stir for 1 minute more.

**3** Spoon sweet potato mixture into wonton shells. Serve immediately. If desired, sprinkle with carrot strips.

nutrition facts per serving: 75 cal., 3 g total fat (2 g sat. fat), 10 mg chol., 83 mg sodium, 10 g carb., 1 g dietary fiber, 1 g protein.

\*test kitchen tip: For cooked sweet potato, peel and cut one 10- to 12-ounce sweet potato into thirds. In a covered small saucepan, cook potato in boiling, lightly salted water for about 20 minutes or just until tender. Drain and chop.

*A tantalizing filling of spinach, feta cheese, dill, and lemon makes up these flaky crusted appetizers. For easy handling, be sure to bring the packaged phyllo to room temperature before using.*

# spinach and feta triangles

prep: 40 minutes   bake: 35 minutes   cool: 20 minutes   oven: 325°F
makes: 48 triangles

2   10-ounce packages frozen chopped spinach, thawed
2   tablespoons butter
1   cup chopped onion
2   cloves garlic, minced
1½   cups crumbled feta cheese (6 ounces)
1   cup cottage cheese
2   eggs, lightly beaten
3   tablespoons snipped fresh dill or 1 tablespoon dried dillweed
2   teaspoons finely shredded lemon peel
⅔   cup butter, melted
24   sheets frozen phyllo dough (14×9-inch rectangles), thawed

**make-ahead directions:**
Prepare as above through Step 1. Transfer filling to an airtight container. Cover and refrigerate for up to 24 hours. Continue as directed.

**1** For filling, press spinach with clean paper towels to remove as much liquid as possible. In a large skillet melt 2 tablespoons butter over medium heat. Cook onion and garlic in hot butter until onion is tender. Remove skillet from heat. Stir in spinach, feta cheese, cottage cheese, eggs, dill, and lemon peel; set aside.

**2** Preheat oven to 325°F. Brush a 13×9×2-inch baking pan with some of the ⅔ cup melted butter. Unfold phyllo dough. Keep phyllo covered with plastic wrap to prevent it from drying out, removing sheets as you need them. Lay one sheet of phyllo in the baking pan. Lightly brush with some of the butter. Top with another phyllo sheet, brushing top with melted butter. Repeat until 12 of the phyllo sheets are layered, generously brushing each sheet with butter as you layer.

**3** Carefully spread filling evenly over phyllo in pan. Layer remaining phyllo sheets on top of filling, brushing each sheet with melted butter as you layer. Drizzle top phyllo sheet with remaining butter. Using a sharp knife, cut through the layers to make 24 squares. Cut each square diagonally in half to make triangle-shape pieces.

**4** Bake for 35 to 45 minutes or until golden. Cool in pan on a wire rack for 20 minutes. Recut triangles along same cut lines to separate completely. Serve warm.

nutrition facts per triangle: 66 cal., 5 g total fat (3 g sat. fat), 22 mg chol., 134 mg sodium, 3 g carb., 0 g dietary fiber, 2 g protein.

*Fold a spoonful of seasoned ricotta and roasted red pepper in puff pastry and get ready for a soft, savory flavor. A couple of these rich-flavored bites are terrific with a simple salad of mixed greens.*

# ricotta puffs

**prep:** 30 minutes **bake:** 20 minutes **cool:** 5 minutes **oven:** 400°F **makes:** 18 puffs

½ cup ricotta cheese
½ cup chopped bottled roasted red sweet pepper
3 tablespoons grated Romano or Parmesan cheese
1 tablespoon snipped fresh Italian parsley
1 teaspoon dried oregano, crushed
½ teaspoon ground black pepper
1 17.3-ounce package frozen puff pastry (2 sheets), thawed
Milk
Grated Romano or Parmesan cheese

**1** Preheat oven to 400°F. Line a large baking sheet with parchment paper or foil. For filling, in a small bowl combine ricotta cheese, sweet pepper, the 3 tablespoons Romano cheese, the parsley, oregano, and black pepper.

**2** On a lightly floured surface unfold pastry sheets. Using a sharp knife or pizza cutter, cut each pastry sheet into nine 3-inch squares.

**3** Working one square at a time, moisten the edges of each pastry square with milk. Spoon about 2 teaspoons filling onto half of each pastry square. Fold each pastry square in half diagonally over the filling to form a triangle. Seal edges by pressing with the tines of a fork. Using fork, prick holes in the top of each pastry puff. Brush with milk. Sprinkle with additional Romano cheese. Arrange pastry bundles on prepared baking sheet.

**4** Bake for about 20 minutes or until golden brown. Transfer to a wire rack. Let cool for 5 minutes. Serve warm.

nutrition facts per puff: 137 cal., 10 g total fat (1 g sat. fat), 3 mg chol., 137 mg sodium, 10 g carb., 0 g dietary fiber, 3 g protein.

**make-ahead directions:** Cover and freeze unbaked puffs in an airtight container for up to 1 month. Thaw puffs in refrigerator for about 4 hours. Place on an ungreased baking sheet. Brush with milk and Romano cheese and bake as directed.

*These mushroom-packed triangles will boost your reputation as a sensational cook if you include them as part of your next hors d'oeuvre buffet.*

# mushroom pastry puffs

prep: 45 minutes  bake: 15 minutes  stand: 10 minutes
cool: 5 minutes  oven: 400°F  makes: 24 puffs

2  teaspoons butter
2  teaspoons olive oil
¾  cup chopped onion
12  ounces button, cremini, and/or stemmed shiitake mushrooms, chopped
1  teaspoon dried thyme, crushed
¼  teaspoon salt
⅛  teaspoon ground black pepper
1  egg
1  tablespoon water
1  17.3-ounce package frozen puff pastry (2 sheets), thawed

**1** For filling, in a large nonstick skillet heat butter and olive oil over medium-high heat. Cook onion for 5 to 7 minutes or until tender, stirring occasionally. Add mushrooms, thyme, salt, and pepper. Cook for 5 to 8 minutes more or until mushrooms are tender and any liquid has evaporated, stirring occasionally. Remove from heat. Let stand for 10 minutes.

**2** Preheat oven to 400°F. Line two large baking sheets with foil; set aside. In a small bowl combine egg and the water. Beat with a fork; set aside. On a lightly floured surface unfold pastry. Roll one pastry sheet into a 15×10-inch rectangle (keep the other pastry sheet in the refrigerator until ready to use). Cut the rectangle crosswise into quarters. Cut each quarter lengthwise into thirds to make 12 rectangles.

**3** Place 1 tablespoon filling in the center of each rectangle. Using a pastry brush, lightly moisten edges of each pastry rectangle with the egg mixture. Fold one corner of each rectangle diagonally over filling to form a triangle. Seal edges by pressing with the tines of a fork. Lightly brush with egg mixture. Place about 1 inch apart on a prepared baking sheet. Repeat with remaining pastry sheet, mushroom filling, and egg mixture, placing pastries about 1 inch apart on the second prepared baking sheet.

**4** Bake, one sheet at a time, for 15 to 20 minutes or until pastries are puffed and golden. Transfer to a wire rack. Let cool for 5 minutes. Serve warm.

nutrition facts per puff: 105 cal., 8 g total fat (3 g sat. fat), 10 mg chol., 107 mg sodium, 8 g carb., 0 g dietary fiber, 2 g protein.

**make-ahead directions:** Cool the baked puffs. Layer between waxed paper in an airtight container. Cover and freeze for up to 3 months. To serve, preheat oven to 400°F. Place frozen puffs on a baking sheet. Bake for about 18 minutes or until heated through. Transfer to a wire rack. Cool for 5 minutes. Serve warm.

*Making a rustic, free-form tart is simpler than you might think—and it's even easier when you start with a ready-made piecrust.*

# swiss olive galette

prep: 25 minutes  bake: 30 minutes  oven: 375°F  makes: 6 to 8 servings

½  of a 15-ounce package
    rolled refrigerated
    unbaked pie crust
    (1 crust)
1  tablespoon olive oil
1  cup finely chopped
    leek (white part
    only)
½  cup finely chopped
    fresh fennel
¾  cup coarsely chopped
    kalamata olives
1  tablespoon snipped
    fresh thyme
4  ounces Gruyère
    cheese, shredded
    (1 cup)
    Snipped fresh fennel
    tops (optional)

1 Allow piecrust to stand at room temperature according to package directions. Preheat oven to 375°F. Line a large baking sheet with parchment paper. Roll pastry into an 11-inch circle on prepared baking sheet.

2 In a medium skillet heat oil over medium heat. Cook leek and fennel in hot oil for 5 to 6 minutes or until tender but not brown. Remove from heat. Stir in olives and thyme. Cool slightly.

3 Spread mixture in the center of the pastry, leaving a 1½-inch rim uncovered on the edge. Fold uncovered pasty up over filling. Top with Gruyère cheese.

4 Bake for 30 to 35 minutes or until pastry is golden. If desired, sprinkle with snipped fennel tops. Cut into wedges and serve warm.

nutrition facts per serving: 296 cal., 20 g total fat (7 g sat. fat), 24 mg chol., 404 mg sodium, 22 g carb., 1 g dietary fiber, 7 g protein.

**make-ahead directions:** Prepare as directed through Step 3. Cover and chill for up to 24 hours. Continue as directed in Step 4.

# artichoke and tomato
## empanadas

prep: 45 minutes   chill: 30 minutes (dough)   bake: 22 minutes   oven: 375°F
makes: 24 empanadas

| | |
|---|---|
| 1 | tablespoon olive oil |
| ½ | cup finely chopped onion |
| 4 | cloves garlic, minced |
| 1 | 9-ounce package frozen artichoke hearts, cooked and drained |
| 3 | plum tomatoes, chopped |
| 2 | teaspoons snipped fresh thyme |
| ⅛ | teaspoon ground black pepper |
| ½ | cup shredded Gruyère or Swiss cheese (2 ounces) |
| 2 | tablespoons finely shredded Parmesan cheese |
| 1 | recipe Empanada Pastry |
| 1 | egg yolk |
| 1 | tablespoon water |

**1** For filling, in a medium skillet heat oil over medium heat. Cook onion and garlic in hot oil until onion is tender. Stir in artichoke hearts, tomatoes, thyme, and pepper. Cook and stir for 3 to 5 minutes or until most of the liquid has evaporated. Cool. Transfer filling to food processor. Cover and process until mixture is finely chopped. Transfer to a small bowl. Stir in Gruyère and Parmesan cheeses.

**2** Preheat oven to 375°F. Lightly grease two large baking sheets; set aside.

**3** Unwrap Empanada Pastry dough. On a lightly floured surface roll one portion of the dough to ⅛-inch thickness. Using a 3½-inch round cutter, cut dough into circles. Reroll scraps and cut enough additional circles to make 12 circles. Repeat with remaining dough portion (24 circles total). Place a rounded teaspoon of the filling in the center of each dough circle. In a small bowl combine egg yolk and the water. Beat with a fork. Brush edges of the dough circles with the egg yolk mixture. Fold each dough circle in half. Seal edges with tines of a fork (empanadas will be very full). Place on prepared baking sheets. Brush tops with egg yolk mixture.

**4** Bake for 22 to 25 minutes or until golden. Cool slightly. Serve warm.

nutrition facts per empanada: 104 cal., 6 g total fat (3 g sat. fat), 19 mg chol., 141 mg sodium, 10 g carb., 1 g dietary fiber, 2 g protein.

empanada pastry: In a food processor combine 2 cups all-purpose flour, 1 tablespoon sugar, and 1 teaspoon salt. Cover; pulse until combined. Add 6 tablespoons cold butter, cut up, and 3 tablespoons shortening. Cover; pulse until mixture resembles cornmeal but a few large pieces remain. With food processor running, quickly add 5 tablespoons cold water and 1½ teaspoons white vinegar through the feed tube. Stop processor; scrape down side. Cover and process with two more pulses. Remove dough; shape into a ball. Divide dough in half. Wrap each half in plastic wrap; chill about 30 minutes.

*In Mexico, these meat-filled turnovers are called empanaditas. Refrigerated biscuit dough makes them simpler than the traditional pastry—the quicker for you and your guests to enjoy.*

# mexicitos

prep: 50 minutes  bake: 10 minutes oven: 350°F
makes: 40 turnovers

1¼ pounds lean ground beef
1 15-ounce can tomato sauce
2 teaspoons chili powder
2 teaspoons dried oregano, crushed
1 teaspoon garlic powder
1 tablespoon snipped fresh cilantro
2 10- to 12-ounce packages refrigerated buttermilk biscuits (20 total)
Milk
Salsa (optional)

**1** For filling, in a large skillet cook ground beef until brown; drain off fat. Stir in tomato sauce, chili powder, oregano, and garlic powder. Bring to boiling; reduce heat. Simmer, uncovered, for 5 minutes. Remove skillet from heat. Stir in cilantro.

**2** Preheat oven to 350°F. Lightly grease a large baking sheet; set aside. Separate biscuits; cut each biscuit in half horizontally. On a lightly floured surface roll each piece of biscuit dough into a 4-inch circle. Place about 1 tablespoon filling onto half of each circle. Brush edges with a little milk. Fold dough in half over filling. Seal edges by pressing with the tines of a fork. Place filled turnovers 1 inch apart on prepared baking sheet; brush with milk.

**3** Bake for 10 to 12 minutes or until golden. Immediately remove from baking sheet and cool slightly on a wire rack. Serve warm. If desired, serve with salsa for dipping.

nutrition facts per turnover: 60 cal., 2 g total fat (1 g sat. fat), 9 mg chol., 175 mg sodium, 7 g carb., 0 g dietary fiber, 4 g protein.

*The distinct flavors of lamb and saffron are rounded out by the unexpected addition of chopped hard-boiled eggs in these pastry triangles.*

## saffron-scented
# lamb pastry puffs

prep: 40 minutes   bake: 18 minutes   stand: 5 minutes   oven: 400°F
makes: 24 puffs

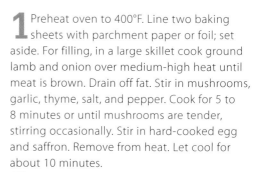

8   ounces ground lamb
1   small onion, chopped
1½  cups coarsely
      chopped fresh
      mushrooms
3   cloves garlic, minced
1   teaspoon snipped
      fresh thyme
½   teaspoon salt
¼   teaspoon ground
      black pepper
1   hard-cooked egg,
      finely chopped
      Dash saffron threads,
      crushed, or ground
      saffron
1   17.3-ounce package
      frozen puff pastry
      sheets (2 sheets),
      thawed
1   egg, lightly beaten
1   tablespoon water

**1** Preheat oven to 400°F. Line two baking sheets with parchment paper or foil; set aside. For filling, in a large skillet cook ground lamb and onion over medium-high heat until meat is brown. Drain off fat. Stir in mushrooms, garlic, thyme, salt, and pepper. Cook for 5 to 8 minutes or until mushrooms are tender, stirring occasionally. Stir in hard-cooked egg and saffron. Remove from heat. Let cool for about 10 minutes.

**2** Meanwhile, on a lightly floured surface unfold one sheet of puff pastry. Roll pastry sheet into a 14x10½-inch rectangle. Cut rectangle into twelve 3½-inch squares. Repeat with second pastry sheet (24 squares total).

**3** Spoon a scant 2 tablespoons of the filling onto each pastry square. In a small bowl combine egg and the water. Lightly brush edges of pastry squares with egg mixture. Fold one corner of each square diagonally over filling to make a triangle. Seal edges by pressing with the tines of a fork. Place on the prepared baking sheets. Lightly brush tops and sides with egg mixture.

**4** Bake for 18 to 20 minutes or until pastries are puffed and golden brown. Let stand for 5 minutes before serving.

nutrition facts per puff: 126 cal., 9 g total fat (1 g sat. fat), 25 mg chol., 138 mg sodium, 8 g carb., 0 g dietary fiber, 3 g protein.

*Crackly, crisp layers of phyllo make any appetizer extra special. Fill layers with savory lamb or beef and feta cheese, and you'll have a winner every time.*

# lamb and feta strudel

prep: 30 minutes  bake: 15 minutes  stand: 15 minutes  oven: 400°F
makes: 16 to 20 appetizers

8   ounces lean ground
      lamb or ground beef
¼   cup finely chopped
      onion
½   of a 10-ounce package
      frozen chopped
      spinach, thawed
      and well drained
5   ounces feta cheese,
      crumbled (1¼ cups)
1   tablespoon milk
1   teaspoon finely
      shredded lemon peel
¼   teaspoon salt
¼   teaspoon ground
      nutmeg
6   sheets frozen phyllo
      dough (14×9-inch
      rectangles), thawed
¼   cup butter, melted
      Ground nutmeg

**make-ahead directions:**
Prepare phyllo rolls as directed through Step 4. Wrap rolls in plastic wrap. Freeze for up to 1 month. To serve, preheat oven to 400°F. Place frozen rolls, seam sides down, on a large baking sheet. Bake for 25 to 30 minutes or until golden. Let stand for 15 minutes before serving. To serve, slice rolls along scored lines.

**1** For filling, in a medium skillet cook ground meat and onion over medium-high heat until brown. Remove from heat. Drain off fat. Add spinach, cheese, milk, lemon peel, salt, and the ¼ teaspoon nutmeg to meat mixture. Stir until combined; set aside.

**2** Preheat oven to 400°F. Unfold phyllo dough. Keep phyllo covered with plastic wrap to prevent it from drying, removing sheets as you need them. Lay one sheet of phyllo on a flat work surface. Lightly brush with some of the butter. Top with another phyllo sheet, matching edges and corners and brushing top with melted butter. Repeat, generously brushing each sheet with butter as you layer.

**3** Using a sharp knife, cut the phyllo stack in half crosswise. Spread half of the filling evenly on each phyllo stack, leaving a 1½- to 2-inch border around the edges. Fold short edges of phyllo over filling. Fold a narrow edge of phyllo lengthwise over filling. Roll up.

**4** Place phyllo rolls, seam sides down, on a baking sheet. Brush with any remaining melted butter; sprinkle with additional nutmeg. Using a serrated knife, make diagonal cuts about ¼ inch deep and 1 inch apart across each phyllo roll. (Do not cut completely through all phyllo layers.)

**5** Bake phyllo rolls for 15 to 18 minutes or until golden. Let rolls stand for 15 minutes before serving. To serve, slice phyllo rolls along scored lines.

nutrition facts per appetizer: 115 cal., 9 g total fat (5 g sat. fat), 26 mg chol., 205 mg sodium, 5 g carb., 0 g dietary fiber, 5 g protein.

*The distinctive shape of these slices is similar to the crisp European pastries known as palmiers. Here, a savory filling replaces the traditional sprinkling of sugar.*

# spinach-prosciutto
## palmiers

prep: 25 minutes  bake: 20 minutes  oven: 400°F  makes: 16 palmiers

½  of a 17.3-ounce package frozen puff pastry sheet (1 sheet), thawed

⅓  cup refrigerated basil pesto

½  of a 10-ounce package frozen chopped spinach, thawed and well drained

¾  cup bottled roasted red sweet pepper, drained and finely chopped

¼  cup grated Parmesan cheese

2  ounces thinly sliced prosciutto or thinly sliced cooked ham

1  egg

1  tablespoon water

**1** Preheat oven to 400°F. Line a very large baking sheet with parchment paper; set aside. On a lightly floured surface unfold pastry. Roll pastry into an 11-inch square. Spread basil pesto on the puff pastry. Top with spinach and pepper. Sprinkle with Parmesan cheese. Cover evenly with prosciutto. Lightly press top with fingers.

**2** Beginning on the right side, roll up into a spiral. Stop in the middle. Repeat rolling, beginning on the left side, until rolls of dough meet and touch in the center. Using a serrated knife in a sawing motion, cut roll crosswise into ½-inch-thick slices. Place slices on prepared baking sheet, reshaping as necessary. In a small bowl combine egg and the water. Beat with fork. Brush egg mixture over the slices.

**3** Bake for about 20 minutes or until puffed and browned. Serve warm or cooled to room temperature.

nutrition facts per palmier: 114 cal., 7 g total fat (2 g sat. fat), 29 mg chol., 180 mg sodium, 8 g carb., 1 g dietary fiber, 5 g protein.

**make-ahead directions:** Layer cooled palmiers between waxed paper in an airtight container. Cover. Freeze for up to 1 month. To reheat, preheat oven to 400°F. Line a large baking sheet with parchment paper. Place frozen palmiers in a single layer on prepared baking sheet. Bake for about 8 minutes or until heated through.

*Tapenade is a thick, nearly smooth spread of seasoned ripe olives—
just spread it between layers of puff pastry for an awesome bite.*

# tapenade-filled palmiers

prep: 40 minutes   freeze: 1 hour   bake: 12 minutes   oven: 400°F
makes: 80 palmiers

1   17.3-ounce package
    frozen puff pastry
    (2 sheets), thawed
⅔   cup purchased olive
    tapenade

**1** On a lightly floured surface unfold pastry. Roll one pastry sheet into a 14×10-inch rectangle. Spread ⅓ cup of the tapenade over the pastry. Beginning at a short side, loosely roll up into a spiral. Stop in the middle. Repeat rolling, beginning at the other short side. Repeat with remaining pastry sheet and tapenade. Wrap each roll in plastic wrap. Freeze for about 1 hour.

**2** Preheat oven to 400°F. Line baking sheets with parchment paper or foil; set aside. Unwrap rolls and place on a cutting board. Using a serrated knife and a sawing motion, trim ends of pastry rolls and cut crosswise into ¼-inch-thick slices. Place slices 1 inch apart on prepared baking sheets, reshaping as necessary.

**3** Bake for 12 to 15 minutes or until puffed and golden. Transfer to a wire rack. Cool slightly. Serve warm.

nutrition facts per palmier: 39 cal., 3 g total fat
(0 g sat. fat), 0 mg chol., 78 mg sodium, 2 g carb.,
0 g dietary fiber, 0 g protein.

**make-ahead directions:** Layer baked and cooled palmiers between pieces of waxed paper and freeze in an airtight container for up to 1 month. To reheat, preheat oven to 400°F. Thaw palmiers at room temperature on a large baking sheet lined with parchment paper for about 30 minutes. Bake for about 5 minutes or until crisp.

*Bake the golden pastries ahead so you can assemble the zesty bites just before the party begins. A garlicky horseradish sauce adds extra kick.*

# peppercorn pastries
## with beef

prep: 35 minutes  bake: 8 minutes  oven: 375°F
makes: 54 appetizers

1  17.3-ounce package frozen puff pastry sheets (2 sheets), thawed
1  egg, lightly beaten
1  teaspoon water
1  8-ounce carton dairy sour cream
2  tablespoons assorted snipped fresh herbs (basil, oregano, thyme, dill, and/or parsley)
4  teaspoons prepared horseradish
1  clove garlic, minced
8  ounces very thinly sliced deli roast beef, torn into pieces
1  teaspoon cracked peppercorn mélange or cracked black pepper
   Assorted fresh herbs

**1** Preheat oven to 375°F. Lightly grease two baking sheets or line with parchment paper or foil; set aside. On a lightly floured surface unfold one sheet of pastry. Roll into a 15×10-inch rectangle. Cut rectangle crosswise into nine 1½-inch-wide strips. Cut strips crosswise into thirds. Repeat with second pastry sheet (54 rectangles total). Place rectangles about 1 inch apart on the prepared baking sheets.

**2** Combine egg and the water. Lightly brush pastry rectangles with egg mixture. Bake for 8 to 10 minutes or until lightly browned. Cool on wire racks.

**3** For topping, in a small bowl stir together sour cream, the 2 tablespoons herbs, the horseradish, and garlic.

**4** To serve, spread about 1 teaspoon of the topping on each pastry rectangle. Mound beef on top of pastry. Sprinkle with peppercorn mélange and garnish with additional fresh herbs.

nutrition facts per appetizer: 57 cal., 4 g total fat (1 g sat. fat), 8 mg chol., 85 mg sodium, 4 g carb., 0 g dietary fiber, 1 g protein.

**make-ahead directions:** Prepare pastry as directed through Step 2. Layer pastry rectangles between waxed paper in an airtight container. Cover and store at room temperature for up to 3 days or freeze for up to 3 months. Prepare topping and assemble as directed.

*Make quick work of spreading the herbed cheese onto the puff pastry circles by putting the cheese mixture into a plastic sandwich bag. Snip a small hole in one corner of the bag and squeeze the cheese mixture onto the puff pastry circles.*

# garden-style
## puff pastry sandwiches

prep: 45 minutes   bake: 10 minutes   oven: 375°F   makes: 32 sandwiches

1⅓ cups soft herbed goat cheese (chèvre) or two 5-ounce containers semisoft cheese with garlic and herbs

2 tablespoons finely chopped green onion

6 to 8 teaspoons hot-style prepared horseradish

1 17.3-ounce package frozen puff pastry (2 sheets), thawed

1 tablespoon milk
Coarse salt (optional)

1 large English cucumber, very thinly sliced

10 radishes, very thinly sliced
Small fresh thyme sprigs (optional)

**1** In a medium bowl combine cheese, green onion, and horseradish; cover and chill until ready to use.

**2** Preheat oven to 375°F. On a lightly floured surface unfold one pastry sheet. Using the tines of a fork, generously prick the pastry. Using a 2-inch triangle, square, or round cutter, cut pastry into 16 shapes. (Do not reroll pastry scraps.) Repeat with second puff pastry sheet.

**3** Transfer pastries to an ungreased baking sheet. Lightly brush each pastry with milk. If desired, sprinkle with salt. Bake for 10 to 12 minutes or until golden. Cool on a wire rack.

**4** To assemble, use a knife to split the baked pastries horizontally. Spread about 1 teaspoon of the cheese mixture onto the cut side of each bottom pastry. Top with a cucumber slice and some radish slices. Spread about 1 teaspoon of the cheese mixture onto the cut side of each pastry top. Place on top of radish slices. If desired, garnish each sandwich with a thyme sprig.

nutrition facts per sandwich: 112 cal., 8 g total fat (3 g sat. fat), 4 mg chol., 75 mg sodium, 8 g carb., 0 g dietary fiber, 3 g protein.

fanciful **pastries**

*This delightful twist on pastry-wrapped Brie features a dried cherry–pecan mixture sweetened with a touch of honey.*

# brie en croute
## with cherries and pecans

prep: 20 minutes  bake: 20 minutes  cool: 10 minutes  oven: 375°F
makes: 12 servings

½  of a 17.3-ounce package frozen puff pastry (1 sheet), thawed
½  cup chopped pecans
⅓  cup snipped dried tart cherries
2  tablespoons honey
2  4½-ounce rounds Brie cheese
1  egg, lightly beaten
1  tablespoon water
   Apple slices, pear slices, and/or seedless grapes

**1** Preheat oven to 375°F. Line a baking sheet with parchment paper; set aside. On a lightly floured surface unfold puff pastry. Roll pastry sheet into a 16×10-inch rectangle. Cut two 8-inch circles from rectangle; set scraps aside.

**2** In a small bowl combine pecans, dried cherries, and honey. Divide cherry mixture between the two pastry circles, spooning mixture into the center of each circle. Place one cheese round on top of each cherry mixture, pressing down to spread cherry mixture. Bring pastry up around cheese to enclose it completely, pleating and pinching edges to cover and seal. Place rounds, sealed sides down, on prepared baking sheet. Combine egg and the water; set aside.

**3** Using a small sharp knife or small cookie cutters, cut reserved pastry trimmings into desired shapes such as leaves. Brush egg mixture onto wrapped cheese rounds; top with pastry shapes and brush again.

**4** Bake for 20 to 25 minutes or until pastry is deep golden brown. Let stand for 10 minutes before serving. Serve with fruit.

nutrition facts per serving: 220 cal., 16 g total fat (4 g sat. fat), 39 mg chol., 217 mg sodium, 14 g carb., 1 g dietary fiber, 6 g protein.

brie en croute with apricots and almonds: Prepare Brie as above, except substitute chopped hazelnuts (filberts) or almonds for the pecans, finely snipped dried apricots for the dried cherries, and apricot preserves for the honey.

*Refrigerated piecrust cradles the blue cheese and mushroom-egg filling for these tiny tarts. Use a measuring spoon so that you add the right amount of filling to the pastry cups.*

# mini quiches

prep: 45 minutes   bake: 18 minutes   cool: 5 minutes   oven: 425°F/350°F
makes: 24 servings

1   15-ounce package rolled refrigerated unbaked piecrust (2 crusts)
3   slices bacon
1   cup finely chopped mushrooms
1   egg
⅓   cup milk
    Dash ground black pepper
⅓   cup crumbled blue cheese or finely shredded Swiss cheese
2   tablespoons snipped fresh chives or chopped green onion
    Red sweet pepper strips (optional)
    Snipped fresh chives or chopped green onion (optional)

1 Preheat oven to 425°F. Lightly coat twenty-four 1¾-inch muffin cups with nonstick cooking spray; set aside. On a lightly floured surface unroll both piecrusts. Using a 2¾-inch round cutter, cut 24 circles of dough from piecrusts, discarding scraps. Gently press circles into prepared muffin cups, pleating as necessary to fit. Do not prick pastry. Bake for 6 to 7 minutes or just until pastry cups begin to brown. Remove muffin pans from oven; place on wire racks to cool. Reduce oven temperature to 350°F.

2 For filling, in a large skillet cook bacon over medium heat until crisp. Drain bacon on paper towels, reserving 1 tablespoon of the drippings in the skillet. When cool, crumble bacon; set aside. Add mushrooms to reserved drippings in skillet. Cook and stir over medium heat for about 3 minutes or until tender. Remove skillet from heat. In a small bowl lightly whisk together egg, milk, and black pepper. Stir in bacon, cooked mushrooms, cheese, and the 2 tablespoons chives.

3 Fill each pastry cup with about 1 teaspoon of the filling. Bake in the 350°F oven for about 18 minutes or until filling is puffed and set. Cool in muffin cups for 5 minutes. Carefully remove quiches from muffin cups; place on a serving platter. If desired, garnish with sweet pepper strips and additional chives. Serve warm.

nutrition facts per serving: 95 cal., 6 g total fat (4 g sat. fat), 15 mg chol., 121 mg sodium, 9 g carb., 0 g dietary fiber, 1 g protein.

*Because the flaky crust is frozen puff pastry, you can assemble these cheese-and bacon-filled bites in minutes.*

# cheese puffs

prep: 30 minutes  bake: 12 minutes  oven: 400°F  makes: 32 puffs

1  3-ounce package cream cheese, softened
1  egg yolk
1  teaspoon lemon juice
1  teaspoon snipped fresh chives
   Dash ground black pepper
½  cup shredded white cheddar cheese (2 ounces)
2  slices bacon, crisp cooked and crumbled
1  17.3-ounce package frozen puff pastry (2 sheets), thawed
   Milk

**1** For filling, in a small mixing bowl combine cream cheese, egg yolk, lemon juice, chives, and pepper. Beat with an electric mixer on medium speed until nearly smooth. Stir in cheddar cheese and bacon.

**2** Preheat oven to 400°F. On a lightly floured surface roll one sheet of the puff pastry into a 12-inch square. Cut into sixteen 3-inch squares. Top each square with about 1 teaspoon of the filling. Brush pastry edges with milk. Fold each square in half diagonally to make a triangle. Seal edges by pressing with the tines of a fork or your fingers. Place on an ungreased baking sheet. Repeat with remaining pastry sheet and filling.

**3** Bake for 12 to 15 minutes or until golden. Serve warm.

nutrition facts per puff: 87 cal., 7 g total fat (1 g sat. fat), 12 mg chol., 83 mg sodium, 6 g carb., 0 g dietary fiber, 1 g protein.

**make-ahead directions:** Prepare as directed through Step 2. Cover and chill in the refrigerator for up to 4 hours. Bake as directed in Step 3.

*Ratatouille, the classic Provencal vegetable mélange, serves as a lively filling in these tempting appetizers. Assembled napoleons will hold for up to 1 hour.*

# ratatouille napoleons

prep: 40 minutes  bake: 12 minutes  broil: 1 minute per batch  oven: 400°F/ Broil  makes: 30 servings

2 tablespoons olive oil
1½ cups chopped peeled eggplant
1½ cups coarsely chopped zucchini (1 large)
½ cup chopped onion
1 clove garlic, minced
1 14½-ounce can diced tomatoes, undrained
½ cup snipped fresh basil
½ teaspoon salt
¼ teaspoon ground black pepper
1 17.3-ounce package frozen puff pastry sheets (2 sheets), thawed
1 egg, lightly beaten
1 tablespoon water
8 ounces fresh mozzarella cheese, thinly sliced

**1** Preheat oven to 400°F. For ratatouille, in a large skillet heat oil over medium heat. Cook eggplant, zucchini, onion, and garlic in hot oil for about 5 minutes or until onion is tender, stirring occasionally. Stir in tomatoes. Bring to boiling; reduce heat. Simmer, uncovered, for about 5 minutes or until most of the liquid evaporates. Stir in basil, salt, and pepper. Cool.

**2** Meanwhile, on a lightly floured surface unfold puff pastry. Cut each sheet along the folds into three portions. Cut each portion crosswise into five rectangles (30 total). Place pastry rectangles on two ungreased baking sheets. In a small bowl combine egg and the water. Lightly brush pastry rectangles with egg mixture.

**3** Bake for 12 to 14 minutes or until golden brown. Transfer to wire racks; cool. Split pastry rectangles in half horizontally.

**4** Preheat broiler. Place bottoms of pastry rectangles on two ungreased baking sheets. Top each with a well rounded tablespoon of the ratatouille. Add a thin slice of cheese. Broil 3 to 4 inches from the heat for 1 to 2 minutes or just until cheese starts to melt. Replace tops of pastry rectangles. Serve warm.

nutrition facts per serving: 112 cal., 8 g total fat (1 g sat. fat), 13 mg chol., 179 mg sodium, 7 g carb., 0 g dietary fiber, 3 g protein.

**make-ahead directions:** Prepare as directed, except do not broil pastries. Let stand at room temperature for up to 30 minutes. Broil as directed.

*Layers of flaky phyllo encase a savory garlic-and-herb cheese filling in these savory appetizers.*

# cheese-and-walnut-
## stuffed mushroom bundles

prep: 30 minutes    cook: 6 minutes    bake: 10 minutes    oven: 400°F
makes: 12 bundles

| | |
|---|---|
| 12 | mushrooms (about 1½ inches in diameter) |
| 8 | sheets frozen phyllo dough (14×9 inches), thawed |
| ¼ | cup butter, melted |
| ½ | of a 5.2-ounce package semisoft cheese with garlic and herbs (about ⅓ cup) |
| ¼ | cup chopped toasted walnuts |

**1** Preheat oven to 400°F. Remove stems from mushrooms; discard or set aside for another use. Cook mushroom caps in a small amount of boiling water in a covered saucepan for 6 to 8 minutes or until soft. Drain and invert caps on paper towels.

**2** Unfold phyllo dough. Keep covered with plastic wrap to prevent it from drying out, removing sheets as you need them. Lay one sheet of phyllo on a flat work surface. Lightly brush with some of the butter. Top with another phyllo sheet, brushing top with melted butter. Repeat with 2 more phyllo sheets, generously brushing each sheet with butter as you layer. Using a sharp knife, cut phyllo stack in half lengthwise; cut each half crosswise into three squares, making six squares. Repeat with remaining phyllo and butter to make 12 squares total.

**3** Place a mushroom, stem side up, on each phyllo square. Top each mushroom with about 1 teaspoon cheese and about 1 teaspoon walnuts. Bring corners of phyllo together on top of mushrooms and filling and pinch to seal. Place bundles on an ungreased baking sheet. Brush with remaining melted butter. Bake for 10 to 12 minutes or until pastry is golden. Serve warm.

nutrition facts per bundle: 114 cal., 8 g total fat (4 g sat. fat), 16 mg chol., 89 mg sodium, 8 g carb., 1 g dietary fiber, 2 g protein.

**make-ahead directions:** Place unbaked phyllo bundles in a single layer in an airtight container. Cover and freeze for up to 1 month. Bake as directed (do not thaw before baking).

*Set aside a few of these rich cheese-topped pastries and tuck them away in the freezer for up to a month. Enjoy them with soups and stews in cold months.*

# caraway-cheese crisps

prep: 10 minutes  bake: 10 minutes  oven: 400°F  makes: 27 crisps

½  of a 17.3-ounce package frozen puff pastry (1 sheet), thawed
1  egg white, slightly beaten
1  tablespoon water
½  cup shredded Swiss cheese (2 ounces)
2  teaspoons caraway seeds, crushed

**1** Preheat oven to 400°F. Grease a large baking sheet; set aside.

**2** On a lightly floured surface unfold pastry sheet. In a small bowl combine egg white and the water. Brush pastry with egg white mixture. Sprinkle with Swiss cheese and caraway seeds. Cut pastry crosswise into nine 1-inch strips. Cut pastry lengthwise into thirds, making a total of twenty-seven 3×1-inch strips. Place on prepared baking sheet.

**3** Bake for 10 to 12 minutes or until puffed and golden. Cool on wire racks.

nutrition facts per crisp: 93 cal., 6 g total fat (2 g sat. fat), 2 mg chol., 45 mg sodium, 7 g carb., 0 g dietary fiber, 2 g protein.

> **make-ahead directions:** Place baked and cooled crisps in layers separated by waxed paper in an airtight storage container. Cover and freeze for up to 1 month. Thaw pastry at room temperature for 30 minutes. Preheat oven to 400°F. Place crisps on a baking sheet lined with parchment paper. Bake for about 5 minutes or until crisp.

## freeze with ease

*Follow these simple tips to ensure your savory pastries retain top-quality flavor and texture after freezing.*

- *Most pastries can be frozen. However, do not freeze those that are filled with hard-cooked eggs, mayonnaise, or fresh vegetables. These ingredients do not hold up well when frozen.*

- *Freeze fragile pastries that can break or crumble in single layers on baking sheets until firm. Then place them in freezer bags or airtight containers and return them to the freezer for longer storage.*

- *If you must stack the pastries, separate layers with waxed paper.*

- *Use frozen pastries within 1 month.*

fanciful **pastries**

*This elegant version of the classic Gruyère cheese and bacon pie, from the Lorraine region in France, is cut into bite-size squares.*

# quiche lorraine squares

prep: 30 minutes  bake: 23 minutes + 25 minutes  cool: 15 minutes
oven: 425°F/350°F  makes: 54 servings

1    recipe Quiche Pastry
     Dough
2    slices bacon
1    cup chopped onion
8    eggs
2    cups half-and-half or
     light cream
¼    teaspoon ground
     black pepper
     Dash ground nutmeg
2    cups shredded
     Gruyère or Swiss
     cheese, (8 ounces)

**1** Preheat oven to 425°F. On a lightly floured surface using a floured rolling pin, roll dough into a 17×12-inch rectangle. Fold dough in half; fold in half again. Transfer to a 15×10×1-inch baking pan. Gently unfold dough; ease into pan, allowing extra pastry to hang over edge. Fold extra pastry under, pressing onto edge of the pan.

**2** Line pastry with foil. Bake for 15 minutes. Remove foil. Bake for about 8 minutes more or until pastry is golden. Cool on a wire rack. Reduce oven temperature to 350°F.

**3** In a medium skillet cook bacon over medium heat until crisp. Drain bacon on paper towels, reserving drippings in skillet. Crumble bacon; set aside. Add onion to the reserved drippings in skillet. Cook for about 4 minutes or until tender, stirring occasionally; set aside.

**4** For filling, in a large bowl whisk together eggs, half-and-half, pepper, and nutmeg. Sprinkle Gruyère cheese, bacon, and onion evenly over crust. Slowly pour egg mixture over.

**5** Bake in the 350°F oven for about 25 minutes or until filling is set and puffed around the edges. Cool in pan on a wire rack for 15 minutes. Cut into squares. Serve warm.

quiche pastry dough: In a medium bowl stir together 2 cups all-purpose flour and ½ teaspoon salt. Using a pastry blender, cut in ½ cup shortening and ¼ cup cold butter until pieces are size of peas. Sprinkle 1 tablespoon cold water over part of the mixture; gently toss with a fork. Push moistened dough to the side of the bowl. Repeat moistening dough, using 1 tablespoon water at a time, until all the dough is moistened (6 to 7 tablespoons cold water total). Form dough into a ball.

nutrition facts per serving: 90 cal., 6 g total fat (3 g sat. fat), 42 mg chol., 82 mg sodium, 4 g carb., 2 g dietary fiber, 3 g protein.

*Mini phyllo shells can be used as a vessel to hold other salads too, such as tuna, ham, and seafood, available at supermarket delis.*

# turkey salad tartlets

start to finish: 25 minutes  makes: 30 tartlets

1¼ cups finely chopped cooked turkey breast*

3 slices packaged ready-to-serve cooked bacon, chopped, or 3 slices bacon, crisp cooked and crumbled

2 tablespoons finely chopped shallot or onion

2 tablespoons mayonnaise

2 tablespoons dairy sour cream

2 teaspoons lime juice

1 teaspoon Dijon-style mustard
  Salt
  Ground black pepper

1 avocado, halved, pitted, peeled, and chopped

2 2.1-ounce packages baked miniature phyllo dough shells (30 shells)

8 grape tomatoes, quartered lengthwise

pineapple-almond turkey salad: Prepare as directed, except omit mustard and substitute ½ cup drained pineapple tidbits for the avocado and ¼ cup toasted sliced almonds for the tomatoes.

**1** In a medium bowl combine turkey, bacon, and shallot; set aside.

**2** In a small bowl stir together mayonnaise, sour cream, lime juice, mustard, and salt and pepper to taste. Add mayonnaise mixture to turkey mixture, stirring to combine. Add avocado to turkey salad, gently tossing to combine.

**3** Spoon turkey salad into each phyllo shell. Garnish each tart with a tomato wedge.

nutrition facts per tartlet: 52 cal., 3 g total fat (0 g sat. fat), 6 mg chol., 52 mg sodium, 3 g carb., 0 g dietary fiber, 3 g protein.

*note: To save time, coarsely chop the turkey in a food processor: cover and pulse until finely chopped.

**make-ahead directions:** Prepare turkey salad through Step 2. Cover and chill for up to 24 hours. Just before serving, stir in avocado and spoon salad into tart shells.

Whether melted to oozy goodness in sand-wiches, served on a stick, or formed into a classic ball, cheese lends a rich, flavorful bite that's sure to bring smiles to your guests.

say che

ese

say cheese

*Due to its mild flavor, warm gooey Brie goes well with tangy chutney and crunchy crackers, making this the perfect party pleaser.*

# brie with chutney

prep: 5 minutes   bake: 15 minutes   oven: 325°F   makes: 4 to 6 servings

1   8-ounce round Brie cheese
5   tablespoons mango chutney
    Assorted crackers

**1** Preheat oven to 325°F. Split Brie cheese in half horizontally. Snip any large mango pieces in chutney. Place bottom half of cheese, cut side up, in a small shallow ovenproof dish. Top with 4 tablespoons chutney. Top with the remaining cheese half, cut side down. Spread the remaining chutney over top of cheese.

**2** Bake for 15 to 20 minutes or until cheese is softened but not runny. Serve with crackers.

nutrition facts per serving: 239 cal., 16 g total fat (10 g sat. fat), 57 mg chol., 519 mg sodium, 12 g carb., 0 g dietary fiber, 12 g protein.

*Three rich and luscious fruits flavor a soft, mellow cheese blend that is rolled in toasted almonds. Served alongside crackers or apple slices, the logs are beautiful to behold.*

# fruited cheese logs

prep: 30 minutes   chill: 4 hours   stand: 30 minutes   makes: 32 servings

½ cup snipped dried apricots

⅓ cup snipped golden raisins

¼ cup snipped pitted whole dates

Warm water

2 cups shredded Monterey Jack cheese (8 ounces)

½ of an 8-ounce package cream cheese

2 tablespoons orange juice

¼ teaspoon salt

½ cup chopped almonds, toasted*

Assorted crackers and/or apple slices

1 In a small bowl soak apricots, raisins, and dates in enough warm water to cover for about 30 minutes or until softened. Drain well; set aside. Meanwhile, place Monterey Jack cheese and cream cheese in a medium mixing bowl. Let stand at room temperature for 30 minutes.

2 Add orange juice to cheeses in bowl. Beat with an electric mixer until well combined. Stir in drained apricots, raisins, dates, and salt. Divide cheese mixture in half. On a large piece of waxed paper shape one portion of the cheese mixture into a log about 5 inches long. Repeat with remaining cheese mixture. Place waxed paper with logs on baking sheet.

3 Cover and chill logs for 4 to 24 hours. Before serving, roll each log in nuts. Serve with assorted crackers and/or apple slices.

nutrition facts per 1 tablespoon: 95 cal., 6 g total fat (3 g sat. fat), 16 mg chol., 107 mg sodium, 6 g carb., 1 g dietary fiber, 4 g protein.

*note: To toast nuts, spread them in a single layer in a shallow baking pan. Bake in a preheated 350°F oven for 5 to 10 minutes or until pieces are golden brown, stirring once or twice. Cool completely.

**make-ahead directions:** Prepare as directed through Step 2. Wrap cheese logs in moisture- and vapor-proof plastic wrap. Freeze for up to 1 month. To serve, thaw the cheese logs in the refrigerator overnight. Unwrap and roll in nuts. Let stand for 15 minutes at room temperature before serving.

*Look for Manchego—a mild and nutty sheep's milk cheese from Spain—at specialty cheese counters. Its crosshatched pattern on the rind makes it easy to spot.*

# manchego bites

prep: 25 minutes   chill: 15 minutes   bake: 18 minutes   oven: 400°F
makes: 15 servings

1   egg
1   tablespoon water
½   of a 17.3-ounce
     package frozen
     puff pastry sheet
     (1 sheet), thawed
4   ounces Manchego
     cheese, shredded
     (1 cup)
¼   cup finely chopped
     red sweet pepper
1   cup shredded arugula

**1** Line a baking sheet with parchment paper or foil; set aside. In a small bowl whisk together egg and the water; set aside. On a lightly floured surface unfold pastry. Brush with egg mixture. Cover and refrigerate remaining egg mixture.

**2** In a bowl combine Manchego cheese, pepper, and arugula. Spread evenly over pastry. Roll up pastry starting with a short side. Wrap and refrigerate for 15 minutes or for up to 2 hours.

**3** Preheat oven to 400°F. Slice the pastry crosswise into 15 slices that are a little thicker than ½ inch each. Place slices, cut sides up, on prepared baking sheet; brush tops with egg mixture. Bake for 18 to 20 minutes or until golden. Serve warm.

nutrition facts per serving: 125 cal., 9 g total fat (3 g sat. fat), 22 mg chol., 137 mg sodium, 8 g carb., 0 g dietary fiber, 4 g protein.

**make-ahead directions:** Place slices on a baking sheet. Brush with egg mixture. Freeze for 2 hours. Transfer to a freezer container. Cover and freeze for up to 1 month. To bake, place frozen bites on parchment-lined baking sheet and bake as directed.

say **cheese**

*Delight cheese lovers with this decadent melted Brie appetizer. The white rind is also edible and is usually eaten along with the soft interior.*

# praline-topped brie

prep: 5 minutes   bake: 15 minutes   oven: 350°F   makes: 10 servings

1   13-ounce round Brie
     or Camembert
     cheese
½   cup orange
     marmalade
2   tablespoons packed
     brown sugar
⅓   cup coarsely chopped
     toasted pecans
     Apple slices and/
     or baguette slices,
     toasted

**1** Preheat oven to 350°F. Place cheese in a shallow ovenproof serving dish or pie plate. In a small bowl stir together orange marmalade and brown sugar. Spread on top of cheese. Sprinkle with pecans.

**2** Bake for about 15 minutes or until cheese is slightly softened and topping is bubbly. Serve with apple and/or baguette slices.

nutrition facts per serving: 198 cal., 13 g total fat (7 g sat. fat), 37 mg chol., 242 mg sodium, 14 g carb., 0 g dietary fiber, 8 g protein.

*Cheesemakers in our nation's heartland produce some of the best blue cheese in the world. These mini cream puffs are an excellent way to show off this flavorful cheese.*

# blue cheese puffs

prep: 45 minutes  bake: 25 minutes  oven: 400°F  makes: about 30 puffs

1  cup water
½  cup butter
⅛  teaspoon salt
1  cup all-purpose flour
4  eggs
1  cup crumbled blue cheese (4 ounces)
½  cup mayonnaise
1  tablespoon snipped fresh chives
30  fresh spinach leaves (about 1 cup)
12  ounces deli-sliced roast beef or smoked turkey, cut into thin bite-size strips

1 Preheat oven to 400°F. Grease two baking sheets; set aside. In a medium saucepan combine the water, butter, and salt. Cook and stir over medium heat until mixture is boiling. Add flour all at once, stirring vigorously. Cook and stir until mixture forms a ball. Remove from heat. Cool for 10 minutes.

2 Add eggs, one at a time, beating with a wooden spoon after each addition until smooth. Stir in ¾ cup of the blue cheese, stirring until combined.

3 Drop batter by rounded teaspoons about 2 inches apart onto prepared baking sheets. Bake for 25 to 30 minutes or until golden. Transfer to a wire rack; cool.

4 In a small bowl stir together the remaining ¼ cup blue cheese, mayonnaise, and chives.

5 To serve, cut tops from puffs. Place a spinach leaf in the bottom of each puff. Top each with some of the roast beef strips and about 1 teaspoon of the mayonnaise mixture. Replace tops.

nutrition facts per puff: 116 cal., 9 g total fat (3 g sat. fat), 49 mg chol., 123 mg sodium, 3 g carb., 0 g dietary fiber, 5 g protein.

*Bring out a couple of party platters and showcase the cheese balls on beds of fresh basil leaves. Add a few serve-along ingredients to each platter and let guests help themselves.*

## ripe olive
# cheese balls

prep: 15 minutes   chill: 4 hours   stand: 45 minutes   makes: 2 balls (3½ cups)

2   8-ounce packages cream cheese
½   cup butter
½   cup crumbled blue cheese (2 ounces)
1   4¼-ounce can sliced pitted ripe olives, drained
2   tablespoons chopped green onion or snipped fresh chives
    Assorted crackers, flatbread, dried dates and/or dried apricots, and walnut halves

**1** Place cream cheese, butter, and blue cheese in a large mixing bowl. Let stand for 30 minutes to reach room temperature. Beat with an electric mixer on low speed until smooth. Stir in olives and green onion. Cover and chill for at least 4 hours or up to 24 hours.

**2** Shape mixture loosely into 2 balls. Cover and chill until serving time. Serve cheese balls with assorted crackers and/or dried fruits.

nutrition facts per 1 tablespoon: 55 cal., 6 g total fat (3 g sat. fat), 14 mg chol., 69 mg sodium, 1 g carb., 0 g dietary fiber, 1 g protein.

**make-ahead directions:** Prepare as directed. Place in a freezer container. Cover and freeze for up to 3 months. Let thaw in refrigerator overnight before serving.

*Toasting the pine nuts enhances flavor. Place them on a baking sheet in a 350°F oven for about 10 minutes, shaking halfway through. Or toast them in a heavy skillet on the stove top over medium heat, stirring often until they turn golden.*

# prosciutto-basil
## cheese ball

prep: 35 minutes   chill: 4 hours   stand: 15 minutes   makes: about 2 cups

1   8-ounce package cream cheese
4   ounces fontina cheese, finely shredded (1 cup)
¼   cup butter
1   tablespoon milk
½   teaspoon Worcestershire marinade for chicken
2   ounces prosciutto, chopped
2   tablespoons thinly sliced green onion
2   tablespoons snipped fresh basil
½   cup chopped toasted pine nuts
    Assorted apples, crackers, and/or flatbread

**1** In a large mixing bowl let cream cheese, shredded cheese, and butter stand at room temperature for 30 minutes. Add milk and Worcestershire sauce. Beat with an electric mixer on medium speed until light and fluffy. Stir in prosciutto, green onion, and basil. Cover and chill for 4 to 24 hours.

**2** Before serving, shape mixture into a ball. Roll ball in nuts and let stand 15 minutes. Serve with apples, crackers, and/or flatbread.

nutrition facts per 1 tablespoon: 63 cal., 6 g total fat (3 g sat. fat), 16 mg chol., 62 mg sodium, 1 g carb., 0 g dietary fiber, 2 g protein.

**make-ahead directions:** Prepare as directed in Step 1. Wrap cheese ball in moisture- and vapor-proof plastic wrap. Freeze for up to 1 month. To serve, thaw the cheese ball in the refrigerator overnight. Unwrap and roll in nuts. Let stand for 15 minutes at room temperature before serving.

*Mixing your own cheese ball is much more fun than purchasing one from a mall shop or kiosk. This one blends taco cheese, jalapeño peppers, and crushed corn chips.*

# spicy taco cheese log

prep: 35 minutes   chill: 4 hours   stand: 15 minutes
makes: about 2 cups

1   8-ounce package
    cream cheese
1   cup shredded taco
    cheese
¼   cup butter or
    margarine
1   tablespoon milk
½   teaspoon
    Worcestershire
    marinade for
    chicken
2   tablespoons thinly
    sliced green onion
2   tablespoons canned
    chopped green
    jalapeño chile
    peppers (see note,
    page 52)
½   cup crushed corn
    chips
1   tablespoon snipped
    fresh cilantro
1   recipe Baked Tortilla
    Chips

**1** In a large mixing bowl let cream cheese, taco cheese, and butter stand at room temperature for 30 minutes. Add milk and Worcestershire sauce. Beat with an electric mixer on medium speed until light and fluffy. Stir in green onion and chile peppers. Cover and chill for 4 to 24 hours.

**2** Shape cheese mixture into a log about 9 inches long. Combine corn chips and cilantro; roll cheese log in corn chip mixture. Let stand for 15 minutes before serving. Serve with Baked Tortilla Chips.

nutrition facts per 1 tablespoon: 81 cal., 6 g total fat (3 g sat. fat), 15 mg chol., 135 mg sodium, 5 g carb., 0 g dietary fiber, 2 g protein.

**make-ahead directions:** Prepare as directed in a cheese log. Wrap cheese log in moisture- and vapor-proof plastic wrap. Freeze for up to 1 month. To serve, thaw the cheese log in the refrigerator overnight. Unwrap and roll in corn chip mixture. Let stand for 15 minutes at room temperature before serving. Store tortilla chips in an airtight container at room temperature for up to 3 days.

baked tortilla chips: Preheat oven to 350°F. Lightly coat a baking sheet with nonstick cooking spray; set aside. Lightly coat both sides of four 8-inch flour tortillas with nonstick cooking spray. Cut each tortilla into 8 wedges; sprinkle lightly with salt. Arrange wedges in a single layer on baking sheet. Bake for 12 to 15 minutes or until crisp and light brown.

*Vary the shape of the cheese mixture if you like. Make one large ball or log or divide the mixture into smaller portions, making two or three cheese balls.*

# dilled onion cheese ball

prep: 35 minutes   chill: 4 hours   stand: 15 minutes
makes: about 2 cups

1   8-ounce package
     cream cheese
4   ounces Gouda
     cheese, finely
     shredded (1 cup)
¼   cup butter
1   tablespoon milk
½   teaspoon
     Worcestershire
     marinade for
     chicken
2   tablespoons thinly
     sliced green onion
2   tablespoons snipped
     fresh dill or 2
     teaspoons dried
     dillweed
½   cup chopped toasted
     almonds
     Assorted crackers
     and/or flatbread

**1** In a large mixing bowl let cream cheese, shredded cheese, and butter stand at room temperature for 30 minutes. Add milk and Worcestershire sauce. Beat with an electric mixer on medium speed until light and fluffy. Stir in green onion and dill. Cover and chill for 4 to 24 hours.

**2** Before serving, shape mixture into a ball. Roll ball in nuts and let stand 15 minutes. Serve with crackers and/or flatbread.

nutrition facts per 1 tablespoon: 63 cal., 6 g total fat (3 g sat. fat), 16 mg chol., 62 mg sodium, 1 g carb., 0 g dietary fiber, 2 g protein.

**make-ahead directions:** Prepare as directed in Step 1. Wrap cheese ball in moisture- and vapor-proof plastic wrap. Freeze for up to 1 month. To serve, thaw the cheese ball in the refrigerator overnight. Unwrap and roll in nuts. Let stand for 15 minutes at room temperature before serving.

*Horseradish-chive Havarti cheese lets you add a windfall of flavors with just one ingredient. If you can't find it, see the recipe Note for an easy substitution.*

# crab and
# horseradish havarti dip

prep: 15 minutes   bake: 25 minutes   oven: 350°F
makes: 3 cups

1   8-ounce package
      cream cheese,
      softened
1¼  cups shredded
      horseradish and
      chive Havarti
      cheese (5 ounces)*
⅓   cup dairy sour cream
¼   cup mayonnaise
6   ounces cooked lump
      crabmeat, flaked,
      or one 6-ounce can
      crabmeat, drained,
      flaked, and cartilage
      removed
1   cup shredded fresh
      baby spinach
      Breadsticks and/
      or other assorted
      breads

1 Preheat oven to 350°F. In a large mixing
bowl combine cream cheese, Havarti cheese, sour cream, and mayonnaise. Beat with an electric mixer on medium speed until well mixed. Fold in crabmeat and spinach.

2 Transfer mixture to a 1-quart soufflé dish or shallow baking dish. Bake for about 25 minutes or until mixture is heated through. Serve dip with assorted breads.

nutrition facts per ¼ cup: 175 cal., 16 g total fat (6 g sat. fat), 47 mg chol., 296 mg sodium, 1 g carb., 0 g dietary fiber, 7 g protein.

*note: If you can't find the horseradish and chive Havarti cheese, substitute 1¼ cups shredded Havarti cheese and add 1 tablespoon snipped fresh chives and 2 teaspoons prepared horseradish with the sour cream.

*Serve this rich, tangy cheesecake with cucumber slices and crackers or bagel crisps. If you chill the cheesecake overnight, set it out 30 minutes before serving, because cheesecakes tastes best when brought to room temperature.*

# salmon-dill cheesecake

bake: 30 minutes  cool: 1 hour 45 minutes  chill: 2 hours  oven: 350°F
makes: 16 servings

1½ cups finely crushed crispy rye or sesame crackers
6 tablespoons butter, melted
2 tablespoons grated Parmesan cheese
1 8-ounce package cream cheese, softened
2 eggs
½ of an 8-ounce tub cream cheese with salmon or plain tub cream cheese
1 tablespoon white wine vinegar or lemon juice
1 8-ounce carton dairy sour cream
4 ounces dry-smoked salmon, skin and bones removed, flaked
1 tablespoon snipped fresh dill
Dill sprigs (optional)
Salmon caviar (optional)

1 For crust, combine crushed crackers, melted butter, and Parmesan cheese in a medium bowl. Press mixture evenly on the bottom and about 1 inch up the sides of a 9-inch springform pan. Set pan aside.

2 Preheat oven to 350°F. For filling, in a large mixing bowl beat softened cream cheese with an electric mixer on low to medium speed until smooth. Add eggs all at once. Beat on low speed just until combined. Add tub cream cheese and vinegar. Beat on low speed just until combined. Stir in sour cream, smoked salmon, and 1 tablespoon snipped dill.

3 Pour into crust-lined springform pan. Place the springform pan on a shallow baking pan on the oven rack. Bake for 30 to 35 minutes or until center appears nearly set when gently shaken.

4 Remove springform pan from baking pan. Cool cheesecake on a wire rack for 15 minutes. Use a small metal spatula to loosen crust from sides of pan. Cool 30 minutes more. Remove sides of the springform pan. Cool for 1 hour. Cover and chill in the refrigerator for at least 2 hours. If desired, garnish with fresh dill sprigs and salmon caviar.

nutrition facts per serving: 196 cal., 15 g total fat (9 g sat. fat), 70 mg chol., 235 mg sodium, 10 g carb., 2 g dietary fiber, 5 g protein.

**make-ahead directions:** Prepare and bake cheesecake as directed. Cover and chill in the refrigerator for up to 24 hours. To serve, garnish cheesecake as directed.

*Use your fingers to lightly press the Parmesan mixture so the crumbs adhere to the chicken. Spreading the chicken pieces out on the baking sheet gives them a nice crisp coating.*

# parmesan-crusted
## chicken bites

prep: 20 minutes   bake: 10 minutes   oven: 425°F   makes: about 40 servings

1¼ pounds skinless, boneless chicken breasts
2 egg whites
1 cup finely shredded Parmigiano-Reggiano cheese or Parmesan cheese (4 ounces)
1 cup panko (Japanese-style breadcrumbs)
¼ teaspoon ground black pepper
1 cup bottled marinara sauce

**1** Heat oven to 425°F. Line a large baking sheet with parchment paper or foil; set aside. Cut chicken into 1-inch pieces.

**2** In a medium bowl whisk egg whites until frothy. In another medium bowl combine Parmigiano-Reggiano cheese, breadcrumbs, and pepper.

**3** Add chicken to egg whites. Toss gently to coat. Transfer chicken, a few pieces at a time, to cheese mixture; toss gently to coat. Place chicken, without touching, on prepared baking sheet. Lightly coat chicken with nonstick cooking spray.

**4** Bake, uncovered, for 10 to 15 minutes or until chicken is no longer pink and coating is lightly browned. Meanwhile, heat marinara sauce. Serve marinara sauce with chicken for dipping.

nutrition facts per serving: 34 cal., 1 g total fat (0 g sat. fat), 10 mg chol., 77 mg sodium, 2 g carb., 0 g dietary fiber, 5 g protein.

*Soft, moist, and easy-to-use canned bread can be found in the baked goods aisle of your supermarket.*

# grilled goat cheese
## sandwiches

start to finish: 20 minutes  makes: 8 servings

1  4-ounce package goat cheese (chèvre), softened
1  tablespoon honey
¼  teaspoon finely shredded lemon peel
1  16-ounce can Boston brown bread, cut into 12 slices
2  tablespoons fig jam
¼  cup small fresh basil leaves

1 In a small bowl combine goat cheese, honey, and lemon peel.

2 Divide half of the cheese mixture among four bread slices, spreading to edges. Top with half of the fig jam. Add half of the basil. Top with four more bread slices. Top with the remaining cheese mixture and the remaining fig jam. Add the remaining basil. Cover with the remaining four bread slices. Lightly coat the outsides of sandwiches with cooking spray.

3 Coat a large skillet with cooking spray; heat over medium heat. Add sandwiches. Cook about 6 minutes or until lightly toasted, turning once. Cut each sandwich in half.

nutrition facts per serving: 171 cal., 4 g total fat (2 g sat. fat), 7 mg chol., 412 mg sodium, 30 g carb., 3 g dietary fiber, 6 g protein.

*Colorful vegetables, aromatic herbs, and outstanding cheeses make up the green, white, and red layers of this easy party spread.*

# layered pesto-and-cheese spread

prep: 30 minutes   chill: 8 to 24 hours   makes: 16 servings

8    ounces goat cheese
     (chèvre)
1    8-ounce package
     cream cheese,
     softened
¼    cup purchased basil
     pesto
½    cup snipped fresh
     basil leaves
½    cup chopped bottled
     roasted sweet red
     peppers
¼    cup tomato paste
¼    cup snipped dried
     tomato (not oil
     packed)
     Toasted Italian bread
     slices, crackers,
     and/or sliced pears
     Bottled roasted sweet
     red peppers, cut
     into strips (optional)
     Small basil leaves
     (optional)

1 Line one 7½×3½×2½-inch loaf pan with plastic wrap, letting enough excess hang over the sides to cover finished spread. To help keep the wrap in place while spreading, tape down the sides.

2 In a food processor combine goat cheese and cream cheese. Cover and process until smooth. Divide mixture into three equal portions (a generous ½ cup each).

3 To one portion of cheese mixture stir in the pesto; spread in bottom of prepared pan. Sprinkle snipped basil on top. Spoon another portion of cheese mixture over basil and spread carefully. Top with the ½ cup chopped pepper. Stir tomato paste and dried tomato into remaining portion of cheese mixture. Spoon into pan and spread carefully.

4 Cover with plastic wrap and chill for at least 8 hours or up to 24 hours.

5 To serve, fold back plastic wrap and invert onto a small serving platter. Remove and discard plastic wrap. Serve spread with bread slices, crackers and/or pears. If desired, garnish with pepper strips and small basil leaves.

nutrition facts per serving: 122 cal., 11 g total fat (5 g sat. fat), 23 mg chol., 144 mg sodium, 3 g carb., 0 g dietary fiber, 5 g protein.

*Keep this zesty dip warm in a 1- to 2-quart slow cooker. On the warm or low heat setting, it will hold for up to 3 hours.*

# cheese and chorizo dip

start to finish: 20 minutes  makes: 3½ cups

8 ounces uncooked
  chorizo sausage
4 cups shredded sharp
  cheddar cheese
  (1 pound)
½ cup dairy sour cream
½ cup half-and-half or
  light cream
¼ teaspoon crushed
  red pepper
  Tortilla chips

**1** In a heavy large saucepan cook chorizo over medium heat for about 5 minutes or until browned. Drain off fat.

**2** Stir cheese, sour cream, half-and-half, and pepper into chorizo. Cook and stir over low heat until cheese is melted and mixture is combined. Serve with chips.

nutrition facts per ¼ cup: 230 cal., 19 g total fat (11 g sat. fat), 54 mg chol., 408 mg sodium, 1 g carb., 0 g dietary fiber, 12 g protein.

*These quesadillas brim with character thanks to the deep, nutty, and rich flavor of Manchego.*

# manchego-mushroom
## quesadillas

prep: 25 minutes    cook: 2 minutes per batch    oven: 300°F
makes: 4 servings

4   slices bacon, chopped
¼   cup chopped onion
1   clove garlic, minced
8   ounces portobello or
    button mushrooms,
    cut into bite-size
    pieces
¼   teaspoon crushed
    red pepper
¼   teaspoon
    Worcestershire
    sauce
2   tablespoons snipped
    fresh cilantro
1   tablespoon butter,
    cut into 4 pieces
4   ounces Manchego
    or Monterey Jack
    cheese, shredded
    (1 cup)
4   7- or 8-inch flour
    tortillas
½   cup dairy sour cream
⅓   cup chopped tomato
⅓   cup chopped green
    sweet pepper
2   tablespoons sliced
    green onion

1 Preheat oven to 300°F. In a large skillet cook bacon over medium heat until bacon starts to crisp, stirring often. Add onion and garlic. Cook and stir for 5 minutes or until onion is tender. Add mushrooms. Cook and stir until tender. Remove from heat. Stir in crushed red pepper, Worcestershire, and cilantro.

2 In another large skillet or on a griddle melt one piece of the butter over medium heat. For quesadillas, sprinkle ¼ cup cheese over half of each tortilla. Top cheese with ⅓ cup of the mushroom mixture. Fold tortillas in half, pressing gently.

3 In prepared skillet cook one quesadilla for 2 to 3 minutes or until lightly browned, turning once. Remove quesadilla from skillet; place on baking sheet. Keep warm in the oven. Repeat with remaining butter and quesadillas. Place sour cream into a bowl. Sprinkle with tomato, sweet pepper, and green onion. Cut quesadillas into wedges. Serve with sour cream mixture.

nutrition facts per serving: 392 cal., 28 g total fat (14 g sat. fat), 52 mg chol., 683 mg sodium, 23 g carb., 2 g dietary fiber, 13 g protein.

*To sample artisanal blue cheeses, use Point Reyes Farmstead or Maytag blue cheese in this fabulous appetizer.*

# blue cheese—onion tart

prep: 45 minutes   bake: 20 minutes   cool: 15 minutes   oven: 450°F/375°F
makes: 12 servings

½ of a 15-ounce package rolled refrigerated unbaked piecrust (1 crust)
2 tablespoons butter
1 tablespoon packed brown sugar
1 teaspoon vinegar
2 medium onions, quartered lengthwise and thinly sliced
1 cup blue cheese, crumbled (4 ounces)
2 eggs
½ teaspoon dried chervil or marjoram, crushed
¼ teaspoon ground black pepper
⅓ cup milk, half-and-half, or light cream
3 tablespoons dry white wine or chicken broth
2 tablespoons snipped fresh parsley

**1** Preheat oven to 450°F. On a lightly floured surface roll piecrust from center to edge to make a circle about 12 inches in diameter. Ease pastry into a 9-inch tart pan with a removable bottom, pressing dough into fluted sides of tart pan. Trim edge. Do not prick pastry. Line pastry with a double thickness of foil. Bake for 8 minutes. Remove foil. Bake for about 4 minutes more or until crust is dry and set. Reduce oven temperature to 375°F.

**2** Meanwhile, for filling, in a medium skillet melt butter over medium-low heat. Cook and stir brown sugar and vinegar in melted butter until thoroughly combined. Add onions. Cook, uncovered, for 12 to 15 minutes or until onions are tender and lightly browned, stirring occasionally. In a medium mixing bowl combine blue cheese, eggs, chervil, and pepper. Beat with an electric mixer on low speed until combined (cheese will be lumpy). Stir in onion mixture, milk, wine, and parsley. Ladle filling evenly into baked tart shell.

**3** Bake tart in the 375°F oven for about 20 minutes or until a knife inserted near the center comes out clean and pastry is golden. Cool in pan on a wire rack for 15 minutes. Carefully remove side of tart pan. Cut tart into wedges. Serve warm.

nutrition facts per serving: 160 cal., 10 g total fat (3 g sat. fat), 51 mg chol., 234 mg sodium, 12 g carb., 0 g dietary fiber, 4 g protein.

*These appetizers pack all the flavor of a delicious cheese pizza into bite-size puffs.*

# italian
# pepperoni-cheese puffs

prep: 30 minutes   bake: 15 minutes per batch   oven: 450°F
makes: about 40 puffs

1¼  cups water
⅓  cup shortening
1½  cups all-purpose flour
4  eggs
¾  cup finely chopped
    pepperoni
    (3 ounces)
¾  cup finely shredded
    Pecorino-Romano or
    Parmesan cheese
    (3 ounces)
2  tablespoons snipped
    fresh parsley
⅛  teaspoon garlic
    powder
⅛  teaspoon ground
    black pepper
    Purchased pizza
    sauce, warmed
    (optional)

1 Preheat oven to 450°F. Lightly grease two large baking sheets. In a large saucepan combine the water and shortening. Bring to boiling. Add flour all at once, stirring vigorously. Cook and stir until mixture forms a ball. Remove from heat. Cool for 10 minutes. Add eggs, one at a time, beating well with a wooden spoon after each addition. Stir in pepperoni, cheese, parsley, garlic powder, and pepper.

2 Drop dough by rounded teaspoons into small mounds 2 inches apart on prepared baking sheets. Position the two baking sheets on separate oven racks. Bake for 15 to 17 minutes or until firm and golden brown, switching sheets between oven racks halfway through baking. Transfer to a wire rack. Repeat, as needed, for remaining dough. Serve warm. If desired, serve with pizza sauce.

nutrition facts per puff: 57 cal., 4 g total fat (1 g sat. fat), 25 mg chol., 81 mg sodium, 4 g carb., 0 g dietary fiber, 2 g protein.

**make-ahead directions:** Prepare puffs as directed. Cool completely. Place in an airtight container. Cover and freeze for up to 1 month. To serve, thaw in the refrigerator overnight. Arrange puffs on baking sheet. Heat in a 325°F oven for 10 to 15 minutes or until warm.

*It's hard to resist these cheesy, nutty rounds. If you have any left over, crumble them into salads or serve them in place of bread with your favorite soup.*

# cheddar-pecan crackers

prep: 20 minutes   chill: 4 hours   bake: 10 minutes per batch
stand: 30 minutes   oven: 350°F   makes: about 60 crackers

1   cup shredded
     cheddar cheese
     (4 ounces)
¼   cup butter
¼   teaspoon dried
     thyme, crushed
⅛   teaspoon cayenne
     pepper
¾   cup all-purpose flour
½   cup finely chopped
     pecans

**make-ahead directions:**
Layer cooled crackers between waxed paper in an airtight container. Cover and freeze for up to 2 weeks.

**1** In a medium mixing bowl let cheddar cheese and butter stand at room temperature for 30 minutes.

**2** Beat the cheese and butter with an electric mixer on medium speed until well mixed. Add thyme and cayenne pepper. Beat until combined.

**3** Use a wooden spoon to stir in flour and pecans until combined. Form into a ball, using your hands to knead gently if necessary. Shape into an 8-inch-long log. Wrap dough with plastic wrap. Chill about 4 hours or until firm.

**4** Preheat oven to 350°F. Lightly coat a large baking sheet with nonstick cooking spray; set aside. Using a sharp knife, cut log into ⅛-inch-thick slices. Place on prepared baking sheet. Bake about 10 minutes or until lightly browned. Transfer crackers to a wire rack; cool.

nutrition facts per cracker: 26 cal., 2 g total fat (1 g sat. fat), 4 mg chol., 20 mg sodium, 1 g carb., 0 g dietary fiber, 1 g protein.

*Offer these enticing cheese wedges at your next gathering. The rich cheese filling gets a flavor boost from olives, sweet pepper, and green onion.*

# three-cheese quesadillas

start to finish: 30 minutes   makes: 12 servings

3 cups shredded Monterey Jack, Colby Jack, and/or cheddar cheese (12 ounces)

1 3-ounce package cream cheese, softened

⅓ cup crumbled feta cheese (about 1½ ounces)

1 tablespoon snipped fresh oregano or 1 teaspoon dried oregano, crushed

4 8- to 10-inch jalapeno, tomato, and/or plain flour tortillas
Olive oil (optional)

½ cup pitted ripe or pitted kalamata olives, coarsely chopped

¼ cup finely chopped red sweet pepper

2 tablespoons thinly sliced green onion
Fresh oregano sprigs, sliced pitted ripe olives, sliced green onions, and/or sliced cherry tomatoes (optional)
Dairy sour cream, guacamole, and/or salsa (optional)

**1** For filling, in a medium bowl stir together shredded cheese, cream cheese, feta cheese, and snipped or dried oregano. If desired, lightly brush one side of each tortilla with oil.

**2** Divide filling among tortillas, spreading over one half of the side without oil. Top filling with olives, pepper, and green onion. Fold tortillas in half, pressing gently.

**3** Preheat an indoor electric grill. If using a covered grill, place 1 tortilla on grill rack; close lid. Grill for 4 minutes or until golden brown and cheese is melted. Repeat with remaining tortillas. For an uncovered grill, place 2 tortillas on grill rack. Grill over medium heat for 6 minutes or until golden brown and cheese is melted, turning once. Repeat with remaining tortillas. Cut each tortilla into three wedges.

**4** If desired, garnish quesadillas with sprigs of fresh oregano, sliced olives, additional green onion, and/or cherry tomatoes. If desired, serve warm with sour cream, guacamole, and/or salsa.

nutrition facts per serving: 179 cal., 13 g total fat (8 g sat. fat), 37 mg chol., 310 mg sodium, 6 g carb., 0 g dietary fiber, 9 g protein.

*The special salty bite from the golden Parmesan shells complements the peppery arugula mixture that goes inside. Using finely shredded cheese creates crispy shells.*

# arugula salad with pancetta
# in parmesan crisps

prep: 45 minutes   bake: 12 minutes per batch   oven: 300°F
makes: 12 servings

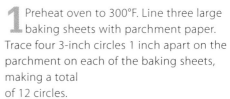

2   6-ounce packages
    finely shredded
    Parmesan cheese
    (3 cups)
¼   teaspoon ground
    black pepper
4   ounces pancetta,
    chopped
4   teaspoons olive oil
1   tablespoon fig
    vinegar, port wine
    vinegar, or raspberry
    balsamic vinegar
1½  teaspoons chopped
    shallot
¼   teaspoon Dijon-style
    mustard
    Salt
    Ground black pepper
2   cups arugula
3   hard-cooked eggs,
    quartered

**1** Preheat oven to 300°F. Line three large baking sheets with parchment paper. Trace four 3-inch circles 1 inch apart on the parchment on each of the baking sheets, making a total of 12 circles.

**2** For crisps, in a medium bowl combine Parmesan cheese and ¼ teaspoon pepper. Divide ¼ cup each of mixture among circles. Bake, one baking sheet at a time, for about 12 minutes or until golden. Balance two long-handled wooden spoons across a 15×10×1-inch baking pan. Quickly drape baked circles over spoon handles. Cool for 10 minutes. Carefully transfer to a wire rack; cool completely.

**3** In a large skillet cook pancetta over medium heat until crisp. Drain pancetta on paper towels.

**4** For dressing, in a small screw-top jar combine olive oil, vinegar, shallot, and mustard. Cover and shake well. Season to taste with salt and pepper.

**5** In a large bowl toss arugula with dressing. Divide arugula among baked crisps. Sprinkle each serving with some of the pancetta; top each with an egg quarter.

nutrition facts per serving: 185 cal., 14 g total fat (7 g sat. fat), 80 mg chol., 722 mg sodium, 1 g carb., 0 g dietary fiber, 14 g protein.

*The French call these little cheese-flavored pastries* gougère, *and they're a classic hors d'oeuvre. Crisp on the outside and soft and custardy on the inside, they're terrific hot out of the oven with chilled white wine or Champagne.*

# mini gruyère puffs

prep: 15 minutes  bake: 20 minutes  stand: 3 minutes  oven: 450°F/375°F
makes: about 20 puffs

½  cup water
¼  cup butter
½  teaspoon dried basil, crushed
¼  teaspoon garlic salt
   Dash ground red pepper
½  cup all-purpose flour
2  eggs
½  cup shredded Gruyère or Swiss cheese (2 ounces)
2  tablespoons grated Parmesan cheese

**1** Preheat oven to 450°F. In a small saucepan combine the water and butter. Add basil, garlic salt, and red pepper. Bring to boiling over medium heat, stirring to melt butter. Add flour all at once, stirring vigorously. Cook and stir until mixture forms a ball that doesn't separate. Remove from heat. Cool 5 minutes.

**2** Grease a baking sheet. Add eggs, one at a time, to saucepan, beating with a spoon after each addition until smooth. Stir in Gruyère cheese. Drop mounds of dough by rounded teaspoons, about 2 inches apart, on a prepared baking sheet. Sprinkle with Parmesan cheese.

**3** Bake for 10 minutes. Reduce oven temperature to 375°F. Bake puffs for 10 to 12 minutes more or until puffed and golden. Turn off oven. Let puffs remain in oven for 3 minutes. Serve hot.

nutrition facts per puff: 53 cal., 4 g total fat (2 g sat. fat), 31 mg chol., 76 mg sodium, 2 g carb., 0 g dietary fiber, 2 g protein.

**make-ahead directions:** Prepare puffs as directed. Cool completely. Place in an airtight container. Cover and freeze for up to 1 month. To serve, thaw in the refrigerator overnight. Arrange puffs on baking sheet. Heat in a 325°F oven for 10 to 15 minutes or until warm.

*Be sure to serve these morsels fresh from the broiler to assure the cheese mixture is at its most flavorful and retains its melt-in-the-mouth texture.*

# brandied blue cheese, walnut, and pear crostini

prep: 10 minutes   broil: 2 minutes   stand: 30 minutes
makes: 8 to 12 servings

| | |
|---|---|
| ½ | cup crumbled blue cheese (4 ounces) |
| 2 | tablespoons butter |
| 1 | to 2 tablespoons brandy |
| ¼ | cup chopped walnuts |
| 16 | ¼-inch-thick baguette-style French bread slices, toasted |
| 1 | ripe medium pear, cored and thinly sliced |
| ½ | cup shredded white cheddar cheese or mozzarella cheese (2 ounces) |

**1** In a small bowl let blue cheese and butter stand at room temperature for 30 minutes. Mash with a fork until well mixed. Stir in brandy and walnuts.

**2** Preheat broiler. Top bread slices with pear slices. Spoon about 1 tablespoon of the blue cheese mixture over the pear on each bread slice. Sprinkle each with cheddar cheese.

**3** Place bread slices on a baking sheet. Broil 4 to 5 inches from heat for about 2 minutes or until the cheese is bubbly. Serve warm.

nutrition facts per serving: 282 cal., 13 g total fat (7 g sat. fat), 26 mg chol., 566 mg sodium, 30 g carb., 2 g dietary fiber, 10 g protein.

**make-ahead directions:** Toast French bread slices and place in an airtight container. Cover and store at room temperature for up to 2 days. Prepare blue cheese mixture as directed in Step 1. Spoon into an airtight container. Cover. Store in the refrigerator for up to 2 days. Assemble as directed.

*Use olive oil infused with herbs or roasted garlic for extra flavor in these crowd-pleasing morsels.*

# marinated mozzarella
## with basil

prep: 25 minutes  stand: 30 minutes  makes: 15 servings

¼ cup fresh basil leaves
¼ cup olive oil
2 tablespoons balsamic vinegar
1 teaspoon coarsely ground black pepper
1 teaspoon finely shredded lemon peel
¼ teaspoon salt
1 pound fresh mozzarella cheese
Tomato slices (optional)
Baguette-style French bread slices or crackers

**1** Set aside several whole basil leaves for garnish. Using a sharp knife, chop remaining basil. In a medium bowl combine chopped basil, oil, vinegar, pepper, lemon peel, and salt. Cut mozzarella into 1-inch cubes; toss cheese cubes gently with herb and oil mixture until cheese is well coated. Cover and let stand for 30 minutes before serving.

**2** Transfer cheese mixture to a serving dish. Garnish with reserved basil leaves and tomato slices, if desired. Serve with baguette slices or crackers.

nutrition facts per serving: 121 cal., 10 g total fat (5 g sat. fat), 21 mg chol., 130 mg sodium, 1 g carb., 0 g dietary fiber, 5 g protein.

**make-ahead directions:** Prepare as directed in Step 1. Cover and chill for up to 5 days. Let stand at room temperature for 30 minutes before serving.

*Make an extra batch of these to munch on as snacks. Store the toasts in an airtight container for up to 3 days.*

# parmesan toasts

start to finish: 25 minutes  oven: 400°F  makes: about 36 toasts

2  tablespoons butter
2  tablespoons olive oil
1  clove garlic, minced
1  10-ounce loaf
   baguette-style
   French bread, cut
   diagonally into
   ¼-inch-thick slices
½  cup finely shredded
   Parmigiano-
   Reggiano cheese
   (2 ounces)

**1** Preheat oven to 400°F. In a small saucepan combine butter, oil, and garlic. Cook over medium heat until butter melts. Remove from heat.

**2** Brush butter mixture lightly over both sides of bread slices. Arrange bread slices in a single layer on a large baking sheet. Sprinkle with Parmigiano-Reggiano cheese.

**3** Bake for 8 to 10 minutes or until bread slices are lightly browned and crisp. Serve warm or at room temperature.

nutrition facts per toast: 38 cal., 2 g total fat (1 g sat. fat), 2 mg chol., 69 mg sodium, 4 g carb., 0 g dietary fiber, 1 g protein.

*You'll find Armenian cracker bread in the cracker or specialty bread section of your supermarket.*

# pear-walnut
## cheese spirals

prep: 25 minutes  chill: 4 hours  stand: 45 minutes  makes: about 20 spirals

1   15-inch round
    Armenian cracker
    bread (lahvosh)
6   cups fresh spinach
    leaves
1   ripe medium pear
2   tablespoons butter
⅓   cup finely chopped
    green onion or
    shallot
⅓   cup finely chopped
    walnuts, toasted
1½  8-ounce tubs cream
    cheese with chive
    and onion
½   teaspoon salt
¼   to ½ teaspoon freshly
    cracked black
    pepper
    Fresh spinach leaves
    (optional)

**1** Hold cracker bread under cool running water until thoroughly wet. Place between wet, clean kitchen towels; let stand for about 45 minutes or until soft enough to fold without breaking.

**2** Meanwhile, finely chop the 6 cups spinach leaves. Peel, core, and finely chop pear. In a large skillet melt butter over medium heat. Cook and stir spinach, pear, and green onion in hot butter until spinach wilts and pear is tender. Stir in nuts. Remove from skillet. Cool.

**3** In a medium bowl combine cream cheese, salt, and pepper. Spread onto cracker bread. Carefully spread spinach mixture onto cream cheese. Roll up cracker bread; wrap in plastic wrap. Chill for 4 hours.

**4** To serve, cut roll into ½-inch-thick slices. If desired, line serving platter with additional spinach leaves; arrange spirals on platter.

nutrition facts per spiral: 117 cal., 8 g total fat (5 g sat. fat), 20 mg chol., 180 mg sodium, 8 g carb., 2 g dietary fiber, 2 g protein.

**make-ahead directions:** Prepare as directed through Step 3, except chill for up to 24 hours. Serve as directed in Step 4.

*The bold mouthwatering taste of these savory bites comes from the rich smoky cheddar. If you're not fond of smoked cheese, use an aged or sharp cheddar for an intense flavor.*

# smoked cheese
# triangles

prep: 25 minutes    bake: 12 minutes per batch    oven: 400°F
makes: 32 triangles

2    cups all-purpose flour
2    teaspoons baking powder
¾    teaspoon lemon-pepper seasoning (optional)
⅛    teaspoon salt
3    tablespoons butter
4    ounces smoked cheddar cheese, finely shredded (1 cup)
¾    cup milk
1    tablespoon milk

**1** Preheat oven to 400°F. Lightly grease two baking sheets. In a large bowl stir together flour, baking powder, lemon-pepper seasoning (if desired), and salt. Using a pastry blender, cut in butter until coarse crumbs form. Stir in half of the cheese. Add the ³/₄ cup milk, stirring just until flour mixture is moistened. Form into a ball, using your hands to knead gently if necessary.

**2** On a lightly floured surface roll dough to a 10-inch square about ¼ inch thick. Brush with the 1 tablespoon milk. Sprinkle with remaining cheese; lightly press cheese into dough. Cut into sixteen 2½-inch squares. Cut each square in half diagonally to make 32 triangles. Place on the prepared baking sheets.

**3** Bake for 12 to 15 minutes or until golden. Serve warm.

nutrition facts per triangle: 53 cal., 2 g total fat (1 g sat. fat), 7 mg chol., 56 mg sodium, 6 g carb., 0 g dietary fiber, 2 g protein.

**make-ahead directions:** Prepare as directed, except cool completely on a wire rack. Layer between waxed paper in an airtight container. Cover. Store in the refrigerator for up to 2 days or freeze for up to 1 month. To serve, preheat oven to 325°F. Arrange chilled or frozen triangles on an ungreased baking sheet. Bake for 6 to 8 minutes or until heated through. Serve warm.

*Two 7- to 8-ounce rounds of Brie can be used instead of the larger cheese round. Bake them for 10 to 12 minutes or until the cheese is softened. That way you can serve one round and then replenish with the second warmed cheese.*

# baked brie with caramelized
# onions and hazelnuts

prep: 25 minutes  bake: 15 minutes  oven: 325°F  makes: 8 to 10 servings

2 tablespoons butter
½ cup chopped yellow onion
1 15-ounce round Brie cheese
3 tablespoons apricot preserves
¼ cup chopped hazelnuts (filberts) or pecans
  Baguette-style French bread slices and/or sliced apples or pears

**1** For caramelized onion, in a small saucepan melt butter over low heat. Cover and cook onion in hot butter for 10 to 15 minutes or until tender and golden, stirring occasionally.

**2** Preheat oven to 325°F. Place Brie on an ovenproof plate or baking sheet. Spread apricot preserves on top. Top with caramelized onion and sprinkle with nuts.

**3** Bake for 15 to 20 minutes or until cheese softens. If baked on baking sheet, carefully transfer warm Brie from baking sheet to a serving platter. Serve with French bread slices and/or sliced fruit.

nutrition facts per serving: 254 cal., 20 g total fat (11 g sat. fat), 61 mg chol., 355 mg sodium, 7 g carb., 1 g dietary fiber, 12 g protein.

**make-ahead directions:** Prepare caramelized onions as directed in Step 1. Cover and chill for up to 24 hours. Allow to stand at room temperature for 30 minutes. Bake Brie as directed. For the Cranberry-Onion Chutney, prepare as directed. Cover and chill for up to 24 hours. Allow to stand at room temperature for 1 hour before using. Serve as directed over warm plain Brie.

**baked brie with cranberry-onion chutney and pistachios:** Prepare caramelized onions as directed in Step 1, except for Cranberry-Onion Chutney, after cooking the onions for only 5 minutes, stir in ²/₃ cup fresh cranberries, 3 tablespoons sugar, 1 tablespoon pepper jelly, 1 tablespoon water, and ¹/₂ teaspoon finely shredded orange peel. Simmer, uncovered, for 10 to 15 minutes or until cranberries pop and mixture thickens, stirring occasionally. Set chutney mixture aside. Place Brie on the ovenproof plate. Omit the preserves and hazelnuts in Step 2. Bake the plain Brie as directed in Step 3. Top the warm Brie with the chutney and sprinkle with ¹/₄ cup chopped pistachio. Serve with French bread slices.

*Slow-roasted garlic, sweet onions, and balsamic vinegar blend to make an irresistible jam topping for tangy blue cheese and walnut crackers.*

# walnut-gorgonzola coins

chill: 1 hour  bake: 8 minutes  oven: 425°F  makes: 75 appetizers

1½ cups all-purpose flour
¼ teaspoon ground black pepper
½ cup butter, softened
4 ounces Gorgonzola or blue cheese, crumbled (1 cup)
¼ cup finely chopped toasted walnuts
2 teaspoons Dijon-style mustard
1 recipe Sweet Onion Jam

**1** In a medium mixing bowl combine flour and pepper. Add butter, Gorgonzola cheese, walnuts, and mustard. Beat with an electric mixer on medium speed until the dough comes together. Divide the dough into thirds and roll each portion into an 8×1-inch log. Wrap logs in plastic wrap and chill for at least 1 hour or freeze for up to 2 months.

**2** Preheat oven to 425°F. Line 2 baking sheets with parchment paper. Slice logs into ¼-inch slices. Place slices 1 inch apart on prepared baking sheets. Bake 8 to 10 minutes or until golden brown. Cool on wire racks. Top coins with Sweet Onion Jam and serve immediately.

nutrition facts per appetizer: 38 cal., 2 g total fat (1 g sat. fat), 5 mg chol., 33 mg sodium, 4 g carb., 0 g dietary fiber, 1 g protein.

sweet onion jam: Preheat oven to 325°F. Cut off about ¼ inch of the pointed top of one whole garlic bulb to expose individual cloves. Place bulb, cut end up, in a custard cup. Drizzle with 1 teaspoon olive oil. Cover with foil and bake for 45 to 60 minutes or until garlic cloves feel soft when pressed. Cool. Gently squeeze garlic paste from individual cloves into a saucepan. Stir in 1 cup finely chopped sweet onion, ½ cup finely chopped Granny Smith apple, ½ cup balsamic vinegar, and ½ cup sugar. Bring to boiling over medium-high heat, stirring occasionally; reduce heat. Simmer, uncovered, about 30 minutes, stirring occasionally, until onion and apple turn transparent and mixture thickens. Cool. Transfer to a covered container and chill up to 1 week. Makes about ¾ cup.

**make-ahead directions:** Prepare coins as directed. Cool completely. Layer between sheets of waxed paper in an airtight container. Cover and freeze for up to 3 months. To thaw, let stand at room temperature for 15 minutes. Prepare Sweet Onion Jam. Cover and refrigerate for up to 1 week.

*Chipotle peppers are dried, smoked jalapeños. They're most often sold packed in cans in adobo sauce—a tomato-based sauce that also usually contains garlic, herbs, and vinegar. Look for chipotles in adobo sauce in the Latin or Mexican section of your supermarket.*

# chipotle-cheddar
## cheesecake with chunky salsa

prep: 50 minutes   chill: 4 hours   bake: 32 minutes   stand: 1 hour
oven: 375°F   makes: 16 servings

4   8-inch flour tortillas
3   tablespoons butter, melted
2   8-ounce packages cream cheese, softened
1   cup finely shredded cheddar cheese
¼   cup milk
1   canned chipotle chile pepper in adobo sauce, drained and finely chopped
½   teaspoon dried oregano, crushed
2   eggs, lightly beaten
1   recipe Chunky Salsa
1   recipe Chipotle Chips

**make-ahead directions:**
Prepare Chunky Salsa. Cover and chill for up to 24 hours. Prepare Chipotle Chips. Store in an airtight container for up to 3 days.

**1** Preheat oven to 375°F. Place tortillas on a baking sheet. Bake for 12 to 14 minutes or until golden brown. Cool. Cut tortillas into pieces. Transfer to a food processor or blender. Cover and process or blend until finely ground. Measure 1 cup of the tortilla crumbs, discarding any remaining crumbs.

**2** In a small bowl combine the tortilla crumbs and melted butter. Press crumb mixture onto the bottom of a greased 9-inch springform pan.

**3** For filling, in a large mixing bowl beat cream cheese, cheddar cheese, milk, chipotle pepper, and oregano with an electric mixer until well combined. Mix in eggs just until combined. Carefully spread filling evenly into crust-lined pan. Bake for about 20 minutes or until center is just set.

**4** Cool in pan on a wire rack for 15 minutes. Loosen crust from sides of pan. Cool for 30 minutes more. Remove sides of pan. Cool completely on a wire rack. Cover and chill for at least 4 hours or up to 48 hours.

**5** Let cheesecake stand at room temperature for 1 hour before serving. Using a slotted spoon, spread the Chunky Salsa over the cheesecake. Serve with Chipotle Chips.

nutrition facts per serving: 263 cal., 20 g total fat (10 g sat. fat), 71 mg chol., 289 mg sodium, 14 g carb., 1 g dietary fiber, 7 g protein.

chunky salsa: In a medium bowl combine 4 roma tomatoes, seeded and chopped; ⅓ cup chopped red onion; 2 green onions, thinly sliced; 2 tablespoons snipped fresh cilantro or parsley; 1 clove garlic, minced; 1 tablespoon lime juice; ¼ teaspoon salt; and ⅛ teaspoon ground black pepper.

chipotle chips: Preheat oven to 375°F. In a small bowl combine ¼ cup cooking oil and 1 to 2 teaspoons drained and finely chopped canned chipotle peppers in adobo sauce; brush over one side of eight 8-inch flour tortillas. Cut each tortilla into 8 wedges. Arrange wedges in a single layer on baking sheets. Bake for 12 to 14 minutes or until light brown. Transfer to a wire rack and let cool.

8

embellished

bre

From breadsticks and bruschetta to pizza and flatbread, these hearty appetizers come with fresh, invigorating toppers and serve-along dips that add unexpected flair to a gathering.

ads

_Your guests will think you spent hours on these tasty, flaky gems. Using refrigerated crescent rolls is your shortcut secret._

## creamy bacon-filled
# crescents

prep: 25 minutes  bake: 12 minutes  oven: 375°F  makes: 16 crescents

4  slices bacon, finely chopped
1  8-ounce package cream cheese, softened
½  cup freshly grated Parmesan cheese
¼  cup thinly sliced green onion
1  tablespoon milk
2  8-ounce packages refrigerated crescent rolls (8 rolls each)
1  egg
1  tablespoon water
1  to 2 teaspoons poppy seeds
   Fresh chives (optional)

**1** Preheat oven to 375°F. In a skillet, cook bacon until crisp. Drain on paper towels. Line a large baking sheet with parchment paper. In a medium bowl combine bacon, cream cheese, Parmesan cheese, green onion, and milk until mixture is nearly smooth; set aside.

**2** Unroll and separate crescent rolls into 16 triangles. Spread each triangle with some of the cream cheese mixture. Roll up from the wide end of the triangle. Place on prepared baking sheet.

**3** In a small bowl beat egg with the water until combined. Brush crescents with the egg mixture; sprinkle with poppy seeds.

**4** Bake for about 12 minutes or until puffed and light golden brown. If desired, garnish with chives. Serve warm.

nutrition facts per crescent: 188 cal., 13 g total fat (6 g sat. fat), 33 mg chol., 358 mg sodium, 12 g carb., 0 g dietary fiber, 5 g protein.

**make-ahead directions:** Prepare as directed through Step 2. Cover and chill on prepared baking sheet for up to 5 hours. (Or, freeze in a single layer until firm. Place in a self-sealing plastic freezer bag and freeze for up to 1 month. To bake, line a baking sheet with parchment paper. Arrange frozen filled crescents in a single layer on prepared baking sheet.) To bake chilled or frozen crescents, preheat oven to 375°F. Bake crescents for 14 to 16 minutes or until golden and heated through.

*Kalamata olives are an imported Greek black olive that you may wish to include in the tapenade. The three colors come from the green and black olives and the red sweet pepper.*

# tricolor **tapenade** toasts

start to finish: 20 minutes  makes: 12 toasts

¼ cup pitted ripe olives, such as kalamata
¼ cup pimiento-stuffed green olives
¼ cup bottled roasted red sweet pepper
1 teaspoon snipped fresh oregano
1 teaspoon olive oil
¼ teaspoon ground black pepper
12 baguette-style French bread slices, toasted, or melba toast rounds
6 ounces soft goat cheese (chèvre)

**1** For tapenade, in a food processor combine olives, sweet pepper, oregano, oil, and black pepper. Cover and pulse until coarsely chopped.

**2** To serve, spread toasted bread slices with goat cheese. Top with the tapenade.

nutrition facts per toast: 65 cal., 4 g total fat (2 g sat. fat), 7 mg chol., 171 mg sodium, 4 g carb., 1 g dietary fiber, 3 g protein.

**make-ahead directions:** Prepare tapenade as directed in Step 1. Transfer to an airtight container. Cover. Chill for up to 2 days. Toast French bread slices and store in an airtight container at room temperature for up to 2 days.

*Four easy flavor-packed toppers make classic bruschetta different and delicious. Part of the fun will be presenting party guests with an array of choices.*

# bruschetta sampler

prep: 25 minutes   bake: 7 minutes   oven: 425°F   makes: 8 to 10 servings

1   8-ounce loaf
      baguette-style
      French bread
2   tablespoons olive oil
      Ground black pepper
1   recipe Fresh Tomato
      and Olive Topping;
      Shrimp Topping;
      Basil, Pesto, and
      White Bean Topping;
      and/or Dried Fig and
      Pistachio Topping

**1** Preheat oven to 425°F. For crostini, bias-slice bread into ½-inch-thick slices. Arrange slices in a single layer on an ungreased baking sheet. Lightly brush one side of each bread slice with oil. Lightly sprinkle oiled side of bread with pepper. Bake, uncovered, for 4 minutes. Turn slices over and bake for 3 to 4 minutes more or until crisp and light brown.

**2** Prepare one or more of the toppings. Spoon onto toasted bread just before serving.

nutrition facts per serving with basil, pesto, and white bean topping: 282 cal., 18 g total fat (4 g sat. fat), 36 mg chol., 503 mg sodium, 24 g carb., 3 g dietary fiber, 9 g protein.

**make-ahead directions:** Cool toasts. Place in an airtight container and store at room temperature for up to 24 hours.

**fresh tomato and olive topping:** *In a small bowl combine 1 cup seeded and finely chopped tomato (2 medium); 1 cup coarsely chopped assorted pitted ripe olives (such as kalamata, Greek, or Mission); 1/3 cup finely chopped red onion; 2 tablespoons snipped fresh cilantro or parsley; 2 tablespoons balsamic vinegar or red wine vinegar; and 2 cloves garlic, minced.*

**shrimp topping:** *In a medium bowl combine 8 ounces peeled and deveined cooked shrimp, chopped; 1 tablespoon olive oil; 2 teaspoons white wine vinegar, 1/4 teaspoon salt, and 1/4 teaspoon ground black pepper; set aside. Halve 2 large cloves of garlic and rub toasts with cut sides before topping with shrimp mixture.*

**basil, pesto, and white bean topping:** *In a small bowl combine a 9-ounce container (1 cup) basil pesto; 1 finely chopped hard-cooked egg; and 1 teaspoon lemon juice, sherry vinegar, or red wine vinegar. In another small bowl combine 1/2 of a 19-ounce can cannellini (white kidney) beans or 1/2 of a 15-ounce can Great Northern beans, rinsed and drained (1 cup); 1 tablespoon thinly sliced green onion or chopped shallot; 1 tablespoon olive oil; and 1/8 teaspoon crushed red pepper.*

**dried fig and pistachio topping:** *In a medium mixing bowl combine 3-ounces cream cheese, 2 ounces fontina or provolone cheese, and 3 ounces goat cheese (chèvre). Let stand at room temperature for 30 minutes. In a small bowl combine 1/4 cup snipped dried figs and 1 tablespoon balsamic vinegar. Let stand at room temperature for 30 minutes. Beat cheese mixture with an electric mixer on low speed until well combined. Stir in figs. Serve with 1/4 cup chopped pistachios.*

*Traditional panzanella, a bread salad, combines pieces of bread with veggies, herbs, and dressing. The bread and salad notion takes to savory pita chips topped with a salad of shredded greens and a Mediterranean mix of chopped veggies and seasonings.*

# panzanella bruschetta

prep: 25 minutes   stand: 15 minutes   makes: about 30 servings

1½   cups shredded baby salad greens
8   small red and/or yellow cherry or pear-shape tomatoes, quartered, or ½ cup chopped seeded tomato
¼   cup finely shredded Parmesan cheese
¼   cup chopped seeded cucumber
2   tablespoons finely chopped red onion
2   tablespoons snipped fresh basil
1   tablespoon capers, rinsed and drained
1   small clove garlic, minced
2   teaspoons red wine vinegar
2   teaspoons olive oil
    Dash salt
    Dash ground black pepper
1   recipe Baked Pita Chips

**1** In a medium bowl combine salad greens, tomatoes, Parmesan cheese, cucumber, onion, basil, capers, and garlic. Sprinkle with vinegar, oil, salt, and pepper; toss gently to coat. Let stand for 15 to 30 minutes for flavors to blend.

**2** to serve, top Baked Pita Chips with the greens mixture.

nutrition facts per serving: 24 cal., 1 g total fat (0 g sat. fat), 0 mg chol., 57 mg sodium, 4 g carb., 0 g dietary fiber, 1 g protein.

**make-ahead directions:** Store Baked Pita Chips in an airtight container at room temperature for up to 1 week or freeze for up to 3 months. Thaw chips, covered, at room temperature.

baked pita chips: Preheat oven to 350°F. Split three large pita bread rounds in half horizontally. Lightly coat the rough sides of each pita bread half with nonstick cooking spray; sprinkle each half with ½ to ³/₄ teaspoon onion powder, garlic powder, or ground black pepper. Cut each half into six wedges. Arrange wedges in a single layer on baking sheets. Bake for 10 to 12 minutes or until crisp; cool on wire racks.

*Crostini is a fancy name for baguette slices that have been brushed with oil and baked until golden brown. For a quick and easy appetizer, layer this tasty combo on the toasts.*

# ham and brie crostini

prep: 15 minutes  bake: 11 minutes  oven: 425°F  makes: 30 servings

1  16-ounce loaf baguette-style French bread, cut into ½-inch-thick slices
   Olive oil
1  4½- to 5-ounce round Brie cheese
1½ cups chopped, seeded roma tomato
1  cup finely chopped cooked ham (about 6 ounces)
2  tablespoons olive oil
2  tablespoons white balsamic vinegar
1  teaspoon dried oregano, crushed
1  teaspoon bottled minced garlic or 2 cloves garlic, minced
½  cup finely shredded Italian-blend cheese (2 ounces)

**1** Preheat oven to 425°F. For crostini, lightly brush both sides of each bread slice with oil. Place slices on an ungreased baking sheet. Bake for 5 to 7 minutes or until crisp and light brown, turning once.

**2** Meanwhile, use a vegetable peeler to remove edible rind from Brie cheese. Finely cube cheese. In a medium bowl combine Brie, tomato, ham, 2 tablespoons oil, vinegar, oregano, and garlic. Toss to combine. Spoon mixture onto bread slices. Sprinkle with Italian-blend cheese. Bake for 6 to 8 minutes or until heated through.

nutrition facts per serving: 93 cal., 4 g total fat (1 g sat. fat), 8 mg chol., 246 mg sodium, 11 g carb., 1 g dietary fiber, 5 g protein.

**make-ahead directions:** Slice and bake bread as directed. Store in a large resealable plastic bag for up to 24 hours.

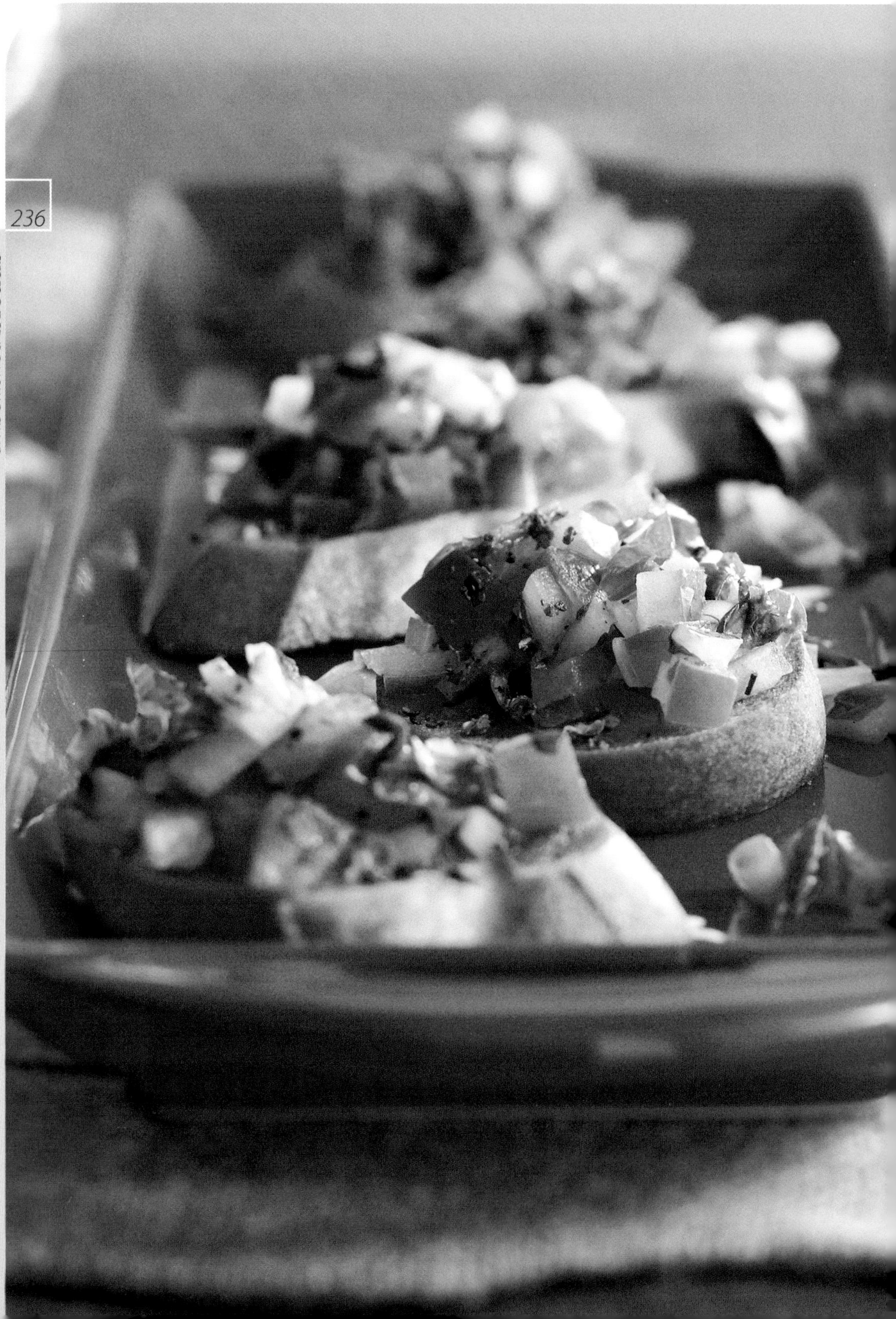

*This Italian-inspired appetizer—toasted bread with a tomato-relish topper—makes a fresh, flavorful addition to a party buffet.*

# bruschetta with
# tomato and arugula

prep: 25 minutes  stand: 1 hour  bake: 7 minutes  oven: 425°F
makes: 24 servings

2   medium tomatoes,
      seeded and
      chopped (1½ cups)
½   cup chopped arugula
      leaves
1   small onion, finely
      chopped
¼   cup snipped fresh
      basil
1   clove garlic, minced
1   tablespoon olive oil
1   tablespoon balsamic
      vinegar
¼   teaspoon salt
¼   teaspoon ground
      black pepper
1   8-ounce loaf
      baguette-style
      French bread
2   to 3 tablespoons
      olive oil

**1** In a medium bowl combine tomatoes, arugula, onion, basil, garlic, 1 tablespoon olive oil, balsamic vinegar, salt, and pepper. Let stand at room temperature for 1 hour.

**2** Meanwhile, preheat oven to 425°F. Slice bread diagonally into ½-inch slices. Lightly brush both sides with the 2 to 3 tablespoons olive oil. Place on a baking sheet. Bake for 5 to 7 minutes or until crisp and light brown, turning once. Cool on a wire rack.

**3** To serve, top toasted bread slices with tomato mixture. Serve immediately.

nutrition facts per serving: 46 cal., 2 g total fat (0 g sat. fat), 0 mg chol., 87 mg sodium, 6 g carb., 0 g dietary fiber, 1 g protein.

**make-ahead directions:** Toast bread slices as directed in Step 2. Place in an airtight container. Cover. Store at room temperature for up to 24 hours.

*Mascarpone cheese, commonly used in tiramisu, a popular Italian dessert, adds rich and creamy qualities to the bean dip. Many supermarkets carry the specialty cheese in small tubs in the refrigerator section.*

# crostini with shrimp and white bean puree

start to finish: 30 minutes   makes: 24 servings

1   8-ounce loaf baguette-style French bread, cut diagonally into ½-inch-thick slices
     Olive oil
24   fresh or frozen large shrimp in shells (about 1 pound)
1   15-ounce can cannellini (white kidney) beans, rinsed and drained
½   cup finely chopped yellow sweet pepper
3   tablespoons snipped fresh chives
2   cloves garlic, minced
⅓   cup mascarpone cheese or cream cheese
¼   teaspoon salt
     Dash ground white pepper
     Fresh chives, cut into ½-inch pieces

**1** Preheat oven to 400°F. Lightly brush both sides of bread slices with oil. Arrange bread slices on baking sheets. Bake for about 8 minutes or until lightly browned, turning once. Cool.

**2** Thaw shrimp, if frozen. Peel and devein shrimp, leaving tails intact, if desired. Rinse shrimp. In a large saucepan cook shrimp in a large amount of boiling salted water for 1 to 3 minutes or until shrimp are opaque. Drain. Rinse shrimp with cold water; drain well. Transfer to a serving bowl. Cover and chill until needed.

**3** Meanwhile, in a food processor or blender combine beans, sweet pepper, snipped chives, and garlic. Cover and process for 1 to 2 minutes or until creamy. Add mascarpone cheese, salt, and white pepper. Cover and process until well mixed. Transfer to a serving bowl.

**4** Spoon about 1 rounded teaspoon of the bean mixture onto each crostini and top with a shrimp. Garnish with chive pieces.

nutrition facts per serving: 64 cal., 2 g total fat (1 g sat. fat), 13 mg chol., 125 mg sodium, 8 g carb., 1 g dietary fiber, 4 g protein.

**make-ahead directions:** Prepare baguette as directed in Step 1. Place in an airtight container and store at room temperature for up to 3 days. Prepare shrimp as directed in Step 2. Cover and store in the refrigerator for up to 3 days.

*Tangy goat cheese, sautéed mushrooms and shallots, and a balsamic reduction give the toasted baguettes many layers of flavor.*

# goat cheese and
# fresh mushroom crostini

prep: 30 minutes   bake: 15 minutes   cook: 8 minutes   oven: 425°F/375°F
makes: 30 servings

1   8-ounce loaf
    baguette-style
    French bread, cut
    into ⅛-inch-thick
    slices
2   tablespoons olive oil
2   tablespoons butter
4   shallots, coarsely
    chopped (about
    1½ cups), or 1½
    cups coarsely
    chopped onion
8   ounces fresh cremini
    mushrooms,
    coarsely chopped
    (about 1½ cups)
1   tablespoon packed
    brown sugar
3   tablespoons balsamic
    vinegar
1   tablespoon snipped
    fresh fresh thyme
¼   teaspoon salt
¼   teaspoon ground
    black pepper
6   ounces goat cheese
    (chèvre)
2   tablespoons snipped
    fresh parsley
    (optional)

**1** Preheat oven to 425°F. Arrange baguette slices on a large baking sheet. Lightly brush one side of each slice with some of the oil. Bake for 5 minutes. Turn slices over and bake 2 to 4 minutes more or until light brown. Remove from oven. Cool. Reduce oven temperature to 375°F.

**2** Meanwhile, in a medium saucepan melt butter over medium-high heat. Cook shallots in hot butter for 3 minutes. Add the mushrooms and brown sugar. Cook and stir for 1 minute. Add the balsamic vinegar, thyme, salt, and pepper. Bring to boiling; reduce heat. Cook, uncovered, for 4 minutes or until most of the liquid evaporates, stirring frequently.

**3** Spread some of the goat cheese on each bread slice. Bake for about 8 minutes or until cheese is warmed through. Remove from oven. Top each with some of the mushroom-shallot mixture. Drizzle any remaining cooking liquid over crostini. If desired, sprinkle each with parsley. Serve immediately.

nutrition facts per serving: 63 cal., 3 g total fat (2 g sat. fat), 5 mg chol., 94 mg sodium, 6 g carb., 0 g dietary fiber, 2 g protein.

*Firm-textured bread creates a sturdy base for the lemon-cucumber sandwiches, making them easy to pick up so your guests can mingle.*

# cucumber canapés

start to finish: 30 minutes  makes: 24 appetizers

½ of a medium English cucumber, very thinly sliced (1 cup)
½ cup thinly sliced red onion
½ teaspoon finely shredded lemon peel
2 teaspoons lemon juice
¼ teaspoon salt
¼ teaspoon ground black pepper
6 slices firm-textured white and/or whole wheat bread
¼ cup butter, softened
½ cup dairy sour cream
1 tablespoon snipped fresh chives

**1** In a medium bowl combine cucumber, onion, lemon peel, lemon juice, salt, and pepper; toss gently to combine.

**2** If desired, remove crusts from bread slices. Cut each bread slice diagonally into quarters. (Or use 2- to 2½-inch decorative cutters to cut shapes from bread slices.) Spread butter onto one side of each piece of bread; top each with some of the cucumber mixture.

**3** In a small bowl combine sour cream and chives. Spoon a little of the sour cream mixture on top of each canapé. If desired, garnish each canapé with additional finely shredded lemon peel. Serve immediately or cover and chill for up to 2 hours.

nutrition facts per appetizer: 45 cal., 3 g total fat (2 g sat. fat), 7 mg chol., 74 mg sodium, 4 g carb., 0 g dietary fiber, 1 g protein.

*Toast points can serve as a versatile base for all types of appetizers. Try different kinds of bread. For make-ahead ease, make the toast points ahead of time and store in an airtight container for up to 24 hours.*

# smoked salmon toasts

prep: 20 minutes  bake: 14 minutes  oven: 325°F  makes: 32 toasts

8   slices pumpernickel
    bread
2   tablespoons butter,
    melted
1   8-ounce package
    cream cheese,
    softened
1   tablespoon lemon
    juice
1   4-ounce piece
    smoked salmon,
    skin and bones
    removed, flaked
1   3.5-ounce jar capers,
    drained
1   hard-cooked egg,
    chopped
¼   cup finely chopped
    red onion
    Fresh dill sprigs
    (optional)

1 Preheat oven to 325°F. Remove crusts from bread slices. Flatten bread slices with a rolling pin. Cut each slice into four squares. Brush each bread piece on both sides with melted butter. Press each bread piece into a 1³/₄-inch muffin cup. Bake for 14 minutes. Remove toast cups immediately from muffin cups and place on a wire rack to cool.

2 In a medium bowl combine cream cheese and lemon juice. Fold in salmon, capers, egg, and onion until combined. Spoon heaping tablespoons of salmon mixture into toast cups. Serve immediately or chill for 1 to 2 hours. If desired, garnish with dill sprigs.

nutrition facts per toast: 59 cal., 4 g total fat (2 g sat. fat), 17 mg chol., 201 mg sodium, 4 g carb., 1 g dietary fiber, 2 g protein.

*A nice toasted-cheese flavor makes these an impressive appetizer, especially if you serve them with dipping sauce. Freeze leftover breadsticks to serve another day with soup or salad.*

## easy parmesan
# breadsticks

prep: 15 minutes  bake: 10 minutes  oven: 375°F  makes: 6 to 8 servings

½  of a 12-ounce loaf
   baguette-style
   French bread
¼  cup olive oil
6  tablespoons grated
   or finely shredded
   Parmesan cheese
   Purchased marinara
   sauce, warmed,
   and/or flavored oils
   (such as lemon-,
   basil-, or garlic-
   flavored)

**1** Preheat oven to 375°F. Line a 15×10×1-inch baking pan with foil; lightly coat foil with cooking spray.

**2** Cut bread in half lengthwise, then cut into ¼- to ½-inch strips. (Cut bread so there is crust on each strip.) Place bread strips on the prepared baking sheet. Drizzle with oil; turn to coat. Sprinkle with Parmesan cheese.

**3** Bake for 10 to 12 minutes or until browned and crisp. Serve with marinara sauce and/or flavored oils for dipping.

nutrition facts per serving: 219 cal., 13 g total fat (3 g sat. fat), 4 mg chol., 539 mg sodium, 20 g carb., 2 g dietary fiber, 5 g protein.

*Pepper adds the bite to these breadsticks. Gauge your tolerance for heat as you decide how much pepper to use.*

# cracked pepper
## breadsticks

prep: 25 minutes  bake: 10 minutes  oven: 450°F  makes: 32 breadsticks

2   cups all-purpose flour
1   tablespoon baking
      powder
1   to 1½ teaspoons
      cracked black
      pepper
¼   teaspoon salt
⅓   cup butter
⅔   cup beef or chicken
      broth

**1** Preheat oven to 450°F. In a medium bowl stir together flour, baking powder, pepper, and salt. Cut in butter until mixture resembles coarse crumbs. Make a well in the center. Add broth; stir just until dough clings together.

**2** Turn dough out onto a lightly floured surface. Knead gently for 10 to 12 strokes. Divide dough into 8 equal portions. Divide each portion into fourths. Roll each piece into a 10-inch-long rope. Fold each rope in half; twist 2 or 3 times. Arrange twists on an ungreased baking sheet.

**3** Bake for 5 minutes. Turn and bake for 5 to 6 minutes more or until brown. Serve warm or cool completely on a wire rack before serving.

nutrition facts per breadstick: 44 cal., 2 g total fat (1 g sat. fat), 5 mg chol., 54 mg sodium, 6 g carb., 0 g dietary fiber, 1 g protein.

**make-ahead directions:** Wrap cooled breadsticks in foil. Freeze for up to 1 week. To reheat, bake wrapped breadsticks in 350°F oven for about 10 minutes or until warm.

*Buttery sweet yet enticingly salty, prosciutto di Parma is a salt-cured, air-dried ham available in large supermarkets and gourmet specialty shops.*

# prosciutto- and basil-wrapped
# breadsticks

prep: 20 minutes  bake: 12 minutes  oven: 375°F
makes: 12 breadsticks

1  11-ounce package refrigerated breadsticks (12)
1  to 3 tablespoons desired toppings (dried basil or dried thyme, crushed; dried minced onion; paprika; and/ or cracked black pepper)
4  ounces very thinly sliced prosciutto
  Tiny fresh basil leaves (optional)

**1** Preheat oven to 375°F. Line a baking sheet with parchment paper or foil. Shape each breadstick into a 12-inch-long rope. Sprinkle desired toppings on pieces of waxed paper; roll breadsticks in toppings to coat.

**2** Place breadsticks on the prepared baking sheet, twisting several times and pressing ends slightly onto baking sheet. Bake for about 12 minutes or until golden brown.

**3** Cut prosciutto lengthwise into 1-inch-wide strips. Wrap prosciutto strips loosely around breadsticks. If desired, garnish with fresh basil leaves.

nutrition facts per breadstick: 89 cal., 2 g total fat (1 g sat. fat), 7 mg chol., 440 mg sodium, 13 g carb., 0 g dietary fiber, 5 g protein.

*Infused with natural hardwood smoke, smoked cheddar adds a bold, mouthwatering taste to these spunky little muffins. Use regular cheddar cheese for milder flavor.*

# smoked cheddar
## mini muffins

prep: 25 minutes  bake: 8 minutes  cool: 5 minutes  oven: 425°F
makes: 18 to 20 mini muffins

½ cup all-purpose flour
½ cup yellow cornmeal
2 tablespoons sugar
1½ teaspoons baking
   powder
⅛ teaspoon salt
   Dash cayenne pepper
¾ cup shredded smoked
   cheddar cheese
   (3 ounces)
1 egg
½ cup milk
2 tablespoons cooking
   oil or 2 tablespoons
   butter, melted
   Assorted toppings
   (poppy seeds,
   sesame seeds, thin
   strips bottled roasted
   red sweet pepper,
   shredded smoked
   cheddar cheese)

1 Preheat oven to 425°F. Lightly grease eighteen to twenty 1¾-inch muffin cups; set aside.

2 In a medium bowl combine flour, cornmeal, sugar, baking powder, salt, and cayenne pepper. Stir in the ¾ cup cheese. In a small bowl combine egg, milk, and oil. Add egg mixture all at once to flour mixture. Stir just until moistened (batter should be lumpy). Batter will thicken upon standing.

3 Spoon batter into prepared muffin cups, filling three-fourths full. Sprinkle with desired topping.

4 Bake for 8 to 10 minutes or until a wooden toothpick inserted in centers comes out clean. Cool in muffin cups on a wire rack for 5 minutes. Remove from muffin cups. Serve warm.

nutrition facts per mini muffin: 71 cal., 4 g total fat (1 g sat. fat), 17 mg chol., 86 mg sodium, 7 g carb., 0 g dietary fiber, 2 g protein.

**make-ahead directions:** Prepare as directed. Store in an airtight container at room temperature for up to 24 hours. To reheat, preheat oven to 350°F. Wrap muffins in foil. Bake for about 10 minutes or until warmed. Serve immediately.

*Lemon- and dill-flavored crab on melted Swiss cheese toasts—the perfect cocktail companions. You can also cook the sandwiches on a panini press.*

# toasted crab
## sandwiches

prep: 30 minutes   cook: 6 minutes   broil: 1 minute   makes: 16 servings

1   8-ounce package flake-style imitation crabmeat, broken up
2   tablespoons mayonnaise
2   tablespoons dairy sour cream
2   tablespoons chopped green onion
1   tablespoon snipped fresh dill
2   teaspoons lemon juice
3   tablespoons butter, softened
⅛   teaspoon cayenne pepper
4   English muffins, split
4   slices Swiss cheese

**1** Preheat broiler. In a medium bowl combine imitation crabmeat, mayonnaise, sour cream, green onion, dill, and lemon juice; set aside. In a small bowl combine butter and cayenne pepper.

**2** Generously spread outsides of English muffin halves with butter mixture. Place four of the muffin halves, buttered sides down, on a baking sheet. Top with cheese. Broil 4 to 5 inches from the heat for 1 to 2 minutes or until cheese starts to melt.

**3** Spoon crab mixture onto cheese-topped muffin halves, spreading to edges. Top with the remaining muffin halves, buttered sides up.

**4** Heat a large griddle or skillet over medium heat. Add sandwiches; cook for about 6 minutes or until muffins are golden brown, turning once. Cut each sandwich into four portions.

nutrition facts per serving: 109 cal., 6 g total fat (3 g sat. fat), 16 mg chol., 224 mg sodium, 9 g carb., 0 g dietary fiber, 4 g protein.

*These open-face treats have the delicious flavor of a classic grilled Reuben and then some, thanks to the addition of caramelized onions tinged with cream and sherry.*

# mini **reuben** melts

prep: 30 minutes  bake: 30 minutes  broil: 4 minutes  oven: 375°F
makes: 16 servings

32  slices party pumpernickel bread
1  to 2 tablespoons olive oil
6  ounces thinly sliced corned beef
1  recipe Creamy Caramelized Onions
4  ounces thinly sliced Gruyère cheese, cut into 2-inch squares
⅓  cup bottled Thousand Island salad dressing

1 Preheat broiler.

2 Brush one side of each bread slice with oil. Place half of bread slices oiled side up on a large baking sheet. Broil about 5 inches from the heat for 1 to 2 minutes or until lightly toasted. Remove from oven. Turn bread slices over. Divide corned beef and caramelized onions equally among bottom slices. Top with Gruyère cheese. Broil for 2 to 3 minutes or until heated through and cheese starts to melt. Transfer to a serving platter.

3 Place the remaining bread slices oiled side up on the baking sheet. Broil for 1 to 2 minutes or until lightly toasted.

4 Spoon a small amount of salad dressing onto the bottom of each sandwich. Top with the remaining bread slices.

nutrition facts per serving: 142 cal., 9 g total fat (3 g sat. fat), 21 mg chol., 324 mg sodium, 10 g carb., 1 g dietary fiber, 6 g protein.

creamy caramelized onions: Preheat oven to 375°F. In a large heavy ovenproof skillet heat 4 teaspoons olive oil over medium-high heat. Add 1 pound onions, thinly sliced; cook for 8 to 10 minutes or until lightly browned, stirring frequently. In a small bowl combine ⅓ cup whipping cream; ¼ cup dry sherry; 2 tablespoons Dijon-style mustard; 1 tablespoon packed brown sugar; 1 clove garlic, minced; ¼ teaspoon salt; ¼ teaspoon ground allspice; and ¼ teaspoon ground black pepper. Pour mixture over onions. Stir to combine. Bake for about 30 minutes or until golden brown and bubbly.

*Add a sophisticated note to your appetizer assortment with toasted date bread slices topped with sweet persimmon and sharp blue cheese. Your shortcut secret is using a bread mix.*

# fruit, cheese, and **bread** bites

prep: 20 minutes  bake: per package directions  broil: 6 minutes
cool: 10 minutes  oven: 375°F  makes: about 30 appetizers

1   16.6-ounce package date quick bread mix
2   medium ripe persimmons or pears, cored and thinly sliced
8   ounces blue cheese, sliced or crumbled
¼   cup honey

**1** Preheat oven to 375°F. Grease the bottoms of three 5x3x2-inch loaf pans; set aside. Prepare quick bread mix according to package directions. Pour batter into the prepared pans, spreading evenly. Bake according to package directions. Cool in pans on wire racks for 10 minutes. Remove from pans. Cool completely on wire racks.

**2** Preheat broiler. Cut bread loaves into ½-inch-thick slices. Arrange slices on a large baking sheet. Broil 3 to 4 inches from the heat for 4 to 6 minutes or until toasted, turning once.

**3** Arrange persimmon slices on top of toasted bread slices. Add cheese. Broil for about 2 minutes more or until cheese melts. Before serving, drizzle with honey.

nutrition facts per appetizer: 115 cal., 4 g total fat (2 g sat. fat), 20 mg chol., 171 mg sodium, 17 g carb., 1 g dietary fiber, 3 g protein.

*Assemble this hero-size crowd-pleasing sandwich ahead so you can bake and slice it just before guests arrive. Raisins lend a pleasing sweetness to the savory ham-and-cheese filling.*

# ham **stromboli** spirals

prep: 45 minutes  rise: 30 minutes  bake: 30 minutes  cool: 30 minutes
oven: 350°F  makes: 24 servings

| | |
|---|---|
| 1 | 16-ounce package bread roll mix |
| ½ | teaspoon dried basil, crushed |
| 8 | ounces cooked ham, chopped (2 cups) |
| 1½ | cups shredded baby Swiss or Gouda cheese (6 ounces) |
| ⅔ | cup raisins or dried cranberries |
| 2 | tablespoons butter, softened |
| 1 | egg |
| 1 | tablespoon water Bottled marinara sauce (optional) |

**1** Line a 15×10×1-inch baking pan with foil; grease foil. Set aside. Prepare hot roll mix according to package directions, except stir the basil into the flour mixture. Knead as directed. Divide dough in half. Cover. Let rest for 5 minutes.

**2** Meanwhile, for filling, in a medium bowl combine ham, Swiss cheese, and raisins. Gently toss to mix.

**3** On a lightly floured surface roll each dough half into a 10x8-inch rectangle. Spread 1 tablespoon of the butter over each dough rectangle, leaving a 1-inch plain border. Sprinkle each rectangle evenly with filling.

**4** Carefully fold edges of short sides over filling about 1 or 2 inches. Roll up, beginning from a long side. Lightly moisten edges and ends with water and pinch to seal. Carefully place loaves, seam side down, on the prepared baking pan. Cover. Let rise in a warm place until nearly double in size (about 30 minutes). (Or cover loaves loosely with plastic wrap; chill overnight. Let stand at room temperature for 20 minutes before baking.)

**5** Preheat oven to 350°F. In a small bowl combine egg and the water. Brush over loaves. Bake for about 30 minutes or until golden brown. Cool on a wire rack for 30 minutes before cutting into ½-inch slices. If desired, serve with marinara sauce for dipping.

nutrition facts per serving: 140 cal., 5 g total fat (2 g sat. fat), 30 mg chol., 303 mg sodium, 18 g carb., 0 g dietary fiber, 7 g protein.

*Crunchy crisp bacon and salty tangy blue cheese complement the sweet onions on toasted baguette slices. Cooking the onions very slowly over low heat makes all the difference.*

# onion, bacon, and blue cheese crisps

start to finish: 35 minutes   makes: 24 servings

4   slices bacon
2   large Vidalia or other sweet onions, quartered and thinly sliced (about 3 cups)
8   ounces baguette-style French bread, cut into ¼-inch-thick slices
2   tablespoons olive oil
⅔   cup crumbled blue cheese
     Fresh thyme leaves

**1** In a large skillet cook bacon over medium heat until crisp. Drain bacon on paper towels, reserving drippings in the skillet. Crumble bacon; set aside. Reduce heat to medium low.

**2** Add onion to reserved drippings. Cook for 15 to 20 minutes or until onion is very tender and golden brown, stirring occasionally.

**3** Meanwhile, preheat broiler. Brush baguette slices on both sides with oil. Arrange in a single layer on a large baking sheet. Broil 3 to 4 inches from heat for 4 minutes, turning once, until lightly toasted.

**4** Divide onion mixture evenly among baguette slices. Sprinkle with blue cheese and crumbled bacon. Broil for 2 to 3 minutes or until cheese begins to melt. Sprinkle with thyme. Serve warm.

nutrition facts per serving: 91 cal., 5 g total fat (2 g sat. fat), 7 mg chol., 169 mg sodium, 8 g carb., 1 g dietary fiber, 3 g protein.

*Even a handful of convenience products can deliver an extraordinary pizza when you add shrimp and roasted red peppers as toppers. Tomato pesto is the hidden ingredient that lends fabulous flavor to the Alfredo sauce.*

# shrimp and roasted pepper pizza

prep: 25 minutes  bake: 20 minutes  oven: 375°F  makes: 32 (2-slice) servings

1 pound fresh or frozen peeled cooked medium shrimp
1 12-ounce jar Alfredo pasta sauce
2 tablespoons purchased dried tomato pesto
1 recipe Homemade Pizza Dough (recipe, page 258)
½ cup grated Parmigiano-Reggiano cheese
1 12-ounce jar roasted red sweet peppers, drained and cut into strips
3 tablespoons pine nuts

1 Thaw shrimp, if frozen. Preheat oven to 375°F.

2 In a small bowl combine Alfredo sauce and pesto. Spread evenly over dough circles. Sprinkle with Parmigiano-Reggiano cheese. Top pizzas with roasted peppers and the shrimp. Sprinkle with pine nuts.

3 Bake for 20 to 25 minutes or until crust bottom is crisp and brown. Cut each pizza into eight wedges. Serve immediately.

nutrition facts per serving: 108 cal., 5 g total fat (2 g sat. fat), 42 mg chol., 152 mg sodium, 11 g carb., 1 g dietary fiber, 6 g protein.

*To pit olives, place one or two at a time under the flat side of a broad knife and press down firmly.*

# lemon-olive-
# cheese toasts

prep: 20 minutes  marinate: 1 to 24 hours  stand: 30 minutes
bake: 5 minutes  oven: 450°F  makes: 26 toasts

1 cup pitted kalamata olives
¾ cup pitted green olives
3 tablespoons capers, rinsed and drained
2 tablespoons lemon juice
2 cloves garlic, quartered
3 tablespoons olive oil
2 teaspoons finely shredded lemon peel
¼ teaspoon crushed red pepper
6 ounces goat cheese (chèvre)
1 8-ounce loaf baguette-style French bread, cut into ¼-inch-thick slices
2 tablespoons olive oil

**1** In a food processor combine kalamata and green olives, capers, lemon juice, and garlic. Cover and process while gradually adding the 3 tablespoons oil, stopping to scrape down side of food processor occasionally. Mixture should be finely chopped, not smooth. Transfer mixture to a medium bowl. Stir in lemon peel and crushed red pepper. Cover and chill for 1 to 24 hours to blend flavors.

**2** Let olive mixture and cheese stand at room temperature for 30 minutes before serving.

**3** Meanwhile, preheat oven to 450°F. Brush both sides of bread slices with the 2 tablespoons oil. Arrange in single layer on baking sheets. Bake for 5 to 7 minutes or until browned.

**4** To serve, spread bread slices with cheese and top with olive mixture.

nutrition facts per toast: 90 cal., 6 g total fat (1 g sat. fat), 3 mg chol., 287 mg sodium, 6 g carb., 1 g dietary fiber, 2 g protein.

*Fans of fresh mushrooms—the more the merrier in this recipe— will devour this scrumptious two-cheese pizza. Try a combination of shiitake, chanterelle, cremini, and portobello.*

# mixed **mushrooms** pizza

prep: 30 minutes  bake: 12 minutes  oven: 425°F  makes: 16 servings

1  16-ounce loaf frozen bread dough, thawed
2  tablespoons olive oil
6  cups sliced assorted fresh mushrooms (about 1 pound)
⅓  cup snipped assorted fresh herbs (oregano, basil, and/or parsley) or 2 teaspoons dried Italian seasoning, crushed
3  cloves garlic, minced
¼  teaspoon salt
1  cup shredded provolone cheese (4 ounces)
¼  cup finely shredded Parmesan cheese

**1** Preheat oven to 425°F. Grease a 15×10×1-inch baking pan. On a lightly floured surface roll bread dough into a 15×10-inch rectangle. (If dough is difficult to roll out, let it rest a few minutes.) Transfer dough to prepared baking pan. Prick dough all over with a fork. Let dough stand for 5 minutes. Bake for about 10 minutes or until lightly browned. Cool slightly.

**2** Meanwhile, in a very large skillet heat oil over medium heat. Cook mushrooms, herbs, garlic, and salt in hot oil for 6 to 8 minutes or just until mushrooms are tender. Sprinkle provolone and Parmesan cheeses over crust. Top with mushroom mixture.

**3** Bake for 12 to 15 minutes more or until the edges turn golden and pizza heats through. Cut into squares.

nutrition facts per serving: 127 cal., 5 g total fat (2 g sat. fat), 6 mg chol., 255 mg sodium, 15 g carb., 1 g dietary fiber, 5 g protein.

*If you're hosting a large gathering, go for a big-batch recipe like this. It's easy to put these rich and cheesy morsels together by the dozens, and each little bite is loaded with flavor.*

# smoked chicken
## and mushroom bites

prep: 25 minutes  bake: 25 minutes  cool: 20 minutes  oven: 375°F
makes: 36 appetizers

1   tablespoon butter
⅔   cup finely chopped onion
1½  cups thinly sliced assorted fresh mushrooms (cremini, chanterelle, and/or button)
3   cloves garlic, minced
1   cup finely chopped smoked chicken
½   cup thinly sliced fresh basil
5   ounces fontina or Havarti cheese, shredded (1¼ cups)
6   eggs
1½  cups half-and-half or light cream
¼   teaspoon salt
¼   teaspoon ground black pepper
36  slices baguette-style French bread, toasted

**1** Preheat oven to 375°F. Line a 13×9×2-inch baking pan with foil; grease foil.* Set aside.

**2** In a large skillet melt butter over medium heat. Cook onion in hot oil for 2 minutes. Add mushrooms and garlic. Cook and stir for about 5 minutes or until mushrooms are tender and any excess water has evaporated. Remove from heat.

**3** In a large bowl combine smoked chicken and basil. Add mushroom mixture. Toss just until mixed. Spoon chicken mixture into prepared baking pan, spreading evenly. Sprinkle with cheese. In another large bowl whisk eggs, half-and-half, salt, and pepper. Carefully pour egg mixture over chicken mixture in baking pan.

**4** Bake for 25 to 30 minutes or until set. Cool in pan on a wire rack for 20 minutes. Cut into 36 squares and serve on toasted baguette slices.

nutrition facts per appetizer: 119 cal., 4 g total fat (2 g sat. fat), 46 mg chol., 259 mg sodium, 15 g carb., 1 g dietary fiber, 6 g protein.

*note: If you prefer, use nonstick foil and omit greasing the foil.

*This quick-to-fix pizza appetizer uses an Italian bread shell for the crust. Prebaking the shell for 5 minutes creates a nice crisp crust.*

# fontina cheese and
# artichoke pizza

prep: 15 minutes  bake: 13 minutes  oven: 450°F  makes: 12 servings

1   tablespoon olive oil or
    cooking oil
1   medium red onion,
    thinly sliced
2   cloves garlic, minced
1   12-inch Italian bread
    shell (such as Boboli
    brand)
1½  cups shredded
    fontina or Swiss
    cheese (6 ounces)
½   of a 9-ounce package
    frozen artichoke
    hearts, thawed and
    cut up
½   cup pitted kalamata
    olives, halved or
    quartered
    Ground black pepper
    Purchased Alfredo
    pasta sauce,
    warmed (optional)

1 Preheat oven to 450°F. In a medium skillet heat oil over medium heat. Cook onion and garlic in hot oil for 2 to 3 minutes or until tender and golden brown, stirring occasionally.

2 Place the bread shell on a lightly greased baking sheet. Bake shell for 5 minutes.

3 Sprinkle hot bread shell with ½ cup of the cheese. Arrange artichokes, olives, and cooked onion mixture on top of cheese. Sprinkle with the remaining cheese. Sprinkle lightly with pepper.

4 Bake for 8 to 10 minutes more or until cheese melts and pizza heats through. Cut into wedges. If desired, serve pizza with warm Alfredo sauce.

nutrition facts per serving: 184 cal., 9 g total fat (3 g sat. fat), 19 mg chol., 390 mg sodium, 19 g carb., 1 g dietary fiber, 8 g protein.

*Start with a single batch of dough and explore a world of flavors with toppings so intriguing and tasty, they'll all become favorites.*

# pick-a-topper
## appetizer flatbreads

prep: 45 minutes (flatbread); 10 to 15 minutes (topper)  rise: 45 minutes
stand: 10 minutes  bake: 10 minutes per batch  oven: 450°F  makes: 9 flatbreads

1¼  cups warm water
     (105°F to 115°F)
  2  tablespoons olive oil
  1  package active dry
     yeast
  1  teaspoon sugar
3¼  to 3½ cups all-
     purpose flour
  1  teaspoon salt
     Cornmeal
     Desired toppings
     (opposite page)

**1** In a medium bowl combine the warm water, oil, yeast, and sugar. Stir to dissolve yeast. Let stand for about 10 minutes or until foamy.

**2** Meanwhile, in a large bowl combine 2¾ cups of the flour and the salt. Stir yeast mixture into flour mixture until combined. Stir in as much of the remaining flour as you can.

**3** Turn dough out onto a lightly floured surface. Knead in enough of the remaining flour to make a soft dough that is smooth and elastic (3 to 5 minutes).

**4** Place dough in an oiled bowl, turning once to grease surface of dough. Cover and let rise in a warm place until double in size (45 to 60 minutes).

**5** Preheat oven to 450°F. Punch down dough. Turn dough out onto a lightly floured surface. Divide dough into nine equal portions. Cover and let rest for 10 minutes. Roll each portion into a 9x4-inch oval. (Cover remaining dough while working so it doesn't dry out.)

**6** Sprinkle a baking sheet with cornmeal. Place three ovals, crosswise, on the prepared baking sheet. Top each oval with desired toppings. Bake for about 10 minutes or until golden brown. Repeat with the remaining dough.

nutrition facts per flatbread without any topper: 202 cal., 4 g total fat (0 g sat. fat), 0 mg chol., 261 mg sodium, 37 g carb., 1 g dietary fiber, 5 g protein.

**sweet potato–sage:** *Brush dough with 2 teaspoons olive oil. Top with 5 to 6 thin slices sweet potato, 2 teaspoons snipped fresh sage, 1 tablespoon crumbled crisp-cooked pancetta, 2 teaspoons maple syrup, and a sprinkle of sea salt and ground black pepper.*

**blue cheese–pear:** *In a medium skillet cook ½ cup thinly sliced sweet onion in 1 tablespoon hot vegetable oil over medium-low heat until tender and golden brown. Spread onions on dough. Top with 5 or 6 slices thinly sliced pear and sprinkle with 2 tablespoons blue cheese.*

**sausage–green olive:** *Spread 2 table-spoons pizza sauce on dough. Top with 2 tablespoons cooked Italian sausage, 1 table-spoon sliced green olives, and 2 tablespoons shredded mozzarella cheese.*

**barbecue chicken:** *Spread 2 tablespoons barbecue sauce on dough. Top with ¼ cup shredded cooked chicken, 1 tablespoon chopped green sweet pepper, and 2 table-spoons shredded Monterey Jack cheese.*

**apple-bacon:** *Top dough with 5 or 6 thin slices apple. Sprinkle with 1 slice crumbled crisp-cooked bacon. Drizzle with 2 teaspoons maple syrup. If desired, sprinkle with 2 tablespoons shredded white cheddar cheese.*

**thai peanut-chicken:** *Combine 2 table-spoons bottled peanut sauce, ¼ cup shredded cooked chicken, and 1 tablespoon shredded carrot. Spoon onto dough. Sprinkle with 1 bias-sliced green onion.*

**rosemary-potato:** *Sprinkle dough with 2 tablespoons shredded Raclette or Gruyère cheese. Top with 5 or 6 slices cooked red-skinned potato. Sprinkle with ½ teaspoon snipped fresh rosemary, dash sea salt, and a few grinds of black pepper. Drizzle with 1 to 2 teaspoons olive oil.*

**chutney-grape-pistachio:** *Spread 2 tablespoons chutney on dough. Top with 10 halved seedless red grapes and 1 table-spoon coarsely chopped pistachios.*

**balsamic–cremini–goat cheese:** *In a medium skillet cook ½ cup sliced cremini mushrooms in 2 teaspoons hot vegetable oil until nearly tender. Add 1 tablespoon balsamic vinegar and continue cooking until liquid evaporates and mushrooms are tender. Spread mushrooms over dough. Sprinkle with 2 tablespoons goat cheese and ½ teaspoon thyme leaves. Just before serving, drizzle with 1 teaspoon balsamic vinegar.*

*Using an egg adds richness to this pizza dough. You'll also note several risings that occur, which yield a lighter, tastier crust. Be sure to cover the dough during risings to keep it moist.*

# homemade pizza dough

prep: 20 minutes  rise: 50 minutes  makes: 8 (7-inch pizzas)

1  package active dry yeast
1  cup warm water (105°F to 115°F)
1  egg
3  tablespoons olive oil
¼  teaspoon salt
3½  to 4 cups all-purpose flour

**1** In a small bowl combine yeast with warm water. Let stand for 5 minutes.

**2** In a large mixing bowl combine egg, oil, and salt. Stir in the yeast mixture. Add 1¼ cups of the flour. Beat with an electric mixer on low speed for 30 seconds, scraping bowl constantly. Beat on high speed for 3 minutes. Using a wooden spoon, stir in as much of the remaining flour as you can.

**3** Turn dough out onto a lightly floured surface. Knead in enough remaining flour to make a moderately stiff dough that is smooth and elastic (6 to 8 minutes total). Lightly grease a large bowl; place dough in bowl. Cover and let dough rise in a warm place until double in size (30 minutes).

**4** Punch dough down. Turn dough out onto a lightly floured surface. Divide dough into 8 portions; roll each portion into a 7-inch circle. Place dough circles on greased baking sheets. Cover and let rise for 20 minutes.

*The peppery bite of arugula teams beautifully with the flavorful prosciutto, crunchy walnuts, and double-cheese topper.*

# prosciutto and arugula
## pizza

prep: 30 minutes   bake: 20 minutes   oven: 375°F   makes: 32 (2-slice) servings

16   thin slices prosciutto di Parma, cut in thin strips
1   recipe Homemade Pizza Dough (recipe, page 258)
3   tablespoons coarsely chopped walnuts
2   cups shredded smoked mozzarella cheese (8 ounces)
¾   cup grated Parmigiano-Reggiano cheese
1   cup arugula, torn if desired

**1** Preheat oven to 375°F. Arrange prosciutto evenly over dough circles. Sprinkle with walnuts. Combine mozzarella and Parmigiano-Reggiano cheeses and sprinkle over each pizza.

**2** Bake for 20 to 25 minutes or until crust bottom is crisp and brown. Cool in pans on a wire rack for 5 minutes. Top with arugula. Cut each pizza into eight wedges. Serve immediately.

nutrition facts per serving: 99 cal., 4 g total fat (2 g sat. fat), 16 mg chol., 214 mg sodium, 10 g carb., 1 g dietary fiber, 5 g protein.

*What's the key to making this savory bread? It's taking advantage of timesaving hot roll mix, already crumbled blue cheese, chopped ripe olives, and bottled minced garlic.*

# easy olive focaccia

prep: 20 minutes   bake: 20 minutes   cool: 10 minutes   oven: 375°F
makes: 32 servings

1   16-ounce package hot
    roll mix
3   tablespoons olive oil
1   teaspoon bottled
    minced garlic
    (2 cloves)
1   tablespoon snipped
    fresh rosemary
½   to 1 teaspoon kosher
    salt
¼   teaspoon ground
    black pepper
½   cup crumbled blue
    cheese (2 ounces)
½   cup chopped pitted
    ripe olives

**1** Lightly grease a 15×10×1-inch baking pan; set aside.

**2** Prepare hot roll mix according to package directions, except substitute 2 tablespoons of the olive oil for the butter or margarine called for on the package. Knead dough and allow to rest as directed. Preheat oven to 375°F.

**3** On a lightly floured surface roll dough to a 15x10-inch rectangle. Carefully transfer dough to prepared baking pan; use your fingers to push dough into corners and sides. Using your fingertips, press indentations randomly into dough.

**4** In a small bowl combine the remaining 1 tablespoon oil and the garlic; brush over dough. In another small bowl combine rosemary, salt, and pepper. Sprinkle over dough. Sprinkle dough with blue cheese and olives. Press cheese and olives gently into the dough. Bake for about 20 minutes or until golden. Cool in pan on a wire rack for 10 minutes. Using a wide spatula, lift focaccia from baking pan; place on a wire rack and cool completely. Serve within 2 hours.

nutrition facts per serving: 73 cal., 2 g total fat (0 g sat. fat), 8 mg chol., 166 mg sodium, 11 g carb., 0 g dietary fiber, 2 g protein.

**make-ahead directions:** Place cooled focaccia in an airtight container or freezer bag; seal bag. Freeze for up to 3 months.

*With a sweet onion and mild, nutty Gouda cheese topper, this pizza is destined to become a party favorite.*

# gouda and red onion
## pizza

prep: 25 minutes   bake: 12 minutes   oven: 400° F   makes: 12 (1-slice) servings

2   tablespoons olive oil
1   large red onion,
       halved lengthwise
       and thinly sliced
       (about 2 cups)
1   tablespoon snipped
       fresh thyme or
       1 teaspoon dried
       thyme, crushed
¼   teaspoon salt
¼   teaspoon ground
       black pepper
1   tablespoon cornmeal
1   13.8-ounce package
       refrigerated pizza
       dough
8   ounces Gouda or
       Edam cheese,
       shredded (2 cups)

**1** Preheat oven to 400°F. In a large skillet heat 1 tablespoon oil over medium heat. Cook onion in hot oil for 5 to 7 minutes until onion is tender but not brown, stirring often. Remove from heat. Stir in thyme, salt, and pepper.

**2** Grease a baking sheet and sprinkle with the cornmeal. Pat pizza dough into a 12x8-inch rectangle on the baking sheet. Brush pizza dough with remaining 1 tablespoon oil. Sprinkle pizza dough with Gouda cheese to within ½ inch of edges. Spoon onion mixture over the cheese.

**3** Bake for 12 to 15 minutes or until crust is golden. Cut into 12 pieces.

nutrition facts per serving: 166 cal., 9 g total fat (4 g sat. fat), 22 mg chol., 308 mg sodium, 15 g carb., 1 g dietary fiber, 7 g protein.

stuffed

mor

Give a new twist to
ever-popular deviled
eggs or stuffed mush-
rooms, or discover
vibrant, fresh-tasting
ways to fill dates,
tomatoes, peppers,
endive, and more.

9

sels

*For a dramatic presentation, nestle red Belgian endive leaves inside regular Belgian endive leaves, then spoon the cheese mixture into the leaves. You'll need two to three heads of each type of Belgian endive.*

# blue cheese–
## stuffed endive

start to finish: 30 minutes   makes: 18 servings (2 filled leaves per serving)

1   8-ounce tub fat-free cream cheese

½   cup crumbled blue cheese (2 ounces)

¼   cup finely chopped green onion or fresh chives

2   slices bacon, crisp cooked, drained, and crumbled

2   tablespoons hazelnuts (filberts) or walnuts, toasted and finely chopped*

36   Belgian endive leaves (about 3 heads)

**1** In a medium bowl combine cream cheese, blue cheese, green onion, bacon, and nuts.

**2** Spoon 2 teaspoons of the cheese mixture into each Belgian endive leaf.

nutrition facts per serving: 35 cal., 2 g total fat (1 g sat. fat), 6 mg chol., 71 mg sodium, 1 g carb., 0 g dietary fiber, 3 g protein.

*note: To toast hazelnuts, preheat oven to 350°F. Spread hazelnuts in a single layer in a shallow baking pan. Bake for about 10 minutes or until toasted, stirring once. Place the warm nuts on a clean kitchen towel. Rub the nuts with the towel to remove the loose skins.

**make-ahead directions:** Prepare as directed in Step 1. Cover and chill for up to 4 hours. Continue as directed in Step 2.

*Score the cucumber for a striking presentation. Simply run a fork lengthwise across the surface to form a decorative pattern.*

# lemon-dill crabmeat
## salad on cucumber rounds

prep: 15 minutes   chill: 1 hour   makes: 6 to 8 servings (about 32 rounds)

1   6½-ounce can lump crabmeat, drained, or 8 ounces peeled, deveined, cooked shrimp, finely chopped, rinsed, and patted dry
¼   cup mayonnaise
1   green onion, finely chopped
1   tablespoon finely snipped fresh dill
1   teaspoon finely shredded lemon peel
¼   teaspoon bottled hot pepper sauce
⅛   teaspoon salt
1   English cucumber, cut into ½-inch-thick slices and chilled
    Paprika
    Fresh dill sprigs (optional)

**1** In a medium bowl combine crabmeat, mayonnaise, green onion, snipped dill, lemon peel, hot pepper sauce, and salt. Cover and chill for 1 hour or up to 8 hours.

**2** If desired, lightly salt cucumber slices. Spoon some of the crabmeat mixture onto chilled cucumber rounds. Sprinkle each with paprika. If desired, garnish with dill sprigs.

nutrition facts per serving: 103 cal., 8 g total fat (1 g sat. fat), 31 mg chol., 203 mg sodium, 1 g carb., 0 g dietary fiber, 7 g protein.

# stuffed mushrooms

oven: 425°F  makes: 24 appetizers

To prepare these appetizers, start with 24 fresh cremini or white mushrooms, 1½ to 2 inches in diameter. Preheat oven to 425°F. Lightly coat a 15×10×1-inch baking pan or baking sheet with nonstick cooking spray; set aside. Rinse and drain mushrooms. Remove stems. Place, stem sides down, in prepared pan. Bake for 5 minutes. Turn mushrooms stem sides up. Divide desired filling among caps. Bake for 8 to 10 minutes more or until heated through.

blackberry mash: *Combine 1½ cups chopped blackberries, ¼ cup chopped toasted walnuts, 2 tablespoons crumbled blue cheese, and 1 teaspoon snipped fresh rosemary.*

curried rice: *Combine ½ cup cooked rice, 1 tablespoon bottled plum sauce, 1 teaspoon seasoned rice vinegar, and ½ teaspoon green curry paste. Top filled caps with cooked shrimp and snipped fresh chives.*

**mustard corn:** *In a small saucepan cook 1 cup fresh or frozen whole kernel corn and ½ cup diced sweet pepper in 1 tablespoon butter or margarine. Stir in ½ cup milk, 1 tablespoon stone-ground mustard, 2 teaspoons all-purpose flour, and ¼ teaspoon salt. Cook and stir until thickened and bubbly.*

**tomato tapenade:** *In a small bowl combine 1 cup chopped, seeded tomato; ½ cup chopped kalamata olives; 2 tablespoons crumbled feta cheese; 1 clove garlic, minced; and 1 teaspoon snipped fresh basil.*

**caramelized onion:** *In a large skillet cook 6 cups thinly sliced onions with 3 tablespoons butter or margarine, 1 tablespoon snipped fresh thyme, and salt and black pepper to taste until onions are golden. Stir in ¼ cup toasted pine nuts.*

**ham and grits:** *Cook ¼ cup regular (hominy) grits according to package directions. Combine grits, ½ cup shredded sharp cheddar cheese, ½ cup diced cooked ham, and ¼ cup sliced green onions.*

*Heaped with a savory cheese and meat or shrimp filling, these*
*sensational appetizers take stuffed mushrooms to a whole new level.*

# spinach-stuffed
## mushrooms

prep: 30 minutes   bake: 10 minutes   oven: 425°F   makes: 24 appetizers

24   large mushrooms
       (1½ to 2 inches in
       diameter)
2   tablespoons olive oil
       Salt
       Ground black pepper
8   ounces bulk hot
       Italian sausage
¼   cup finely chopped
       onion
¼   cup finely chopped
       red sweet pepper
1   clove garlic, minced
1   cup fresh spinach,
       chopped
¼   cup finely shredded
       Parmesan cheese
¼   cup fine dry
       breadcrumbs

**1** Preheat oven to 425°F. Lightly rinse
mushrooms; pat dry with paper towels.
Remove stems and chop; set aside. Lightly
grease a baking sheet. Place mushroom caps
stem side up on prepared baking sheet.
Brush caps with oil. Sprinkle with salt and
black pepper.

**2** In a 12-inch skillet cook chopped
mushroom stems, sausage, onion, sweet
pepper, and garlic over medium heat until
sausage browns, stirring occasionally. Stir in
spinach until wilted. Stir in Parmesan cheese
and breadcrumbs. Remove from heat. Spoon
sausage mixture into mushroom caps.

**3** Bake for 10 to 12 minutes or until stuffing
is brown and mushrooms are tender.

nutrition facts per appetizer: 56 cal., 4 g total fat
(2 g sat. fat), 7 mg chol., 179 mg sodium, 2 g carb.,
0 g dietary fiber, 3 g protein.

chicken-, bacon-, and asiago-stuffed mushrooms: Prepare
as directed, except substitute 8 ounces ground chicken for the
Italian sausage, ¼ cup Asiago cheese for the Parmesan cheese,
and ¼ cup golden raisins for the red sweet pepper. Add 2 slices
bacon, crisp cooked, drained, and crumbled, to the cooked
chicken mixture. Stir in ¼ teaspoon salt.

shrimp- and gouda- stuffed mushrooms: Prepare as
directed, except omit the Italian sausage, red sweet pepper,
spinach, Parmesan cheese, and dry breadcrumbs. Cook chopped
mushroom stems, onion, and garlic over medium heat for 6 to
8 minutes or until tender. Cool slightly. Stir in 8 ounces peeled,
deveined, and cooked shrimp, chopped; ½ cup soft breadcrumbs;
1 egg, slightly beaten; ½ teaspoon finely shredded lemon peel, and
2 ounces Gouda cheese, shredded. (Makes ½ cup.)

*To clean fresh mushrooms, wipe them with a clean, damp cloth or rinse them lightly, then dry gently with paper towels.*

# horseradish-stuffed mushrooms

prep: 30 minutes   bake: 13 minutes   oven: 425°F   makes: 24 appetizers

24   large white or cremini mushrooms (1½ to 2 inches in diameter)
3   tablespoons olive oil
⅓   cup chopped onion
2   3-ounce packages cream cheese, cut up
3   to 4 teaspoons prepared horseradish
    Desired garnishes (snipped fresh chives, Italian parsley, basil, or cooked bacon pieces)

**1** Preheat oven to 425°F. Clean mushrooms. Remove stems and chop. Reserve ¾ cup stems, discarding the rest. Place mushroom caps, stem side down, on a 15×10×1-inch baking pan. Lightly brush mushroom caps with 1 tablespoon of the oil. Bake for 5 minutes. Carefully place mushroom caps, stem side down, on a double thickness of paper towels to drain while preparing filling; set aside.

**2** For filling, in a large skillet heat the remaining 2 tablespoons oil over medium heat. Cook chopped mushroom stems and onion in hot oil for about 8 minutes or until onion is tender, stirring occasionally. Remove from heat. Add cream cheese and horseradish. Let stand for 2 minutes. Stir until combined.

**3** Place mushroom caps, stem sides up, in the same baking pan. Use a spoon to mound filling into mushroom caps. Bake for 8 to 10 minutes or until heated through and cheese is slightly browned. Sprinkle with desired garnishes.

nutrition facts per appetizer: 46 cal., 5 g total fat (2 g sat. fat), 8 mg chol., 24 mg sodium, 1 g carb., 0 g dietary fiber, 1 g protein.

**make-ahead directions:** Clean mushrooms and chop stems and onions several hours ahead. Cover and chill until ready to use.

**stuffed morsels**

*If you can't find mini sweet peppers, roma tomatoes are an excellent alternative. Or use the chicken salad to fill half peppers and half tomatoes for more variety on the party tray.*

# pesto chicken salad
## in mini peppers

start to finish: 35 minutes  makes: 20 servings

20  mini sweet peppers
    (1½ to 2 inches
    long)
1   cup chopped cooked
    chicken
2   tablespoons finely
    chopped onion
2   tablespoons finely
    chopped yellow or
    red sweet pepper
3   tablespoons
    purchased pesto
2   tablespoons
    mayonnaise
⅛   teaspoon ground
    black pepper

**1** To make pepper shells, cut off one-third of peppers lengthwise, leaving stems on shell portion. Finely chop some of the removed pepper and use for the salad (reserve remaining sweet pepper for another use). Remove seeds and membranes from pepper shells.

**2** For salad, in a small bowl combine chicken, onion, and chopped sweet pepper. In a small bowl stir together pesto, mayonnaise, and black pepper. Add mayonnaise mixture to chicken mixture, stirring to combine.

**3** To serve, spoon some chicken mixture into each pepper portion. Arrange on a platter.

nutrition facts per serving: 45 cal., 3 g total fat (0 g sat. fat), 8 mg chol., 32 mg sodium, 2 g carb., 0 g dietary fiber, 3 g protein.

**make-ahead directions:** Prepare filled vegetables as directed. Arrange on a serving platter. Cover with plastic wrap; chill peppers in the refrigerator for up to 2 hours and tomatoes for up to 1 hour.

pesto chicken salad in tomato shells: Cut 8 to 10 small roma tomatoes in half lengthwise. Scoop out and discard the tomato pulp, leaving ¼-inch-thick shells. Place tomato shells, cut sides down, on paper towels to drain. Let stand for 30 minutes. Just before serving, spoon some chicken salad into each tomato shell. Arrange on a serving platter. Makes 16 to 20 appetizers.

*Create a colorful grouping by choosing a small sweet pepper of each color to cradle the tangy goat cheese filling.*

# cheese-piped peppers

start to finish: 20 minutes  makes: 36 servings

6   ounces soft goat
    cheese
1   tablespoon milk
2   tablespoons snipped
    fresh herbs (such as
    chives, basil, and/or
    thyme)
¼   teaspoon ground
    black pepper
2   large red, green, and/
    or yellow sweet
    peppers
    Fresh herb sprigs
    (optional)

**1** In a small bowl combine goat cheese, milk, snipped herbs, and black pepper.

**2** Spoon cheese mixture into a piping bag fitted with a ½-inch star tip (or into a plastic bag with a corner snipped off).

**3** Remove stems, seeds, and membranes from sweet peppers. Cut each pepper into 1-inch-wide strips; cut strips into 1½- to 2-inch-long pieces.

**4** To serve, pipe cheese mixture onto sweet pepper pieces. If desired, garnish with herb sprigs.

nutrition facts per serving: 15 cal., 1 g total fat (1 g sat. fat), 2 mg chol., 18 mg sodium, 1 g carb., 0 g dietary fiber, 1 g protein.

**make-ahead directions:** Prepare as directed in Step 1. Cover and chill for up to 24 hours. Continue as directed.

*This tasty take on stuffed mushrooms will be the biggest hit at your next party. The fine breadcrumbs in the filling add a little crunch to each bite.*

# mushrooms filled with ham and blue cheese

prep: 25 minutes  bake: 13 minutes  oven: 425°F  makes: 24 appetizers

| | |
|---|---|
| 24 | large mushrooms (about 2 inches in diameter) |
| 1 | tablespoon olive oil |
| ½ | cup finely chopped cooked ham |
| ⅓ | cup fine dry breadcrumbs |
| ¼ | cup crumbled blue cheese (1 ounce) |
| 2 | tablespoons snipped fresh parsley |
| 2 | tablespoons olive oil |
| 2 | cloves garlic, minced |
| ⅛ | teaspoon cayenne pepper |

**1** Preheat oven to 425°F. Lightly rinse mushrooms; pat dry with paper towels. Remove stems and reserve for another use. Place mushroom caps, stem side up, in a shallow baking pan. Lightly brush rounded sides of the mushroom caps with the 1 tablespoon oil; set aside.

**2** In a small bowl combine ham, breadcrumbs, blue cheese, parsley, the 2 tablespoons oil, garlic, and cayenne pepper. Spoon ham mixture into mushroom caps.

**3** Bake for 13 to 15 minutes or until mushrooms are tender and filling is hot.

nutrition facts per appetizer: 36 cal., 3 g total fat (1 g sat. fat), 3 mg chol., 72 mg sodium, 2 g carb., 0 g dietary fiber, 2 g protein.

**make-ahead directions:** Prepare as directed through Step 2. Cover and chill for up to 12 hours. Bake as directed in Step 3.

*Stuffed mushrooms take on a meatier, earthier style when prepared with large portobellos. Italian cheese and pesto studded with chopped peppers and nuts fill the mushroom halves.*

## sensational stuffed
# portobellos

prep: 20 minutes  broil: 5 minutes  makes: 12 servings

6   4- to 5-inch fresh portobello mushroom caps
¾   cup bottled roasted red sweet pepper, drained and cut into strips
¼   cup purchased basil pesto
1½  ounces sliced pepperoni, coarsely chopped
⅓   cup walnuts, toasted and chopped
⅛   to ¼ teaspoon crushed red pepper
1   cup shredded Italian cheese blend

**1** Preheat broiler. Remove and discard stems and gills from mushroom caps. Arrange mushroom caps, stem side up, in an shallow baking pan. Broil 3 to 4 inches from the heat for 4 minutes.

**2** Meanwhile, for filling, in a medium bowl combine sweet pepper, pesto, pepperoni, walnuts, and crushed red pepper. Spoon sweet pepper mixture evenly into mushroom caps. Sprinkle with cheese.

**3** Broil for 1 to 2 minutes more or until filling is heated through. To serve, cut each mushroom cap in half.

nutrition facts per serving: 132 cal., 11 g total fat (2 g sat. fat), 12 mg chol., 166 mg sodium, 5 g carb., 1 g dietary fiber, 7 g protein.

*Hailing from France, gougères (goo-ZHAIR) are savory cream puffs traditionally flavored with Gruyére cheese. Each filling below makes enough to fill half the gougères. Choose two fillings to give your guests a duo of irresistible options.*

# gougères
## with assorted fillings

prep: 25 minutes   bake: 20 minutes   cool: 10 minutes   oven: 400°F
makes: 60 puffs

1½   cups water
½   cup butter, cut into pieces
½   teaspoon salt
1½   cups all-purpose flour
5   eggs
1½   cups shredded Gruyère, Comté, Emmentaler, or white cheddar cheese
4   teaspoons Dijon-style mustard
½   teaspoon ground white pepper
⅛   teaspoon cayenne pepper
2   recipes desired filling

1 Preheat oven to 400°F. Lightly grease two large baking sheets; set aside. In a medium saucepan combine the water, butter, and salt. Bring to boiling. Add flour all at once, stirring vigorously. Cook and stir until mixture forms a ball. Remove from heat. Transfer to a large mixing bowl. Cool for 10 minutes.

2 Add eggs, one at a time, beating with a wooden spoon after each addition until well combined. Stir in Gruyère cheese, mustard, white pepper, and cayenne pepper.

3 Drop dough in 1-inch mounds about 1½ inches apart onto the prepared baking sheets. Bake for 20 minutes or until puffed, golden brown, and firm. Transfer puffs to wire racks and cool completely.

4 To fill with desired filling, cut puffs in half horizontally with a serrated knife. Spoon filling into the bottom half of each puff. Replace top. Serve immediately or cover and chill for up to 2 hours.

nutrition facts per puff: 43 cal., 3 g total fat (2 g sat. fat), 25 mg chol., 44 mg sodium, 2 g carb., 0 g dietary fiber, 2 g protein.

cheddar-chicken-pecan filling: Finely chop 1 cup purchased deli chicken salad. Combine ¼ cup chopped toasted pecans, ¼ cup diced cheddar cheese, and chicken salad. Stir in some mayonnaise to moisten. Makes 1¼ cups.

shrimp remoulade filling: Coarsely chop 8 ounces peeled, cooked shrimp. Combine ¼ cup mayonnaise, 2 tablespoons finely chopped celery, 2 tablespoons snipped fresh chives, 1 tablespoon finely chopped onion, 1 tablespoon snipped fresh parsley, 2 teaspoons prepared horseradish, 2 teaspoons lemon juice, ½ teaspoon Worcestershire sauce, 1 teaspoon ketchup, 1 teaspoon Dijon-style mustard, 2 minced garlic cloves, and bottled hot pepper sauce to taste. Add shrimp and stir gently until combined. Makes 1⅓ cups.

chutney, ham, and dried fruit filling: Combine 1 cup finely chopped ham, ¼ cup mayonnaise, ¼ cup chopped dried apricots or cherries, ¼ cup currants or golden raisins, 2 tablespoons mango chutney, 1 minced garlic clove, and ⅛ teaspoon cayenne pepper. Season to taste with salt and ground black pepper. Makes 1⅓ cups.

goat cheese, prosciutto, and pine nut filling: Combine one 3-ounce package cream cheese, 3 ounces soft goat cheese (chèvre), and 3 tablespoons milk. Stir in ½ cup diced prosciutto and ¼ cup toasted pine nuts. Season to taste with salt and ground black pepper. Fill puffs as directed, except before replacing top half of puffs, drizzle the filling with a small amount of honey. Makes about 1½ cups.

**make-ahead directions:** Prepare and bake puffs as directed through Step 3. Place in a container. Cover and refrigerate for up to 24 hours. Or, place baked puffs in a single layer in an airtight container. Cover and freeze for up to 2 weeks. To serve, heat oven to 350°F. Arrange puffs on a baking sheet and bake for 7 to 10 minutes or until crisp.

*When it comes to classic appetizers, this is at the top of the list.*
*The recipe can be changed easily with just a few additions or*
*adjustments to the yolk mixture.*

# deviled eggs

start to finish: 30 minutes   makes: 12 servings

7   hard-cooked eggs,
     peeled
¼   cup mayonnaise
1   to 2 teaspoons Dijon-
     style mustard,
     balsamic herb
     mustard, honey
     mustard, or other
     favorite mustard
½   teaspoon dry mustard
     Salt
     Ground black pepper
     Paprika

**1** Using a sharp knife, halve 6 of the hard-cooked eggs lengthwise. Carefully remove yolks and place in a medium bowl. Cover whites and set aside. Coarsely chop the remaining hard-cooked egg.

**2** In a heavy resealable plastic bag combine the egg yolks, chopped egg, mayonnaise, mustard, and dry mustard; seal bag. Gently squeeze to combine ingredients. Season to taste with salt and pepper.

**3** Cut a small hole in one corner of the bag. Squeeze bag, pushing egg yolk mixture through hole into egg white halves. Sprinkle with paprika. Cover and chill until serving time (up to 12 hours).

nutrition facts per serving: 72 cal., 6 g total fat (1 g sat. fat), 109 mg chol., 63 mg sodium, 0 g carb., 0 g dietary fiber, 3 g protein.

italian-style deviled eggs: Prepare as directed, except omit the mayonnaise, both mustards, and paprika. Add ¼ cup bottled creamy Italian salad dressing and 2 tablespoons grated Parmesan cheese to yolk mixture. Top with additional shredded Parmesan cheese and small fresh basil leaves.

greek-style deviled eggs: Prepare as directed, except add 2 tablespoons crumbled feta cheese, 1 tablespoon finely chopped pitted ripe olives, and 2 teaspoons snipped fresh oregano to yolk mixture.

mexican-style deviled eggs: Prepare as directed, except omit mayonnaise, both mustards, and paprika. Add 3 tablespoons dairy sour cream, 1 tablespoon bottled salsa, and ½ teaspoon ground cumin to yolk mixture. Top with additional salsa and small fresh cilantro leaves.

indian-style deviled eggs: Prepare as directed, except omit mayonnaise, both mustards, and paprika. Add 3 tablespoons plain low-fat yogurt, 1 tablespoon chopped chutney, and ½ teaspoon curry powder to yolk mixture. Sprinkle with chopped peanuts.

**make-ahead directions:**
Prepare deviled eggs as directed. Cover and chill for up to 12 hours.

*Cook a few extra eggs to allow for any that may not peel smoothly. This will assure you that you will have at least 24 intact shells for the filling.*

# bacon-avocado
## deviled eggs

prep: 45 minutes  chill: 4 hours  makes: 24 servings

12  eggs
5  slices thick-sliced
     bacon, chopped
½  cup mayonnaise
1  tablespoon country
     Dijon-style mustard
2  teaspoons caper juice
     or sweet or dill
     pickle juice
¼  teaspoon ground
     black pepper
     Few dashes bottled
     hot pepper sauce
1  ripe but firm avocado,
     halved, pitted, and
     peeled
2  teaspoons lemon
     juice
     Ground black pepper
     (optional)

1 Place eggs in a single layer in a 4-quart saucepan or pot. Add enough cold water to cover the eggs by at least 1 inch. Bring to a rapid boil over high heat (water will have large rapidly breaking bubbles). Remove from heat, cover, and let stand for 10 to 15 minutes; drain. Run cold water over the eggs or place them in ice water until cool enough to handle. Drain. Peel eggs. Using a sharp knife, halve the eggs lengthwise. Carefully remove yolks and place in a medium bowl. Cover the whites and set aside.

2 In a medium skillet cook bacon over medium heat until crisp. Drain bacon on paper towels; set aside. Using a fork, mash egg yolks. Add mayonnaise, mustard, caper juice, the ¼ teaspoon black pepper, and the hot pepper sauce; mix well.

3 Cut avocado into 24 equal pieces. Toss with lemon juice. Pipe or spoon egg yolk mixture into egg white halves. Top with an avocado piece. Sprinkle with bacon pieces. If desired, sprinkle with additional pepper. Cover and chill for up to 4 hours.

nutrition facts per serving: 109 cal., 9 g total fat (2 g sat. fat), 110 mg chol., 112 mg sodium, 1 g carb., 0 g dietary fiber, 9 g protein.

*A savory filling of soft, melty warm cheese flavored with bacon, scallions, and garlic makes these sweet dates irresistible. They will disappear the minute they appear from the oven.*

# bacon- and
# cheese-stuffed dates

prep: 25 minutes   bake: 5 minutes   oven: 350°F   makes: 24 servings

2   slices bacon, crisp
    cooked, drained,
    and finely crumbled,
    or ¼ cup chopped
    prosciutto (2 ounces)
¼   cup thinly sliced
    green onion
2   cloves garlic, minced
½   cup crumbled blue
    cheese (2 ounces)
1   3-ounce package
    cream cheese,
    softened
2   teaspoons Dijon-style
    mustard
⅛   teaspoon ground
    black pepper
24  Medjool dates (about
    1 pound unpitted)

**1** Preheat oven to 350°F. In a medium bowl stir together bacon, green onion, and garlic. Stir in blue cheese, cream cheese, mustard, and pepper.

**2** Using a sharp knife, make a lengthwise slit in each date. Spread each date open slightly. Remove pits. Fill each date with a rounded teaspoon of the bacon mixture.

**3** Place dates, filling sides up, on a baking sheet. Bake, uncovered, for 5 to 8 minutes or until heated through. Serve warm.

nutrition facts per serving: 91 cal., 2 g total fat (1 g sat. fat), 6 mg chol., 66 mg sodium, 18 g carb., 2 g dietary fiber, 2 g protein.

**make-ahead directions:** Prepare as above, except do not bake the dates. Place stuffed dates in an airtight container, cover, and chill for up to 24 hours. Bake as directed just before serving.

*These treats are dangerously addictive—don't say we didn't warn you!*

# parmesan-stuffed
## dates

prep: 20 minutes  bake: 12 minutes  oven: 400°F  makes: 12 servings

12  Medjool dates (about 12 ounces)
2   ounces Parmigiano-Reggiano cheese, cut into 12 small pieces
6   slices bacon, halved crosswise

**1** Preheat oven to 400°F. Using a sharp knife, cut a lengthwise slit in each date. Remove the pit. Stuff each date with a piece of cheese. Wrap each with a bacon half and secure with a wooden toothpick. Place stuffed dates in a 15×10×1-inch baking pan.

**2** Bake for 12 to 14 minutes or until bacon is crisp. Serve warm.

nutrition facts per serving: 172 cal., 10 g total fat (4 g sat. fat), 16 mg chol., 234 mg sodium, 18 g carb., 2 g dietary fiber, 4 g protein.

*Enjoy the fresh garden flavor of these tomato bites any time of year. Prepare them up to 2 hours ahead and refrigerate until serving time.*

# herb-stuffed cherry
# tomatoes

start to finish: 35 minutes  makes: 36 servings

3   dozen cherry tomatoes, (1 to 1½ inches)
2   tablespoons purchased pesto
1   clove garlic, minced
2   tablespoons snipped fresh parsley
2   tablespoons snipped fresh chives
1   tablespoon snipped fresh tarragon or dill
1   8-ounce package cream cheese
4   ounces fresh goat cheese (chèvre) or cream cheese

**1** Using a sharp knife, cut off the top ⅓ of each tomato on the stem end. Set aside the tops for garnish, if desired, or discard. Hollow out tomatoes; invert on paper towels and set aside.

**2** Place pesto, garlic, the 2 tablespoons parsley, chives, and tarragon or dill in a food processor. Cover and process for 15 seconds; add the cream cheese and chèvre. Process 30 to 45 seconds more or until the filling is smooth.

**3** Place the filling in a pastry bag fitted with a star tip and pipe into each cherry tomato. Garnish with reserved tomato tops, if desired.

nutrition facts per serving: 40 cal., 3g total fat (2g sat. fat), 8mg chol., 38mg sodium, 1g carb., 0g dietary fiber, 1g protein.

*This tasty party spud—with a layer of aromatic pesto and a sprinkling of crispy pancetta—will be a hit at every gathering. Best of all, you can assemble the potatoes ahead and chill them for smart party planning.*

# petite pesto-
## parmesan potatoes

prep: 50 minutes   bake: 27 minutes   oven: 425°F   makes: 40 servings

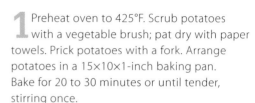

20  tiny new potatoes
     (about 2¼ pounds)
4   ounces pancetta,
     chopped
⅔   cup light dairy sour
     cream
2   teaspoons snipped
     fresh chives
¼   teaspoon salt
¼   teaspoon cracked
     black pepper
¼   cup refrigerated basil
     pesto
¼   cup shredded
     Parmesan cheese
     (1 ounce)
     Snipped fresh chives
     (optional)
     Cracked black pepper
     (optional)

**1** Preheat oven to 425°F. Scrub potatoes with a vegetable brush; pat dry with paper towels. Prick potatoes with a fork. Arrange potatoes in a 15×10×1-inch baking pan. Bake for 20 to 30 minutes or until tender, stirring once.

**2** Meanwhile, in a small skillet cook pancetta over medium heat until crisp. Drain pancetta on paper towels, discarding drippings.

**3** When potatoes are cool enough to handle, cut potatoes in half lengthwise. If necessary, cut a thin slice from each bottom to keep potato upright. Using a very small spoon or a measuring teaspoon, carefully scoop pulp out of each potato half, leaving a ¼-inch-thick shell. Place pulp in a medium bowl.

**4** Mash the potato pulp with a potato masher or an electric mixer on low speed. Add sour cream, the 2 teaspoons chives, the salt, and the ¼ teaspoon pepper. Beat until smooth. Spoon a rounded ¼ teaspoon pesto into potato shells. Top with the mashed potato mixture. Place potato shells in a 3-quart rectangular baking dish. Sprinkle with pancetta.

**5** Bake for about 5 minutes or until heated through. Sprinkle with Parmesan cheese. Bake for about 2 minutes more or until cheese melts. If desired, garnish with additional chives and additional cracked pepper.

nutrition facts per serving: 47 cal., 2 g total fat (1 g sat. fat), 4 mg chol., 90 mg sodium, 5 g carb., 1 g dietary fiber, 1 g protein.

*This recipe rivals the all-out-decadent twice-baked potatoes found at high-end restaurants. The cheese gives this version the edge!*

# twice-baked potatoes with comté cheese

prep: 25 minutes   bake: 1 hour 10 minutes   stand: 10 minutes   oven: 400°F
makes: 8 servings

4   large Yukon gold potatoes (about 2 pounds)
1   tablespoon olive oil
2   tablespoons butter
⅓   cup finely chopped shallot
1   tablespoon snipped fresh chives
1   tablespoon snipped fresh parsley
4   ounces Comté or Gruyère cheese, shredded (1 cup)
⅓   cup snipped prosciutto (about 2 ounces)
¼   cup dairy sour cream
    Milk
    Salt
    Ground black pepper

**1** Preheat oven to 400°F. Scrub potatoes thoroughly with a vegetable brush; pat dry. Rub potatoes with oil. Wrap each potato in foil. Bake potatoes for 50 to 60 minutes or until tender. Remove and discard foil. Let potatoes stand for about 10 minutes to cool slightly. Cut the potatoes in half lengthwise. Using a teaspoon, carefully scoop pulp out of each potato, leaving a ¼- to ½-inch shell. Place pulp in a mixing bowl; set shells aside. Mash pulp with electric mixer on low speed until nearly smooth.

**2** In a small saucepan melt butter over medium heat. Cook shallot in hot butter until are tender but not brown. Add chives and parsley. Cook 30 seconds more. Add shallot mixture to mashed potatoes; mix until smooth. Stir in ¾ cup of the Comté cheese, the prosciutto, and sour cream. If necessary, stir in a little milk to reach desired consistency. Season to taste with salt and pepper. Mound mixture into reserved potato shells and sprinkle with remaining ¼ cup cheese. Place potatoes in a single layer in a 3-quart rectangular baking dish.

**3** Bake, uncovered, for about 20 minutes or until golden brown and heated through.

nutrition facts per serving: 227 cal., 12 g total fat (5 g sat. fat), 26 mg chol., 280 mg sodium, 21 g carb., 3 g dietary fiber, 9 g protein.

**make-ahead directions:** Prepare as directed through Step 2. Place potatoes in a single layer in an airtight container. Cover; chill for up to 1 day. Place potatoes in a 3-quart rectangular baking dish. Bake, covered, in a 325°F oven for 30 minutes. Uncover; bake for 15 minutes more or until potatoes are heated through.

*Gouda and cream cheese melt together with bacon and shrimp, creating a creamy, decadent filling in these tiny twice-baked potatoes.*

# shrimp- and bacon-
## stuffed baby potatoes

prep: 35 minutes  bake: 42 minutes  oven: 425°F  makes: 28 servings

14  tiny new potatoes
(about 1¼ pounds)
2  tablespoons Dijon-
style mustard
1  tablespoon olive oil
2  teaspoons Old Bay
seasoning*
1  7- to 8-ounce package
frozen peeled
cooked shrimp,
thawed, drained,
and chopped
½  of an 8-ounce
package cream
cheese, softened
1  cup shredded Gouda
cheese (4 ounces)
5  slices bacon, crisp
cooked, drained,
and crumbled
¼  cup snipped fresh
chives (optional)

**1** Preheat oven to 425°F. Cut potatoes in half lengthwise. Using a melon baller or a very small spoon, scoop out potato pulp, leaving a ¼-inch shell. Cut a thin slice from each bottom to keep potato upright. Place potatoes, cut side up, in a 15×10×1-inch baking pan.

**2** In a small bowl combine mustard, oil, and 1 teaspoon of the Old Bay seasoning. Brush the hollowed-out portions of potatoes with mustard mixture. Bake about 30 minutes or until potatoes are tender. Remove from oven.

**3** Meanwhile, for filling, in a small bowl combine shrimp, cream cheese, Gouda cheese, bacon, and the remaining 1 teaspoon Old Bay seasoning. Spoon filling into potato shells, mounding slightly.

**4** Bake for 12 to 15 minutes more or until filling is heated through and cheese melts. Serve warm or at room temperature. If desired, garnish with chives.

nutrition facts per serving: 63 cal., 4 g total fat (2 g sat. fat), 24 mg chol., 168 mg sodium, 3 g carb., 0 g dietary fiber, 4 g protein.

*note: If your seasoning is coarse, crush before using.

*Not only do these appetizers brim with great flavor, but they can be made up to 24 hours in advance. Serve them with assorted crackers.*

# stuffed peppers and olives

start to finish: 20 min.  makes: about 50 servings

1   16-ounce jar whole
    cherry peppers
1   10-ounce jar
    pepperoncini salad
    peppers
1   5 ¾-ounce can
    colossal pitted ripe
    olives
2   very thin slices
    prosciutto or
    smoked ham
3   to 4 ounces provolone
    or Asiago cheese
3   to 4 ounces Monterey
    Jack cheese with
    peppers
1   tablespoon olive oil
1   tablespoon balsamic
    vinegar

1 Drain cherry peppers, pepperoncini, and olives. Slit a ½-inch cross in the side of each cherry pepper and a 1-inch cross in the side of each pepperoncini. Drain any juices from inside peppers.

2 Count the number of peppers and cut the prosciutto crosswise into that many thin strips; set aside. Cut provolone and Monterey Jack cheeses into ½-inch cubes.

3 Wrap a prosciutto strip around each piece of provolone. Stuff into prepared peppers. Stuff each olive with a cube of Monterey Jack cheese. Place peppers and olives in a shallow container.

4 Whisk oil and vinegar. Drizzle over olives and peppers.

nutrition facts per serving: 24 cal., 2 g total fat (1 g sat. fat), 3 mg chol., 201 mg sodium, 1 g carb., 0 g dietary fiber, 1 g protein.

# 10

worldly bi

An amazing assortment of global-inspired offerings, including Italian antipasti, Chinese dim sum, and Spanish tapas.

tes

*Inspired by Korean beef, known as Bul-Kogi, these little skewers make a great grilled appetizer.*

# sesame beef kabobs

prep: 20 minutes  marinate: 4 hours  grill: 12 minutes
makes: about 30 servings

12  ounces beef flank steak
2  tablespoons soy sauce
2  tablespoons toasted sesame oil
1  green onion, sliced
1½  teaspoons sugar
1½  teaspoons dry sherry (optional)
2  cloves garlic, minced
½  teaspoon sesame seeds
½  teaspoon crushed red pepper
2  small orange and/or red sweet peppers, quartered
4  limes, each cut into 8 wedges
¾  cup fresh pea pods, trimmed and halved crosswise diagonally
30  grape and/or cherry tomatoes
  Sesame seeds

**1** Trim fat from meat. Score both sides of meat in a diamond pattern by making shallow diagonal cuts at 1-inch intervals. Place meat in a resealable plastic bag set in a shallow dish.

**2** For marinade, in a small bowl combine soy sauce, sesame oil, green onion, sugar, sherry (if desired), garlic, the ½ teaspoon sesame seeds, and the crushed red pepper. Pour marinade over meat; seal bag. Turn to coat meat. Marinate in the refrigerator for 4 to 24 hours, turning bag occasionally. Drain meat, discarding marinade.

**3** For a charcoal grill, place meat on the rack of an uncovered grill directly over medium coals. Grill for 12 to 14 minutes or until medium (160°F), turning once halfway through grilling. While the meat is grilling, add sweet pepper quarters and lime wedges to grill. Grill for 4 to 5 minutes or until lightly charred, turning once halfway through grilling. Cut meat and sweet peppers into 1-inch pieces.

**4** Meanwhile, in a small saucepan cook pea pods in a small amount of boiling water for 2 to 4 minutes or until crisp-tender. Drain.

**5** To serve, thread meat pieces, sweet pepper pieces, pea pods, and tomatoes onto wooden skewers. Sprinkle with additional sesame seeds and serve with the grilled lime wedges.

nutrition facts per serving: 31 cal., 1 g total fat (0 g sat. fat), 4 mg chol., 42 mg sodium, 2 g carb., 1 g dietary fiber, 3 g protein.

*Easy versions of the Asian-style "beggar's purse," these spicy meat dumplings are topped with the crunch of sesame seeds.*

# mandarin beef buns

prep: 40 minutes   rise: 20 minutes   bake: 15 minutes   oven: 375°F
makes: 24 servings

1   tablespoon cooking
     oil
2   cups shredded
     cooked beef or pork
¼   teaspoon crushed red
     pepper
1   cup chopped bok
     choy, napa cabbage,
     or green cabbage
1   tablespoon grated
     fresh ginger
1   teaspoon finely
     shredded orange
     peel
⅓   cup thinly bias-sliced
     green onion
¼   cup bottled hoisin
     sauce
1   16-ounce package hot
     roll mix
1   egg, lightly beaten
1   tablespoon water
     Black and/or white
     sesame seeds

**1** For filling, in a large skillet heat oil over medium heat. Cook and stir meat and crushed red pepper in hot oil for 3 minutes. Add bok choy, ginger, and orange peel. Cook and stir for 2 to 3 minutes or until bok choy wilts. Stir in green onion and hoisin sauce; set aside.

**2** Lightly grease two baking sheets. Prepare hot roll mix according to package directions. Divide dough into 24 portions; shape into balls. On a lightly floured surface roll or pat balls of dough into 3½-inch circles.

**3** For each bun, place about 1 tablespoon of the filling in the center of a dough circle. Moisten edge of dough with a little water. Bring dough up around filling; pinch dough together to seal. Arrange filled buns, seam sides down, on the prepared baking sheets. Cover and let rise in a warm place until nearly double in size (about 20 minutes).

**4** Preheat oven to 375°F. In a small bowl combine egg and the 1 tablespoon water. Brush over buns. Sprinkle with sesame seeds. Bake for about 15 minutes or until golden brown. Serve warm.

nutrition facts per serving: 125 cal., 4 g total fat
(1 g sat. fat), 28 mg chol., 179 mg sodium, 16 g carb.,
0 g dietary fiber, 7 g protein.

**make-ahead directions:** Prepare and bake buns as directed. Transfer to a wire rack. Cool for 30 minutes. Wrap buns in heavy foil and freeze for up to 1 month. To serve, preheat oven to 325°F. Bake the foil-wrapped buns for about 40 minutes or until heated through.

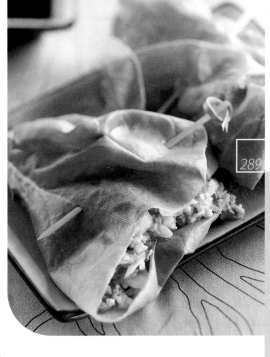

*The key to great lettuce wraps is the contrast of warm, flavorful fillings with the cool crunch of lettuce. For the best results, pick the largest, most pliable lettuce leaves. Besides Boston or Bibb lettuce, try iceberg, red lettuce, radicchio, or large spinach leaves.*

# spicy tofu
## lettuce wraps

start to finish: 20 minutes   makes: 8 servings

12   ounces extra-firm tofu
2    cups shredded
     cabbage with carrot
     (coleslaw mix)
1    8-ounce can sliced
     water chestnuts,
     drained
2    green onions,
     chopped
2    tablespoons snipped
     fresh cilantro
⅓    cup Asian sweet chili
     sauce or bottled
     stir-fry sauce
1    tablespoon lime juice
8    large leaves
     butterhead (Boston
     or Bibb) or green
     leaf lettuce

**1** Drain tofu. Press out excess liquid with paper towels. In a food processor combine about half of each of the following ingredients: tofu, coleslaw mix, water chestnuts, green onions, and cilantro. Cover and pulse until finely chopped. Transfer to a large skillet. Repeat with the remaining tofu, coleslaw mix, water chestnuts, green onions, and cilantro. Stir chili sauce and lime juice into mixture in skillet. Cook and stir over medium heat until heated through.

**2** If present, cut the center veins from lettuce leaves. Divide tofu mixture among lettuce leaves; fold or roll up. Secure with toothpicks.

nutrition facts per serving: 88 cal., 2 g total fat (0 g sat. fat), 0 mg chol., 141 mg sodium, 12 g carb., 3 g dietary fiber, 5 g protein.

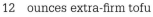

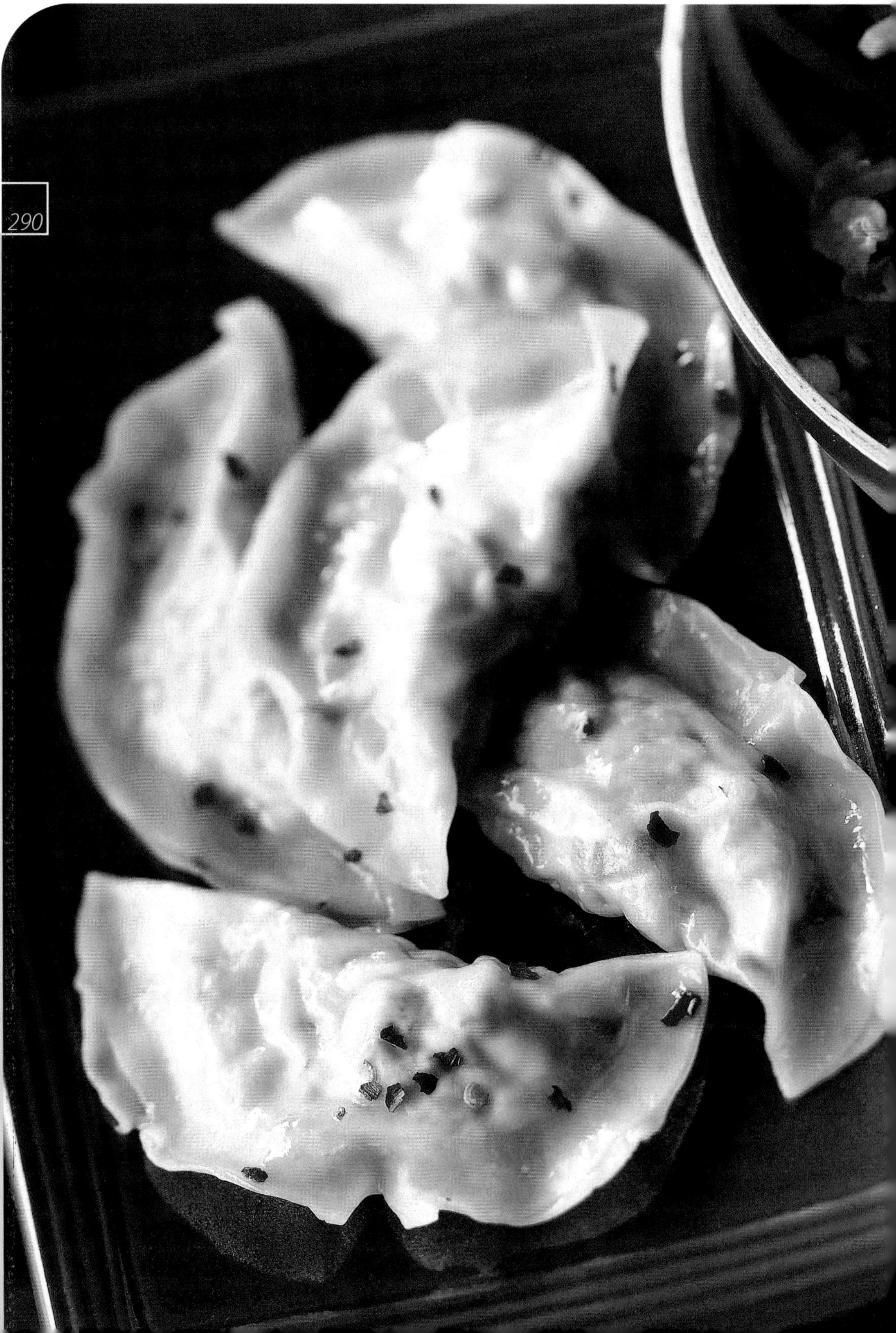

*Gyoza wrappers are similar to wonton wrappers, but slightly thicker. Look for them in the Oriental food section of your supermarket.*

# shrimp pot stickers

prep: 45 minutes  chill: 1 hour  cook: 11 minutes per batch
makes: 32 pot stickers

6   ounces frozen peeled, deveined cooked medium shrimp, thawed, drained, and chopped
½   cup chopped stemmed shiitake mushrooms
¼   cup frozen chopped spinach, thawed and squeezed dry
¼   cup canned water chestnuts, drained and chopped
2   green onions, chopped
1   egg white
2   tablespoons soy sauce
1   tablespoon grated fresh ginger
2   teaspoons finely shredded lemon peel
2   teaspoons sesame oil (not toasted)
¼   to ½ teaspoon crushed red pepper
¼   teaspoon salt
¼   teaspoon ground black pepper
32  gyoza wrappers
¼   cup sesame oil (not toasted)
1⅓  cups water
    Crushed red pepper (optional)

1 For filling, combine shrimp, mushrooms, spinach, water chestnuts, green onions, egg white, soy sauce, ginger, lemon peel, the 2 teaspoons oil, the ¼ to ½ teaspoon crushed red pepper, the salt, and black pepper. Transfer mixture to a food processor. Cover; pulse until well mixed but still slightly chunky. Return to bowl. Cover and chill for at least 1 hour.

2 Lightly flour a baking sheet. For each pot sticker, working on a flat surface, place about 2 teaspoons of the filling in the center of a gyoza wrapper. Moisten edge of wrapper with water. Fold wrapper in half over filling; pinch edges together to seal. Set pot sticker with sealed edge upright and press gently to slightly flatten the bottom. Transfer pot stickers to prepared baking sheet; cover.

3 In a very large skillet heat 2 tablespoons of the oil over medium-high heat about 1 minute or until very hot. Carefully place half of the pot stickers upright in skillet (make sure pot stickers do not touch). Cook the pot stickers in hot oil about 1 minute or until bottoms are lightly browned. Reduce heat.

4 Carefully add ⅔ cup of the water to skillet. Cover and cook for 5 minutes. Cook, uncovered, for 3 to 4 minutes or until water evaporates. Cook, uncovered, for 2 to 3 minutes more or until bottoms are browned and slightly crisp. Gently remove pot stickers from skillet. Carefully wipe any remaining moisture from skillet.

5 Keep pot stickers warm while cooking the remaining pot stickers, using the remaining 2 tablespoons oil and the remaining ⅔ cup water. If desired, sprinkle pot stickers with additional crushed red pepper.

nutrition facts per pot sticker: 40 cal., 2 g total fat (0 g sat. fat), 8 mg chol., 109 mg sodium, 4 g carb., 0 g dietary fiber, 2 g protein.

*Flavor-infused ingredients elevate the crunchy goodness of coleslaw to an intriguing new level. If you're short on time, use packaged coleslaw mix and substitute ⅓ cup bottled ginger vinaigrette salad dressing for the homemade dressing.*

# asian slaw

start to finish: 40 minutes   makes: 8 to 10 servings

2  tablespoons salad oil
1  tablespoon lime juice
1  tablespoon rice
   vinegar
1  teaspoon packed
   brown sugar
1  teaspoon grated fresh
   ginger
1  teaspoon soy sauce
¼  teaspoon salt
¼  teaspoon crushed red
   pepper
4  cups shredded napa
   cabbage
1  cup shredded bok
   choy
1  cup coarsely
   shredded carrot
½  cup thinly sliced
   radish or shredded
   daikon
½  cup bite-size strips
   cucumber
½  cup bite-size strips
   green or orange
   sweet pepper
¼  cup fresh cilantro
   leaves
¼  cup sliced almonds,
   toasted

**1** For dressing, in a small screw-top jar combine oil, lime juice, vinegar, brown sugar, ginger, soy sauce, salt, and crushed red pepper. Cover and shake well. Set aside.

**2** In a large bowl combine cabbage, bok choy, carrot, radish, cucumber, sweet pepper, cilantro, and almonds. Pour dressing over cabbage mixture. Toss gently to coat.

nutrition facts per serving: 70 cal., 5 g total fat (1 g sat. fat), 0 mg chol., 138 mg sodium, 6 g carb., 2 g dietary fiber, 2 g protein.

**make-ahead directions:** Prepare as directed. Cover and chill for up to 6 hours.

## the asian pantry

- chinese rice wine: *Similar to dry sherry and used to flavor dishes as well as diminish strong fish flavors*

- gingerroot: *An Asian staple that adds zest to sauces and salads; best if grated fresh, but also available jarred in minced form*

- hoisin sauce: *Sweet, aromatic dipping sauce made of fermented soybeans, garlic, vinegar, and chili peppers*

- oyster sauce: *A condiment made from boiled oysters and a blend of seasonings, and used to flavor everything from meat to vegetables*

- sesame oil: *A deep brown, rich-tasting oil used to add flavor while sautéing*

- soy sauce: *A pungent, salty concoction made from fermented soybeans and used to flavor sauces, soups, and marinades (also available in a low-sodium form)*

*Slow-roasting the ribs in a bold, sweet, and spicy Chinese sauce makes them extra tender and succulent. Be sure to ask your butcher to cut the ribs into single-rib portions.*

# spicy glazed ribs

prep: 15 minutes  bake: 1½ hours  oven: 350°F  makes: about 12 servings

2 pounds pork loin back ribs or meaty pork spareribs, cut into single-rib portions

1 8-ounce jar hoisin sauce

½ cup sugar

½ cup soy sauce

½ cup tomato paste

¼ cup sweet rice wine (mirin) or sweet white wine

¼ cup bottled minced garlic

1 tablespoon finely shredded orange peel

2 tablespoons orange juice

1 tablespoon bottled hot pepper sauce

**1** Preheat oven to 350°F. Place ribs in a large shallow roasting pan. Bake for 45 minutes. Carefully drain off fat.

**2** Meanwhile, for sauce, in a medium bowl combine hoisin sauce, sugar, soy sauce, tomato paste, wine, garlic, orange peel, orange juice, and hot pepper sauce.

**3** Pour sauce over ribs. Stir to coat. Bake for about 45 minutes or until ribs are tender, stirring every 10 minutes to keep ribs coated with sauce.

nutrition facts per serving: 234 cal., 10 g total fat (3 g sat. fat), 37 mg chol., 1028 mg sodium, 24 g carb., 1 g dietary fiber, 10 g protein.

*Be sure to allow extra time to thaw the frozen phyllo dough. Thaw the phyllo in its original packaging in the refrigerator for 24 hours.*

# asian **vegetable** strudel

**prep:** 45 minutes  **bake:** 15 minutes  **cool:** 10 minutes  **oven:** 400°F
**makes:** 24 servings

| | |
|---|---|
| 2 | tablespoons reduced-sodium soy sauce |
| 1 | teaspoon sugar |
| 1 | teaspoon cornstarch |
| ½ | teaspoon toasted sesame oil |
| ¼ | teaspoon ground black pepper |
| 1 | teaspoon grated fresh ginger |
| 1 | tablespoon butter |
| 1 | cup chopped stemmed shiitake mushrooms |
| 1 | cup coarsely shredded carrot |
| ½ | cup thinly sliced green onion |
| 4 | cups finely shredded napa cabbage |
| 12 | sheets frozen phyllo dough (14×9-inch rectangles), thawed |
| ⅔ | cup butter, melted |
| ⅔ | cup finely chopped peanuts |
| | Sesame seeds (optional) |

**1** For filling, combine soy sauce, sugar, cornstarch, oil, and pepper; set aside. In a large skillet heat 1 tablespoon butter over medium-high heat. Cook and stir ginger in hot butter for 15 seconds. Add mushrooms, carrot, and green onion. Cook and stir for 2 minutes. Stir soy sauce mixture; add to skillet. Cook and stir until thickened and bubbly. Add cabbage. Cook and stir for 1 to 2 minutes or until wilted. Remove from heat.

**2** Preheat oven to 400°F. Line a 15×10×1-inch baking pan with parchment paper. Unfold phyllo dough. (Keep phyllo covered with plastic wrap to prevent it from drying out, removing sheets as you need them.) Lay one sheet of phyllo on a clean work surface. Lightly brush phyllo with some of the ⅔ cup butter. Top with another sheet of phyllo; brush with more butter and sprinkle with about 2 tablespoons peanuts. Repeat with four more phyllo sheets to make a stack of six phyllo sheets, brushing each sheet with melted butter and sprinkling every other sheet with 2 tablespoons peanuts.

**3** Spread 1 cup of the filling over phyllo stack, leaving a 1½-inch border around edges. Fold in short sides of phyllo. Starting with a long side, roll up phyllo to enclose filling. Place rolls, seam side down, in prepared pan. Brush top of roll with more melted butter. Diagonally score top, making the cuts 1 inch apart and about ¼ inch deep. If desired, sprinkle with sesame seeds. Repeat to make another roll, using the remaining phyllo sheets, the melted butter, and peanuts. If desired, sprinkle with sesame seeds.

**4** Bake for 15 to 18 minutes or until golden brown. Cool on a wire rack for 10 minutes. Use a serrated knife to slice strudel.

nutrition facts per serving: 97 cal., 8 g total fat (4 g sat. fat), 15 mg chol., 145 mg sodium, 5 g carb., 0 g dietary fiber, 2 g protein.

*Grilled chicken strips are coated in a marinade of sweet pineapple, aromatic sake, and sesame oil. The result is sizzlingly delicious.*

# chicken sake skewers

prep: 40 minutes  marinate: 1 hour  bake: 12 minutes  oven: 450°F
makes: 26 to 30 servings

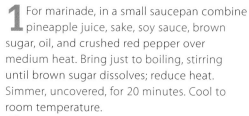

1 cup unsweetened
  pineapple juice
¾ cup sake
¼ cup soy sauce
3 tablespoons packed
  brown sugar
3 tablespoons toasted
  sesame oil
½ teaspoon crushed
  red pepper
2 pounds skinless,
  boneless chicken
  breasts, cut
  lengthwise into
  1-inch-wide strips
1 cup peanut butter
½ cup half-and-half
  or light cream
1½ cups finely chopped
  cashews
  Asian sweet chili
  sauce

**1** For marinade, in a small saucepan combine pineapple juice, sake, soy sauce, brown sugar, oil, and crushed red pepper over medium heat. Bring just to boiling, stirring until brown sugar dissolves; reduce heat. Simmer, uncovered, for 20 minutes. Cool to room temperature.

**2** Place chicken in a large shallow dish. Pour marinade over chicken. Stir gently to coat. Cover and marinate in the refrigerator for 1 to 2 hours, stirring once.

**3** Soak twenty-six to thirty 6-inch wooden skewers in water for at least 30 minutes. Drain before using. Preheat oven to 450°F. Lightly grease a 15×10×1-inch baking pan; set aside.

**4** Drain chicken, discarding marinade. Pat chicken dry with paper towels. In a small bowl combine peanut butter and half-and-half. Place cashews in a shallow dish. Thread each chicken strip lengthwise onto a soaked skewer. Brush chicken with peanut butter mixture. Roll in cashews to coat. Place in the prepared baking pan. Bake about 12 minutes or until chicken is no longer pink, turning once.

**5** Serve chicken skewers with Asian chili sauce.

nutrition facts per serving: 200 cal., 10 g total fat (2 g sat. fat), 22 mg chol., 345 mg sodium, 15 g carb., 1 g dietary fiber, 12 g protein.

*Complement the fiery Asian flavors of these crab wonton crisps with a fruity appetizer or drink.*

# asian crab salad
## on wonton crisps

prep: 20 minutes   bake: 6 minutes   oven: 350°F   makes: 20 servings

10  wonton wrappers, halved diagonally
1   tablespoon vegetable oil
1   teaspoon sesame seeds (optional)
1   3-ounce package cream cheese, softened
⅓   cup mayonnaise
1   tablespoon chopped green onion
2   teaspoons grated fresh ginger
1   teaspoon soy sauce
1   teaspoon rice vinegar
¼   teaspoon toasted sesame oil
⅛   teaspoon bottled hot pepper sauce
1   6-ounce can lump crabmeat, drained, flaked, and cartilage removed
    Chopped green onion

**1** Preheat oven to 350°F. Place wonton wrappers on a lightly greased baking sheet. Brush with vegetable oil. If desired, sprinkle with sesame seeds. Bake for 6 to 8 minutes or until golden and crisp. Cool on a wire rack.

**2** For the salad, in a medium mixing bowl beat cream cheese with an electric mixer on medium to high speed for 30 seconds. Beat in mayonnaise, the 1 tablespoon green onion, the ginger, soy sauce, vinegar, sesame oil, and hot pepper sauce until combined. Fold in the crabmeat.

**3** Spoon about 1 tablespoon of crab salad onto each wonton crisp. Sprinkle with additional chopped green onion.

nutrition facts per serving: 69 cal., 5 g total fat (2 g sat. fat), 15 mg chol., 95 mg sodium, 3 g carb., 0 g dietary fiber, 2 g protein.

**make-ahead directions:** Prepare the wonton crisps and crab salad as directed up to 24 hours before serving. Store the wonton crisps in an airtight container. Cover and chill the crab salad.

*Fill moistened rice papers with a savory shrimp, noodle, and cabbage mixture. Another time, serve the tasty rolls for a light lunch entree.*

# asian shrimp spring rolls

**prep:** 35 minutes  **chill:** 6 hours  **makes:** 12 rolls

12 medium fresh or
     frozen shrimp in
     shells
1 ounce dried rice
     vermicelli noodles
1 tablespoon sesame oil
2 cloves garlic, minced
1 teaspoon sesame
     seeds
¼ teaspoon crushed
     red pepper
1 cup finely shredded
     napa cabbage
1 medium carrot,
     coarsely shredded
2 green onions,
     chopped
¼ cup fresh cilantro
     leaves
¼ cup fresh mint leaves
2 tablespoons chopped
     dry-roasted cashews
1 tablespoon rice vinegar
1 teaspoon packed
     brown sugar
1 teaspoon soy sauce
1 teaspoon grated fresh
     ginger
12 8½-inch round rice
     papers
     Fresh cilantro leaves,
       snipped fresh
       chives, and/or
       crushed red pepper
       (optional)
     Purchased sweet
       Asian chili sauce

**1** Thaw shrimp, if frozen. Peel and devein shrimp. Rinse shrimp; pat dry. In a medium saucepan cook vermicelli in boiling lightly salted water for 2 to 3 minutes or until just tender. Drain; rinse with cold water. Drain well. Snip the noodles into small lengths; set aside.

**2** In a skillet heat oil over medium heat. Cook shrimp, garlic, sesame seeds, and ¼ teaspoon crushed red pepper in hot oil about 3 minutes or until shrimp are opaque, stirring occasionally. Remove from skillet. When cool, halve lengthwise; set aside.

**3** For filling, in a bowl combine vermicelli, cabbage, carrot, green onions, ¼ cup cilantro, mint, and cashews. In a bowl combine rice vinegar, brown sugar, soy sauce, and ginger. Add to cabbage mixture. Toss to coat.

**4** Fill a very large skillet about half full with water. Bring just to simmering; remove from heat. Place one rice paper in the skillet at a time, pushing it down gently to cover with water. Allow to soften about 10 seconds. Using tongs, gently lift the paper from the water and place on a dinner plate (make sure it is laying flat on the plate so the rice paper doesn't stick to itself). Pull gently and carefully on the edges of the paper to straighten while it is still warm.

**5** Spoon a scant ¼ cup of the filling across the lower third of the softened rice paper. Arrange two shrimp halves and fresh herbs on top of the filling. Fold bottom of rice paper over filling; fold in the sides of the rice paper. Tightly roll up. Place, seam side down, on a large plate. Repeat with remaining rice papers, filling, and shrimp. Cover and chill for up to 6 hours. Serve with chili sauce.

nutrition facts per roll: 89 cal., 2 g total fat (0 g sat. fat), 11 mg chol., 79 mg sodium, 15 g carb., 1 g dietary fiber, 3 g protein.

*Every bite of these classic pork-filled egg rolls presents a symphony of tastes and textures: ginger, garlic, and crunchy cabbage. Served with sweet-and-sour sauce (and maybe some head-clearing Chinese mustard), they're sure to make it onto your list of classic favorites.*

# egg rolls

prep: 30 minutes   cook: 2 minutes per batch   oven: 300°F   makes: 8 rolls

8   egg roll wrappers
1   recipe Gingered Pork Filling
     Vegetable oil for deep-fat frying
1   cup bottled sweet-and-sour sauce or ½ cup prepared Chinese-style hot mustard

**1** Preheat oven to 300°F. For each egg roll, place an egg roll wrapper on a flat surface with a corner pointing toward you. Spoon ¼ cup filling across and just below center of egg roll wrapper. Fold bottom corner over filling, tucking it under on the other side. Fold side corners over filling, forming an envelope shape. Roll egg roll toward remaining corner. Moisten top corner with water; press firmly to seal.

**2** In a heavy saucepan or deep-fat fryer heat 1½ inches oil to 365°F. Fry egg rolls, a few at a time, for 2 to 3 minutes or until golden brown. Drain on paper towels. Keep warm in oven while frying remaining egg rolls. Serve warm egg rolls with sweet-and-sour sauce or hot mustard.

nutrition facts per roll: 372 cal., 20 g total fat (3 g sat. fat), 23 mg chol., 841 mg sodium, 38 g carb., 2 g dietary fiber, 10 g protein.

gingered pork filling: In a large skillet cook 8 ounces ground pork until browned. Drain off fat. Add 4 cups packaged shredded cabbage with carrot (coleslaw mix) or 3 cups packaged shredded broccoli (broccoli slaw mix); 2 tablespoons soy sauce; 2 teaspoons grated fresh ginger; 1 clove garlic, minced; and ¼ teaspoon salt. Cook and stir for 2 minutes.

*Biting into a slice of this fragrant condiment cleanses the palate nicely between bites of sushi. You can also use this instead of the bottled pickled ginger in the Shrimp Sushi (page 305) and California Sushi Rolls (page 303).*

# homemade
# pickled ginger

prep: 30 minutes   chill: overnight   cook: 30 minutes   cool: 1 hour
makes: 1 cup

8   to 10 ounces fresh ginger
1   cup rice vinegar
¼   cup sugar
1   small fresh or canned beet, halved, or 6 or 7 drops red food coloring (optional)
1½   teaspoons salt
½   teaspoon ground white pepper

**1** Trim small knobs from ginger. Peel. Using a vegetable peeler or small mandoline, carefully cut enough of the ginger into about ⅛-inch-thick slices to measure 1 cup.

**2** In a medium saucepan combine vinegar, sugar, beet or food coloring (if desired), salt, and white pepper. Bring to boiling. Add ginger; reduce heat. Cover and simmer for 30 to 40 minutes or until softened. Cool for 1 hour. Remove and discard beet (if using). Transfer mixture to an airtight container. Cover and chill overnight before using.

**3** If desired, use a slotted spoon to serve pickled ginger.

nutrition facts per 1 teaspoon: 10 cal., 0 g total fat (0 g sat. fat), 0 mg chol., 74 mg sodium, 2 g carb., 0 g dietary fiber, 0 g protein.

## sushi essentials

- nori: *These paper-thin sheets of dried seaweed range in color from dark green to dark purple and have a sweet, clean taste.*

- rice: *While many larger supermarkets carry sushi-style rice, head to your local Asian market for the best quality and flavor. Also known as Japanese short grain white rice or japonica rice, sushi rice contains the right amount of starch to cook up glossy and sticky but not mushy or dry.*

- rice paddle: *This flat, round wooden paddle comes in handy for turning and cooling the rice after cooking. Soaking it in water before using prevents it from sticking to the rice.*

- sushi mat: *Made from long, slender bamboo sticks held together by cotton string, the sushi mat works as a guide for rolling sushi. Find the thin, square mat at specialty kitchen stores or Asian food stores.*

- wasabi: *Also called Japanese horseradish, wasabi is the root of an Asian plant. It has a sharp, spicy flavor that, when ground into paste, serves as a traditional sushi accompaniment. Look for wasabi powders and pastes at Asian food stores.*

Because the rice is sticky, moisten your fingers with water, then use them to spread the filling over the nori. Leave ½ inch of nori uncovered at one end so you can seal the edge once it is rolled.

Arrange the cucumber strips, crabmeat strips, and avocado slices in a straight line just below the center of the rice-covered nori. This allows you to roll the nori and rice up and over the veggies, enclosing them in the center of the roll.

Using the sushi mat as a guide, start with the filled side and tightly roll the nori toward the unfilled end. Then brush the unfilled end with water and press it against the roll to seal.

Before cutting each piece of sushi, spray a sharp knife with nonstick cooking spray. Use a back-and-forth sawing motion to cut clean, straight-edge slices.

*When cutting the sushi rolls, use a sharp knife. To prevent sticking, coat the knife with nonstick cooking spray.*

# california **sushi rolls**

prep: 30 minutes  cook: 15 minutes  cool: 45 minutes  makes: 12 pieces

1  recipe Sushi Rice
   Filling
2  8-inch square sheets
   nori (seaweed)
2  to 4 thin 8-inch-long
   strips of cucumber
1  to 2 ounces cooked
   crabmeat or leg-
   style imitation
   crabmeat, cut into
   thin strips
¼  of an avocado, pitted,
   peeled, and sliced
   Wasabi paste
   Soy sauce
   Bottled pickled sushi
   ginger (optional)

**1** Line a sushi mat with plastic wrap. Place a sheet of nori on top of plastic wrap. Using moistened fingers, spread 1 cup of the filling over nori, leaving ½ inch uncovered at the far side of the mat. Arrange half of the cucumber, half of the crabmeat, and half of the avocado in strips just below the center.

**2** Using the mat as a guide, roll nori tightly into a spiral, starting with the filled side and rolling toward the unfilled side. Press unfilled edge over top of roll, brushing with water to seal, if necessary. Repeat to make another sushi roll, using the remaining nori, filling, cucumber, crabmeat, and avocado.

**3** To serve, cut each sushi roll into six slices. Serve with wasabi paste, soy sauce, and pickled ginger (if desired).

nutrition facts per piece: 92 cal., 1 g total fat (0 g sat. fat), 3 mg chol., 662 mg sodium, 17 g carb., 1 g dietary fiber, 2 g protein.

**make-ahead directions:** Prepare sushi rolls as directed through Step 2. Cover and chill for up to 4 hours.

sushi rice filling: In a fine-mesh sieve, wash ½ cup uncooked short grain rice under cold running water for about 1 minute or until water runs clear, rubbing grains together with your fingers. Drain. In a small saucepan combine rinsed rice, 1 cup cold water, 2 tablespoons rice vinegar, and ¼ teaspoon salt. Bring to boiling; reduce heat. Cover and simmer for 15 minutes (rice should be sticky). Remove from heat. Stir in 1 tablespoon sugar and 1 tablespoon sake or dry sherry, if desired. Cool for at least 45 minutes or until room temperature. Fluff rice with a fork. Makes about 2 cups.

*Hollowed-out cucumber and summer squash, along with lettuce leaves form attractive bowls for the sushi filling. Just another simple, elegant way to share the popular Japanese cuisine, especially if you're having a sushi party.*

# vegetable sushi

prep: 25 minutes   cook: 15 minutes   cool: 45 minutes   makes: 36 appetizers

36   cucumber, squash,
        and/or lettuce bowls
1   recipe Carrot-Rice
        Filling
      Sesame seeds,
        toasted (optional)
      Fresh cilantro sprigs
        (optional)

**carrot-rice filling:** In a fine-mesh sieve wash 1/2 cup uncooked short grain rice under cold running water for about 1 minute or until water runs clear, rubbing grains together with your fingers; drain. In a small saucepan combine rinsed rice, 1 cup cold water, 2 tablespoons rice vinegar or white wine vinegar, and 1/4 teaspoon salt. Bring to boiling; reduce heat. Cover and simmer for 15 minutes (rice should be sticky). Remove from heat. Stir in 1/4 cup finely shredded carrot, 1 tablespoon sugar, and (if desired) 1 tablespoon sake or dry sherry. Cool for at least 45 minutes or until room temperature. Fluff rice with a fork. Makes about 2 cups.

**1** For cucumber bowls, peel and cut medium cucumbers crosswise into 1-inch-thick pieces. Using a small melon baller or a small spoon, hollow out centers.

**2** For squash bowls, cut baby zucchini in half lengthwise (if necessary, cut a thin slice from each bottom to keep zucchini upright). Cut baby pattypan squash in half lengthwise or crosswise. Cut medium yellow summer squash crosswise into 1-inch-thick pieces. Using the tip of a vegetable peeler, a small melon baller, or a small spoon, hollow out centers. If desired, steam and chill before stuffing; replace tops of pattypan squash after stuffing.

**3** For lettuce bowls, select the smallest romaine or butterhead (Boston or bibb) lettuce leaves. Rinse lettuce; pat dry with paper towels.

**4** Using a measuring teaspoon dipped in water, stuff each vegetable bowl with a scant 2 teaspoons of the filling. If desired, sprinkle with sesame seeds and garnish with cilantro. Serve within 2 hours.

nutrition facts per appetizer: 18 cal., 0 g total fat (0 g sat. fat), 0 mg chol., 18 mg sodium, 4 g carb., 0 g dietary fiber, 0 g protein.

**make-ahead directions:** Prepare the filling as directed. Cover and chill for up to 3 days. Prepare the vegetable bowls as directed. Invert onto paper towels in a storage container. Cover and chill for up to 24 hours.

*Shrimp is one of the most popular toppings for hand-pressed sushi. Since the shrimp are cooked, guests who don't care for raw fish can enjoy this sushi.*

# shrimp sushi

prep: 30 minutes  cook: 15 minutes  cool: 45 minutes  makes: 21 to 25 appetizers

1  medium cucumber
1  recipe Rice Filling
1  pound frozen peeled cooked shrimp with tails (21 to 25 shrimp), thawed
½  cup bottled pickled sushi ginger, cut into small pieces (optional)
   Fresh chives or green onion tops, cut into thin strips
   Wasabi paste (optional)

**1** Using a lemon zester or fork, score cucumber lengthwise. Cut into ¼-inch-thick slices. Using moistened fingers, scoop up a scant tablespoon of the filling and place on top of a cucumber slice. Repeat with the remaining filling and the remaining cucumber slices.

**2** Top each with a shrimp and, if desired, a small piece of pickled ginger. Garnish with chives. If desired, serve with wasabi paste. Serve within 2 hours.

nutrition facts per appetizer: 42 cal., 0 g total fat (0 g sat. fat), 42 mg chol., 76 mg sodium, 5 g carb., 0 g dietary fiber, 5 g protein.

rice filling: In a fine-mesh sieve, wash ½ cup uncooked short grain rice under cold running water for about 1 minute or until water runs clear, rubbing grains together with your fingers; drain. In a small saucepan combine rinsed rice, 1 cup cold water, 4 teaspoons rice vinegar or 1 tablespoon white vinegar, and ¼ teaspoon salt. Bring to boiling; reduce heat. Cover and simmer for 15 minutes (rice should be sticky). Remove from heat. Stir in 1½ teaspoons sugar. Cool for at least 45 minutes or until room temperature. Fluff rice with a fork. Makes about 2 cups.

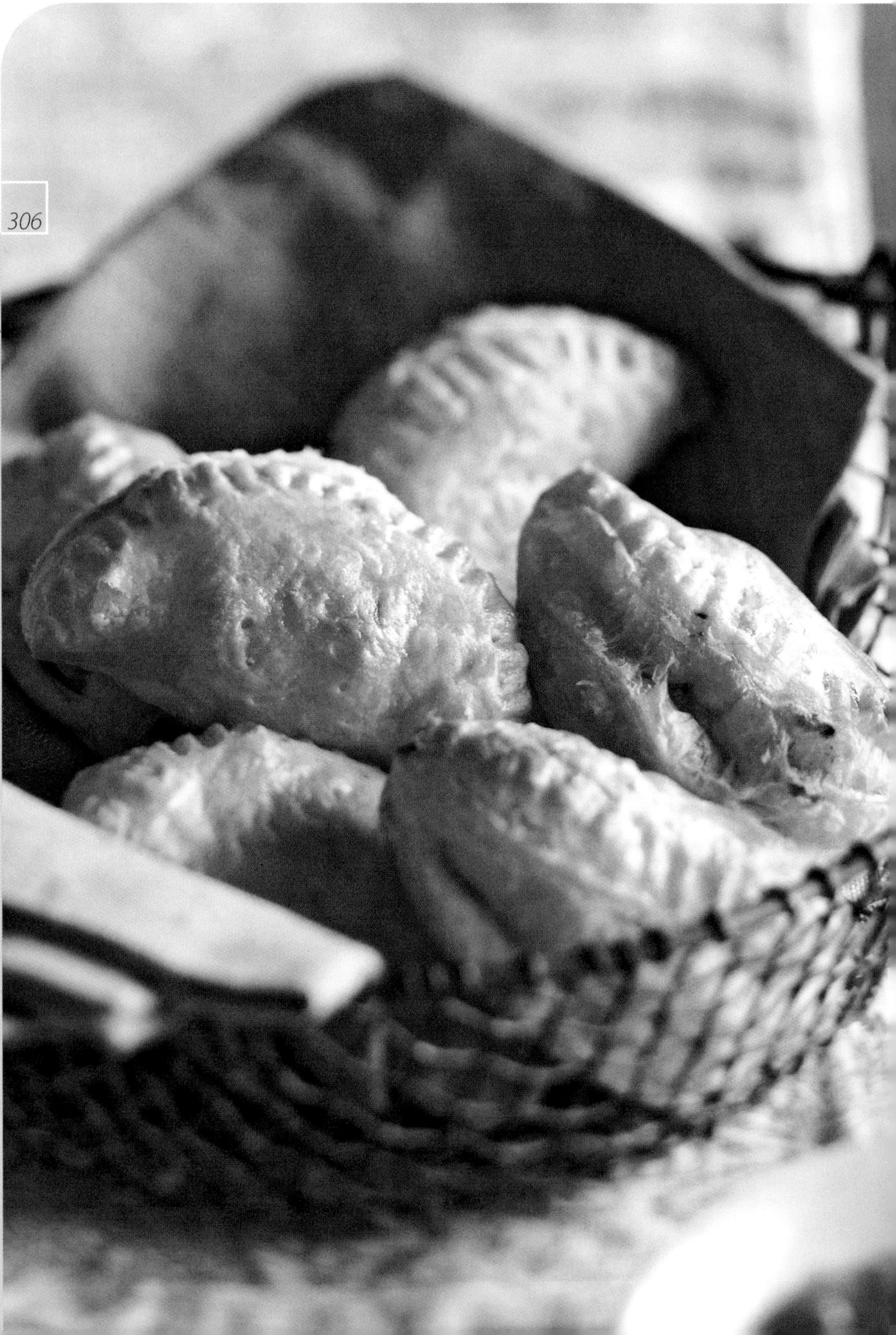

*Tiny in size but huge on flavor, these alluring appetizers are the miniature versions of the classic Spanish empanadas.*

# spicy beef
# empanaditas

prep: 40 minutes  bake: 18 minutes  stand: 5 minutes  oven: 400°F
makes: 18 servings

4 ounces lean ground beef
⅓ cup finely chopped onion
1 clove garlic, finely chopped
¼ teaspoon salt
¼ teaspoon ground cumin
⅛ teaspoon cayenne pepper
¼ cup chopped pitted ripe olives
3 tablespoons tomato puree
1 tablespoon golden raisins
2 teaspoons finely shredded lime peel
1 17.3-ounce package frozen puff pastry sheets (2 sheets), thawed
1 egg, lightly beaten
1 tablespoon water
Bottled green salsa (optional)

**1** Preheat oven to 400°F. Line a large baking sheet with parchment paper or foil; set aside. For filling, in a medium-size skillet cook ground beef, onion, and garlic over medium-high heat until meat is brown. Drain off fat. Stir in salt, cumin, and cayenne pepper. Cook and stir for 2 minutes. Stir in olives, tomato puree, raisins, and lime peel. Remove from heat. Cool for about 10 minutes.

**2** Meanwhile, on a lightly floured surface unfold pastry. Using a 3-inch round cookie cutter, cut each sheet into nine rounds (18 total).

**3** Spoon a scant tablespoon of the filling onto each pastry round. In a small bowl combine egg and the water. Lightly brush edges of pastry rounds with egg mixture. Fold each round in half. Press edges together with a fork to seal. Prick each top several times. Place on the prepared baking sheet. Lightly brush tops and sides with egg mixture.

**4** Bake for 18 to 20 minutes or until pastries are puffed and golden brown. Let stand for 5 minutes before serving. If desired, serve with green salsa.

nutrition facts per serving: 143 cal., 10 g total fat (0 g sat. fat), 16 mg chol., 161 mg sodium, 11 g carb., 0 g dietary fiber, 3 g protein.

*Serve this fiesta food buffet-style. Place an assortment of toppers in small bowls next to the meat-filled corn tortilla cups and let guests add their own toppings.*

# shredded pork chalupas

prep: 1 hour  bake: 23 minutes  cook: 8 to 10 hours (low) or 4 to 5 hours (high)
oven: 375°/350° F  makes: 32 servings

1½  pounds boneless pork shoulder or beef chuck roast, cut into 2-inch chunks
1  8-ounce can tomato sauce
2  canned chipotle chile peppers in adobo sauce
1  teaspoon cumin seeds
4  cloves garlic, minced
2  cups masa harina (corn tortilla flour)
1  cup finely shredded cheddar cheese (4 ounces)
1  teaspoon baking powder
¼  cup lard or shortening
1  egg yolk
1  cup warm water
   Assorted toppers (dairy sour cream, chopped tomatoes, finely shredded cheddar cheese, and/or sliced green onions; optional)

**1** In a 3½- or 4-quart slow cooker combine meat, tomato sauce, peppers, cumin seeds, garlic, ½ cup *water,* and ½ teaspoon *salt.* Cover and cook on low heat setting for 8 to 10 hours or on high heat setting for 4 to 5 hours.

**2** Remove meat; cool until easy to handle. Strain and reserve cooking liquid. Using two forks, shred meat. Stir in enough liquid to moisten. Cover and chill meat mixture and liquid until needed or up to 3 days.

**3** Preheat oven to 375°F. To prepare chalupas, in a medium bowl combine masa harina, cheese, baking powder, and ½ teaspoon *salt.* In a large mixing bowl beat lard and egg yolk with an electric mixer on medium speed until light and fluffy. Alternately add masa mixture and warm water to mixture until soft dough forms. (If necessary, add more water, 1 teaspoon at a time, to make a soft dough that is easy to handle.)

**4** Using a tablespoon of dough each, shape 32 smooth 1-inch balls. Place 3 inches apart on a very large greased baking sheet. Flatten each ball to a 2¾-inch circle and build up edges slightly. Bake, uncovered, about 15 minutes or until set and bottoms are lightly browned. Cool on baking sheet. Use immediately or place in an airtight container and store at room temperature for up to 2 days.

**5** To serve, preheat oven to 350°F. Transfer meat mixture to a large skillet; cook and stir mixture over medium heat until heated through, adding cooking liquid, if necessary, to moisten. Meanwhile, return chalupas to baking sheet. Bake, uncovered, for 8 to 10 minutes or until heated through. Spoon on shredded meat mixture. If desired, add toppers.

nutrition facts per serving: 90 cal., 5 g total fat (2 g sat. fat), 25 mg chol., 157 mg sodium, 7 g carb., 1 g dietary fiber, 6 g protein.

**make-ahead directions:** Prepare meat mixture and chalupas as directed through Step 4. Place in separate freezer containers. Cover and freeze for up to 1 month. Thaw in the refrigerator for 1 to 2 days. Reheat as directed.

*This sweet-tart Sicilian dish (kap-oh-NAH-tah) features sautéed eggplant, sweet pepper, onion, and celery spiked with vinegar and tomatoes. Serve this as an antipasto over Italian bread slices.*

# caponata

prep: 30 minutes   cook: 35 minutes   makes: 16 (¼-cup) servings

2   tablespoons olive oil
1   medium red sweet pepper, cut into bite-size pieces
¾   cup chopped onion (1 large)
⅓   cup chopped celery
½   of a 28-ounce can Italian-style whole peeled tomatoes in puree, drained
½   cup chopped pitted green olives
¼   cup golden raisins
3   tablespoons white wine vinegar
1   tablespoon capers, rinsed and drained
1   teaspoon sugar
¼   teaspoon salt
    Dash cayenne pepper
1   medium eggplant, peeled and cut into 1-inch cubes
2   tablespoons olive oil
¼   cup pine nuts, lightly toasted*
1   recipe Toasted Italian Bread

1 In a large saucepan heat 2 tablespoons oil over medium heat. Cook sweet pepper in hot oil for 5 to 8 minutes or until tender. Using a slotted spoon, remove pepper from pan. Add onion and celery to pan. Cook for 5 to 8 minutes or until just tender.

2 Add tomatoes, olives, raisins, vinegar, capers, sugar, salt, and cayenne pepper to pan. Cook, uncovered, over low heat for 15 minutes, stirring occasionally. Stir in sweet pepper.

3 Meanwhile, in a very large skillet heat 1 tablespoon oil. Cook half eggplant in hot oil over medium heat about 5 minutes or until tender and browned. Transfer eggplant to paper towels to drain. Repeat with remaining 1 tablespoon oil and remaining eggplant. Stir the eggplant into the tomato mixture. Cook, uncovered, for 10 minutes more.

4 Cool mixture to room temperature, or if time permits, cover and refrigerate overnight to allow the flavors to blend. Bring to room temperature before serving. Just before serving, stir in pine nuts. Serve over Toasted Italian Bread.

nutrition facts per serving: 173 cal., 9 g total fat (1 g sat. fat), 0 mg chol., 361 mg sodium, 20 g carb., 2 g dietary fiber, 4 g protein.

*note: To toast pine nuts, spread nuts in a single layer in a shallow baking pan. Bake in a 350°F oven for 4 to 6 minutes or until light golden brown, watching carefully and stirring once or twice so the nuts don't burn.

toasted italian bread: Cut a 1-pound loaf of Italian bread in half lengthwise. Brush cut sides with olive oil. Place on a large baking sheet. Broil 6 inches from the heat for 2 to 3 minutes or until toasted. Cut crosswise into 1-inch slices.

*Tantalize taste buds with a sophisticated tray of bite-size appetizer roll varieties paired with roasted sweet peppers, artichoke hearts, olives, capers, and bread.*

# italian-style relish tray

start to finish: 30 minutes  makes: 12 servings

1  recipe Salami Rolls
1  recipe Italian Cheese Bites
1  7-ounce jar roasted red and/or yellow sweet peppers, drained and cut into strips
2  6-ounce jars marinated artichoke hearts, drained
8  ounces pitted green or ripe olives, drained
   Capers, rinsed and drained
   Thinly sliced ciabatta or Italian bread (optional)

Arrange Salami Rolls, Italian Cheese Bites, sweet pepper strips, artichoke hearts, and olives on a serving platter. Sprinkle capers over artichoke hearts. If desired, serve with ciabatta.

nutrition facts per serving: 426 cal., 37 g total fat (17 g sat. fat), 69 mg chol., 1406 mg sodium, 6 g carb., 1 g dietary fiber, 19 g protein.

salami rolls: Spread 24 thin slices garlic salami (about 4 ounces) with ¼ cup kalamata olive tapenade. Place a roasted red sweet pepper strip along one edge of each salami slice; roll up. Cut in half crosswise.

italian cheese bites: Cut 4 ounces thinly sliced prosciutto into narrow strips. Cut 1½ pounds Taleggio, Asiago, and/or aged provolone cheese into bite-size pieces. Wrap a prosciutto strip around each piece of cheese.

*Serve up medallions of polenta that are crisp on the outside and creamy on the inside, topped with fresh Italian flavors. Find ready-to-cook tubes of polenta in the refrigerated produce section of the supermarket.*

# polenta with peppers and olives

prep: 25 minutes  bake: 10 minutes  oven: 350°F  makes: 12 servings

1  16-ounce tube refrigerated cooked polenta
2  tablespoons olive oil
1  cup red, green, and/or yellow sweet pepper cut into thin strips
⅛  teaspoon salt
⅛  teaspoon crushed red pepper
¼  cup pitted kalamata olives, coarsely chopped
2  tablespoons finely shredded Parmesan cheese
1½  teaspoons snipped fresh rosemary

**1** Preheat oven to 350°F. Trim ends of polenta. Cut polenta into twelve ½-inch-thick slices. Brush polenta slices with 1 tablespoon of the oil. Place polenta slices on a baking sheet. Bake for 10 to 15 minutes or until heated through.

**2** Meanwhile, in a 10-inch skillet heat remaining 1 tablespoon oil over medium heat. Cook and stir sweet pepper strips, salt, and crushed red pepper in hot oil until pepper strips are tender. Stir in the olives.

**3** To serve, spoon pepper mixture over warm polenta slices. Sprinkle with Parmesan cheese and rosemary.

nutrition facts per serving: 52 cal., 4 g total fat (1 g sat. fat), 3 mg chol., 124 mg sodium, 4 g carb., 1 g dietary fiber, 1 g protein.

quick polenta toppers: Prepare polenta as directed above through Step 1 except sprinkle with ½ cup finely shredded Parmesan cheese for the last 5 minutes of baking. To serve, top polenta with desired toppings: ¾ cup marinated artichoke hearts, drained and chopped; ¾ cup pepperoni slices, cut into slivers; 1½ teaspoons snipped fresh rosemary; 1 tablespoon snipped fresh basil; 2 teaspoons snipped fresh oregano; ½ cup pitted kalamata olives, chopped; ½ cup flaked lox-style smoked salmon; or ½ cup salsa mixed with ⅓ cup refried beans.

*Rich feta cheese bites, lusciously topped with olives and basil, are small in size but bold in flavor.*

# tuscan **cheesecake** bites

prep: 25 minutes   bake: 12 minutes   cool: 10 minutes   oven: 350°F
makes: 24 tartlets

⅓   cup panko (Japanese-style breadcrumbs)
⅓   cup ground walnuts
½   teaspoon dried basil, crushed
2   tablespoons butter, melted
1   8-ounce package reduced-fat cream cheese (Neufchâtel), softened
½   of an 8-ounce package feta cheese with basil and tomato, crumbled
1   egg
2   tablespoons dairy sour cream
2   tablespoons chopped pitted ripe olives
2   tablespoons snipped fresh basil

**1** Preheat oven to 350°F. Line twenty-four 1¾-inch muffin cups with paper liners; set aside. In a small bowl combine panko, walnuts, and dried basil. Stir in butter. Spoon a slightly rounded teaspoon of panko mixture onto the bottoms of each lined cup. Press into bottoms using the rounded side of a measuring teaspoon; set aside.

**2** In a medium mixing bowl beat cream cheese with an electric mixer on medium speed until light and fluffy. Add feta and egg. Beat until combined. Stir in sour cream. Spoon about 1 tablespoon filling into each crust-lined muffin cup.

**3** Bake for 12 to 15 minutes or until filling appears set. Cool in pan on a wire rack for 10 minutes. Carefully remove to a serving platter. Serve warm topped with olives and basil.

nutrition facts per tartlet: 64 cal., 6 g total fat (3 g sat. fat), 22 mg chol., 103 mg sodium, 1 g carb., 0 g dietary fiber, 2 g protein.

*It takes only a few minutes to make these little nuggets. To please your vegetarian guests, substitute cherry tomatoes for the pepperoni.*

## olive-pepperoni
# kabobs

start to finish: 20 minutes  makes: 12 appetizers

12  5-inch fresh rosemary
    stems
12  4×1-inch rectangles
    thinly sliced
    provolone cheese
12  2-inch-diameter
    rounds thinly sliced
    pepperoni
12  pitted kalamata
    olives

**1** Strip leaves from rosemary stems, leaving 1-inch of foliage at one end of each stem.

**2** Arrange a piece of provolone, a slice of pepperoni, and an olive on each rosemary skewer.

nutrition facts per appetizer: 85 cal., 7 g total fat (3 g sat. fat), 16 mg chol., 265 mg sodium, 1 g carb., 0 g dietary fiber, 5 g protein.

*Have this ready-to-devour hors d'oeuvre waiting in the fridge when guests arrive. All you'll need for serving is a pretty bowl and frilly toothpicks.*

# marinated feta and olives

prep: 30 minutes  marinate: 4 hours  makes: 20 (¼-cup) servings

1 pound feta cheese, cut into ½-inch cubes
1 cup pitted kalamata olives
1 cup pitted green olives
½ cup bottled roasted red sweet pepper, cut into strips
1 red onion, cut into thin wedges
½ cup olive oil
½ cup balsamic vinegar
4 cloves garlic, minced
1 tablespoon snipped fresh thyme leaves
2 teaspoons snipped fresh oregano
½ teaspoon cracked black pepper

**1** In a large glass or stainless-steel bowl combine cheese, kalamata and green olives, sweet pepper, and onion.

**2** In a screw-top jar combine oil, vinegar, garlic, thyme, oregano, and black pepper. Cover and shake well. Pour over mixture in bowl. Toss gently to coat.

**3** Cover and marinate in the refrigerator for 4 to 6 hours before serving. Serve with toothpicks.

nutrition facts per serving: 138 cal., 12 g total fat (4 g sat. fat), 20 mg chol., 444 mg sodium, 4 g carb., 1 g dietary fiber, 3 g protein.

**make-ahead directions:** Prepare as directed, except cover and store in the refrigerator for up to 2 days.

*Just a handful of ingredients turns a simple jar of olives into a delicacy.*

# mediterranean-spiced olives

prep: 20 minutes  marinate: 24 hours  stand: 1 hour  makes: 16 servings

1  16-ounce jar cracked green olives, drained
⅔  cup bottled roasted red sweet pepper*, drained and thinly sliced
⅓  cup olive oil
3  tablespoons drained capers
3  tablespoons sherry vinegar
2  tablespoons snipped fresh rosemary
1  tablespoon ground cumin
4  cloves garlic, slivered
½  to ¾ teaspoon crushed red pepper

**1** In a medium glass or stainless steel bowl combine olives, sweet pepper, oil, capers, vinegar, rosemary, cumin, garlic, and crushed red pepper. Cover and marinate in the refrigerator for 24 hours.

**2** To serve, let stand at room temperature for 1 hour.

nutrition facts per serving: 87 cal., 9 g total fat (1 g sat. fat), 0 mg chol., 490 mg sodium, 2 g carb., 1 g dietary fiber, 1 g protein.

**make-ahead directions:** Prepare as directed in Step 1, except marinate in refrigerator for up to 7 days. Serve as directed.

**note**

*To roast sweet peppers, preheat oven to 425°F. Quarter 2 sweet peppers lengthwise; remove and discard stems, seeds, and membranes. Place pepper quarters, cut sides down, on a foil-lined baking sheet. Roast for 20 to 25 minutes or until pepper skins are blistered and dark. Bring foil up around peppers to enclose. Let stand for about 15 minutes or until cool. Using a sharp knife, loosen edges of the skins; gently pull off the skin in strips and discard. Chop enough of the roasted peppers to equal 1 cup.*

*Wrapped with goodness, tender turkey encases a savory herbed sweet pepper, dried tomato, and feta cheese filling. The fact that it is rolled makes it a roulade (pronounced roo-LAHD).*

# greek-stuffed turkey roulade

prep: 35 minutes   roast: 30 minutes   stand: 10 minutes   oven: 400°F
makes: about 20 servings

- 2   12- to 14-ounce turkey breast tenderloins
- ½   teaspoon salt
- ¼   teaspoon ground black pepper
- 1   cup chopped roasted yellow sweet pepper* (see note, opposite)
- ½   cup crumbled feta cheese (2 ounces)
- ¼   cup oil-packed dried tomato, drained and chopped
- ¼   cup snipped fresh basil
- 2   teaspoons snipped fresh thyme
- 3   cloves garlic, minced
- 1   tablespoon olive oil
      Fresh basil leaves (optional)

**1** Preheat oven to 400°F. Line a 15×10×1-inch baking pan with foil. Place a rack in the foil-lined pan; set aside. Make a lengthwise cut down the center of each turkey tenderloin, cutting almost to, but not through, the other side. Spread open. Place each tenderloin between two pieces of plastic wrap. Working from the center to the edges, pound turkey lightly with the flat side of a meat mallet until about ¼ inch thick. Remove wrap. Sprinkle turkey with the salt and black pepper.

**2** For stuffing, in a medium bowl combine sweet pepper, cheese, dried tomato, the snipped basil, the thyme, and garlic.

**3** Spread stuffing over turkey portions to within ½ inch of the edges. Starting from a long side, roll up each portion into a spiral. Tie at 2-inch intervals with 100-percent-cotton kitchen string. Brush rolls with oil and sprinkle with additional salt and black pepper. Place rolls on the rack in the prepared baking pan.

**4** Roast, uncovered, for 30 to 35 minutes or until turkey is no longer pink (170°F). Remove from oven. Cover loosely with foil; let stand for 10 minutes before slicing. Remove and discard string. Cut rolls into 1-inch-thick slices. Serve warm. If desired, serve on basil leaves.

nutrition facts per serving: 59 cal., 2 g total fat (1 g sat. fat), 24 mg chol., 146 mg sodium, 1 g carb., 0 g dietary fiber, 9 g protein.

**make-ahead directions:** Prepare as directed, except do not slice turkey rolls. Wrap each roll in plastic wrap and chill for up to 48 hours. Cut into 1-inch-thick slices before serving.

*Roasting the mushrooms brings out their earthiness, while garlic, a splash of sherry, and fresh sage leaves take them one step further to fabulous.*

# roasted mushrooms
## with fresh sage

prep: 30 minutes   roast: 30 minutes   stand: 2 to 6 hours (tapenade)
oven: 450°F   makes: 8 to 10 servings

3   pounds assorted fresh mushrooms (such as chanterelle, shiitake, button, cremini, morel, and/or oyster)
3   heads garlic
3   tablespoons butter, melted
3   tablespoons olive oil
½   teaspoon salt
½   teaspoon ground black pepper
     Dry sherry or port
¼   cup fresh sage leaves, coarsely torn
1   8-ounce carton dairy sour cream
2   to 3 tablespoons prepared horseradish
     Coarsely crushed pink peppercorns
1   recipe Roasted Red Pepper and Black Olive Tapenade
     Toasted baguette slices

**1** Preheat oven to 450°F. If using shiitake and/or oyster mushrooms, remove and discard stems. Brush any dirt off mushrooms, leaving mushrooms whole (you should have about 16 cups). Remove loose outer skins of garlic heads. Trim stem ends to expose cloves; break apart cloves.

**2** Place mushrooms and garlic in a large roasting pan. In a small bowl combine butter and oil. Drizzle over mushrooms and garlic. Toss to coat. Sprinkle with salt and black pepper. Roast about 30 minutes or until mushrooms are tender and garlic cloves are soft, stirring twice. Transfer mushrooms and garlic to a serving platter. Splash with sherry; sprinkle with sage.

**3** In a small bowl combine sour cream and horseradish; sprinkle with crushed peppercorns. Serve mushrooms and garlic with sour cream mixture, Roasted Red Pepper and Black Olive Tapenade, and toasted baguette slices.

nutrition facts per serving: 254 cal., 23 g total fat (8 g sat. fat), 25 mg chol., 301 mg sodium, 11 g carb., 2 g dietary fiber, 7 g protein.

**make-ahead directions:** Prepare Roasted Red Pepper and Black Olive Tapenade as directed, except cover and chill for up to 24 hours. Let stand at room temperature for 30 minutes before serving.

roasted red pepper and black olive tapenade: In a small bowl combine ½ cup coarsely chopped pitted ripe olives, ⅓ cup coarsely chopped roasted red sweet pepper, 2 tablespoons olive oil, 1 tablespoon snipped fresh rosemary, 2 teaspoons snipped fresh oregano, and 1½ teaspoons finely shredded lemon peel. Let stand at room temperature for 2 to 6 hours to allow flavors to blend. Serve at room temperature.

*Accompany this coarse-textured country-style spread with apple or pear slices or toasted baguette rounds.*

# cranberry-pistachio pâté

prep: 30 minutes  chill: 12 hours  bake: 1 hour 30 minutes  oven: 350°F
makes: 24 servings

1   egg, lightly beaten
¾   cup dried cranberries
½   cup chopped shallots or onion
½   cup chopped pistachio
⅓   cup port wine or cranberry juice
¼   cup half-and-half or light cream
¼   cup fine dry breadcrumbs
2   teaspoons dried sage leaves, crushed, or ½ teaspoon ground sage
1   teaspoon salt
1   teaspoon ground black pepper
2   cloves garlic, minced
1   pound lean ground beef
1   pound lean ground pork
    Stone-ground mustard

**1** Preheat oven to 350°F. Lightly coat a 9×5×3-inch loaf pan with cooking spray; set aside.

**2** In a large bowl combine egg, cranberries, shallot, nuts, wine, half-and-half, breadcrumbs, sage, salt, pepper, and garlic; mix well. Add ground beef and pork; mix well. Press mixture into prepared pan. Cover tightly with foil.

**3** Bake for 1½ hours. Remove pan from oven. Cool slightly. Uncover. Carefully pour off drippings, leaving pâté in pan. Cover pâté loosely with foil. Place several heavy cans of food in another 9×5×3-inch loaf pan to serve as a weight. Place pan on top of the covered pâté. Chill for 12 to 24 hours.

**4** Remove weighted pan and foil. If necessary, loosen sides of pâté. Invert onto a serving platter. Cut in half lengthwise and then into thin slices. Serve pâté with stone-ground mustard.

nutrition facts per serving: 135 cal., 9 g total fat (3 g sat. fat), 36 mg chol., 155 mg sodium, 6 g carb., 1 g dietary fiber, 8 g protein.

**make-ahead directions:** Prepare as directed through Step 3. Remove weighted pan and foil. If necessary, loosen sides of pâté. Invert pâté onto a plate. Wrap pâté in plastic wrap and store in the refrigerator for up to 2 days. Serve as directed in Step 4.

*If you love chicken livers, you'll love this elegant spread. Plan ahead for several hours of chilling to let the flavors blend.*

# chicken liver pâté

prep: 15 minutes   chill: 3 hours   cook: 10 minutes
makes: 8 (2-tablespoon) servings

2   slices bacon
8   ounces chicken livers
1   medium onion,
      chopped (½ cup)
4   cloves garlic, minced
2   tablespoons dry
      white wine or milk
¼   teaspoon salt
¼   teaspoon ground
      black pepper
¼   teaspoon ground
      nutmeg or
      ⅛ teaspoon ground
      allspice
      Snipped fresh parsley
      or chives (optional)
      Assorted crackers

**1** In a large skillet cook bacon until crisp. Drain bacon on paper towels, reserving 2 tablespoons drippings in skillet. Crumble bacon; set aside.

**2** Add chicken livers, onion, and garlic to reserved drippings in skillet. Cook and stir over medium heat for about 5 minutes or until livers are no longer pink. Cool slightly.

**3** In a food processor or blender combine crumbled bacon, chicken liver mixture, wine, salt, pepper, and nutmeg. Cover and process or blend just until combined (mixture will be soft). Spoon liver mixture into a crock or several small ramekins. (Or line a 1-cup mold or bowl with plastic wrap; spoon in liver mixture.) Cover and chill for 3 to 24 hours.

**4** To serve, place crock or ramekins on a serving plate. (Or uncover and invert mold or bowl onto a platter.) If desired, sprinkle with parsley. Serve pâté with crackers.

nutrition facts per serving: 84 cal., 5 g total fat (2 g sat. fat), 103 mg chol., 145 mg sodium, 2 g carb., 0 g dietary fiber, 6 g protein.

*The dense, earthy flavor of portobello mushrooms makes this a rave-drawing appetizer. The longer you chill this, the better it will taste.*

# portobello pâté

prep: 35 minutes   chill: 3 hours   makes: 12 to 14 (2-tablespoon) servings

8  ounces portobello
    mushrooms
2  tablespoons butter
¼  cup dry white wine
1  8-ounce package
    cream cheese,
    softened
2  tablespoons butter,
    softened
1½ teaspoons snipped
    fresh rosemary
2  cloves garlic, minced
¼  teaspoon salt
¼  teaspoon white
    pepper
    Toasted baguette-
    style French bread
    slices

**1** Trim down mushroom stems to be even with caps, discarding stems. Lightly rinse mushrooms; pat dry with paper towels. Finely chop mushrooms.

**2** In a large skillet heat 2 tablespoons butter over medium heat. Cook mushrooms in hot butter about 5 minutes or until mushrooms are tender and most of the liquid evaporates. Carefully add wine. Cook for 2 minutes more or until most of the liquid evaporates.

**3** In a medium mixing bowl combine mushrooms, cream cheese, the softened butter, rosemary, garlic, salt, and pepper. Beat with an electric mixer on medium speed until nearly smooth. Cover and chill for 3 to 24 hours.

**4** Serve pâté on toasted baguette slices.

nutrition facts per serving: 109 cal., 10 g total fat (6 g sat. fat), 31 mg chol., 138 mg sodium, 2 g carb., 0 g dietary fiber, 2 g protein.

**make-ahead directions:** Prepare as directed through Step 3, except store in the refrigerator for up to 1 week. Serve as directed.

Bold, exciting flavors make these soups—
from warm, rich bisques and chowders to
cool and chunky gazpacho—stand out at
any gathering or first course.

small bo

11
wls

*Barley adds both a chewy texture and a nutty flavor to this hearty appetizer soup. Look for barley next to the rice at your supermarket.*

# beef and barley soup

prep: 20 minutes   cook: 7 to 8 hours (low) or 3½ to 4 hours (high)
makes: 8 servings

12  ounces boneless
      beef chuck, cut into
      ½-inch cubes
4   cups water
1   10½-ounce can
      condensed French
      onion soup
1   cup shredded carrot
½   cup medium pearl
      barley
1   teaspoon dried thyme
      or oregano, crushed
      Salt
      Ground black pepper

**1** Coat an unheated large skillet with nonstick cooking spray. Preheat over medium heat. Add meat to hot skillet; cook until brown. Drain off fat.

**2** In a 3½- to 4½-quart slow cooker combine meat, the water, French onion soup, carrot, pearl barley, and thyme.

**3** Cover and cook on low heat setting for 7 to 8 hours or on high heat setting for 3½ to 4 hours. Season to taste with salt and pepper.

nutrition facts per serving: 116 cal., 2 g total fat (1 g sat. fat), 26 mg chol., 453 mg sodium, 13 g carb., 3 g dietary fiber, 11 g protein.

**make-ahead directions:** Prepare as directed. Cool slightly. Cover and chill for up to 2 days. Reheat over low heat before serving.

*Create a spectacular first course for a special dinner—small bowls of this rich and creamy soup. The toasted buttery croutons make a great accompaniment for practically any soup.*

# chicken-spinach soup

start to finish: 25 minutes  makes: 8 servings

¼  cup butter
½  cup chopped red
    sweet pepper
½  cup all-purpose flour
6  cups chicken broth*
2  cups chopped cooked
    chicken (10 ounces)
1  10-ounce package
    frozen chopped
    spinach, thawed
    and well drained
¼  teaspoon ground
    nutmeg
1  cup half-and-half
    or light cream
    Ground nutmeg
    (optional)
1  recipe Star-Shaped
    Croutons (optional)

**1** In a large saucepan melt butter over medium heat. Cook pepper in hot butter for 2 to 3 minutes or until tender. Stir in flour. Cook and stir for 1 minute. Stir in chicken broth. Cook and stir until slightly thickened and bubbly.

**2** Add the chicken, spinach, and the ¼ teaspoon nutmeg. Stir in half-and-half. Heat through. If desired, sprinkle individual servings with additional nutmeg. If desired, serve with Star-Shaped Croutons.

nutrition facts per serving: 208 cal., 12 g total fat (7 g sat. fat), 60 mg chol., 853 mg sodium, 9 g carb., 1 g dietary fiber, 14 g protein.

*note: If you'd like to reduce the sodium, use reduced-sodium chicken broth.

**make-ahead directions:** Prepare as directed, except do not add the spinach. Cool slightly. Cover and chill for up to 2 days. Reheat over low heat. Stir in the spinach. Heat through. Serve as directed.

star-shaped croutons:
Preheat oven to 350°F. Using a 1-inch star-shaped cutter, cut out shapes from bread slices. Brush cutouts with melted butter. Bake for 6 to 8 minutes or until toasted, turning once.

*This soup combines wild rice with a rich, creamy blend of chicken, mushrooms, and whipping cream.*

# chicken–wild rice soup

prep: 25 minutes    cook: 35 minutes    makes: 8 servings

3   14-ounce cans chicken broth
1   cup coarsely chopped carrot
½   cup wild rice, rinsed and drained
½   cup chopped celery
½   cup chopped onion
2   cups sliced fresh mushrooms
2   tablespoons butter
¼   cup all-purpose flour
¼   teaspoon salt
¼   teaspoon ground black pepper
1   cup whipping cream
2   cups chopped cooked chicken (10 ounces)
   Snipped fresh chives (optional)
   Sliced baguette-style French bread, toasted (optional)

**1** In a large pot combine 2 cans of the broth, the carrot, rice, celery, and onion. Bring to boiling; reduce heat. Cover and simmer for 35 to 40 minutes or until wild rice is tender but still chewy; add the mushrooms for the last 5 minutes of cooking.

**2** Meanwhile, in a medium saucepan melt butter over medium heat. Stir in flour, salt, and pepper. Add the remaining 1 can broth. Cook and stir until thickened and bubbly. Cook and stir for 1 minute more. Stir in whipping cream.

**3** Add whipping cream mixture to wild rice mixture, stirring constantly. Stir in chicken; heat through. If desired, garnish each serving with chives and serve with bread slices.

nutrition facts per serving: 271 cal., 17 g total fat (12 g sat. fat), 82 mg chol., 749 mg sodium, 15 g carb., 2 g dietary fiber, 14 g protein.

**make-ahead directions:** Prepare as directed. Cool slightly. Cover and chill for up to 2 days. Reheat over low heat before serving.

*This soup owes its extraordinary flavor to Yukon gold potatoes, artichoke hearts, and a blend of seasonings.*

# chicken and artichoke heart soup

prep: 30 minutes   cook: 60 minutes   makes: 6 servings

3   tablespoons butter
1   large onion, finely
      chopped
1   stalk celery, sliced
2   cloves garlic, minced
3   tablespoons all-
      purpose flour
2   14-ounce cans
      reduced-sodium
      chicken broth
1   14½-ounce can
      diced tomatoes,
      undrained
8   ounces skinless,
      boneless chicken
      breast halves, cut
      into 1-inch pieces
1   large Yukon gold
      potato, peeled and
      chopped
1   medium carrot,
      peeled and sliced
½   teaspoon dried
      rosemary, crushed
½   teaspoon dried
      thyme, crushed
½   teaspoon dried
      parsley flakes
¼   teaspoon cayenne
      pepper
1   14-ounce can
      artichoke hearts,
      drained and
      quartered
2   tablespoons grated
      Parmesan cheese

**1** In a large pot melt butter over medium heat. Cook onion and celery in hot butter for about 4 minutes or until tender. Add garlic. Cook for 1 minute. Stir in flour. Cook for about 1 minute or until lightly browned. Stir in broth, 2 cups *water*, tomatoes, chicken, potato, carrot, dried herbs, cayenne pepper, ½ teaspoon *salt*, and ¼ teaspoon *ground black pepper*. Bring to boiling; reduce heat. Cover and simmer for 55 minutes.

**2** Stir in artichoke hearts. Heat through. Serve with grated cheese.

nutrition facts per serving: 193 cal., 7 g total fat (5 g sat. fat), 39 mg chol., 949 mg sodium, 18 g carb., 4 g dietary fiber, 14 g protein.

**make-ahead directions:** Prepare as directed through Step 2, but do not add the Parmesan cheese until serving. Cool slightly. Cover and chill for up to 2 days. Reheat over low heat before serving.

*Rev up this colorful blend of pasta and vegetables by using hot Italian sausage rather than mild.*

# italian sausage soup

prep: 30 minutes   cook: 1½ hours   makes: 8 servings

1 pound Italian sausage (casings removed, if present)
1 large onion, chopped
1 medium carrot, chopped
1 stalk celery, chopped
8 cups chicken broth
1 14½-ounce can diced tomatoes, undrained
1 8-ounce can tomato sauce
1 clove garlic, minced
1 teaspoon dried oregano, crushed
½ teaspoon dried rosemary, crushed
½ teaspoon dried basil, crushed
¼ teaspoon dried thyme, crushed
¼ teaspoon fennel seeds, crushed
1 bay leaf
½ cup dried orzo or finely broken cappellini pasta
Finely shredded Parmesan cheese (optional)

**1** In a 4-quart Dutch oven combine sausage, onion, carrot, and celery. Cook over medium heat until sausage browns. Drain off fat. Add broth, tomatoes, tomato sauce, garlic, oregano, rosemary, basil, thyme, fennel seeds, and bay leaf to sausage mixture. Bring to boiling; reduce heat. Cover and simmer for 1 hour.

**2** Add uncooked pasta to sausage mixture. Return to boiling; reduce heat. Cook, uncovered, for 30 minutes more. Discard bay leaf. If desired, serve with shredded Parmesan cheese.

nutrition facts per serving: 283 cal., 19 g total fat (6 g sat. fat), 46 mg chol., 1635 mg sodium, 17 g carb., 2 g dietary fiber, 12 g protein.

**make-ahead directions:** Prepare as directed in Step 1. Cool slightly. Cover and chill for up to 2 days. Reheat over medium heat until boiling. Add uncooked pasta.

*The flavor of this creamy melted cheese soup depends on the quality of the cheese, so if you can, splurge on a good sharp cheddar. Both wine and beer go well with this soup.*

# cheddar cheese soup

prep: 40 minutes   cook: 25 minutes   makes: 12 servings

1   tablespoon olive oil
½   cup sliced celery
      (1 stalk)
1   cup coarsely chopped
      onion
4   cloves garlic, sliced
3   14-ounce cans
      reduced-sodium
      chicken broth
2   12-ounce cans
      evaporated fat-free
      milk
½   cup all-purpose flour
2   cups shredded
      cheddar cheese
      (8 ounces)
¼   teaspoon ground
      white pepper
      (optional)
    Shredded cheddar
      cheese (optional)

**1** In a large pot heat oil over medium heat. Cook celery, onion, and garlic in hot oil for 3 to 5 minutes or until tender. Add broth. Bring to boiling; reduce heat. Cover and simmer for 25 minutes.

**2** Pour mixture through a fine-mesh strainer. Reserve broth; discard vegetables. Return broth to Dutch oven. In a screw-top jar, combine evaporated milk and flour. Cover and shake well until smooth. Stir into broth. Cook and stir until thickened and bubbly.

**3** Add the 2 cups cheese. Cook and stir over low heat until cheese melts. If desired, stir in white pepper. If desired, sprinkle each serving with additional shredded cheese.

nutrition facts per serving: 163 cal., 8 g total fat (4 g sat. fat), 22 mg chol., 422 mg sodium, 13 g carb., 0 g dietary fiber, 11 g protein.

## soup's on!

*Here are tips for serving party soups.*

- *Use espresso cups, small glass mugs, or small bowls when serving soup as an appetizer.*
- *Set the bowls or cups right next to the soup and provide a ladle or serving spoon appropriate to the size of the bowls or cups.*
- *Consider offering more than one soup. When selecting them, be sure they offer contrasting textures and flavors.*
- *Offer a variety of soup toppings, such as tiny oyster crackers, tortilla strips, small croutons, grated cheeses, miniature cheese crackers, dairy sour cream, sliced green onions, and sliced jalapeño chile peppers.*
- *To keep soup flavorful and safe to eat when your party will last for several hours, regularly refill the serving bowl with hot soup. Keep the remaining soup hot on the stove top or in a slow cooker.*

*The enjoyment-to-effort ratio on this Caribbean-style soup is really high! Just five ingredients and about 15 minutes stack up to a terrific starter for a special meal.*

# shrimp and coconut
## soup

start to finish: 15 minutes   makes: 5 servings

8   ounces fresh or frozen peeled and deveined small shrimp

2   14-ounce cans chicken broth

4   ounces dried angel-hair pasta or vermicelli, broken into 2-inch pieces

1   tablespoon curry powder

1   cup purchased unsweetened coconut milk
    Sliced green onion or snipped fresh chives

**1** Thaw shrimp, if frozen. Rinse shrimp; pat dry with paper towels. Set aside.

**2** In a large saucepan bring broth to boiling. Add pasta and curry powder; return to boiling. Boil gently for 3 minutes. Add shrimp. Cook for 2 to 3 minutes more or until shrimp are opaque and pasta is tender. Stir in coconut milk; heat through. Sprinkle each serving with green onion.

nutrition facts per serving: 268 cal., 14 g total fat (11 g sat. fat), 69 mg chol., 762 mg sodium, 22 g carb., 2 g dietary fiber, 15 g protein.

*The easiest way to clean leeks is to slice them in half lengthwise and hold them under running water, root end up. As you lift and separate the leaves, the water will wash away the grit trapped between the layers.*

# sherried salmon bisque


start to finish: 35 minutes  makes: 8 servings

12 ounces fresh or frozen salmon fillets or steaks, cut ¾ inch thick

2 tablespoons butter

3 cups sliced fresh stemmed shiitake or other mushrooms

¾ cup thinly sliced leek or ½ cup thinly sliced green onion

1 14-ounce can chicken broth or vegetable broth

1½ teaspoons snipped fresh dill or ½ teaspoon dried dill

¼ teaspoon salt
Dash ground black pepper

2 cups half-and-half or light cream

2 tablespoons cornstarch

2 tablespoons dry sherry
Fresh dill sprigs (optional)

**1** Thaw salmon, if frozen. Rinse salmon; pat dry with paper towels. Slice off and discard salmon skin. Remove and discard bones. Cut salmon into ½-inch pieces; set aside. In a large saucepan melt butter over medium heat. Cook mushrooms and leek in hot butter until tender. Stir in broth, dill, salt, and pepper. Bring to boiling.

**2** In a medium bowl combine half-and-half and cornstarch. Stir into mushroom mixture. Cook and stir over medium heat until thickened and bubbly. Add salmon. Cover and simmer for about 4 minutes or until salmon flakes easily when tested with a fork. Gently stir in sherry. If desired, garnish with dill.

nutrition facts per serving: 232 cal., 15 g total fat (7 g sat. fat), 55 mg chol., 345 mg sodium, 14 g carb., 1 g dietary fiber, 11 g protein.

**make-ahead directions:** Prepare as directed. Cool slightly. Transfer to a container. Cover and chill for up to 2 days. Reheat over medium-low heat until heated through, stirring occasionally.

*When you need a terrific main dish, ladle this creamy tempter into bowls and serve it with crusty bread.*

# new england
# clam chowder

start to finish: 40 minutes  makes: 8 servings

1   pint shucked clams or
    two 6½-ounce cans
    minced clams
2   slices bacon
2½  cups finely chopped
    peeled potato
1   cup chopped onion
1   teaspoon instant
    chicken bouillon
    granules
1   teaspoon
    Worcestershire
    sauce
¼   teaspoon dried
    thyme, crushed
⅛   teaspoon ground
    black pepper
2   cups milk
1   cup half-and-half
    or light cream
2   tablespoons
    all-purpose flour

1 If using shucked clams, chop them, reserving the liquid; set clams aside. Strain clam liquid to remove bits of shell. (Or drain canned clams, reserving the liquid.) If necessary, add enough water to reserved clam liquid to measure 1 cup total; set liquid aside.

2 In a large saucepan cook bacon until crisp. Drain bacon on paper towels, reserving 1 tablespoon drippings. Crumble bacon; set aside.

3 Stir reserved 1 cup clam liquid, potato, onion, bouillon granules, Worcestershire sauce, thyme, and pepper into reserved drippings. Bring to boiling; reduce heat. Cover and simmer about 10 minutes or until potatoes are tender. Using the back of a fork, mash potatoes slightly against the side of the pan.

4 In a medium bowl stir together milk, half-and-half, and flour. Add to potato mixture. Cook and stir until slightly thickened and bubbly. Stir in clams. Return to boiling; reduce heat. Cook for 1 to 2 minutes more or until heated through. Sprinkle individual servings with the crumbled bacon.

nutrition facts per serving: 376 cal., 15 g total fat (8 g sat. fat), 76 mg chol., 495 mg sodium, 35 g carb., 2 g dietary fiber, 24 g protein.

**make-ahead directions:** Prepare as directed. Cool slightly. Cover and chill for up to 2 days. Reheat over low heat before serving.

*A generous splash of wine rounds out the flavor of this creamy combo of crab and cauliflower.*

# cauliflower-crab
## chowder

start to finish: 25 minutes   makes: 6 servings

2 cups loose-pack frozen cauliflower
½ cup water
3 tablespoons butter
3 tablespoons all-purpose flour
1 14-ounce can vegetable or chicken broth
1¼ cups milk
1 3-ounce package cream cheese, cubed
2 tablespoons chopped pimiento or bottled roasted red sweet pepper
2 tablespoons snipped fresh parsley
1 tablespoon snipped fresh chives
¼ teaspoon salt
1 6-ounce package frozen crabmeat, thawed and drained
¼ cup dry white wine or dry sherry
Snipped fresh parsley (optional)

1 In a medium saucepan combine cauliflower and the water. Bring to boiling; reduce heat. Cover and simmer for about 4 minutes or just until crisp-tender. Do not drain. Cut up any large pieces of cauliflower; set aside.

2 Meanwhile, in a large saucepan melt butter over medium heat. Stir in flour. Add broth and milk. Cook and stir until slightly thickened and bubbly.

3 Stir in undrained cauliflower, cream cheese, pimiento, parsley, chives, and salt. Stir over low heat until cream cheese melts. Stir in crabmeat; heat through. Stir in wine. If desired, sprinkle with parsley. Serve immediately.

nutrition facts per serving: 192 cal., 12 g total fat (7 g sat. fat), 63 mg chol., 551 mg sodium, 9 g carb., 1 g dietary fiber, 10 g protein.

**make-ahead directions:** Prepare as directed. Cool slightly. Cover and chill for up to 2 days. Reheat over low heat before serving.

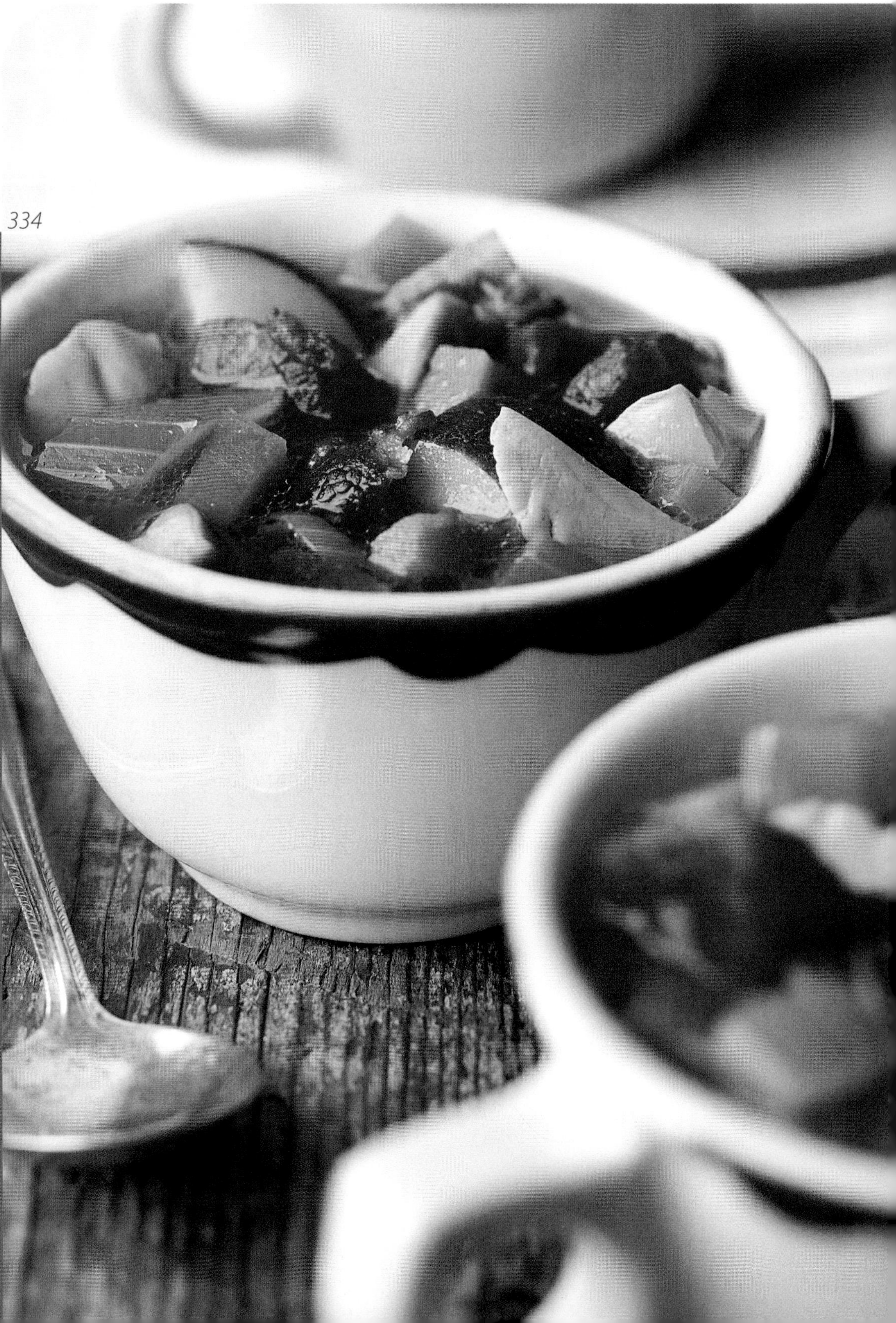

*If you prefer to use purchased bacon pieces instead of regular bacon, use 2 tablespoons olive oil to cook the celery, carrot, and onion.*

# manhattan
# clam chowder

start to finish: 45 minutes  makes: 6 servings

1   pint shucked clams or
    two 6.5-ounce cans
    minced clams
2   slices bacon
1   cup chopped celery
⅓   cup chopped onion
¼   cup chopped carrot
1   8-ounce bottle clam
    juice or 1 cup
    chicken broth
2   cups cubed red-skin
    potatoes
    (2 medium)
1   teaspoon dried
    thyme, crushed
⅛   teaspoon cayenne
    pepper
⅛   teaspoon ground
    black pepper
1   14.5-ounce can
    diced tomatoes,
    undrained

1  If using fresh clams, drain, reserving juice. Chop clams; set aside. Strain clam juice to remove bits of shell. (Or drain canned clams, reserving juice.) If necessary, add enough water to reserved clam juice to make 1½ cups total liquid; set juice aside.

2  In a large saucepan cook bacon over medium heat until crisp. Drain bacon on paper towels, reserving 2 tablespoons drippings. Crumble bacon; set aside.

3  Heat reserved bacon drippings. Add celery, onion, and carrot. Cook for 3 to 5 minutes or until tender. Stir in reserved 1½ cups clam juice and the bottled clam juice. Stir in potato, thyme, cayenne pepper, and black pepper. Bring to boiling; reduce heat. Cover and simmer for 10 minutes.

4  Stir in clams, bacon, and tomatoes. Return to boiling; reduce heat. Cook for 1 to 2 minutes more or until heated through.

nutrition facts per serving: 169 cal., 6 g total fat (1 g sat. fat), 27 mg chol., 338 mg sodium, 16 g carb., 2 g dietary fiber, 13 g protein.

*Once hard to find, authentic Mexican ingredients are now more widely available than ever before. This recipe makes good use of Mexican cheese and poblano chile peppers to enliven this colorful soup. Pictured on page 323.*

# crab and poblano soup

start to finish: 30 minutes   makes: 8 servings

¼   cup butter
2   fresh poblano chile peppers, seeded and chopped (see note, page 52)
¾   cup chopped red sweet pepper
½   cup chopped onion
2   cloves garlic, minced
¼   cup all-purpose flour
¼   teaspoon salt
¼   teaspoon ground black pepper
1   14-ounce can chicken broth
2   cups milk
6   ounces asadero cheese or quesadilla queso, shredded (1½ cups)
1   6.5-ounce can lump crabmeat, drained, or 8 ounces fresh lump crabmeat, picked over and cut into bite-size pieces
1   recipe Fresh Tomato Salsa
1   recipe Crisp Tortilla Strips (optional)

1 In a large saucepan melt butter over medium heat. Cook chile peppers, sweet pepper, onion, and garlic in hot butter until tender, stirring occasionally. Stir in flour, salt, and pepper. Add broth all at once, stirring to combine. Cook and stir until thickened and bubbly. Cook and stir for 1 minute more.

2 Reduce heat to medium low. Stir in milk and cheese. Cook and stir for 3 to 5 minutes or until cheese melts. Stir in crabmeat; heat through.

3 Top each serving with Fresh Tomato Salsa. If desired, serve with Crisp Tortilla Strips.

nutrition facts per serving: 204 cal., 12 g total fat (8 g sat. fat), 60 mg chol., 665 mg sodium, 11 g carb., 1 g dietary fiber, 14 g protein.

fresh tomato salsa: In a small bowl stir together 3 roma tomatoes, seeded and chopped; 1 green onion, thinly sliced; 1 tablespoon snipped fresh cilantro; 2 teaspoons lime juice; and 1 teaspoon finely chopped fresh jalapeño chile pepper (see note, page 52). Season to taste with salt and black pepper. Makes 1 cup.

crisp tortilla strips: Preheat oven to 350°F. Roll up each of 3 flour tortillas; slice crosswise, which will result in long thin strips. Lightly coat tortilla strips with nonstick cooking spray and spread on a baking sheet. Bake for about 5 minutes or until golden. Cool.

*Lemongrass is a unique ingredient in Asian fare. As the name implies, the herb (which resembles a green onion) tastes like lemon. It's worth looking for in an Asian market, but in a pinch, substitute 1 teaspoon finely shredded lemon peel for the 2 tablespoons lemongrass.*

# shiitake
# and lemongrass soup

prep: 20 minutes   cook: 20 minutes   makes: 4 servings

2 tablespoons butter
½ cup finely chopped onion
2 tablespoons finely chopped fresh lemongrass
3 cups mushroom or vegetable broth
8 ounces fresh shiitake mushrooms, stemmed and sliced
1 tablespoon rice vinegar
⅛ teaspoon ground white pepper
1 cup coarsely chopped fresh spinach

1 In a large saucepan melt 1 tablespoon of the butter over medium-high heat. Cook onion and lemongrass in hot butter for about 5 minutes or until tender. Add broth. Bring to boiling; reduce heat. Simmer, uncovered, for 15 minutes. Pour through a fine-mesh strainer. Discard onion and lemongrass.

2 Meanwhile, in a large skillet melt the remaining 1 tablespoon butter over medium-high heat. Cook sliced mushrooms in hot butter for about 5 minutes or until mushrooms are lightly browned on the edges. Remove from heat.

3 Stir vinegar and pepper into broth mixture. Stir in spinach. To serve, ladle broth mixture into bowls. Top with cooked mushrooms.

nutrition facts per serving: 80 cal., 8 g total fat (4 g sat. fat), 16 mg chol., 770 mg sodium, 6 g carb., 2 g dietary fiber, 2 g protein.

*For smooth pureed soups like this one, a handheld immersion blender comes in handy. It allows you to blend the soup right in the saucepan.*

# roasted red pepper soup

prep: 25 minutes   cook: 15 minutes   makes: 4 servings

| | |
|---|---|
| 1 | 12-ounce jar roasted red sweet peppers, drained and sliced |
| 1 | tablespoon olive oil |
| 1 | cup chopped onion |
| 4 | cloves garlic, minced |
| 3 | 14-ounce cans vegetable or chicken broth |
| 1 | cup chopped peeled potato |
| 1 | tablespoon snipped fresh oregano or 1 teaspoon dried oregano, crushed |
| 1 | teaspoon snipped fresh thyme or ½ teaspoon dried thyme, crushed |
| ¼ | cup dairy sour cream |

**1** If desired, reserve some of the sweet pepper slices for garnish. In a large saucepan or pot heat oil over medium heat. Cook onion and garlic in hot oil for 3 to 4 minutes or until tender. Stir in the remaining sweet pepper, the broth, potato, oregano, and thyme. Bring to boiling; reduce heat. Cover and simmer for 15 minutes. Cool mixture slightly.

**2** Using a handheld immersion blender, blend broth mixture until nearly smooth; heat through. (Or place one-third of the broth mixture in a blender. Cover and blend until nearly smooth. Transfer to a bowl. Repeat two more times with the remaining broth mixture. Return all of the broth mixture to saucepan; heat through.)

**3** Top each serving with sour cream and reserved red pepper, if desired.

nutrition facts per serving: 137 cal., 6 g total fat (2 g sat. fat), 5 mg chol., 1178 mg sodium, 18 g carb., 2 g dietary fiber, 2 g protein.

*Yukon gold potatoes have a beautiful golden color and a rich, creamy potato flavor, making soups like this extra delicious.*

# creamy
# potato soup

prep: 25 minutes   cook: 35 minutes   makes: 8 servings

1 tablespoon olive oil
2 cups thinly sliced onion or leek
2 cups milk
3 tablespoons all-purpose flour
1 pound Yukon gold potatoes, peeled and sliced
4 cups reduced-sodium chicken broth
8 ounces Swiss-style cheese such as Gruyére or baby Swiss, shredded (2 cups)
   Salt
   Ground black pepper
   Snipped fresh herbs
2 ounces baby Swiss cheese, thinly sliced (optional)

**1** In a large saucepan or Dutch oven heat oil over medium heat. Cook onion in hot oil for 5 to 10 minutes or until tender. Whisk together milk and flour. Add to saucepan. Cook and stir for 5 minutes.

**2** Add potatoes and chicken broth. Bring to boiling; reduce heat. Cover and cook for 20 minutes or until potatoes are tender. Remove from heat. Cool slightly.

**3** Place half of the soup in a blender. Cover and puree until smooth. Transfer to a bowl. Repeat with the remaining soup. Return all of the soup to saucepan. Add shredded cheese. Cook and stir over medium heat just until cheese melts. Season to taste with salt and pepper. Sprinkle with fresh herbs; garnish with sliced cheese, if desired.

nutrition facts per serving: 220 cal., 11 g total fat (6 g sat. fat), 31 mg chol., 441 mg sodium, 18 g carb., 1 g dietary fiber, 13 g protein.

*So few ingredients, so much flavor! Even better, this soup freezes well, so make an extra batch.*

# butternut squash soup
## with ravioli

start to finish: 35 minutes  makes: 5 servings

2  pounds butternut
    squash
2  14.5-ounce cans
    vegetable broth
½  cup water
⅛  teaspoon cayenne
    pepper
1  tablespoon butter
1  9-ounce package
    refrigerated cheese
    ravioli
1  tablespoon molasses
    (optional)

**1** Peel squash. Halve lengthwise. Remove seeds and discard. Cut squash into ³/₄-inch pieces.

**2** In a large saucepan combine squash, broth, the water, and cayenne pepper. Cover and cook over medium heat for about 20 minutes or until squash is tender.

**3** Place one-fourth of the squash mixture in a blender. Cover and blend until smooth. Transfer to a bowl. Repeat three more times with remaining squash mixture. Return all of the mixture to saucepan.

**4** Bring just to boiling; immediately reduce heat. Simmer, uncovered, for 5 minutes. Add butter, stirring just until melted.

**5** Meanwhile, prepare the ravioli according to package directions. Drain. Ladle hot squash mixture into bowls. Divide cooked ravioli among bowls. If desired, drizzle with molasses.

nutrition facts per serving: 259 cal., 10 g total fat (5 g sat. fat), 52 mg chol., 933 mg sodium, 36 g carb., 2 g dietary fiber, 10 g protein.

**make-ahead directions:** Prepare soup as directed though Step 4. Cool squash mixture. Transfer to a container. Cover and chill for up to 2 days or freeze for up to 2 months. Reheat over medium-low heat for 15 to 20 minutes or until heated through, stirring often. Continue with Step 5.

*Coffee gives a deep, mellow boost to a variety of recipes, including this tomato soup. Top each serving with whipped cream.*

# tomato-joe soup

prep: 30 minutes   cook: 30 minutes   makes: 6 to 8 servings

2   tablespoons butter
1   cup chopped onion
1   cup chopped celery
1   cup chopped carrot
6   medium tomatoes, peeled and quartered (about 2 pounds), or two 14.5-ounce cans diced tomatoes, drained
2   cups strong brewed coffee
½   cup water
1   6-ounce can tomato paste
2   teaspoons sugar
½   teaspoon salt
    Few dashes bottled hot pepper sauce
¾   cup whipping cream

**1** In a saucepan melt butter over medium heat. Cook onion, celery, and carrot in hot butter about 5 minutes or until nearly tender, stirring occasionally. Add tomatoes, coffee, the water, tomato paste, sugar, salt, and hot pepper sauce. Bring to boiling; reduce heat. Cover and simmer for 20 to 25 minutes or until vegetables are tender. Cool slightly.

**2** Place half of the tomato mixture in a blender or food processor. Cover and blend or process until smooth. Transfer to a bowl. Repeat with remaining tomato mixture. Return all of the tomato mixture to saucepan. Stir in ¼ cup of the whipping cream; heat through.

**3** In a medium mixing bowl beat the remaining ½ cup whipping cream with an electric mixer on low speed just until soft peaks form (tips curl). Top each serving with whipped cream.

nutrition facts per serving: 164 cal., 12 g total fat (7 g sat. fat), 39 mg chol., 378 mg sodium, 14 g carb., 3 g dietary fiber, 3 g protein.

*A splash of dry sherry brings out the rich mushroom flavor in this sophisticated first-course soup.*

# wild rice–
# mushroom bisque

prep: 25 minutes   cook: 55 minutes   cool: 5 minutes   makes: 12 servings

1   cup wild rice
2   cups water
1   tablespoon butter
1   pound fresh
     shiitake or cremini
     mushrooms,
     stemmed and sliced
3   medium leeks, sliced
2   tablespoons dry
     sherry (optional)
1   32-ounce box chicken
     broth
2   large russet potatoes,
     peeled and chopped
     (12 ounces)
1   cup half-and-half or
     light cream
1   medium carrot,
     shredded
1   teaspoon snipped
     fresh thyme or
     ¼ teaspoon dried
     thyme, crushed
¼   teaspoon salt
¼   teaspoon ground
     black pepper

**1** Rinse wild rice well. In a small saucepan combine wild rice and the water. Bring to boiling; reduce heat. Cover and simmer for 40 minutes or until most of the water is absorbed. Drain, if necessary.

**2** Meanwhile, in a large pot melt butter over medium heat. Cook mushrooms and leeks in hot butter for about 5 minutes or until tender. If desired, remove pot from heat. Carefully add sherry. Return to heat and cook and stir, uncovered, until all of the sherry evaporates. Remove half of the mushroom mixture from the pot; set aside.

**3** Add chicken broth and potatoes to pot. Bring to boiling; reduce heat. Cover and simmer for 10 minutes or until potatoes are tender. Remove from heat. Cool slightly.

**4** Place one-third of the soup mixture in a food processor or blender. Cover and process or blend until almost smooth. Repeat two more times with remaining soup mixture. Return all the soup mixture to the pot. Stir in wild rice, reserved mushrooms, half-and-half, carrot, thyme, salt, and pepper. Return to boiling; reduce heat. Simmer, uncovered, for 5 minutes or until heated through and carrot is tender.

nutrition facts per serving: 145 cal., 4 g total fat (2 g sat. fat), 11 mg chol., 379 mg sodium, 25 g carb., 3 g dietary fiber, 4 g protein.

**make-ahead directions:** Prepare bisque as directed. Cover and chill for up to 24 hours. Reheat, thinning to desired consistency with additional chicken broth.

*If fresh shiitake mushrooms aren't available, soak dried ones in hot water. Two ounces of dried mushrooms equal 1 cup of the fresh.*

# mushroom-tomato
## bisque

prep: 25 minutes   cook: 30 minutes   makes: 4 servings

2   tablespoons butter
½   cup sliced leek or
       chopped onion
½   cup sliced celery
2   cloves garlic, minced
1½  cups sliced stemmed
       fresh shiitake or
       other mushrooms
1   14.5-ounce can
       diced tomatoes,
       undrained
1   14-ounce can chicken
       or vegetable broth
½   cup whipping cream
½   teaspoon dried
       dillweed
⅛   teaspoon ground
       black pepper
       Sautéed mushrooms
       (optional)

**1** In a large saucepan melt butter over medium heat. Cook leek, celery, and garlic in hot butter for 3 to 5 minutes or until tender. Add the 1½ cups mushrooms. Cook and stir about 5 minutes or until mushrooms are tender. Stir in tomatoes, broth, whipping cream, dillweed, and pepper. Bring to boiling; reduce heat. Cover and simmer for 30 minutes. Cool slightly.

**2** Using a handheld immersion blender, blend soup mixture until nearly smooth; heat through. (Or let soup mixture cool slightly. Place half of the mixture in a blender or food processor. Cover and blend or process until smooth. Transfer to a bowl. Repeat with the remaining soup mixture. Return all of the soup to saucepan and heat through.)

**3** If desired, top each serving with sautéed mushrooms.

nutrition facts per serving: 193 cal., 13 g total fat (8 g sat. fat), 47 mg chol., 607 mg sodium, 17 g carb., 2 g dietary fiber, 3 g protein.

*This make-ahead chilled soup is a colorful blend of tomatoes,*
*tomatillos, cucumber, and cilantro—it's as refreshing as it is easy.*

# red and green gazpacho

prep: 30 minutes   chill: 1 hour   makes: 6 servings

3 cups chopped red
  and/or partially
  green tomato
  (3 large)
2 11.5-ounce cans
  tomato juice (about
  3 cups)
½ cup chopped tomatillo
  (2 medium; optional)
½ cup chopped
  cucumber
1 large fresh jalapeño
  chile pepper,
  seeded and finely
  chopped (see note,
  page 52)
¼ cup finely chopped
  green onion
1 clove garlic, minced
¼ cup finely snipped
  fresh cilantro
1 tablespoon olive oil
1 tablespoon lime juice
¼ teaspoon salt
¼ teaspoon bottled hot
  pepper sauce
1 avocado, halved,
  pitted, peeled, and
  chopped (optional)
  Snipped fresh cilantro
  (optional)

**1** In a large bowl combine tomato, tomato
juice, tomatillo (if desired), cucumber, chile
pepper, green onion, garlic, the ¼ cup cilantro,
the oil, lime juice, salt, and hot pepper sauce.
Cover. Chill for at least 1 hour.

**2** If desired, top each serving with avocado
and additional cilantro.

nutrition facts per serving: 60 cal., 3 g total fat (0 g sat.
fat), 0 mg chol., 398 mg sodium, 9 g carb., 2 g dietary fiber,
2 g protein.

shrimp gazpacho: Prepare as directed. Just before serving, stir
8 ounces cooked, peeled, deveined, and chopped shrimp into
the gazpacho mixture.

nutrition facts per serving: 98 cal., 3 g total fat (0 g sat. fat), 74 mg chol.,
483 mg sodium, 9 g carb., 2 g dietary fiber, 10 g protein.

# 12

veggie

tw

Whether marinated, wrapped, stuffed, or oven-roasted, garden-fresh beauties—from asparagus to sweet potatoes—show simple ways to add color and crunch.

*The secret to the light, crispy crust on the asparagus is Japanese breadcrumbs, panko. Made from wheat and honey, the crumbs are very large and flaky, unlike traditional breadcrumbs.*

# panko-roasted
# asparagus

prep: 20 minutes   roast: 12 minutes   oven: 425°F   makes: 16 to 20 servings

½   cup mayonnaise
¼   cup Dijon-style
     mustard
2   teaspoons lemon
     juice
1   cup panko (Japanese-
     style breadcrumbs)
1   pound thick
     asparagus spears,
     trimmed
2   tablespoons peanut
     oil

**1** Preheat oven to 425°F. In a small bowl combine mayonnaise, mustard, and lemon juice. Transfer half of the mixture to a small serving bowl. Cover and chill until ready to serve.

**2** Place breadcrumbs in a shallow dish. Spread the remaining mayonnaise mixture over asparagus spears. Roll in breadcrumbs to coat. Place in an ungreased 15×10×1-inch baking pan. Drizzle with oil.

**3** Roast about 12 minutes or until asparagus is crisp-tender and breadcrumbs are golden brown. Serve asparagus with the reserved mayonnaise mixture.

nutrition facts per serving: 88 cal., 7 g total fat (1 g sat. fat), 3 mg chol., 139 mg sodium, 4 g carb., 1 g dietary fiber, 1 g protein.

*Though the pickled radishes will remain crunchy, they may lose some of their bright color over time. Any beauty lost will be more than made up for by the delicious flavor they pick up from the pickling juice.*

# pickled radishes

prep: 20 minutes   chill: 8 hours   makes: 2 cups

| | |
|---|---|
| 8 | ounces radishes |
| 1 | small red onion, cut into thin wedges and separated |
| ½ | cup white vinegar |
| ½ | cup sugar |
| 1½ | teaspoon salt |
| 6 | heads fresh dill |
| 1 | tablespoon whole pink peppercorns or whole black peppercorns |

**1** Slice radishes with a knife or use the slicing blade in a food processor. You should have about 2 cups sliced radishes. Place radish slices and onion in a 1-quart jar. In another bowl stir together vinegar, sugar, and salt until sugar dissolves. Pour mixture over radishes and onions. Add dill and peppercorns.

**2** Cover and refrigerate for at least 8 hours or overnight before serving. (Radish mixture will have a very pungent aroma.)

nutrition facts per 2-tablespoon: 31 cal., 0 g total fat (0 g sat. fat), 0 mg chol., 224 mg sodium, 7 g carb., 0 g dietary fiber, 0 g protein.

*Easy to make and fun to eat, these bite-size delights cook unattended in a slow cooker.*

# hoisin-garlic mushrooms

prep: 15 minutes   cook: 5 to 6 hours (low) or 2½ to 3 hours (high)   makes: 10 servings

| | |
|---|---|
| ½ | cup bottled hoisin sauce |
| ¼ | cup water |
| 2 | tablespoons bottled minced garlic |
| ¼ | to ½ teaspoon crushed red pepper |
| 24 | ounces whole fresh button mushrooms, trimmed |

**1** In a 3½- or 4-quart slow cooker combine hoisin sauce, the water, garlic, and crushed red pepper. Add mushrooms, stirring to coat.

**2** Cover and cook on low heat setting for 5 to 6 hours or on high heat setting for 2½ to 3 hours. To serve, remove mushrooms from cooker with a slotted spoon. Discard cooking liquid. Serve warm mushrooms with decorative toothpicks.

nutrition facts per serving: 43 cal., 1 g total fat (0 g sat. fat), 0 mg chol., 211 mg sodium, 9 g carb., 1 g dietary fiber, 3 g protein.

*Even a dip like this one, created for health-conscious eaters, is bound to be a hit at parties. It's full of garden-fresh flavors and paired with nutritious dippers.*

# very veggie dip

start to finish: 20 minutes   makes: 16 (2-tablespoon) servings

1   8-ounce carton light
    dairy sour cream
½   of an 8-ounce package
    reduced-fat cream
    cheese (Neufchâtel)
1   tablespoon fat-free
    milk
¼   cup finely chopped
    red or yellow sweet
    pepper
¼   cup finely chopped
    zucchini
2   tablespoons shredded
    carrot
1   tablespoon snipped
    fresh chives or
    green onion tops
¼   teaspoon salt
¼   teaspoon ground
    black pepper
    Fresh vegetable
    dippers, whole
    grain crackers,
    and/or multigrain
    tortilla chips

**1** In a medium mixing bowl beat sour cream, cream cheese, and milk with an electric mixer on low to medium speed until smooth. Stir in sweet pepper, zucchini, carrot, and chives. Stir in salt and pepper.

**2** To serve, stir dip. Serve with vegetables, crackers, and/or tortilla chips.

nutrition facts per serving: 39 cal., 3 g total fat (2 g sat. fat), 10 mg chol., 76 mg sodium, 2 g carb., 0 g dietary fiber, 1 g protein.

make-ahead directions: Prepare as directed in Step 1. Cover and chill for up to 3 days. Serve as directed.

italian veggie dip: Prepare as directed, except omit the sweet pepper, carrot, and chives. Stir in ¼ cup seeded and finely chopped tomato and 1 clove garlic, minced. Stir in 1 tablespoon snipped fresh basil, oregano, and/or thyme or 1 teaspoon dried Italian seasoning, crushed.

south-of-the-border veggie dip: Prepare as directed, except omit the sweet pepper, zucchini, carrot, and chives. Stir in ⅔ cup purchased salsa.

*"Shocking" the asparagus in ice water preserves its vibrant color and tender-crisp texture.*

# prosciutto-wrapped
## asparagus

start to finish: 25 minutes  makes: 8 servings

24  asparagus spears
     (1 to 1¼ pounds),
     trimmed to 6-inch
     lengths
24  thin slices provolone
     cheese (12 to 14
     ounces)
12  very thin slices
     prosciutto (8 to 10
     ounces), halved
     lengthwise
     Cracked black pepper
 1   to 2 tablespoons
     olive oil
 1   to 2 tablespoons
     balsamic vinegar

**1** Place a steamer basket in a large skillet. Add water to reach just below bottom of basket. Bring to boiling. Place asparagus in basket. Reduce heat to medium low. Cover and steam for 4 minutes. Immerse asparagus in ice water. Drain asparagus. Pat dry with paper towels.

**2** Wrap a slice of cheese and a half-slice of prosciutto around each asparagus spear. Arrange wrapped asparagus on a serving platter.

**3** Before serving, sprinkle with cracked pepper. Drizzle with oil and balsamic vinegar.

nutrition facts per serving: 268 cal., 20 g total fat (8 g sat. fat), 29 mg chol., 876 mg sodium, 4 g carb., 1 g dietary fiber, 19 g protein.

**make-ahead directions:** Prepare as directed through Step 2. Cover and chill for up to 24 hours. Serve as directed.

*If you find yourself falling for the intensely bright chimichurri sauce—an Argentine specialty—keep the recipe close by to work its magic on grilled meats, chicken, and fish.*

# veggie spring rolls
## with chimichurri sauce

prep: 30 minutes   stand: 15 minutes   makes: 6 rolls

1 recipe Chimichurri Sauce
1 cup shredded romaine lettuce
¾ cup packaged coarsely shredded carrots
½ cup bite-size strips zucchini
½ cup bite-size strips peeled jicama
2 green onions, cut into thin bite-size strips
6 8-inch rice papers
6 sprigs fresh Italian parsley

**1** In a medium bowl combine half of the sauce, the lettuce, carrots, zucchini, jicama, and green onions. Let stand for 15 to 30 minutes to allow vegetables to soften slightly and absorb flavor from the sauce, stirring occasionally. Cover and chill the remaining sauce until ready to serve.

**2** To assemble, pour warm water into a pie plate. Carefully dip a rice paper into the water; transfer to a clean kitchen towel. Let stand for several seconds to soften. Place a parsley sprig in the center of the paper. Spoon about ⅓ cup of the vegetable mixture just below the center. Tightly roll up rice paper from the bottom, tucking in one side as you roll.

**3** Repeat with the remaining rice papers, parsley sprigs, and vegetable mixture. Serve spring rolls with the remaining sauce.

nutrition facts per roll: 152 cal., 9 g total fat (1 g sat. fat), 0 mg chol., 125 mg sodium, 15 g carb., 2 g dietary fiber, 2 g protein.

chimichurri sauce: In a blender or food processor combine 1½ cups lightly packed fresh flat-leaf parsley; ¼ cup olive oil; ¼ cup rice vinegar; 6 cloves garlic, minced; ¼ teaspoon salt; ¼ black pepper; and ¼ teaspoon crushed red pepper. Cover and blend or process with several on/off pulses until chopped but not pureed. Makes about ½ cup.

make-ahead directions: Prepare as directed. Layer spring rolls between damp paper towels in an airtight container. Store in the refrigerator for up to 4 hours. Store the remaining sauce in the refrigerator for up to 4 hours.

*Instead of serving veggies and a cheese spread, provide marinated veggies with plenty of crunch and flavor all their own.*

# caraway **veggies**

prep: 45 minutes   chill: 2 hours   makes: 12 servings

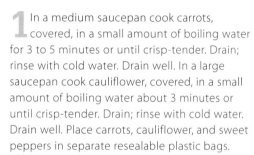

1½   pounds small carrots with tops, trimmed and peeled, or 12 ounces packaged peeled fresh baby carrots

6   cups cauliflower florets

2   medium red and/or green sweet peppers, cut into wedges

¾   cup salad oil

1   tablespoon caraway seeds, crushed

1   cup white wine vinegar

½   teaspoon salt

½   teaspoon crushed red pepper

**1** In a medium saucepan cook carrots, covered, in a small amount of boiling water for 3 to 5 minutes or until crisp-tender. Drain; rinse with cold water. Drain well. In a large saucepan cook cauliflower, covered, in a small amount of boiling water about 3 minutes or until crisp-tender. Drain; rinse with cold water. Drain well. Place carrots, cauliflower, and sweet peppers in separate resealable plastic bags.

**2** For marinade, in a small saucepan combine oil and caraway seeds. Cook and stir over low heat for 4 to 5 minutes or until oil is warm and slightly fragrant. Cool slightly. In a large glass measure whisk together the oil mixture, vinegar, salt, and crushed red pepper.

**3** Pour about ½ cup of the marinade over the carrots, about 1 cup of the marinade over the cauliflower, and the remaining marinade over the sweet peppers; seal bags. Turn to coat. Chill for 2 to 6 hours, turning bags often.

**4** To serve, drain vegetables, discarding marinade. Arrange vegetables on a serving platter.

nutrition facts per serving: 85 cal., 5 g total fat (1 g sat. fat), 0 mg chol., 85 mg sodium, 9 g carb., 3 g dietary fiber, 2 g protein.

*Choose plump cherry tomatoes to hold the irresistible filling. When filling the tomatoes, use a piping bag for something decorative. Or just spoon the filling in if it doesn't have to be fancy. Garnish the filled tomatoes with snipped fresh basil.*

# avocado-pesto
# stuffed tomatoes

prep: 40 minutes  stand: 30 minutes  makes: 30 servings

30  cherry tomatoes
    (about 1¼ pints)
½  medium avocado,
    pitted, peeled, and
    chopped
2  ounces cream cheese,
    softened
2  tablespoons
    purchased basil
    pesto
1  teaspoon lemon juice

**1** Line a large baking sheet with paper towels; set aside. Cut a thin slice from the bottom of each tomato so it stands upright. Cut a thin slice from the top of each tomato. Carefully hollow out the cherry tomatoes with a small measuring spoon or small melon baller. Invert tomatoes onto prepared baking sheet. Let stand for 30 minutes.

**2** In a food processor combine avocado, cream cheese, pesto, and lemon juice. Cover and process until mixture is smooth. Spoon into a pastry bag fitted with a large plain round or open star tip.

**3** Place tomatoes, open sides up, onto a serving platter. Pipe avocado mixture into the tomato shells. Serve immediately or cover loosely and chill for up to 4 hours.

nutrition facts per serving: 18 cal., 1 g total fat (1 g sat. fat), 2 mg chol., 16 mg sodium, 1 g carb., 0 g dietary fiber, 0 g protein.

*Enlist the help of a food processor to shred the vegetables quickly. If you end up with extra zucchini, store it in the refrigerator to use later in a pasta sauce.*

# potato pancakes
## with herbed crème

prep: 30 minutes  bake: 14 minutes  oven: 425°F  makes: about 22 servings

1 egg, lightly beaten
2 tablespoons all-purpose flour
1 teaspoon salt
½ teaspoon ground black pepper
1 pound russet potatoes
1½ cups finely shredded zucchini
1 cup finely shredded carrots
½ cup plain low-fat yogurt
2 tablespoons finely snipped fresh basil
1 tablespoon finely snipped fresh chives

1 Preheat oven to 425°F. Line a very large baking sheet with parchment paper or foil; coat with cooking spray. Set aside. In a medium bowl whisk together egg, flour, salt, and pepper; set aside.

2 Peel and finely shred potatoes. Press shredded potatoes between several layers of paper towels to remove any excess moisture. In a large bowl combine shredded potatoes, zucchini, and carrots. Add egg mixture. Stir just until combined.

3 Drop potato mixture by rounded tablespoons onto the prepared baking sheet. Using the back of a spoon, flatten mounds slightly. Coat mounds with cooking spray. Bake for 7 minutes. Turn pancakes over. Bake about 7 minutes more or until lightly browned.

4 Meanwhile, for herbed crème, in a small bowl combine yogurt, basil, and chives. Serve warm potato pancakes with herbed crème.

nutrition facts per serving: 25 cal., 0 g total fat (0 g sat. fat), 10 mg chol., 118 mg sodium, 4 g carb., 1 g dietary fiber, 1 g protein.

*Try this healthier version of a classic Japanese favorite. Instead of deep-frying the batter-dipped veggies, oven roast them at high heat for a nice crisp coating.*

# baked vegetable
## tempura

prep: 30 minutes   bake: 9 minutes   oven: 450°F   makes: 10 servings

2    eggs
1½   cups panko
       (Japanese-style
       breadcrumbs)
¼    teaspoon salt
1½   cups cauliflower
       florets
1½   cups small fresh
       mushrooms, stems
       removed
1    medium sweet
       potato, peeled and
       cut into 3½-inch
       strips
1    small zucchini, cut
       into ¼-inch-thick
       slices
1    small red onion,
       cut into ½-inch-
       thick slices and
       separated into rings
1    cup fresh green
       beans
1    cup sugar snap peas
¼    cup all-purpose flour
2    tablespoons butter,
       melted
1    recipe Honey-
       Mustard Sauce

**1** Preheat oven to 450°F. Coat a 15×10×1-inch baking pan with nonstick cooking spray. In a shallow bowl beat eggs with a fork. In a medium bowl combine breadcrumbs and salt.

**2** In a large bowl toss the vegetables in flour, shaking to remove any excess flour. Dip the vegetables, a few at a time, into the eggs; dip into the crumb mixture to coat. Place the vegetables in a single layer in the prepared pan.

**3** Drizzle the vegetables with melted butter. Bake for 9 to 11 minutes or until vegetables are golden brown, gently stirring twice. Serve immediately with Honey-Mustard Sauce.

nutrition facts per serving: 148 cal., 4 g total fat (2 g sat. fat), 49 mg chol., 702 mg sodium, 23 g carb., 2 g dietary fiber, 9 g protein.

make-ahead directions: Prepare as directed through Step 2. Cover and chill for up to 3 hours. Honey-Mustard Sauce may be prepared up to 3 days ahead. Stir before serving.

honey-mustard sauce: In a small bowl stir together 1 cup Dijon-style mustard and 2 tablespoons honey.

*Tahini, a main ingredient in hummus, is a thick paste made from ground sesame seeds. Look for tahini near the peanut butter or in your supermarket's ethnic section.*

# sweet potato sticks
## with hummus

prep: 30 minutes   bake: 25 minutes   oven: 450°F   makes: 8 to 10 servings

5   large sweet potatoes
3   tablespoons olive oil
1   teaspoon ground cumin
½   teaspoon salt
½   teaspoon garlic powder
½   teaspoon paprika
⅓   cup water
3   tablespoons lime or lemon juice
3   tablespoons tahini (sesame seed paste)
1½   teaspoons ground coriander
1   teaspoon cumin seeds, toasted
½   teaspoon cayenne pepper
1   15-ounce can garbanzo beans (chickpeas), rinsed and drained
2   cloves garlic, minced

1 Preheat oven to 450°F. Cut each sweet potato lengthwise into eight wedges. Place potato wedges in a very large bowl. In a small bowl stir together oil, the ground cumin, the salt, and garlic powder. Drizzle over potato wedges; toss gently to coat.

2 Arrange potato wedges in a single layer on a very large baking sheet. Sprinkle with paprika. Bake for 25 to 35 minutes or until potatoes are tender and lightly browned on the edges.

3 Meanwhile, for hummus, in a food processor combine the water, lime juice, tahini, coriander, cumin seeds, and cayenne pepper. Add garbanzo beans and garlic. Cover and process until smooth, scraping down sides of bowl as necessary. Transfer to a serving bowl. Serve sweet potato wedges with hummus.

nutrition facts per serving: 242 cal., 9 g total fat (1 g sat. fat), 0 mg chol., 368 mg sodium, 36 g carb., 6 g dietary fiber, 6 g protein.

*Look for a sweet onion, such as Vidalia, to use in these classic rings.*
*Keep the fried rings warm and crisp in a 300°F oven.*

# onion rings

prep: 15 minutes   cook: 2 to 3 minutes per batch   makes: 6 servings

¾   cup all-purpose flour
⅔   cup milk
1   egg
1   tablespoon vegetable
    oil
¼   teaspoon salt
    Vegetable oil for
    deep-fat frying
4   medium mild yellow
    or white onions,
    sliced ¼ inch thick
    and separated into
    rings (1¼ pounds)
    Salt
1   recipe Chipotle
    Ketchup (optional)

**1** In a medium bowl combine flour, milk, egg, the 1 tablespoon oil, and the ¼ teaspoon salt. Using a whisk or rotary beater, beat just until smooth.

**2** In a deep-fat fryer or large deep skillet heat 1 inch oil to 365°F. Using a fork, dip onion rings into batter; drain off excess batter. Fry onion rings, a few at a time, in a single layer in hot oil for 2 to 3 minutes or until golden, stirring once or twice with a fork to separate rings. Remove rings from oil. Drain on paper towels. Sprinkle with additional salt. If desired, serve with Chipotle Ketchup.

nutrition facts per serving: 657 cal., 58 g total fat (5 g sat. fat), 37 mg chol., 771 mg sodium, 31 g carb., 2 g dietary fiber, 5 g protein.

chipotle ketchup: In a small bowl stir together 1 cup ketchup and 2 teaspoons finely chopped chipotle chile peppers in adobo sauce. Makes 1 cup.

*These earthy beauties will have friends and family in awe. Use a mixture of red, gold, and blue fingerlings for the most striking appearance.*

## sage-embossed
# fingerling potatoes

prep: 15 minutes   bake: 15 minutes   oven: 425°F   makes: 30 servings

| | |
|---|---|
| 15 | fingerling potatoes and/or small new potatoes |
| 2 | tablespoons olive oil |
| ¼ | teaspoon hickory smoked salt or seasoned salt |
| 30 | fresh sage leaves |

**1** Preheat oven to 425°F. Line a baking sheet with parchment paper or foil; grease foil (if using). Set aside.

**2** Cut potatoes in half lengthwise. In a medium bowl combine potatoes, oil, and salt. Toss gently to coat. Press a sage leaf against the cut side of each potato half. Arrange potatoes, cut side down, on the prepared baking sheet.

**3** Bake for 15 to 20 minutes or until potatoes are tender. Serve warm or at room temperature.

nutrition facts per serving: 19 cal., 1 g total fat (0 g sat. fat), 0 mg chol., 14 mg sodium, 3 g carb., 0 g dietary fiber, 0 g protein.

*Serve these sports-bar favorites at your next bowl-game party. Make them up to a day ahead, and you'll be able to spend that much more time cheering on your favorite team.*

# loaded potato skins

prep: 20 minutes   bake: 50 minutes   oven: 425°F   makes: 24 wedges

6   large baking potatoes (such as russet or long white)
1   tablespoon cooking oil
1   to 1½ teaspoons chili powder
     Several drops bottled hot pepper sauce
     Salt
8   slices cooked bacon, drained and crumbled
⅔   cup finely chopped tomato (1 medium)
2   tablespoons finely chopped green onion
1   cup shredded cheddar cheese (4 ounces)
½   cup dairy sour cream

1 Preheat oven to 425°F. Prick potatoes with a fork. Bake for 40 to 45 minutes or until tender. Cool.

2 Cut each potato lengthwise into 4 wedges. Using a teaspoon, carefully scoop pulp out of each potato wedge, leaving a ¼-inch shell. Cover and chill scooped pulp for another use.

3 Line a very large baking sheet with foil. In a small bowl combine the oil, chili powder, and hot pepper sauce. Using a pastry brush, brush the insides of the potato wedges with the oil mixture. Sprinkle with salt. Place the potato wedges in a single layer on the prepared baking sheet. Sprinkle wedges with bacon, tomato, and green onion. Top with cheese.

4 Bake for about 10 minutes or until cheese melts and potatoes are heated through. Serve with sour cream.

nutrition facts per 2 wedges: 64 cal., 4 g total fat (2 g sat. fat), 10 mg chol., 146 mg sodium, 4 g carb., 1 g dietary fiber, 3 g protein.

make-ahead directions: Prepare as above through Step 3. Cover and chill potato wedges for up to 24 hours. Uncover and bake as directed.

crunchy

mun

Ideal to have on hand for impromptu get-togethers, this eclectic assortment of pick-up-and-mingle party foods includes flavored popcorn, crunchy nuts and snack mixes, and savory biscotti.

13

chies

*No one can eat just one of these crispy triangles. Look for wonton wrappers in the refrigerator area of the produce section.*

# crispy
# parmesan
# chips

prep: 15 minutes  bake: 8 minutes per batch  oven: 350°F
makes: 15 (4-chip) servings

30  wonton wrappers, cut
    in half diagonally
2  tablespoons olive oil
1  clove garlic, minced
½  teaspoon dried basil,
    crushed
¼  cup grated Parmesan
    or Romano cheese

**1** Preheat oven to 350°F. Coat a baking sheet with cooking spray. Arrange one-third of the wonton triangles in a single layer on prepared baking sheet.

**2** In a small bowl combine oil, garlic, and basil. Lightly brush the wonton triangles on baking sheet with some of the oil mixture. Sprinkle with one-third of the cheese.

**3** Bake for 8 to 9 minutes or until golden. Cool completely on a wire rack. Repeat with the remaining wonton triangles, oil mixture, and cheese.

nutrition facts per serving: 69 cal., 2 g total fat (1 g sat. fat), 3 mg chol., 112 mg sodium, 9 g carb., 0 g dietary fiber, 2 g protein.

**make-ahead directions:** Store in a tightly sealed container at room temperature for up to 3 days.

*If you're wanting to add fun colors to your party spread, try this with different colors of flour tortillas.*

# crispy tortilla chips

prep: 10 minutes   bake: 8 minutes per batch   oven: 425°F
makes: 8 (6-chip) servings

8    6-inch corn tortillas
     Nonstick cooking
        spray
2    teaspoons garlic-
        pepper blend
½    teaspoon coarse salt

1 Preheat oven to 425°F. Lightly coat tortillas on both sides with cooking spray. Sprinkle tortillas on both sides with pepper blend and coarse salt. Make 2 stacks of 4 tortillas each. Using a sharp knife, cut each stack into 6 pieces. Arrange half of the pieces in a single layer on baking sheet.

2 Bake for 8 to 10 minutes or until lightly browned and crisp. Cool on wire rack. Repeat with remaining tortilla pieces.

nutrition facts per serving: 69 cal., 1 g total fat (0 g sat. fat), 0 mg chol., 362 mg sodium, 15 g carb., 1 g dietary fiber, 2 g protein.

**make-ahead directions:** Store in a tightly sealed container at room temperature for up to 3 days.

*Vary the flavor of this snack mix depending on the salad dressing mix you choose.*

# crunchy cracker snack mix

prep: 10 minutes  bake: 25 minutes  oven: 300°F  makes: 13 cups

4 cups bite-size cheese crackers
5 cups wheat stick crackers
3 cups pretzel twists
2 cups mixed nuts
½ cup butter, melted
1 0.6 to 0.7-ounce envelope cheese-garlic or Italian dry salad dressing mix

**1** Preheat oven to 300°F. Place cheese crackers and wheat crackers in a large roasting pan. Bake for about 5 minutes or until warm.

**2** Add pretzel twists and nuts to pan. Pour melted butter over mixture. Sprinkle with salad dressing mix. Stir well to coat. Bake for 20 minutes more, stirring once. Spread mixture on a large piece of foil. Cool.

nutrition facts per ¼ cup: 80 cal., 6 g total fat (2 g sat. fat), 5 mg chol., 165 mg sodium, 5 g carb., 1 g dietary fiber, 2 g protein.

**make-ahead directions:** Store in an airtight container at room temperature for up to 1 week.

*Combine savory snack mix with sweet nuts and chocolate and fruity banana chips for a winning flavor combination.*

# sweet and salty party mix

prep: 10 minutes  makes: 14 cups

2  8.6- to 8.75-ounce packages party snack mix (original flavor)

2  cups honey and nut bite-size shredded wheat cereal

1  cup plain or honey-roasted mixed nuts

1  cup plain candy-coated milk chocolate pieces

½  cup peanuts in crunchy sugar coating (French burnt peanuts)

½  cup dried banana chips

In a very large bowl combine packaged snack mix, shredded wheat cereal, mixed nuts, candy-coated milk chocolate pieces, peanut candy, and banana chips. Toss gently until well combined.

nutrition facts ½ cup: 176 cal., 8 g total fat (2 g sat. fat), 1 mg chol., 265 mg sodium, 33 g carb., 2 g dietary fiber, 3 g protein.

**make-ahead directions:** Store in an airtight container at room temperature for up to 2 weeks.

# fruit and nut crunch

prep: 20 minutes  bake: 15 minutes  oven: 325° F  makes: about 6 cups

¼  cup jalapeño pepper jelly

2  tablespoons butter

¼  teaspoon five-spice powder

¼  teaspoon salt

¼  teaspoon bottled hot pepper sauce

2  cups whole cashews or dry-roasted peanuts

1  cup dried banana chips

1  cup dried pineapple chunks, cut up

1  cup chopped pitted dates

1  cup chow mein noodles

1  Preheat oven to 325°F. In a saucepan combine jelly, butter, five-spice powder, salt, and hot pepper sauce over low heat. Cook for 5 minutes or until jelly melts. Add remaining ingredients, stirring well to coat. Pour mixture into a large roasting pan.

2  Bake for 15 to 20 minutes or until cashews are lightly browned, stirring once. Remove from oven. Spread mixture on foil; cool.

nutrition facts per serving: 232 cal., 13 g total fat (4 g sat. fat), 4 mg chol., 131 mg sodium, 29 g carb., 2 g dietary fiber, 4 g protein.

**make-ahead directions:** Store in an airtight container at room temperature for up to 3 days.

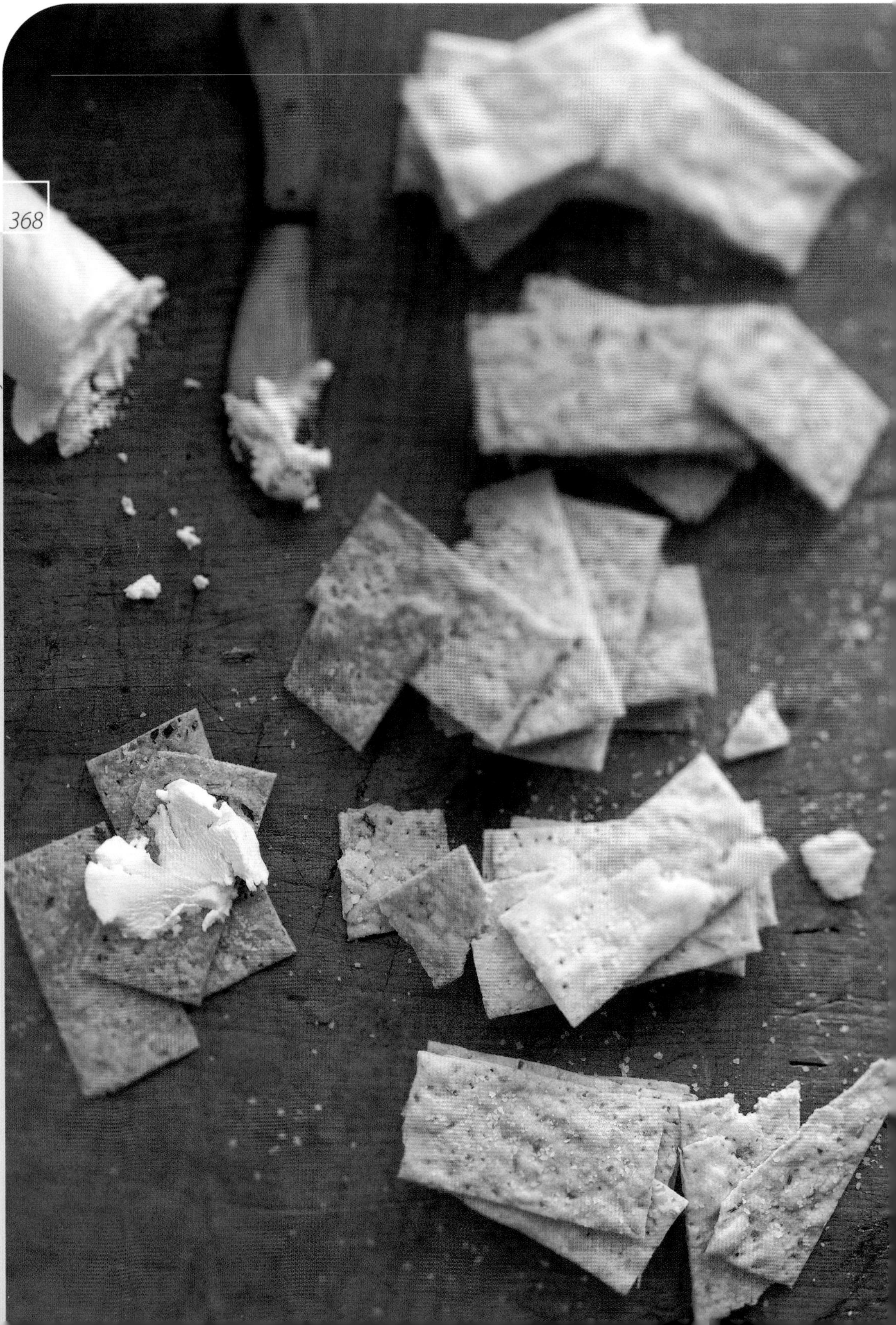

*These crackers are as versatile as the party calls for. Simply prepare the crackers with your choice of wine and the spice or herb combinations listed.*

# sublime wine crackers

prep: 20 minutes  bake: 18 minutes  oven: 325°F
makes: 6 (4-cracker) servings

1  cup all-purpose flour
   Desired herb/spice
     (see below)
½  teaspoon salt
¼  teaspoon ground
     black pepper
3  tablespoons desired
     wine (see below)
2  tablespoons olive oil
   Kosher salt

basil and sauvignon blanc: ¼ cup snipped fresh basil and 2 tablespoons pine nuts, finely ground

tarragon and riesling: 2 teaspoons snipped fresh tarragon and ¼ teaspoon paprika

rosemary and cabernet sauvignon: 2 tablespoons snipped fresh rosemary

mustard and champagne: 2 teaspoons dry mustard

fennel and chardonnay: 2 teaspoons fennel seed, crushed; reduce black pepper to ⅛ teaspoon

**1** Preheat oven to 325°F. In a medium bowl combine flour, desired herb/spice, salt, and pepper. In a small bowl combine desired wine and oil. Gradually add wine mixture to flour mixture, tossing with a fork until combined. Shape dough into a ball. (Dough will appear dry but will come together when gently worked with hands. Avoid adding more liquid as this will make the crackers tough.)

**2** Transfer dough to a lightly floured surface. Using hands or a rolling pin, pat or roll into a 12×9-inch rectangle, ⅛ to ¹⁄₁₆ inch thick. Trim edges. Using a fork, prick pastry. Using a pizza cutter or sharp knife, cut dough into 3×1½-inch rectangles. Gently transfer rectangles to an ungreased baking sheet. Sprinkle with kosher salt.

**3** Bake for about 18 minutes or just until crackers are firm to the touch and start to brown. Transfer crackers to wire racks; cool.

nutrition facts per serving: 33 cal., 2 g total fat (0 g sat. fat), 0 mg chol., 209 mg sodium, 4 g carb., 0 g dietary fiber, 1 g protein.

*food processor method: In a food processor combine flour, salt, and pepper. Cover and process just until combined. Add desired herb/spice, desired wine, and olive oil. Cover and process just until combined (dough will look crumbly). Form dough into a ball. Continue as directed in Step 2.

**make-ahead directions:** Store in an airtight container at room temperature for up to 1 week or freeze for up to 3 months.

crunchy **munchies**

*Crispy, crunchy, and fruity in every bite. Add the sesame sticks and crackers just before serving so they stay crisp.*

# **salty** and **fruity** snack mix

start to finish: 10 minutes  makes: 4 cups

In large bowl combine cereal, pretzels, dried fruit, and fish-shape crackers.

1   cup round toasted-
      oat cereal with nuts
      and honey
1   cup pretzel sticks
      or twists
1   cup raisins, dried
      tart cherries, dried
      cranberries, and/
      or chopped dried
      pineapple
1   cup bite-size fish-
      shape crackers

nutrition facts per ½ cup: 121 cal., 2 g total fat (0 g sat. fat), 2 mg chol., 173 mg sodium, 26 g carb., 1 g dietary fiber, 2 g protein.

**make-ahead directions:** Store in an airtight container at room temperature for up to 1 week.

*The cereals and pecans soak up the maple and cinnamon flavors as they roast, producing a sweet sensation in every bite.*

# maple-spiced snack mix

prep: 10 minutes   bake: 45 minutes   oven: 300°F   makes: 7½ cups

2   cups round toasted multigrain cereal or round toasted-oat cereal
2   cups bite-size wheat or rice square cereal
2   cups bite-size corn or oat square cereal
1½  cups coarsely chopped pecans
½   cup butter
½   cup packed brown sugar
⅓   cup maple-flavor syrup
¼   teaspoon ground cinnamon
1   teaspoon vanilla

**1** Preheat oven to 300°F. In a 13×9×2-inch baking pan, combine cereals and pecans.

**2** In a medium saucepan combine butter, brown sugar, syrup, and cinnamon. Cook and stir over medium heat until sugar dissolves. Stir in vanilla. Pour over cereal mixture in pan. Toss to coat well.

**3** Bake for 45 minutes, stirring every 15 minutes. Spread baked mixture on foil. Cool. Break into bite-size pieces.

nutrition facts per ½ cup: 232 cal., 15 g total fat (4 g sat. fat), 17 mg chol., 175 mg sodium, 25 g carb., 2 g dietary fiber, 2 g protein.

**make-ahead directions:** Store in an airtight container at room temperature for up to 5 days.

*Crunchy and spicy, this snack mix has it all. Customize the mix by substituting your favorite type of nut for the almonds and peanuts specified in the recipe.*

# honey-mustard
## snack mix

prep: 10 minutes  bake: 20 minutes  oven: 300°F  makes: 7½ cups

1½ cups crispy corn-and-
    rice cereal
1 cup bite-size
    shredded wheat
    biscuits
¾ cup unblanched
    whole almonds
½ cup peanuts
2 tablespoons butter
3 tablespoons honey
    mustard
1 teaspoon
    Worcestershire
    sauce
¼ teaspoon garlic
    powder
⅛ teaspoon cayenne
    pepper
4 cups plain popped
    popcorn

**1** Preheat oven to 300°F. Line a 13×9×2-inch baking pan with foil. Place cereal, wheat biscuits, almonds, and peanuts in prepared pan. Toss. In small saucepan melt butter. Remove from heat. Add mustard, Worcestershire sauce, garlic powder, and cayenne pepper, stirring to combine. Drizzle over cereal mixture in pan. Gently toss to coat.

**2** Bake, uncovered, for 20 minutes, gently stirring after 10 minutes. Stir in popcorn. Remove from pan by lifting the foil edges; cool. Serve immediately.

nutrition facts per ½ cup: 113 cal., 8 g total fat (2 g sat. fat), 4 mg chol., 87 mg sodium, 9 g carb., 2 g dietary fiber, 3 g protein.

**make-ahead directions:** Store in an airtight container at room temperature for up to 3 days.

*Show off your knack for snacks with a fancy popcorn-and-cashew mix. Ginger and sesame seeds provide it with an Asian influence.*

# sesame-ginger popcorn

prep: 15 minutes   bake: 20 minutes   oven: 300°F   makes: 8½ cups

6  cups popped popcorn
1½  cups lightly salted cashews
⅔  cup packed brown sugar
2  tablespoons butter
2  tablespoons light corn syrup
1  tablespoon grated fresh ginger
2  teaspoons toasted sesame oil
2  tablespoons sesame seeds
1  teaspoon vanilla
⅛  teaspoon baking soda

**1** Grease a 17×12×2-inch baking pan or roasting pan. Remove all unpopped kernels from popped popcorn. Place popcorn and cashews in prepared pan.

**2** In a medium saucepan combine brown sugar, butter, corn syrup, ginger, and sesame oil over medium heat. Cook and stir until butter melts and mixture boils. Continue boiling at a moderate rate, without stirring, for 5 minutes. Remove pan from heat. Stir in sesame seeds, vanilla, and baking soda. Pour mixture over popcorn and cashews. Stir gently to coat.

**3** Bake for 20 to 25 minutes or until popcorn mixture is golden brown, stirring twice. Spread popcorn mixture on a large piece of buttered foil to cool. Store in a tightly covered container for up to 3 days.

nutrition facts per ¾ cup: 203 cal., 12 g total fat (3 g sat. fat), 5 mg chol., 49 mg sodium, 23 g carb., 1 g dietary fiber, 3 g protein.

*Sweet and savory seasonings mingle in one great snack that's fun to munch and crunch.*

# mexican-spiced
# popcorn

start to finish: 15 minutes  makes: 12 cups

½   teaspoon ground
      cumin
½   teaspoon chili
      powder
¼   to ½ teaspoon salt
      Dash cayenne pepper
      Dash ground
      cinnamon
12   cups plain popped
       popcorn
       Nonstick cooking
       spray

**1** In a small bowl combine cumin, chili powder, salt, cayenne pepper, and cinnamon.

**2** Remove uncooked kernels from popped corn. Spread popcorn in an even layer in a large shallow baking pan. Lightly coat popcorn with cooking spray. Sprinkle cumin mixture evenly over popcorn. Toss gently to coat.

nutrition facts per 1 cup: 31 cal., 0 g total fat (0 g sat. fat), 0 mg chol., 50 mg sodium, 6 g carb., 1 g dietary fiber, 1 g protein.

**make-ahead directions:** Store in an airtight container at room temperature for up to 3 days.

*A crunchy snack mix meant to be casually nibbled over cocktails makes for an inviting way to kick off a party. With a good amount of lively flavors in the mix, this one will really get guests talking!*

# spicy lime snack mix

prep: 20 minutes  bake: 20 minutes  oven: 300°F
makes: about 8 cups

4 cups bite-size shredded wheat biscuits
1½ cups chow mein noodles or pretzel sticks
1 cup peanuts
1 cup cashews
1 cup whole almonds
¼ cup butter, melted
¼ cup finely chopped shallots
1 tablespoon finely shredded lime peel
2 tablespoons lime juice
½ teaspoon crushed red pepper
1 tablespoon dried cilantro
1 teaspoon garlic salt
½ teaspoon onion salt
½ teaspoon ground ancho chile pepper or chili powder

**1** Preheat oven to 300°F. Line a 15×10×1-inch baking pan with foil; set aside.

**2** In a large bowl combine shredded wheat biscuits, chow mein noodles, peanuts, cashews, and almonds.

**3** In a small saucepan heat butter over medium heat. Cook shallots in hot butter for 3 to 5 minutes or until tender. Stir in lime peel, lime juice, crushed red pepper, cilantro, garlic salt, onion salt, and ground ancho chile pepper. Cook and stir for 1 minute. Pour over cereal-nut mixture. Toss to coat. Pour into prepared pan.

**4** Bake for 20 minutes, stirring twice. Remove from oven. Spread mixture on a large piece of buttered foil to cool.

nutrition facts ½ cup: 242 cal., 18 g total fat (4 g sat. fat), 8 mg chol., 229 mg sodium, 16 g carb., 3 g dietary fiber, 7 g protein.

**make-ahead directions:** Store in an airtight container at room temperature for up to 3 days.

*This chili- and cheese-spiced popcorn is a cinch to make. If you want an easy shortcut, purchase popped popcorn instead of popping it yourself.*

# cheesy chili popcorn

start to finish: 10 minutes   makes: 8 cups

8   cups plain popped
      popcorn
2   tablespoons butter,
      melted
1   teaspoon chili
      powder
⅛   teaspoon garlic
      powder
2   tablespoons grated
      Parmesan cheese

Place popcorn in a large bowl. In a small bowl combine butter, chili powder, and garlic powder. Drizzle over popcorn. Toss gently to coat. Sprinkle with Parmesan cheese. Toss to coat.

nutrition facts per 1 cup: 51 cal., 3 g total fat (2 g sat. fat), 7 mg chol., 46 mg sodium, 5 g carb., 1 g dietary fiber, 1 g protein.

**make-ahead directions:** Store in an airtight container at room temperature for up to 3 days.

*Here's a nice twist on popcorn, perfect for munching on during parties, movies, or anytime you're craving a snack.*

# italian-seasoned
# popcorn

start to finish: 5 minutes   makes: 6 cups

¼   cup grated Parmesan
    cheese
1   teaspoon Italian
    seasoning, crushed
¼   teaspoon crushed red
    pepper (optional)
6   cups popped popcorn
1   to 2 tablespoons
    butter, melted, or
    nonstick cooking
    spray

In a small bowl stir together Parmesan cheese, Italian seasoning, and crushed red pepper, if desired. Place popcorn in a large bowl or in a large shallow baking pan. Add melted butter. Toss. Sprinkle with seasoning mixture and lightly toss again. Serve immediately.

nutrition facts per 1 cup: 63 cal., 3 g total fat (2 g sat. fat), 8 mg chol., 65 mg sodium, 6 g carb., 1 g dietary fiber, 2 g protein.

*Five different seasonings accent popcorn for a terrific savory snack that's fun to munch and crunch.*

# indian-spiced popcorn

start to finish: 10 minutes   makes: 12 cups

½   teaspoon curry
    powder
½   teaspoon garam
    masala
¼   to ½ teaspoon salt
¼   teaspoon ground
    turmeric
¼   teaspoon ground
    black pepper
12  cups popped popcorn
    Nonstick cooking
    spray

1 In a small bowl stir together curry powder, garam masala, salt, turmuric, and pepper.
2 Spread popcorn in an even layer in a large shallow baking pan. Lightly coat popcorn with nonstick cooking spray. Sprinkle the cumin mixture evenly over popcorn. Toss to coat.

nutrition facts per 1 cup: 31 cal., 0 g total fat (0 g sat. fat), 0 mg chol., 49 mg sodium, 6 g carb., 1 g dietary fiber, 1 g protein.

*Dried cherries are a colorful and chewy substitute for nuts in this simple caramel corn recipe.*

# cherry caramel corn

prep: 10 minutes  bake: 15 minutes  oven: 325°F  makes: 16 cups

3 tablespoons butter
¼ cup light corn syrup
1 tablespoon molasses
½ teaspoon baking soda
15 cups plain popped popcorn
1 cup dried tart red cherries

**1** Preheat oven to 325°F. In small saucepan melt butter over medium-low heat. Remove from heat. Add corn syrup, molasses, and baking soda and stir until baking soda dissolves. Place popcorn in a large roasting pan. Drizzle molasses mixture over popcorn. Toss gently to coat.

**2** Bake popcorn mixture for 15 minutes, stirring twice. Transfer mixture to a very large serving bowl. Stir in cherries. Cool.

nutrition facts per ½ cup: 74 cal., 2 g total fat (1 g sat. fat), 5 mg chol., 49 mg sodium, 14 g carb., 1 g dietary fiber, 1 g protein.

**make-ahead directions:** Store in an airtight container in the freezer for up to 2 weeks.

*Prepare the Orange-Pecan Crunch ahead of time so you can toss together this great-tasting snack at the last minute.*

# orange-pecan
## crunch mix

start to finish: 20 minutes  makes: about 7 cups (16 servings)

1 recipe Orange-Pecan Crunch
2 cups dried apricots
1½ cups sesame sticks or sesame oat bran sticks
1 5-ounce package yogurt-covered raisins (¾ cup)
1 cup whole hazelnuts

In a large bowl combine Orange-Pecan Crunch, apricots, sesame sticks, yogurt-covered raisins, and hazelnuts.

nutrition facts per serving: 297 cal., 20 g total fat (3 g sat. fat), 4 mg chol., 129 mg sodium, 30 g carb., 3 g dietary fiber, 5 g protein.

orange-pecan crunch: Line a baking sheet with foil; grease foil with butter. Set aside. Combine $1^1/2$ cups pecan halves, $^1/2$ cup sugar, 2 tablespoons butter or margarine, and $^1/2$ teaspoon vanilla in a large heavy skillet. Cook over medium-high heat, shaking skillet occasionally; do not stir. When most of the sugar melts, reduce heat to low. Cook, stirring frequently, until sugar has completely melted and is golden brown. Stir in $1^1/2$ teaspoons finely shredded orange peel. Spread onto prepared baking sheet. Cool. Break up into bite-size pieces. Store, covered, in a cool, dry place for up to 1 week.

*Chock-full of flavor, the delectable layers include Jamaican-seasoned shrimp, sweet mango salsa, and pepper Jack cheese.*

# spicy shrimp nachos

broil: 1 minute  start to finish: 35 minutes  makes: 8 servings

1  pound fresh or frozen peeled, deveined medium shrimp
1  cup fresh mango, seeded, peeled, and chopped
1  medium red sweet pepper, chopped
2  tablespoons finely chopped red onion
1  fresh jalapeño chile pepper, seeded and finely chopped (see note, page 52)
2  tablespoons packed brown sugar
2  tablespoons Jamaican jerk seasoning
8  ounces tortilla chips (about 8 cups)
4  ounces Monterey Jack cheese with jalapeño peppers or Monterey Jack cheese, shredded (1 cup)

**1** Thaw shrimp, if frozen. Rinse shrimp; pat dry with paper towels. Set aside. Preheat broiler.

**2** In a small bowl stir together mango, sweet pepper, onion, and jalapeño pepper; set aside.

**3** In a large bowl combine brown sugar and jerk seasoning. Add shrimp. Toss gently to coat. Coat a grill pan or large skillet with cooking spray. Heat over medium-high heat. Add half of the shrimp to the pan. Cook for 2 to 3 minutes or until shrimp are opaque, turning the shrimp once. Remove; set aside. Repeat with remaining shrimp. If desired, coarsely chop shrimp.

**4** Arrange tortilla chips on a broiler-safe platter or baking sheet. Top with shrimp and mango salsa. Sprinkle with Monterey Jack cheese. Broil 4 inches from heat for 1 to 2 minutes or until mixture heats through and cheese melts.

nutrition facts per serving: 283 cal., 12 g total fat (4 g sat. fat), 99 mg chol., 507 mg sodium, 27 g carb., 2 g dietary fiber, 17 g protein.

*Every appetizer spread needs one extra-hearty dish for guests
who nibble their way through an evening. Loaded with satisfying
ingredients, these nachos will do the trick.*

# party nachos

prep: 10 minutes  bake: 5 minutes per batch  oven: 400°F
makes: 8 to 10 servings

8   ounces tortilla chips
    (about 8 cups)
2   cups shredded
    cheddar cheese
    (8 ounces)
2   cups shredded
    Monterey Jack
    cheese (8 ounces)
⅓   cup sliced green
    onion
1   cup chopped seeded
    tomato (2 medium)
1   4-ounce can diced
    green chile peppers,
    drained
1   2.25-ounce can sliced
    pitted ripe olives,
    drained
1   15-ounce can black
    beans, rinsed and
    drained
    Purchased salsa
    (optional)
    Dairy sour cream
    (optional)
    Purchased guacamole
    (optional)

**1** Preheat oven to 400°F. Divide tortilla chips
between two 12-inch round pizza pans.
Top chips with half of the cheddar cheese, half
of the Monterey Jack cheese, the green onion,
tomato, and chile peppers. Sprinkle with the
remaining cheeses, the olives, and black beans.

**2** Bake, uncovered, one pan at a time, for
5 to 7 minutes or until cheese melts. Serve
immediately. If desired, serve with salsa, sour
cream, and/or guacamole.

nutrition facts per serving: 414 cal., 27 g total fat
(13 g sat. fat), 55 mg chol., 720 mg sodium, 28 g carb.,
5 g dietary fiber, 20 g protein.

*Mix up this herbed nut snack with just one kind of nut or your preferred medley.*

# savory walnuts

prep: 10 minutes  bake: 12 minutes  oven: 350°F  makes: 8 (¼-cup) servings

2 cups walnut halves
2 tablespoons Worcestershire-style marinade for chicken
1 tablespoon olive oil
2 teaspoons snipped fresh thyme or ½ teaspoon dried thyme, crushed
1 teaspoon snipped fresh rosemary or ¼ teaspoon dried rosemary, crushed
¼ teaspoon salt
⅛ teaspoon cayenne pepper

**1** Preheat oven to 350°F. Spread walnuts in an even layer in a 13×9×2-inch baking pan. In a small bowl combine Worcestershire sauce, oil, thyme, rosemary, salt, and cayenne pepper. Drizzle over nuts. Toss gently to coat.

**2** Bake for 12 to 15 minutes or until nuts are toasted, stirring occasionally. Spread nuts on a large sheet of foil. Cool.

nutrition facts per serving: 259 cal., 27 g total fat (4 g sat. fat), 0 mg chol., 191 mg sodium, 5 g carb., 3 g dietary fiber, 3 g protein.

**make-ahead directions:** Store in an airtight container or resealable plastic bag at room temperature for up to 1 week.

*Orange flavoring, sugar, and spice make these fragrant nuts irresistible.*

# orange-spiced hazelnuts

prep: 15 minutes  bake: 20 minutes  oven: 300°F  makes: 20 (¼-cup) servings

¾ cup sugar
1 tablespoon ground cinnamon
1 teaspoon salt
½ teaspoon ground allspice
½ teaspoon ground ginger
⅛ teaspoon ground cloves
2 egg whites
2 tablespoons water
½ teaspoon orange extract
3 cups hazelnuts (filberts), toasted

**1** Preheat oven to 300°F. Line a 15×10×1-inch baking pan with parchment paper or foil; grease foil (if using). Set aside. In a large resealable plastic bag combine sugar, cinnamon, salt, allspice, ginger, and cloves; seal bag. Shake to mix; set aside.

**2** In a large bowl whisk together egg whites, the water, and orange extract. Add hazelnuts. Toss gently to coat. Transfer nuts to a large colander. Drain for 2 minutes.

**3** Add drained hazelnuts to sugar mixture; seal bag. Shake to coat. Spread hazelnuts in an even layer in the prepared baking pan. Bake for 20 minutes. Spread nuts on a large sheet of waxed paper. Cool.

nutrition facts per serving: 159 cal., 12 g total fat (1 g sat. fat), 0 mg chol., 122 mg sodium, 11 g carb., 2 g dietary fiber, 3 g protein.

*Here's a creative change of pace for using the same seasonings enjoyed in a popular sour cream dip. Toss the seasonings with buttery rich macadamia nuts for an unbeatable snack.*

## onion-garlic
# macadamia nuts

prep: 10 minutes   cook: 5 minutes   makes: 12 (¼-cup) servings

3   tablespoons olive oil
1   tablespoon dried
     parsley flakes
1   tablespoon onion salt
1½  teaspoons sugar
1½  teaspoons lemon
     juice
¾   teaspoon garlic
     powder
3   cups macadamia nuts
     (about 14 ounces)

**1** In a large skillet heat oil over medium heat for 1 to 2 minutes or until very hot. Carefully add parsley, onion salt, sugar, lemon juice, and garlic powder, stirring until combined. Add macadamia nuts.

**2** Cook and stir for 5 minutes. Drain nuts on paper towels. Cool.

nutrition facts per serving: 274 cal., 29 g total fat (5 g sat. fat), 0 mg chol., 402 mg sodium, 5 g carb., 3 g dietary fiber, 3 g protein.

**make-ahead directions:** Store in an airtight container or resealable plastic bag in the refrigerator for up to 2 weeks or freeze for up to 6 months.

*No pumpkin pie spice? No worries. Use what you have in the pantry to make the spice blend. Combine 1 teaspoon ground cinnamon, ½ teaspoon each of ground ginger and ground allspice, and ¼ teaspoon ground nutmeg.*

# sugar-and-spice pecans

prep: 10 minutes  bake: 20 minutes  oven: 325°F  makes: 28 (¼-cup) servings

1   egg white
5   cups pecan halves
¾   cup sugar
2   teaspoons pumpkin
     pie spice
¼   teaspoon salt

**1** Preheat oven to 325°F. Lightly coat a 15×10×1-inch baking pan with cooking spray; set aside.

**2** In a large bowl lightly beat egg white with a fork. Add pecans. Toss gently to coat. In a small bowl stir together sugar, pumpkin pie spice, and salt. Sprinkle over pecans. Toss gently to coat.

**3** Spread pecans in an even layer in the prepared baking pan. Bake for 20 minutes. Spread nuts on a large sheet of foil. Cool.

nutrition facts per serving: 156 cal., 14 g total fat (1 g sat. fat), 0 mg chol., 23 mg sodium, 8 g carb., 2 g dietary fiber, 2 g protein.

**make-ahead directions:** Store in an airtight container or resealable plastic bag at room temperature for up to 2 weeks.

*Your garlic-loving guests will savor this crunchy snack, which gets a kick from adding cayenne pepper.*

# spicy roast almonds

prep: 10 minutes  bake: 17 minutes  oven: 350°F  makes: 12 (¼-cup) servings

3 cups whole almonds
1 tablespoon butter
1 tablespoon olive oil
2 tablespoons Worcestershire sauce
1 teaspoon ground cumin
1 teaspoon garlic powder
½ teaspoon kosher salt
½ teaspoon cayenne pepper

**1** Preheat oven to 350°F. Spread almonds in a single layer in a 15×10×1-inch baking pan. Bake about 10 minutes or until lightly toasted, stirring once.

**2** Meanwhile, in a small saucepan heat butter and oil over medium-low heat. Add Worcestershire sauce, cumin, garlic powder, salt, and cayenne pepper. Stir. Drizzle over almonds. Toss gently to coat. Bake for 7 minutes more.

**3** Spread nuts on a large sheet of foil. Cool.

nutrition facts per serving: 229 cal., 20 g total fat (2 g sat. fat), 3 mg chol., 116 mg sodium, 7 g carb., 4 g dietary fiber, 8 g protein.

**make-ahead directions:** Store in an airtight container or resealable plastic bag at room temperature for up to 3 weeks.

*Sweet, salty, and spicy cashews add delightful crunch to the party buffet. Chop up leftover nuts and sprinkle on soups or salads.*

# curried cashews

prep: 10 minutes   bake: 22 minutes   oven: 350°F   makes: 14 (¼-cup) servings

3   cups raw cashews
      (about 1 pound)
3   tablespoons packed
      brown sugar
2   teaspoons kosher salt
2   teaspoons curry
      powder
½   teaspoon ground
      cumin
¼   teaspoon cayenne
      pepper
¼   cup water
1   tablespoon butter

1 Preheat oven to 350°F. Line a 15×10×1-inch baking pan with parchment paper or foil. Spread cashews in a single layer in the prepared baking pan. Bake about 10 minutes or until lightly browned.

2 Meanwhile, in a small bowl combine 2 tablespoons of the brown sugar, the salt, curry powder, cumin, and cayenne pepper; set aside.

3 In a large saucepan combine the remaining 1 tablespoon brown sugar, the water, and butter. Bring to boiling, stirring constantly. Add cashews, stirring to coat. Cook and stir for about 2 minutes or until liquid evaporates. Remove from heat. Add curry mixture. Toss gently to coat.

4 Spread nuts in an even layer in the same baking pan. Bake for 12 to 15 minutes or until golden brown, stirring once. Cool in pan on a wire rack.

nutrition facts per serving: 188 cal., 14 g total fat (3 g sat. fat), 2 mg chol., 287 mg sodium, 13 g carb., 1 g dietary fiber, 5 g protein.

**make-ahead directions:** Store in an airtight container or resealable plastic bag at room temperature for up to 1 week.

*Serve these spicy nuts in paper baking cups. Guests will love having their own serving-size portions.*

# chili-toasted
# pecans
## with dried cherries

prep: 15 minutes  bake: 12 minutes  oven: 325°F  makes: 10 (¼-cup) servings

| | |
|---|---|
| 1 | tablespoon cooking oil |
| ¼ | teaspoon bottled hot pepper sauce |
| 2 | cups pecan halves (8 ounces) |
| 1½ | teaspoons chili powder |
| 1 | teaspoon ground black pepper |
| ¾ | teaspoon salt |
| ½ | teaspoon ground cumin |
| ¼ | teaspoon dried oregano, crushed |
| ¾ | cup dried cherries (4 ounces)* |

**1** Preheat oven to 325°F. In a large bowl combine oil and hot pepper sauce. Add pecans. Toss to coat evenly; set aside.

**2** In a small bowl combine chili powder, black pepper, salt, cumin, and oregano. Add to pecans. Toss well to coat.

**3** Arrange pecans in a single layer in a 15×10×1-inch pan. Bake for 12 to 15 minutes or until toasted, stirring every 5 minutes. Stir in dried cherries. Serve warm or cooled to room temperature.

nutrition facts per serving: 196 cal., 17 g total fat (2 g sat. fat), 0 mg chol., 182 mg sodium, 11 g carb., 3 g dietary fiber, 2 g protein.

**\*note:** If you have other dried fruits on hand, such as raisins and dried cranberries, add them to this mix. Just use ¾ cup dried fruit total.

**make-ahead directions:** Store in an airtight container at room temperature for up to 1 week.

*Chipotle chile powder, made from finely ground smoked jalapeño peppers, adds wonderful hot, smoky bite to the oven-roasted nuts.*

# sweet-hot peanuts

prep: 10 minutes  bake: 30 minutes  oven: 250°F  makes: 12 (¼-cup) servings

2 tablespoons sugar
2 tablespoons olive oil
1 to 2 teaspoons ground chipotle chile pepper
1½ teaspoons chili powder
1 teaspoon five-spice powder
3 cups dry-roasted peanuts

**1** Preheat oven to 250°F. Line a 15×10×1-inch baking pan with parchment paper or foil; set aside.

**2** In a large bowl combine sugar, oil, chipotle chile powder, chili powder, and five-spice powder. Add peanuts. Toss gently to coat.

**3** Spread peanuts in a single layer in the prepared baking pan. Bake for 30 minutes, stirring twice. Cool in pan on a wire rack.

nutrition facts per serving: 244 cal., 20 g total fat (3 g sat. fat), 0 mg chol., 302 mg sodium, 10 g carb., 0 g dietary fiber, 9 g protein.

**make-ahead directions:** Store in an airtight container or resealable plastic bag at room temperature for up to 1 week.

*These savory cookies get a spicy kick from crushed red pepper. For a mellower flavor, substitute paprika.*

# dried tomato biscotti

prep: 30 minutes  bake: 32 minutes  stand: 6 to 24 hours  cool: 30 minutes
oven: 375°F/325°F  makes: about 32 biscotti

½  cup butter, softened
½  cup packed brown sugar
¼  cup grated Parmesan cheese
2  teaspoons baking powder
½  teaspoon salt
¼  teaspoon crushed red pepper
¼  teaspoon ground black pepper
2  eggs
2  cups all-purpose flour
¼  cup snipped dried tomato
1  egg, lightly beaten
1  recipe Roasted Garlic–Parmesan Oil

1 Preheat oven to 375°F. Lightly grease a cookie sheet; set aside.

2 In a large mixing bowl beat butter with an electric mixer on medium to high speed for 30 seconds. Add brown sugar, Parmesan cheese, baking powder, salt, crushed red pepper, and black pepper. Beat until combined, scraping side of bowl occasionally. Beat in the 2 eggs until combined. Beat in as much of the flour as you can with the mixer. Use a wooden spoon to stir in any remaining flour and the dried tomato.

3 Divide dough in half. Shape into two 9-inch-long loaves. Place loaves on prepared cookie sheet. Flatten slightly until about 2 inches wide. Brush loaves with the lightly beaten egg.

4 Bake for 18 to 20 minutes or until a toothpick inserted near the centers comes out clean. Cool on cookie sheet for 30 minutes. Wrap in plastic wrap and let stand at room temperature for 6 to 24 hours to make biscotti easier to slice.

5 Preheat oven to 325°F. Using a serrated knife, cut loaves into ¼-inch-thick slices. Place slices on an ungreased cookie sheet. Bake for 6 minutes. Turn slices over. Bake for about 8 minutes or until crisp and dry (do not overbake). Transfer slices to wire racks. Cool.

6 Serve biscotti with Roasted Garlic–Parmesan Oil for dipping.

**make-ahead directions:** Layer biscotti between waxed paper in an airtight container. Store at room temperature for up to 3 days or freeze for up to 3 months.

roasted garlic–parmesan oil: In a small bowl combine ½ cup olive oil, 2 tablespoons grated Parmesan cheese, 1 teaspoon bottled minced roasted garlic, and ⅛ teaspoon ground black pepper.

nutrition facts per slice: 109 cal., 7 g total fat (3 g sat. fat), 28 mg chol., 110 mg sodium, 10 g carb., 0 g dietary fiber, 2 g protein.

*Turn the twice-baked Italian cookies into a savory delight with onions and herb. Topping the slices with goat cheese makes these even more impressive.*

# caramelized onion–
## tarragon biscotti

prep: 30 minutes   bake: 32 minutes   cool: 1 hour   oven: 350°F/325°F
makes: about 40 biscotti

1  tablespoon butter
1  cup finely chopped
   onion
1  teaspoon honey
½  teaspoon salt
½  cup butter, softened
1  tablespoon sugar
1  teaspoon baking
   powder
½  teaspoon salt
2  eggs
2  cups all-purpose flour
2  tablespoons snipped
   fresh tarragon or
   2 teaspoons dried
   tarragon, crushed
1  tablespoon finely
   shredded lemon
   peel
   Goat cheese (chèvre;
   optional)

**1** Preheat oven to 350°F. Lightly grease a cookie sheet; set aside. For caramelized onion, in a medium skillet heat the 1 tablespoon butter over medium heat. Cook onion, honey, and ½ teaspoon salt in hot butter for about 10 minutes or until onion is golden brown, stirring occasionally. Cool.

**2** In a large mixing bowl beat the ½ cup butter with an electric mixer on medium to high speed for 30 seconds. Add sugar, baking powder, and ½ teaspoon salt. Beat until combined, scraping side of bowl occasionally. Beat in eggs until combined. Beat in as much of the flour as you can with the mixer. Use a wooden spoon to stir in any remaining flour. Stir in caramelized onion, tarragon, and lemon peel.

**3** Divide dough in half. Shape into two 10-inch-long loaves. Place loaves on the prepared cookie sheet. Flatten slightly.

**4** Bake for 20 to 25 minutes or until a toothpick inserted near the centers comes out clean. Cool on cookie sheet for 1 hour.

**5** Preheat oven to 325°F. Using a serrated knife, cut loaves diagonally into slightly less than ½-inch-thick slices. Place slices on an ungreased cookie sheet. Bake for 6 minutes. Turn slices over. Bake for 6 to 8 minutes or until crisp and dry (do not overbake). Transfer slices to wire racks. Cool.

**6** If desired, serve biscotti with goat cheese.

nutrition facts per slice: 53 cal., 3 g total fat (2 g sat. fat), 17 mg chol., 86 mg sodium, 6 g carb., 0 g dietary fiber, 1 g protein.

**make-ahead directions:** Layer biscotti between waxed paper in an airtight container. Store at room temperature for up to 3 days or freeze for up to 1 month.

# fennel-asiago biscotti

prep: 30 minutes  bake: 39 minutes  stand: 15 minutes  cool: 25 minutes
oven: 350°F/325°F  makes: about 80 biscotti

2 cups all-purpose flour
¼ cup white cornmeal
1 teaspoon baking powder
1 teaspoon salt
½ teaspoon coarsely ground black pepper
⅛ teaspoon baking soda
  Dash cayenne pepper
¾ cup grated Asiago cheese (3 ounces)
½ cup pine nuts, toasted and chopped*
2 teaspoons fennel seeds
2 eggs, lightly beaten
½ cup buttermilk
  Parmigiano-Reggiano cheese (optional)
  Dried apricots and/or dried figs (optional)
  Pear slices (optional)

**make-ahead directions:** Layer biscotti between waxed paper in an airtight container. Store in the refrigerator for up to 3 days or freeze for up to 2 weeks.

1 Preheat oven to 350°F. Line a large cookie sheet with parchment paper or foil; set aside. In a medium bowl stir together flour, cornmeal, baking powder, salt, black pepper, baking soda, and cayenne pepper. Stir in Asiago cheese, pine nuts, and fennel seeds.

2 In a small bowl combine eggs and buttermilk. Add egg mixture to flour mixture. Stir until dough clings together. Turn out onto a lightly floured surface. Gently knead just until dough is smooth (dough may still be slightly sticky). Shape dough into a ball. Wrap in plastic wrap and let stand at room temperature for 15 minutes to make dough easier to shape.

3 Divide dough into thirds. Shape into three 7-inch-long loaves. Place loaves 2 inches apart on the prepared cookie sheet.

4 Bake for about 25 minutes or until golden brown. (The tops may split as the biscotti bake.) Cool on cookie sheet for 5 minutes. Carefully transfer loaves to a wire rack. Cool for 20 minutes.

5 Reduce oven temperature to 325°F. Line another cookie sheet with parchment paper or foil. Use a serrated knife to cut loaves diagonally into ¼-inch-thick slices. Place slices on the prepared cookie sheet. Bake for 6 minutes. Turn slices over. Bake for about 8 minutes or until crisp and dry (do not overbake). Transfer slices to wire racks. Cool.

6 If desired, serve biscotti with Parmigiano-Reggiano cheese, dried apricots and/or figs, and pear slices.

nutrition facts per slice: 25 cal., 1 g total fat (0 g sat. fat), 6 mg chol., 49 mg sodium, 3 g carb., 0 g dietary fiber, 1 g protein.

*note: To toast nuts, preheat oven to 350°F. Spread nuts in a single layer in a shallow baking pan. Bake for 5 to 10 minutes or until golden, stirring once or twice. Cool nuts on a wire rack.

*Spiked with a medley of Italian flavors, these are a treat on their own. But for something special, team them up with an antipasto platter.*

# pepperoni biscotti

prep: 30 minutes  bake: 37 minutes  cool: 1 hour  oven: 350°F/325°F
makes: about 24 biscotti

⅓  cup butter, softened
¼  cup grated Parmesan
    cheese
1  tablespoon sugar
4  cloves garlic, minced
1  teaspoon baking
    powder
1  teaspoon dried Italian
    seasoning, crushed
1  egg
1  tablespoon milk
1½  cups all-purpose flour
½  cup finely chopped
    pepperoni
¼  cup finely chopped
    red sweet pepper
2  tablespoons finely
    chopped onion
2  tablespoons snipped
    fresh parsley
2  tablespoons grated
    Parmesan cheese
    Bottled pepperoncini
    salad peppers
    (optional)
    Assorted pitted olives
    (optional)

**1** Preheat oven to 350°F. Lightly grease a cookie sheet; set aside.

**2** In a large mixing bowl beat butter with an electric mixer on medium to high speed for 30 seconds. Add the ¼ cup Parmesan cheese, the sugar, garlic, baking powder, and Italian seasoning. Beat until combined, scraping side of bowl occasionally. Beat in egg and milk until combined. Beat in as much of the flour as you can with the mixer. Use a wooden spoon to stir in any remaining flour. Stir in pepperoni, sweet pepper, onion, and parsley to form a crumbly dough.

**3** Turn dough out onto a lightly floured surface. Gently knead until dough clings together. Divide dough in half. Shape into two 9-inch-long loaves. Place the 2 tablespoons Parmesan cheese on a piece of waxed paper. Roll loaves in cheese to coat. Place loaves on the prepared cookie sheet. Flatten slightly.

**4** Bake for 25 to 30 minutes or until a toothpick inserted near the centers comes out clean. Cool on cookie sheet for 1 hour.

**5** Preheat oven to 325°F. Using a serrated knife, cut loaves into about ⅜-inch-thick slices. Place slices on an ungreased cookie sheet. Bake for 6 minutes. Turn slices over. Bake for 6 to 8 minutes or until crisp and dry (do not overbake). Transfer slices to wire racks. Cool. If desired, serve biscotti with pepperoncini peppers and olives.

nutrition facts per slice: 75 cal., 4 g total fat (2 g sat. fat), 19 mg chol., 90 mg sodium, 7 g carb., 0 g dietary fiber, 2 g protein.

**make-ahead directions:** Layer biscotti between waxed paper in an airtight container. Store in the refrigerator for up to 3 days or freeze for up to 2 weeks.

*Three kinds of peppers lend zest to this crisp, twice-baked cookie.*

# chile pepper–cheese
## biscotti

prep: 30 minutes   bake: 57 minutes   cool: 1 hour   oven: 350°F/325°F
makes: about 56 biscotti

1   cup shredded white
     cheddar cheese
     (4 ounces)
¼   cup butter, softened
1   4-ounce can diced
     green chile peppers,
     undrained
2½  teaspoons baking
     powder
¼   teaspoon salt
¼   teaspoon ground
     black pepper
2   eggs
½   cup yellow cornmeal
2   cups all-purpose flour
     Sliced Monterey
       Jack cheese with
       jalapeño peppers
       (optional)
     Bottled sliced pickled
       jalapeño chile
       peppers (optional)

**1** Preheat oven to 350°F. Lightly grease a cookie sheet; set aside.

**2** In a large mixing bowl combine cheddar cheese and butter. Beat with an electric mixer on medium to high speed for 30 seconds. Add diced chile peppers, baking powder, salt, and black pepper. Beat until combined, scraping side of bowl occasionally. Beat in eggs until combined. Beat in cornmeal. Beat in as much of the flour as you can with the mixer. Use a wooden spoon or your hands to stir or knead in any remaining flour.

**3** Divide dough in half. Shape into two 9-inch-long loaves. Place loaves about 5 inches apart on the prepared cookie sheet. Flatten slightly until about 3 inches wide.

**4** Bake for 30 to 35 minutes or until lightly browned. Cool on cookie sheet for 1 hour.

**5** Preheat oven to 325°F. Use a serrated knife to cut loaves diagonally into ¼-inch-thick slices. Place slices on an ungreased cookie sheet. Bake for 15 minutes. Turn slices over. Bake for 12 to 15 minutes or until crisp and dry (do not overbake). Transfer slices to wire racks. Cool.

**6** If desired, serve biscotti with Monterey Jack cheese and pickled jalapeño peppers.

nutrition facts per slice: 39 cal., 2 g total fat (1 g sat. fat), 12 mg chol., 48 mg sodium, 4 g carb., 0 g dietary fiber, 1 g protein.

**make-ahead directions:** Layer biscotti between waxed paper in an airtight container. Store in the refrigerator for up to 3 days or freeze for up to 2 weeks.

*A healthful combination of seeds adds satisfying crunch and complexity to this rustic biscotti recipe.*

# seeded cheddar biscotti

prep: 30 minutes  bake: 40 minutes  cool: 1 hour  oven: 375°F/325°F
makes: about 50 biscotti

2¼ cups all-purpose flour
⅓ cup yellow cornmeal
1½ teaspoons sugar
1½ teaspoons salt
1½ teaspoons baking powder
½ teaspoon baking soda
½ teaspoon dry mustard
½ teaspoon coarsely ground black pepper
Dash cayenne pepper
¾ cup shredded sharp cheddar cheese (3 ounces)
7 teaspoons assorted seeds (such as poppy seeds, dill seeds, celery seeds, sesame seeds, and/or flax seeds) or purchased bread topping seed mix
2 eggs, lightly beaten
½ cup buttermilk
2 tablespoons butter, melted
Very thin slices prosciutto and/or salami (optional)

1 Preheat oven to 375°F. Line a very large cookie sheet with parchment paper or foil; set aside. In a medium bowl combine flour, cornmeal, sugar, salt, baking powder, baking soda, dry mustard, black pepper, and cayenne pepper. Stir in cheese and seeds.

2 In a small bowl combine eggs, buttermilk, and melted butter. Add egg mixture to flour mixture. Stir to form a crumbly dough.

3 Turn dough out onto a lightly floured surface. Gently knead until dough clings together. Divide dough into thirds. Shape into three 10-inch-long loaves. Place loaves on the prepared cookie sheet. Flatten slightly.

4 Bake for about 20 minutes or until a toothpick inserted near the center comes out clean. Cool on cookie sheet for 1 hour.

5 Preheat oven to 325°F. Use a serrated knife to cut loaves into ¼-inch-thick slices. Place slices on an ungreased cookie sheet. Bake for 10 minutes. Turn slices over. Bake for 10 to 12 minutes or until crisp and dry (do not overbake). Transfer slices to wire racks. Cool.

6 If desired, serve biscotti with prosciutto and/or salami.

nutrition facts per slice: 39 cal., 1 g total fat (1 g sat. fat), 12 mg chol., 109 mg sodium, 5 g carb., 0 g dietary fiber, 1 g protein.

**make-ahead directions:** Layer biscotti between waxed paper in an airtight container. Store in the refrigerator for up to 3 days or freeze for up to 2 weeks.

Double baking rids biscotti of excess moisture, making them light, airy, and crisp.

14

fresh

Si

Complement party nibbles with punches, cocktails, or a rainbow of other fun-loving drinks. Whether hot or cold, spiked or alcohol-free, any of these will make a great thirst impression.

ps

*Cuba is the birthplace of the Mojito, the rum-based cocktail that inspired this alcohol-free punch. Pictured on page 397.*

# raspberry mojito punch

start to finish: 15 minutes   makes: 8 (1-cup) servings

⅓ cup sugar
¼ cup lightly packed
   fresh mint leaves
3 cups cold water
1 12-ounce can frozen
   raspberry juice
   blend concentrate
   (1⅓ cups), thawed
½ cup lime juice, chilled
3 cups club soda,
   chilled
1 cup ice cubes
1 cup fresh raspberries
   Key lime slices or
   lime slices

**1** In a punch bowl combine sugar and mint. Using the back of a wooden spoon, lightly mash the mint by pressing it against the side of the bowl. Add the cold water, raspberry juice blend, and lime juice, stirring until sugar dissolves.

**2** Stir in club soda and ice cubes. Add raspberries and lime slices. Serve at once.

nutrition facts per serving: 139 cal., 0 g total fat (0 g sat. fat), 0 mg chol., 38 mg sodium, 34 g carb., 1 g dietary fiber, 0 g protein.

*Spicy, sweet, and refreshing—combine the fruitiness of pineapple with the peppery bite of ginger. This also has a splash of lime-flavored vodka for extra sipping pleasure.*

# ginger, lime, and pineapple punch

prep: 25 minutes   chill: 2 hours   stand: 30 minutes
makes: 8 to 10 (1- to 1¼-cup) servings

1½   cups water
1   cup sugar
1   cup thinly sliced
      unpeeled fresh
      ginger (about
      4 ounces)
3   cups pineapple juice,
      chilled
1½   cups lime vodka
¼   cup lemon juice
¼   cup lime juice
1   1-liter bottle club
      soda, chilled
      Ice cubes
      Lime slices

**1** In a small saucepan combine the water, sugar, and ginger. Bring to boiling, stirring until sugar dissolves; reduce heat. Simmer for 10 minutes. Cool ginger mixture to room temperature. Strain through a fine-mesh sieve into a bowl. Cover with plastic wrap and chill for at least 2 hours.

**2** In a large punch bowl or pitcher combine chilled ginger mixture, pineapple juice, vodka, lemon juice, and lime juice. Stir in club soda. Add ice cubes and lime slices.

nutrition facts per serving: 258 cal., 0 g total fat (0 g sat. fat), 0 mg chol., 32 mg sodium, 41 g carb., 1 g dietary fiber, 1 g protein.

fresh **sips**

*For holiday parties and open houses, here is a drink that should be on everyone's Christmas list. Creamy, minty, and absolutely delightful, this ice cream concoction goes does down very smoothly.*

# peppermint-
## eggnog punch

start to finish: 15 minutes  makes: 18 (½-cup) servings

1 quart peppermint ice cream
1 quart dairy or canned eggnog
1 cup rum (optional)
1 to 2 10-ounce bottles (1¼ to 2½ cups) ginger ale, chilled
Additional peppermint ice cream (optional)
Peppermint sticks (optional)

**1** Place ice cream in a large chilled bowl; stir until softened. Gradually stir in eggnog. If desired, stir in rum.

**2** Transfer to a punch bowl. Add desired amount of ginger ale to reach desired consistency. If desired, top each serving with additional peppermint ice cream and peppermint sticks.

nutrition facts per serving: 148 cal., 7 g total fat (5 g sat. fat), 47 mg chol., 63 mg sodium, 17 g carb., 0 g dietary fiber, 3 g protein.

*A whisper of cinnamon and cloves spices up this warm beverage. For a special occasion, garnish each cup with a few cranberries threaded like beads onto cinnamon sticks.*

# hot scarlet wine punch

prep: 10 minutes   cook: 3 to 4 hours (low) or 1 to 1½ hours (high), plus 30 minutes (high)
makes: 14 (½-cup) servings

1   2-inch cinnamon stick
    broken in half
4   whole cloves
1   32-ounce bottle
    (4 cups) cranberry
    juice
⅓   cup packed brown
    sugar
1   750-milliliter bottle
    white Zinfandel or
    dry white wine

**1** For spice bag, cut a double thickness of 100-percent-cotton cheesecloth into a 6-inch square. Place cinnamon and cloves in center of cheesecloth square. Bring up corners of cheesecloth and tie closed with clean 100-percent-cotton kitchen string.

**2** In a 3½- or 4-quart slow cooker, combine spice bag, cranberry juice, and brown sugar. Cover and cook on low heat setting for 3 to 4 hours or on high heat setting for 1 to 1½ hours. Remove spice bag.

**3** If using low heat setting, turn to high heat setting. Stir wine into mixture in cooker. Cover and cook for 30 minutes more.

**4** Serve immediately or cover and keep warm on warm setting or low heat setting for up to 2 hours. Stir occasionally.

nutrition facts per serving: 99 cal., 0 g total fat (0 g sat. fat), 0 mg chol., 6 mg sodium, 16 g carb., 0 g dietary fiber, 0 g protein.

### hot drink tips

· *When welcoming guests with warm punches, be sure to ladle the brew into thick, heatproof cups.*

· *For casual gatherings, invite guests to replenish their drinks directly from a stockpot kept over low heat on the stove.*

· *If serving hot punch from a bowl, use a small one and refill it frequently to make sure portions are piping hot. Be certain that the bowl and ladle are heat-resistant.*

· *For carefree elegance, consider renting a silver electric coffee percolator that will keep punch hot for long periods and allow guests to serve themselves.*

· *Do not allow alcohol-spiked punches to boil—the alcohol will evaporate.*

*This recipe makes the most of inexpensive Champagne or sparkling wine—no need to spend more than $10 per bottle.*

# champagne-citrus
## punch

start to finish: 20 minutes   makes: about 10 (³/₄-cup) servings

1   6-ounce can frozen
    orange juice
    concentrate,
    thawed
½   of a 6-ounce can
    frozen lemonade
    concentrate,
    thawed
½   of a 750-milliliter
    bottle (about
    1⅔ cups) sweet
    white wine or
    blush wine (such
    as Riesling or white
    Zinfandel), chilled
1   cup cold water
1   750-milliliter bottle
    Champagne or
    sparkling wine,
    chilled
    Fruited Ice (optional)

In a large punch bowl combine orange juice concentrate and lemonade concentrate. Add wine and the cold water, stirring to combine. Carefully add Champagne, but do not stir. If desired, float Fruited Ice in punch.

nutrition facts per serving: 126 cal., 0 g total fat (0 g sat. fat), 0 mg chol., 3 mg sodium, 13 g carb., 0 g dietary fiber, 0 g protein.

fruited ice: Cut several pieces of fruit (such as limes, key limes, kumquats, oranges, blood oranges, lemons, and/or blackberries) into halves, quarters, or slices. Arrange in an 8-inch square baking pan. Pour enough ginger ale (about 2¹/₂ cups) over the fruit in the pan to cover. Cover and freeze for 6 hours or until firm. Remove from freezer and let stand 20 to 30 minutes. Break into chunks. Add to punch bowl.

### punch bowl options

*If you don't own a traditional punch bowl (or even if you do), try one of these fresh options for serving plenty of guests.*

- *Try something a little shabby chic and use a large ceramic or pottery mixing-style bowl instead of the classic glass bowl.*

- *Use a large bowl that doesn't match the style of your party as a liner placed inside a basket.*

- *For enticing whimsy, use a gallon-size jar or crock. Make sure the ladle is long enough to dip down inside.*

- *If a bowl and ladle are not to your liking, opt for a pitcher. Any pitcher will do as long as it is large enough to hold several servings.*

*Do you love fancy drinks but detest the work of making individual cocktails? Serve Cosmopolitans in a punch! Set citrus twists in a tiny bowl alongside the glasses.*

# cosmo fruit punch

start to finish: 10 minutes   makes: 14 (³/₄-cup) servings

4   cups cranberry juice, chilled
½   of a 12-ounce can frozen limeade concentrate, thawed
4   cups lemon-lime soda, chilled
2   cups orange vodka or vodka
⅓   cup orange liqueur
    Ice cubes
    Lime or orange slices (optional)

**1** In a large pitcher or punch bowl combine cranberry juice and limeade concentrate. Slowly pour lemon-lime soda down side of pitcher. Add vodka and liqueur. Stir gently to mix.

**2** Serve over ice. If desired, garnish each serving with lime slices.

nutrition facts per serving: 180 cal., 0 g total fat (0 g sat. fat), 0 mg chol., 17 mg sodium, 26 g carb., 0 g dietary fiber, 0 g protein.

*Citrus and berry concentrates make this pleasingly refreshing. Ginger ale turns the fruity blend into a bubbly sensation, especially when the ale is well chilled and added just before serving.*

# easy party punch

start to finish: 10 minutes   makes: 25 (³/₄-cup) servings

1  12-ounce can frozen citrus blend juice concentrate, thawed
1  12-ounce can frozen berry blend juice concentrate, thawed
2  2-liter bottles ginger ale, chilled
   Ice cubes or ice ring
   Halved orange slices (optional)
   Strawberries, sliced (optional)

In a very large punch bowl combine citrus and berry juice concentrates. Slowly pour ginger ale down side of bowl. Stir gently to mix. Add ice. If desired, garnish with orange slices and strawberries.

nutrition facts per serving: 101 cal., 0 g total fat (0 g sat. fat), 0 mg chol., 13 mg sodium, 26 g carb., 0 g dietary fiber, 0 g protein.

**serving drinks**

*A mix-and-match collection of taste-size containers, such as shot glasses or espresso cups, adds a touch of charm and whimsy to your party. Even votive candleholders make cute glasses—and usually cost less than true barware.*

*This spiced milk-and-tea blend hails from India and is especially soothing on chilly nights.*

# chai punch

prep: 15 minutes   cook: 15 minutes   stand: 30 minutes
makes: 8 (1-cup) servings

6   cups water
2   teaspoons fennel
     seeds
12   whole cloves
½   teaspoon whole
     cardamom pods
2   4-inch cinnamon
     sticks
2   2-inch slices fresh
     ginger
⅓   cup Darjeeling loose
     tea leaves
2   cups milk
½   cup raw sugar or
     granulated sugar
     Orange peel strips
     Cinnamon sticks,
     crushed

**1** In a large saucepan combine the water, fennel seeds, cloves, cardamom, the 4-inch cinnamon sticks, and ginger. Bring to boiling; reduce heat. Cover and simmer for 15 minutes.

**2** Remove saucepan from heat. Add tea leaves. Cover and allow to steep for 30 minutes.

**3** Strain mixture through a fine-mesh sieve. Return to saucepan. Add milk and sugar. Cook and stir over medium heat until sugar dissolves.

**4** Pour punch into heatproof cups or glasses. Garnish glasses with orange peel strips and crushed cinnamon sticks.

nutrition facts per serving: 82 cal., 1 g total fat (1 g sat. fat), 5 mg chol., 31 mg sodium, 16 g carb., 0 g dietary fiber, 2 g protein.

*If you run short on time, serve this colorful three-fruit sipper over ice cubes instead of the Winter Fruit Brittle.*

# berry holiday punch

prep: 20 minutes  chill: 4 hours  freeze: 4 hours (fruit brittle)
makes: 16 (³⁄₄-cup) servings

2   10-ounce packages
    frozen red
    raspberries in
    syrup, thawed
1   16-ounce can jellied
    cranberry sauce
2   cups blood orange
    juice or regular
    orange juice
2   1-liter bottles
    carbonated water or
    ginger ale, chilled
1   recipe Winter Fruit
    Brittle

**1** Place a fine-mesh sieve over a 4-cup glass measure. Drain raspberries in sieve, pressing with the back of a spoon to mash and remove all of the juice. Discard seeds. In a blender combine the raspberry liquid and the cranberry sauce. Cover and blend until smooth. Transfer mixture back to the glass measure. Cover and chill for 4 hours.

**2** In a large punch bowl combine cranberry mixture and orange juice. Slowly pour carbonated water or ginger ale down the side of the bowl. Stir gently to combine. Add Winter Fruit Brittle to the punch bowl.

**3** To serve, ladle punch and some of the brittle into each glass.

nutrition facts per serving: 113 cal., 0 g total fat (0 g sat. fat), 0 mg chol., 50 mg sodium, 18 g carb., 2 g dietary fiber, 1 g protein.

> **make-ahead directions:** Prepare as directed in Step 1, except chill for up to 3 days. Continue as directed.

**winter fruit brittle:** Line a 15×10×1-inch baking pan with foil, extending the foil up over the edges of the pan. Add water (about 2 cups) to prepared pan to ¼-inch depth. Arrange fresh rosemary sprigs and leaves, fresh raspberries, and halved thinly sliced blood oranges and/or regular oranges in the water. Carefully transfer the baking sheet to the freezer. Freeze until completely firm (4 hours). Just before serving, remove brittle from pan by lifting up foil. Twist the pan to help loosen the brittle if necessary. Remove foil from brittle. Break brittle into large, irregularly shaped pieces.

*Coffee liqueur mixed with brewed coffee and coffee ice cream packs a triple-coffee punch. For a nonalcoholic version, substitute ½ cup strong brewed coffee, chilled, for the liqueur.*

# coffeehouse
# mocha punch

start to finish: 15 minutes   makes: 6 (about 9-ounce) servings

2   cups chocolate milk
1   cup strong brewed
      coffee, chilled
½   cup coffee liqueur
      or ¼ cup coffee
      liqueur plus ¼ cup
      chocolate liqueur
1   pint coffee or
      chocolate ice cream
      (2 cups)
1   pint vanilla ice cream
      (2 cups)
      Whipped cream
      (optional)
      Ground cinnamon
      (optional)

**1** In a large punch bowl combine chocolate milk, coffee, and liqueur. Stir coffee ice cream and vanilla ice cream until softened. Spoon small scoops of ice cream into milk mixture; whisk lightly until smooth.

**2** If desired, top each serving with whipped cream and sprinkle with cinnamon.

nutrition facts per serving: 325 cal., 12 g total fat (8 g sat. fat), 44 mg chol., 123 mg sodium, 39 g carb., 1 g dietary fiber, 6 g protein.

*Bottled blends of black tea and fruit juices are all the rage. This fresh punch takes off on that trend. Use a medium-grade black tea, such as an orange pekoe.*

# lime-tea
## punch

prep: 10 minutes  chill: 4 hours  cool: 15 minutes  makes: 16 (²/₃-cup) servings

8 individual-size black tea bags
6 cups boiling water
2 tablespoons honey
1 12-ounce can frozen limeade concentrate
1 liter (about 4 cups) ginger ale, chilled
  Ice cubes
1 lime, cut into wedges

**1** Steep tea bags in boiling water for 5 minutes. Remove tea bags and discard. Let mixture cool for 15 minutes. Add honey. Stir until dissolved. Add limeade concentrate. Stir until melted. Cover and chill mixture for at least 4 hours.

**2** To serve, transfer tea mixture to a punch bowl. Add ginger ale and ice. Garnish each serving with lime wedges.

nutrition facts per serving: 73 cal., 0 g total fat (0 g sat. fat), 0 mg chol., 9 mg sodium, 19 g carb., 0 g dietary fiber, 0 g protein.

**make-ahead directions:** Prepare tea mixture as directed in Step 1. Cover and chill for up to 48 hours. Continue as directed.

Ladle up some cheer!

*To preserve any leftover fresh ginger, freeze it. Slice or grate the frozen ginger when you want to use it.*

# tango with the tropics
## sipper

prep: 25 minutes   chill: 2 hours   makes: 16 (1-cup) servings

½   cup water
⅓   cup sugar
12   inches stick
      cinnamon
2   ¼-inch-thick slices
      fresh ginger
½   teaspoon whole
      cloves
1   64-ounce carton
      refrigerated
      pineapple-orange-
      banana juice
1   6-ounce can
      lemonade
      concentrate,
      thawed
1   1-liter bottle lemon-
      lime soda, chilled
3   cups light rum
      Orange slices and/
      or kumquat slices
      (optional)
      Crushed ice (optional)

**1** In a small saucepan combine the water, sugar, cinnamon, ginger, and cloves. Bring to boiling; reduce heat. Cover and simmer for 10 minutes. Remove from heat. Transfer to a small bowl. Cover and chill for 2 hours.

**2** Using a fine-mesh sieve, strain spices from sugar syrup. In a large punch bowl combine sugar syrup, pineapple-orange-banana juice, and lemonade concentrate, stirring to mix. Slowly pour the lemon-lime soda and rum down the side of the punch bowl. Stir gently to mix. If desired, garnish with orange and/or kumquat slices and serve over crushed ice.

nutrition facts per serving: 226 cal., 0 g total fat, 0 mg chol., 22 mg sodium, 33 g carb., 0 g dietary fiber, 0 g protein.

**make-ahead directions:** Prepare as directed in Step 1, except chill for up to 24 hours. Continue as directed.

*This tangy, fizzy refresher suits all ages and goes down as smoothly at an evening cocktail party as it does at a lazy afternoon lakeside gathering.*

# apple-lemon sparkler

start to finish: 10 minutes   makes: 18 (³/₄-cup) servings

8   cups apple juice or
      apple cider, chilled
½   of a 12-ounce can
      frozen lemonade
      concentrate,
      thawed
1   1-liter bottle
      carbonated water,
      chilled
      Ice cubes
      Red and/or green
      apple wedges
      (optional)

**1** In a punch bowl or large pitcher combine apple juice and lemonade concentrate. Slowly pour carbonated water down side of bowl. Stir gently to mix.

**2** Serve over ice. If desired, garnish each serving with apple wedges.

nutrition facts per serving: 69 cal., 0 g total fat (0 g sat. fat), 0 mg chol., 15 mg sodium, 17 g carb., 0 g dietary fiber, 0 g protein.

*Grenadine, a pomegranate syrup, is used in many mixed drinks and cocktails, but pomegranate juice is the star of this sprightly drink, combined with carbonated water and mint.*

# pomegranate fizzes

prep: 20 minutes  chill: 2 hours  makes: about 20 (¹/₂-cup) servings

¼  cup fresh mint leaves
4  cups pomegranate
    juice or cranberry
    juice
¼  cup sugar
2  1-liter bottles
    carbonated water
    Ice cubes
    Mint sprigs (optional)
    Pomegranate seeds
    (optional)

**1** In a pitcher place mint leaves. Using a wooden spoon, bruise leaves. Add pomegranate juice and sugar, stirring until sugar dissolves. Cover and chill syrup for 2 to 4 hours. Using a slotted spoon, remove and discard mint leaves.

**2** For each serving, in a small glass combine ¼ cup syrup and ½ cup carbonated water over ice cubes. If desired, garnish with mint sprigs and pomegranate seeds. Serve immediately.

nutrition facts per serving: 40 cal., 0 g total fat (0 g sat. fat), 0 mg chol., 21 mg sodium, 10 g carb., 0 g dietary fiber, 0 g protein.

**make-ahead directions:** Prepare syrup, chill, and remove mint as directed. Syrup may be stored for up to 48 hours after mint has been removed.

*Just as baking spices and brown sugar add warmth and fragrance to baked goodies, they add flavor to this warm toddy.*

## spiced buttered
# rum toddy

prep: 20 minutes  chill: overnight  makes: 4 servings

3  tablespoons butter, softened
3  tablespoons packed brown sugar
¼  teaspoon ground cloves
¼  teaspoon ground cinnamon
   Dash ground nutmeg
   Orange wedge
¼  cup turbinado sugar
¾  cup amber rum, such as Mount Gay
¼  cup Grand Marnier
1½  cups boiling water
   Sweetened whipped cream
4  cinnamon sticks

**1** In a small mixing bowl beat butter and brown sugar with an electric mixer on medium speed until combined. Add cloves, ground cinnamon, and nutmeg, beating to combine. Refrigerate overnight or until ready to use.

**2** When ready to serve, moisten rims of four heatproof mugs with the orange wedge. Place turbinado sugar in a small plate. Dip rims of mugs in sugar to coat.

**3** Place 1 tablespoon of butter-spice mixture in each sugar-rimmed mug. Add 1½ ounces rum and ½ ounce Grand Marnier to each mug. Divide boiling water evenly among mugs and stir to combine. Float a spoonful of whipped cream on the top and garnish with a cinnamon stick.

nutrition facts per serving: 336 cal., 11 g total fat (7 g sat. fat), 33 mg chol., 71 mg sodium, 30 g carb., 0 g dietary fiber, 0 g protein.

*Two of winter's most beloved fruits star in this creative and elegant cupful.*

# cranberry-pear toddy

start to finish: 10 minutes   makes: 4 (1-cup) servings

3   cups cranberry nectar
     or cranberry juice
½   cup pear brandy
½   cup Cointreau or
     other orange
     liqueur
     Fresh cranberries

**1** In a large saucepan heat the cranberry nectar over low to medium-low heat until simmering (do not boil). Remove from heat. Add pear brandy and Cointreau.

**2** Pour juice mixture into four heatproof punch cups or mugs. Garnish each with a cocktail pick threaded with cranberries.

nutrition facts per serving: 271 cal., 0 g total fat (0 g sat. fat), 0 mg chol., 31 mg sodium, 43 g carb., 0 g dietary fiber, 0 g protein.

*Welcome guests to an autumn gathering with this hot spiced cider. The drink not only warms the heart but also adds a cinnamon-and-clove aroma to your kitchen.*

# warming wassail

prep: 20 minutes   cook: 30 minutes   makes: about 16 (1-cup) servings

1   1-gallon bottle apple
     cider
1   cup lemon juice
⅓   cup sugar
10  2-inch cinnamon
     sticks, broken in
     half
6   oranges
     Whole cloves

**1** In a 6-quart Dutch oven combine apple cider, lemon juice, and sugar. Add cinnamon sticks. Stud each orange with 6 cloves. Cut each orange into 6 wedges. Add orange wedges to cider mixture.

**2** Bring to boiling; reduce heat. Cover and simmer for 30 minutes. If desired, remove orange wedges and cinnamon sticks with a slotted spoon before serving. Ladle into mugs.

nutrition facts per serving: 136 cal., 0 g total fat (0 g sat. fat), 0 mg chol., 8 mg sodium, 34 g carb., 0 g dietary fiber, 0 g protein.

*This versatile sip can be served warm on a chilly autumn day or chilled on a balmy summer afternoon.*

# spiced cranberry cider

start to finish: 15 minutes   makes: 8 (about 11-ounce) servings

5 cups apple cider or apple juice
5 cups cranberry juice
1½ cups guava juice or mango nectar
¼ cup lime juice
1 teaspoon ground ginger
½ teaspoon ground cinnamon
½ teaspoon ground allspice
Honey (optional)
Lime slices (optional)
8 cinnamon sticks (optional)
Cranberries (optional)

**1** In a 4-quart Dutch oven combine apple cider, cranberry juice, guava juice, lime juice, ginger, cinnamon, and allspice. Bring to boiling; reduce heat. Simmer, uncovered, for 5 minutes, stirring occasionally. If desired, sweeten to taste with honey.

**2** To serve, ladle into mugs. If desired, garnish with cinnamon sticks and a few cranberries.

nutrition facts per serving: 182 cal., 0 g total fat (0 g sat. fat), 0 mg chol., 28 mg sodium, 46 g carb., 0 g dietary fiber, 0 g protein.

*With Cognac and raspberry liqueur, this is a very sophisticated rendition of apple cider.*

# hot apple-raspberry cider

start to finish: 15 minutes    makes: 6 (about 7-ounce) servings

3  cups apple cider
1  tablespoon finely shredded orange peel
⅛  teaspoon ground cinnamon
⅛  teaspoon ground cloves
⅛  teaspoon ground cardamom
1  cup Cognac
⅓  cup raspberry liqueur, such as Chambord
   Whipped cream
   Ground cinnamon
   Finely shredded orange peel

**1** In a small saucepan combine the cider, orange peel, cinnamon, cloves, and cardamom. Heat the mixture until steam rises from the surface (do not boil). Strain through a fine-mesh sieve, discarding orange peel. Return cider mixture to pan; heat through (if necessary).

**2** Remove from heat. Stir in the Cognac and liqueur. Pour the hot cider into six heatproof mugs. Garnish with whipped cream, additional cinnamon, and orange peel.

nutrition facts per serving: 208 cal., 3 g total fat (2 g sat. fat), 10 mg chol., 3 mg sodium, 6 g carb., 0 g dietary fiber, 0 g protein.

*If you plan to use the Vanilla Sugar coating on the glass rims, make it several weeks ahead of the time you'll need it. Prepare the vodka mixture 3 days ahead as well.*

# cranberry martini

prep: 20 minutes   freeze: 3 days   cool: 30 minutes   makes: 8 servings

1   cup cranberries
1   cup granulated sugar
1   cup water
1   750-milliliter bottle
     vodka
1   recipe Vanilla Sugar
     (optional)
     Ice cubes
     Cranberries (optional)

**1** To make cranberry-flavored vodka, in a 1½-quart saucepan combine 1 cup cranberries, granulated sugar, and the water. Bring to boiling, stirring until sugar dissolves. Continue to cook just until cranberries start to burst. Remove from heat. Cool 30 minutes. Strain cranberry mixture, reserving cranberries and liquid. In a large glass pitcher combine vodka, reserved strained cranberries, and ⅔ cup of the reserved liquid (discard remaining liquid). Cover and freeze for 3 days.

**2** Strain cranberries out of vodka, discarding cranberries (you should have about 4 cups vodka mixture). If desired, moisten rims of eight martini glasses with water. Place some Vanilla Sugar on a small plate. Dip rims of martini glasses in Vanilla Sugar.

**3** In a cocktail shaker place ice cubes. For four drinks, add 2 cups vodka mixture; shake until very cold. Strain into four of the prepared glasses; repeat. If desired, garnish with additional cranberries threaded onto small skewers.

nutrition facts per serving: 296 cal., 0 g total fat (0 g sat. fat), 0 mg chol., 1 mg sodium, 24 g carb., 0 g dietary fiber, 0 g protein.

vanilla sugar: Fill a quart jar with 4 cups granulated sugar. Cut a vanilla bean in half lengthwise and insert both halves into sugar. Secure lid and store in a cool dry place for several weeks before using.

*Serve this fruity libation in icy cold martini glasses. Place the glasses in the freezer about 30 minutes before you're ready to make and shake the drinks.*

# continental martini

start to finish: 10 minutes    makes: 4 (½-cup) servings

Ice cubes
1½  cups citrus-flavored vodka
½  cup raspberry liqueur
Fresh raspberries (optional)

In a cocktail shaker place ice cubes. Add citrus-flavored vodka and raspberry liqueur; shake until very cold. Strain into four chilled martini glasses. If desired, garnish each with a fresh raspberry.

nutrition facts per serving: 273 cal., 0 g total fat (0 g sat. fat), 0 mg chol., 1 mg sodium, 10 g carb., 0 g dietary fiber, 0 g protein.

*The curaçao adds an orange flavor and tropical blue hue to this special cocktail.*

# blue hawaii martini

start to finish: 10 minutes    makes: 4 (3-ounce) servings

1  cup vodka
¼  cup blue curaçao
¼  cup pineapple juice
Ice cubes
Orange wedges (optional)

In a pitcher combine vodka, blue curaçao, and pineapple juice. In a cocktail shaker place ice cubes. Add the liqueur mixture; shake until very cold. Strain into four chilled martini glasses. If desired, garnish each serving with an orange wedge.

nutrition facts per serving: 178 cal., 0 g total fat (0 g sat. fat), 0 mg chol., 1 mg sodium, 6 g carb., 0 g dietary fiber, 0 g protein.

*To garnish these beverages, you can dip the rims of each martini glass in chocolate-flavored hard-shell-style ice cream coating and drizzle a little in the bottom of each glass.*

# chocolate martini

start to finish: 10 minutes  makes: 4 to 6 servings

¾ cup half-and-half or
  light cream
1 cup dark chocolate
  liqueur
¼ cup vodka
  Ice cubes

In a pitcher stir together the half-and-half, chocolate liqueur, and vodka. In a cocktail shaker place ice cubes. Add liqueur mixture; shake until very cold. Strain into four to six chilled martini glasses.

nutrition facts per serving: 297 cal., 5 g total fat (3 g sat. fat), 17 mg chol., 19 mg sodium, 24 g carb., 0 g dietary fiber, 1 g protein.

chocolate-raspberry martinis: Prepare as directed, except substitute raspberry vodka for the regular vodka.

white chocolate martinis: Prepare as directed, except substitute white or clear chocolate liqueur for the dark chocolate liqueur.

# manhattan

start to finish: 5 minutes  makes: 1 (2½-ounce) serving

¼ cup bourbon
1 tablespoon sweet
  vermouth
  Dash bitters
½ cup ice cubes
  Maraschino cherry

In a cocktail shaker combine bourbon, vermouth, and bitters. Add ice cubes; shake until very cold. Strain into a chilled glass or a glass filled with additional ice cubes. Garnish with cherry.

nutrition facts per serving: 171 cal., 0 g total fat (0 g sat. fat), 0 mg chol., 0 mg sodium, 4 g carb., 0 g dietary fiber, 0 g protein.

*Sangria is essentially a blend of wine, spirits, and fruit served over ice. Since wine is the dominant ingredient, it should be something you like. For authentic flavor, use a fruity Spanish red such as Gran Sangre de Toro.*

# sangria
## sparkler

prep: 10 minutes   chill: 2 hours   makes: 6 (about 1-cup) servings

1   750-milliliter bottle
     dry red wine
1   cup orange juice
¼   cup sugar
¼   cup Cognac or other
     brandy
¼   cup orange liqueur
1   medium orange,
     sliced
1   medium blood
     orange, sliced
1   medium lime, sliced
2   cups club soda,
     chilled
     Crushed ice (optional)
     Orange peel twists
     (optional)

**1** In a large pitcher combine wine, orange juice, sugar, Cognac, and liqueur. Stir in orange and lime slices. Cover and chill for at least 2 hours.

**2** Before serving, slowly pour club soda down side of pitcher. Stir gently to mix. If desired, serve over crushed ice and garnish with orange peel twist.

nutrition facts per serving: 232 cal., 0 g total fat (0 g sat. fat), 0 mg chol., 30 mg sodium, 25 g carb., 1 g dietary fiber, 1 g protein.

*This drink is traditionally made with prepared horseradish, but try a new twist—use wasabi (Japanese horseradish) as a substitute.*

# bloody mary

start to finish: 10 minutes   makes: 4 (½- to ⅔-cup) servings

In a pitcher, combine tomato juice, lime juice, Worcestershire sauce, horseradish, hot pepper sauce, celery salt, and pepper. Stir well. Pour into four glasses filled with ice cubes. If desired, stir vodka into individual servings (3 tablespoons per serving). Garnish each serving with a celery stalk, green onion, or broccoli stalk.

2   cups tomato juice or vegetable juice cocktail, chilled
3   tablespoons lime juice
1   tablespoon Worcestershire sauce
1   teaspoon prepared horseradish
½   to ¾ teaspoon bottled hot pepper sauce
¼   teaspoon celery salt or garlic salt
¼   teaspoon ground black pepper
    Ice cubes
    Vodka (optional)
    Celery stalks with leaves, green onions, or broccoli stalks

nutrition facts per serving: 29 cal., 0 g total fat (0 g sat. fat), 0 mg chol., 484 mg sodium, 7 g carb., 1 g dietary fiber, 1 g protein.

bloody maria: Prepare as above, except add ¼ teaspoon ground cumin to the tomato juice and substitute tequila for the vodka.

wasabi mary: Prepare as above, except substitute 1 teaspoon wasabi paste for the hot pepper sauce.

*Cognac, a French brandy, is considered the finest of all brandies, but other less expensive kinds may be substituted, as well as Scotch. Or use peach, apricot, or pear juice.*

# blackberry fizz

start to finish: 10 minutes   makes: 1 (5-ounce) serving

4   or 5 fresh
     blackberries
     or frozen
     unsweetened
     blackberries,
     thawed
1   tablespoon lime juice
1   teaspoon superfine
     sugar
     Ice cubes
3   tablespoons Cognac
     or other brandy
3   tablespoons
     Champagne or
     sparkling wine,
     chilled
     Blackberries
     Fresh mint sprig
     (optional)

**1** In a chilled cocktail glass combine the 4 or 5 blackberries, the lime juice, and sugar. Gently crush berries with the back of a spoon.

**2** Fill a cocktail shaker three-fourths full with ice. Add Cognac. Cover and shake until the outside of the shaker becomes frosty. Strain into the cocktail glass. Pour in Champagne. Garnish with additional blackberries and a mint sprig, if desired.

nutrition facts per serving: 167 cal., 0 g total fat (0 g sat. fat), 0 mg chol., 1 mg sodium, 8 g carb., 1 g dietary fiber, 0 g protein.

fresh **sips**

*The original version of the gimlet was described as a straight-up combination of gin, a spot of lime, and soda. Now a three-to-one combination of alcohol to lime juice, the vodka gimlet just switches out the gin. Pictured opposite.*

# vodka gimlet

start to finish: 10 minutes  makes: 1 (⅓-cup) serving

|  | Ice cubes |
|---|---|
| 3 | tablespoons vodka or gin |
| 1 | tablespoon bottled sweetened lime juice |
|  | Fresh lime peel twist (optional) |

In a cocktail shaker place ice cubes. Add vodka and lime juice; shake until very cold. Strain into a chilled cocktail glass. Garnish with lime peel twist, if desired.

nutrition facts per serving: 100 cal., 0 g total fat (0 g sat. fat), 0 mg chol., 2 mg sodium, 1 g carb., 0 g dietary fiber, 0 g protein.

*Grapefruit is an excellent citrus that adds a touch of sour to drinks. Fresh juice makes the best cocktail and is easy to extract from the fruit if you have a good juicer.*

# cognac-grapefruit cocktail

start to finish: 10 minutes  makes: 1 (5-ounce) serving

|  | Lemon wedge |
|---|---|
|  | Coarse decorating sugar |
|  | Ice cubes |
| ¼ | cup grapefruit juice |
| 3 | tablespoons Cognac or other brandy |
| 1 | tablespoon limoncello |
| 1 | tablespoon Cointreau or other orange liqueur |
| 1 | tablespoon lemon juice |
|  | Orange slices and/ or lemon slices (optional) |

1 Moisten the rim of a chilled cocktail glass with a lemon wedge. Place decorating sugar in a small plate. Dip rim of glass in sugar.

2 Fill a cocktail shaker three-fourths full with ice cubes. Add grapefruit juice, Cognac, limoncello, Cointreau, and lemon juice; shake until the outside of the shaker becomes frosty. Strain into the cocktail glass. If desired, garnish with orange and/or lemon slices.

nutrition facts per serving: 230 cal., 0 g total fat (0 g sat. fat), 0 mg chol., 1 mg sodium, 20 g carb., 0 g dietary fiber, 1 g protein.

*Margaritas come in many shapes, sizes, and colors, but a basic margarita is made with three ingredients—tequila, orange liqueur, and lime juice. Start with the basic margarita to create the frozen and fruity combos on the opposite page.*

# margarita cocktails

start to finish: 15 minutes   makes: 8 (³/₄-cup) servings

1   lime wedge
¼   cup kosher salt
1½  cups triple sec
    or other orange
    liqueur
1   to 1½ cups tequila
¾   cup lime juice
½   cup superfine sugar
    or powdered sugar
    Ice cubes
8   lime wedges

**1** Rub the rims of eight margarita glasses with the lime wedge. Place salt on a small plate. Dip rims of glasses in salt; set aside.

**2** In a pitcher combine triple sec, tequila, lime juice, and sugar. Stir to dissolve sugar. Chill until ready to serve.

**3** Strain into salt-rimmed glasses filled with ice cubes. Garnish with lime wedges.

nutrition facts per serving: 242 cal., 0 g total fat (0 g sat. fat), 0 mg chol., 725 mg sodium, 31 g carb., 0 g dietary fiber, 0 g protein.

**frozen margaritas:** *In a blender place half of the Margarita mixture. With the motor running, add 3 cups ice cubes through the opening in the lid, one at a time, until mixture is thick and slushy. Repeat with remaining Margarita mixture and 3 cups additional ice.*

**strawberry-banana margaritas:** *Dip rims of glasses in sugar to coat. In a blender place one 16-ounce package thawed frozen unsweetened strawberries and 1 medium sliced banana. Cover and blend until smooth. If desired, strain to remove seeds. Add to Margarita mixture. Garnish with fresh strawberries.*

**mango margaritas:** *In a blender place 3 cups bottled refrigerated mango slices. Cover and blend until smooth. Add to Margarita mixture. If desired, replace triple sec with coconut-flavored rum. Garnish with fresh mango wedges.*

**blackberry margaritas:** *In a blender place one 16-ounce package thawed frozen unsweetened blackberries. Cover and blend until smooth. If desired, strain to remove seeds. Add to Margarita mixture. If desired, replace half of the triple sec with blackberry brandy.*

*Typically, a martini is made with gin and vermouth. It's called a vodka martini when vodka is used in place of gin. An olive or lemon peel twist is the classic garnish.*

# classic
# dry martini

start to finish: 10 minutes   makes: 4 (½-cup) servings

1  **cup gin or vodka**
2  **tablespoons dry vermouth**
   **Ice cubes**
   **Pimiento-stuffed olives (optional)**
   **Fresh lemon peel twists (optional)**

In a cocktail shaker combine gin and vermouth. Add ice cubes; shake until very cold. Strain into four chilled martini glasses. If desired, garnish each with a skewered olive or lemon peel twist.

# cosmopolitan

start to finish: 5 minutes
makes: 1 (4½-ounce) serving

¼  **cup vodka**
2  **tablespoons orange liqueur**
2  **tablespoons cranberry juice**
1  **tablespoon lime juice**
   **Ice cubes**
   **Fresh lime peel twist**

In a cocktail shaker combine vodka, orange liqueur, cranberry juice, and lime juice. Add ice cubes; shake until very cold. Strain into a chilled martini glass. Garnish with lime peel twist.

# daiquiri

start to finish: 5 minutes
makes: 1 (2½-ounce) serving

- 3 tablespoons rum
- 2 tablespoons lime juice
- 1 teaspoon superfine sugar
  Ice cubes
  Lime wedge

In a cocktail shaker combine rum, lime juice, and sugar. Add ice cubes; shake until sugar dissolves and drink is very cold. Strain into a chilled glass. Garnish with lime wedge.

# kamikaze

start to finish: 10 minutes
makes: 1 (5-ounce) serving

- ¼ cup vodka
- ¼ cup lime juice
- 2 tablespoons orange liqueur
- ½ cup ice cubes
  Lime wedge

In a cocktail shaker combine vodka, lime juice, and orange liqueur. Add ice cubes; shake until very cold. Strain into a vodka glass set in a bowl of ice or, if desired, into a glass filled with ice cubes. Garnish with lime wedge.

# mint julep

start to finish: 10 minutes
makes: 1 (¼-cup) serving

1 teaspoon sugar
1 to 2 fresh mint leaves
¼ cup bourbon
Ice cubes
Crushed ice
Mint sprigs

In a cocktail shaker combine sugar and mint leaves; crush mint with the back of a spoon. Add bourbon and ice cubes; shake until sugar dissolves and drink is very cold. Strain into an 8-ounce glass filled with crushed ice. Garnish with mint sprigs.

# screwdriver

start to finish: 5 minutes
makes: 1 (¾-cup) serving

Ice cubes
3 to 4 tablespoons vodka
½ to ¾ cup orange juice
Orange slice (optional)

Fill a tall glass with ice cubes. Add vodka. Pour in orange juice. Stir to mix. If desired, garnish with orange slice.

# tom collins

start to finish: 10 minutes
makes: 1 (1-cup) serving

¼ cup gin
3 tablespoons lemon juice
1½ teaspoons sugar
½ cup ice cubes
Crushed ice
1 or 2 lemon slices
Sparkling water

In a cocktail shaker combine gin, lemon juice, and sugar. Add ice cubes; shake until sugar dissolves and drink is very cold. Strain into a glass filled with crushed ice and lemon slices. Add a splash of sparkling water. Stir.

# whiskey sour

start to finish: 10 minutes
makes: 1 (½-cup) serving

¼ cup bourbon
2 tablespoons lime juice
2 tablespoons lemon juice
1 tablespoon sugar
Ice cubes
Orange slice
Maraschino cherry

In a rocks glass combine bourbon, lime juice, lemon juice, and sugar. Using a spoon, stir until combined and sugar dissolves. Add ice cubes. Garnish with orange slice and maraschino cherry.

15

dessert

daz

End a party on an extra-sweet note with luscious bite-size treats or drinkable concoctions—something guests are sure to crave after indulging in a savory spread.

zlers

*Firm-textured pound cake has a buttery flavor that pairs deliciously with creamy fillings and fresh fruit. Another time, try this with lemon curd and fresh raspberries.*

# fruit-and-cream tortes

start to finish: 20 minutes  makes: 6 servings

1  10-ounce frozen pound cake, thawed

2  cups frozen whipped dessert topping, thawed

1  10-ounce jar lime curd

1½  cups assorted fresh fruit (strawberry slices, kiwi slices, and/or blueberries)

Using a serrated knife, slice pound cake into 4 horizontal slices. Using a 2½-inch scalloped cutter, cut 12 rounds. In a medium bowl combine dessert topping and lime curd; mix until smooth. Spoon lime mixture onto half of the cake rounds; top with remaining rounds. Top with additional lime mixture and fresh fruits.

nutrition facts per serving: 943 cal., 54 g total fat (32 g sat. fat), 377 mg chol., 498 mg sodium, 147 g carb., 4 g dietary fiber, 12 g protein.

*For easy handling, let the pastry stand at room temperature according to package directions before unrolling it. To prevent sticking, sprinkle the work surface lightly with flour.*

# mini fruit pies

prep: 20 minutes   bake: 22 minutes   oven: 375°F   makes: 4 servings

1  21-ounce can apricot
   pie filling
¼  cup dried fruit bits
¼  teaspoon ground
   ginger
½  of a 15-ounce
   package rolled
   refrigerated
   unbaked piecrust
   (1 crust)
   Milk
   Coarse sugar

Preheat oven to 375°F. Combine pie filling, dried fruit bits, and ginger. Divide mixture among four custard cups. Unroll piecrust. Cut into star shapes; place on a baking sheet. Brush with milk; sprinkle with coarse sugar. Bake fruit-filled cups and stars for 22 to 25 minutes or until fruit mixture is bubbly and stars are golden brown. Serve warm fruit with star toppers.

nutrition facts per serving: 432 cal., 14 g total fat (5 g sat. fat), 5 mg chol., 232 mg sodium, 71 g carb., 2 g dietary fiber, 1 g protein.

*Plan ahead for thawing the puff pastry. Figure that it will take about 4 hours in the refrigerator or 30 minutes at room temperature to thaw a sheet of pastry.*

# gooey galette

prep: 15 minutes   bake: 17 minutes   oven: 400°F   makes: 9 servings

½   of a 17.3-ounce
     package frozen puff
     pastry (1 sheet),
     thawed
½   cup semisweet
     chocolate pieces
½   cup butterscotch-
     flavor pieces
¼   cup coconut
¼   cup chopped pecans
     Caramel ice cream
     topping

Preheat oven to 400°F. Place unrolled sheet puff pastry on a baking sheet. Bake for 15 minutes. Sprinkle with chocolate and butterscotch pieces. Bake for 2 minutes. Sprinkle with coconut and pecans. Drizzle with ice cream topping. Cut into 9 squares.

nutrition facts per serving: 301 cal., 18 g total fat (6 g sat. fat), 0 mg chol., 143 mg sodium, 33 g carb., 1 g dietary fiber, 3 g protein.

*Be adventurous and use other flavors of ice cream to make these simple treats. For other embellishments, try coconut, miniature chocolate pieces, or toffee bits.*

# puffwiches

prep: 20 minutes   bake: 12 minutes   oven: 400°F   makes: 9 servings

½  of a 17.3-ounce package frozen puff pastry (1 sheet), thawed

1  ½-gallon carton chocolate ice cream

Crushed peppermint candies or chopped toasted almonds

Powdered sugar

Preheat oven to 400°F. Unroll pastry sheet. Cut into 9 squares. Place on a baking sheet and bake for 12 to 15 minutes or until golden. Cool. Cut squares in half horizontally. Remove block of ice cream from box; cut into 1½-inch-thick slices. (Reserve remaining ice cream for another use.) Place slices on bottom half of pastry squares; top with top halves. Roll in crushed peppermint candies. Freeze. Sprinkle with powdered sugar.

nutrition facts per serving: 334 cal., 18 g total fat (6 g sat. fat), 30 mg chol., 173 mg sodium, 40 g carb., 1 g dietary fiber, 4 g protein.

*Sugar-glazed almonds and refreshing orange-flavored icing contrast pleasantly with the buttery, rich cookies.*

# glazed almond
## shortbread stacks

prep: 50 minutes  bake: 20 minutes  oven: 325°F  makes: about 28 cookies

1¼  cups all-purpose flour
3  tablespoons packed brown sugar
½  cup butter
2  tablespoons sliced almonds, finely chopped
1  3-ounce package cream cheese, softened
4  teaspoons powdered sugar
¼  teaspoon finely shredded orange peel
1  teaspoon orange juice
1  recipe Sugar-Glazed Almonds (opposite)

**1** Preheat oven to 325°F. In a medium bowl combine flour and brown sugar. Using a pastry blender, cut in the ½ cup butter until mixture resembles fine crumbs and starts to cling. Stir in the finely chopped almonds. Knead until smooth and shape into a ball. On a lightly floured surface roll or pat dough to a ¼-inch thickness. Use a 1½-inch scalloped round cookie cutter to cut dough. Place 1 inch apart on an ungreased cookie sheet.

**2** Bake about 20 minutes or until bottoms just start to brown and cookies are set. Transfer to a wire rack; cool.

**3** For frosting, in a small mixing bowl combine cream cheese and powdered sugar. Beat with an electric mixer on medium speed until smooth. Add orange peel and orange juice. Beat until combined. If necessary, stir in additional orange juice to make a frosting of spreading consistency.

**4** To assemble, spread shortbread rounds with frosting. Top with Sugar-Glazed Almonds.

nutrition facts per cookie: 87 cal., 6 g total fat (3 g sat. fat), 13 mg chol., 35 mg sodium, 8 g carb., 0 g dietary fiber, 1 g protein.

**make-ahead directions:** Layer unfrosted cookies between waxed paper in an airtight container. Store at room temperature for up to 2 days or freeze for up to 1 month. To serve, thaw cookies if frozen. Prepare frosting and assemble as directed.

*If you're not nuts about peanuts, try almonds or cashews. Toasting the nuts makes these taste even better.*

# peanut bites

start to finish: 30 minutes  makes: 36 servings

1  10-ounce frozen
    pound cake, thawed
1  16-ounce container
    vanilla frosting
¾  cup chopped salted
    peanuts
    Whole peanuts

Cut pound cake into 1-inch cubes. In a small saucepan melt frosting over low heat. Using a skewer, dip cake cubes into frosting; roll sides of cubes in chopped salted peanuts. Top each with whole peanuts. Let stand until set.

nutrition facts per serving: 199 cal., 13 g total fat (6 g sat. fat), 57 mg chol., 142 mg sodium, 27 g carb., 0 g dietary fiber, 3 g protein.

sugar-glazed almonds: Line a baking sheet with foil; lightly butter foil. Set aside. In a heavy, medium skillet heat 3 tablespoons granulated sugar over medium-high heat, shaking skillet several times to heat sugar evenly (do not stir). Heat until some of the sugar melts (it should look syrupy). Start to stir only the melted sugar to keep it from overbrowning. Stir in the remaining sugar as it melts. Reduce heat to low. Continue to stir until all of the sugar melts and turns golden brown. Add 2 teaspoons butter, stirring until butter melts. Add ½ cup sliced almonds. Stir to coat. Pour nut mixture onto the prepared baking sheet. Using two forks, separate nut mixture into small clusters while still warm. Cool.

*To make the crumbs for these no-bake treats, place the wafers in a resealable plastic bag and crush them with a rolling pin.*

# chocolate
# **bourbon**
# **balls**

prep: 20 minutes   stand: 30 minutes   makes: about 50 balls

1   cup semisweet
    chocolate pieces
¼   cup sugar
3   tablespoons light
    corn syrup
⅓   cup bourbon
2½   cups finely crushed
    vanilla wafers
    (about 55 wafers)
½   cup finely chopped
    walnuts
    Powdered sugar,
    unsweetened cocoa
    powder, grated milk
    chocolate, or white
    baking chocolate

**1** In a heavy medium saucepan heat and stir the 1 cup chocolate pieces over low heat until chocolate melts. Remove from heat.

**2** Stir in sugar and corn syrup. Add bourbon. Stir to combine. Add vanilla wafers and walnuts to chocolate mixture. Stir to combine. Let stand at room temperature for 30 minutes.

**3** Shape mixture into 1-inch balls. Roll balls in powdered sugar, unsweetened cocoa powder, grated milk chocolate, or white baking chocolate.

nutrition facts per ball: 65 cal., 3 g total fat (1 g sat. fat), 0 mg chol., 17 mg sodium, 9 g carb., 0 g dietary fiber, 1 g protein.

**make-ahead directions:** Layer balls between waxed paper in an airtight container. Store at room temperature for up to 1 week.

*Puff pastry is easy to work with, and the results are impressive because of its buttery, flaky layers. Handle the pastry as little as possible to ensure tenderness.*

# lemon-berry bites

start to finish: 30 minutes   oven: 400°F   makes: 22 servings

½ of a 17.3-ounce package frozen puff pastry (1 sheet), thawed

2 tablespoons sugar

¾ teaspoon ground cinnamon

2 cups purchased lemon pudding

⅔ cup Strawberry ice cream topping

2 cups frozen whipped dessert topping, thawed

22 fresh strawberries

Preheat oven to 400°F. Unfold pastry sheet. Using a 2-inch scalloped cutter, cut pastry into 22 rounds. Combine sugar and cinnamon. Sprinkle mixture over pastry rounds. Bake for 12 to 15 minutes or until golden. Cool. Cut rounds in half horizontally. Fill each with 2 tablespoons purchased lemon pudding. Drizzle with strawberry ice cream topping. Spoon on whipped topping and add fresh strawberry to each.

nutrition facts per serving: 105 cal., 5 g total fat (1 g sat. fat), 2 mg chol., 114 mg sodium, 13 g carb., 0 g dietary fiber, 1 g protein.

*These exquisite mini desserts boast three kinds of chocolate—cocoa powder in the pastry, unsweetened chocolate in the brownie layer, and semisweet chocolate in the velvety ganache.*

# raspberry brownie tartlets

prep: 45 minutes  bake: 12 minutes  cool: 20 minutes  oven: 375°F
makes: 24 tartlets

| | |
|---|---|
| 1 | recipe Chocolate Pastry |
| 1 | ounce unsweetened chocolate, chopped |
| 2 | tablespoons butter |
| ⅓ | cup sugar |
| ¼ | cup seedless red raspberry jam |
| 1 | egg, lightly beaten |
| ⅓ | cup all-purpose flour |
| ¼ | teaspoon baking powder |
| ⅛ | teaspoon salt |
| 24 | fresh red raspberries |
| 1 | recipe Chocolate Ganache |

**1** Preheat oven to 375°F. On a lightly floured surface roll the pastry to ⅛-inch thickness. Using a 2¾-inch round cookie cutter, cut pastry into 24 rounds. Fit rounds into 24 ungreased 1¾-inch muffin cups, pressing pastry onto bottoms and up the sides. Bake for 5 minutes.

**2** Meanwhile, for filling, in a small saucepan combine unsweetened chocolate and butter. Cook and stir over low heat until mixture melts. Remove from heat. Stir in sugar, jam, and egg just until combined. Stir in flour, baking powder, and salt. Spoon a scant 1 tablespoon of the filling into each pastry-lined muffin cup.

**3** Bake for 12 to 15 minutes or until filling sets. Cool in muffin cups on a wire rack for 5 minutes. Remove from muffin cups; cool on wire rack.

**4** Top each tartlet with a raspberry. Spoon Chocolate Ganache over berry.

nutrition facts per tartlet: 145 cal., 8 g total fat (5 g sat. fat), 34 mg chol., 56 mg sodium, 18 g carb., 1 g dietary fiber, 2 g protein.

chocolate pastry: In a medium bowl stir together 1¼ cups all-purpose flour, ⅓ cup sugar, and ¼ cup unsweetened cocoa powder. Using a pastry blender, cut in ½ cup cold butter until mixture is crumbly. In a small bowl, whisk together 1 egg yolk and 2 tablespoons cold water. Gradually stir egg yolk mixture into flour mixture. Gently knead dough just until a ball forms. If necessary, cover dough with plastic wrap and chill for 30 to 60 minutes or until dough is easy to handle.

chocolate ganache: In a small saucepan heat ¼ cup whipping cream over medium-high heat just until boiling. Remove from heat. Add ½ cup semisweet chocolate pieces (do not stir). Let stand for 5 minutes. Stir until smooth. Cool for 15 minutes before using. Makes 1 cup.

**make-ahead directions:** Layer plain baked tartlets between waxed paper in an airtight container. Store at room temperature for up to 2 days or freeze for up to 1 month. To serve, thaw tartlets if frozen. Prepare Chocolate Ganache. Top tartlets with raspberries and spoon ganache over as directed.

*Starting with phyllo tart shells saves time and effort; filling with fresh berries and sweetened sour cream makes these elegant enough for even the fanciest gathering.*

## bite-size
# berry pies

start to finish: 15 minutes  makes: 15 servings

| | |
|---|---|
| ⅓ | cup dairy sour cream |
| 1 | teaspoon powdered sugar |
| 15 | mini phyllo dough tart shells |
| ⅓ | cup strawberry or raspberry preserves |
| ¾ | cup assorted fresh berries (blueberries, raspberries, and/or sliced strawberries) |

In a small bowl combine sour cream and powdered sugar. Place a spoonful of the sour cream mixture into the bottoms of tart shells. Top with 1 teaspoon preserves and mixture of berries.

nutrition facts per serving: 55 cal., 2 g total fat (0 g sat. fat), 2 mg chol., 16 mg sodium, 9 g carb., 0 g dietary fiber, 1 g protein.

*Look for a high-quality caramel sauce in specialty food stores. Select one with butter or cream as an ingredient listing.*

## caramel-almond
# profiteroles

prep: 50 minutes   chill: up to 24 hours   bake: 25 minutes   oven: 400°F
makes: 24 servings

½   of an 8-ounce carton
     mascarpone cheese
½   cup whipping cream
2   tablespoons
     powdered sugar
2   tablespoons orange
     marmalade
¼   teaspoon vanilla
½   cup water
¼   cup butter
     Dash salt
½   cup all-purpose flour
2   eggs
1   cup caramel sauce
2   tablespoons orange
     liqueur, such as
     Grand Marnier or
     triple sec
¼   cup sliced almonds,
     toasted

**make-ahead directions:**
Prepare and bake puffs as
directed through Step 3.
Place baked puffs in a single
layer in an airtight container.
Freeze for up to 2 weeks.
To serve, preheat oven to
350°F. Arrange puffs on a
baking sheet and bake for
7 to 10 minutes or until crisp.

**1** For filling, in a medium mixing bowl beat mascarpone cheese, whipping cream, powdered sugar, orange marmalade, and vanilla with an electric mixer on medium speed just until stiff peaks form, scraping side of bowl occasionally. Cover and chill for up to 24 hours.

**2** Preheat oven to 400°F. Grease a large baking sheet. In a small saucepan combine the water, butter, and salt. Bring to boiling. Add flour all at once, stirring vigorously. Cook and stir until mixture forms a ball. Remove from heat. Cool for 10 minutes. Add eggs, one at a time, beating with a wooden spoon after each addition until well combined.

**3** Place dough into a pastry bag fitted with a ½-inch open star tip. Pipe onto prepared baking sheet, making a total of 24 puffs, or drop mounds of dough by rounded teaspoons 2 inches apart onto the prepared baking sheet. (If you need to use two baking sheets, keep second sheet covered while baking first batch.) Bake for 25 minutes. Transfer puffs to wire racks. Cool completely.

**4** For sauce, just before serving, in a small saucepan gently heat and stir caramel sauce over medium heat just until warm. Remove from heat. Stir in liqueur. Set aside.

**5** To serve, cut tops from puffs. Remove soft dough from inside. Spoon filling into bottom half of each puff; replace tops. Drizzle each puff with sauce and sprinkle with almonds.

nutrition facts per serving: 126 cal., 7 g total fat (4 g sat. fat), 36 mg chol., 61 mg sodium, 14 g carb., 0 g dietary fiber, 3 g protein.

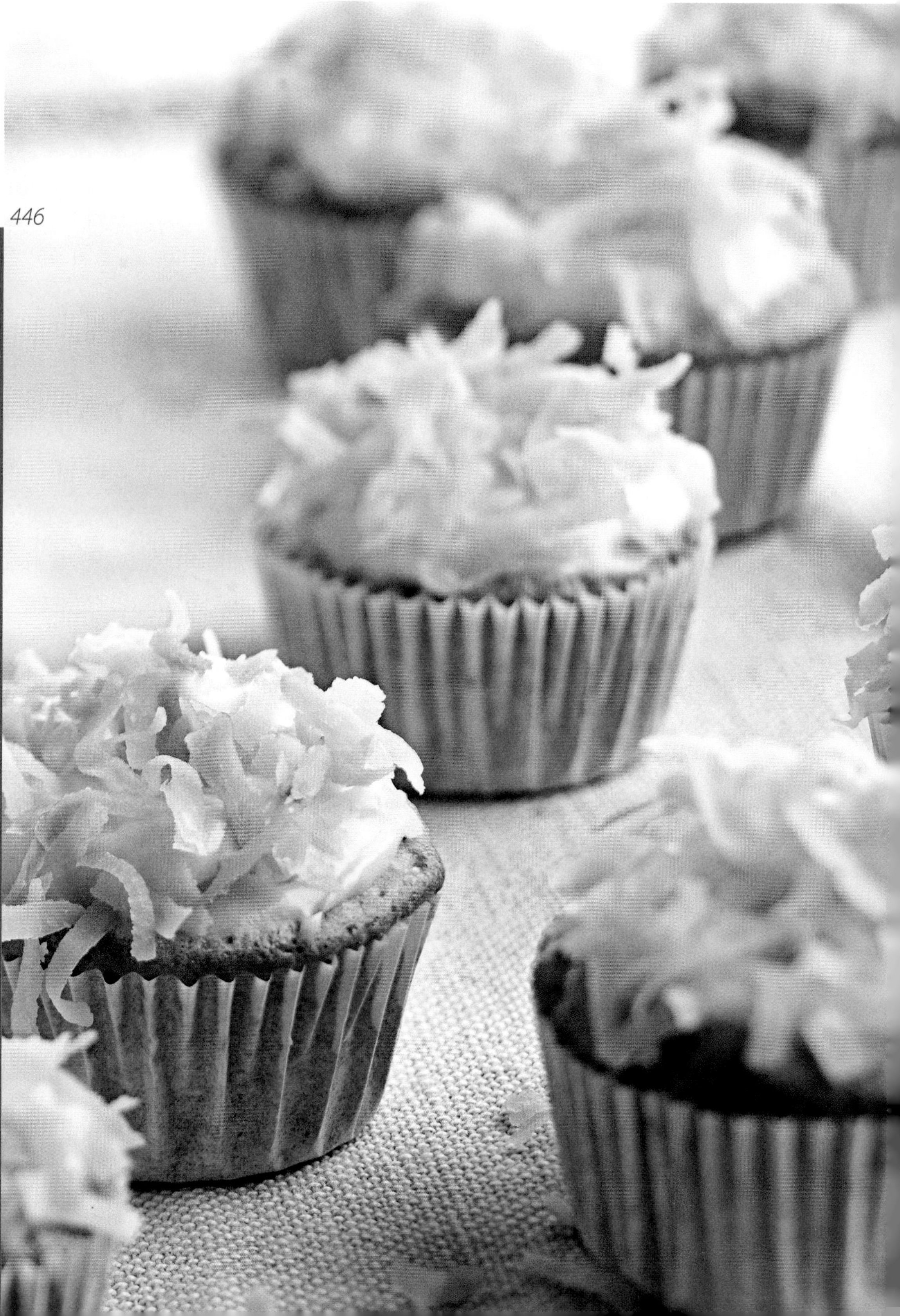

*To soften the cream cheese for the frosting, let it stand at room temperature for about 30 minutes. Or unwrap it and microwave it, uncovered, on 100 percent power (high) for 10 seconds or until softened.*

# mini coconut cakes

prep: 40 minutes  bake: 10 minutes  cool: 5 minutes  oven: 350°F
makes: 36 mini cakes

1 package 1-layer-size white cake mix
½ cup half-and-half or light cream
1 egg
1 teaspoon vanilla
⅛ teaspoon ground nutmeg
¾ cup shredded coconut
  Food coloring (optional)
1 3-ounce package cream cheese, softened
2 tablespoons butter, softened
¾ cup powdered sugar
½ teaspoon vanilla
1 to 2 tablespoons half-and-half or light cream

**1** Preheat oven to 350°F. Lightly coat thirty-six 1¾-inch muffin cups with cooking spray or line muffin cups with paper bake cups.

**2** In a medium bowl combine cake mix, the ½ cup half-and-half, the egg, the 1 teaspoon vanilla, and the nutmeg. Beat with an electric mixer on low speed just until combined. Beat on medium speed for 2 minutes, scraping side of bowl frequently. Divide batter evenly among the prepared muffin cups, filling each about two-thirds full (about 1 rounded teaspoon in each). Bake for 10 to 12 minutes or until a toothpick inserted in the centers comes out clean. Cool in muffin cups on a wire rack for 5 minutes. Remove from muffin cups. Cool on wire rack.

**3** If desired, tint coconut: In a small resealable plastic bag, combine desired amount of coconut and several drops of food coloring. Seal bag. Use your hands to knead the bag until all of the coconut is tinted, adding more food coloring as necessary to reach desired color. Set aside.

**4** For frosting, in a medium mixing bowl combine cream cheese and butter. Beat with an electric mixer on medium speed until combined. Beat in powdered sugar and ½ teaspoon vanilla. Beat in enough of the 1 to 2 tablespoons half-and-half, 1 teaspoon at a time, to make a frosting of spreading consistency.

**5** Dip tops of mini cakes into frosting, then into coconut.

nutrition facts per mini cake: 64 cal., 3 g total fat (2 g sat. fat), 12 mg chol., 60 mg sodium, 9 g carb., 0 g dietary fiber, 1 g protein.

*Refresh party-goers' palates with this intensely flavored ice dessert. Even when served after a heavy meal or in between courses, it's a lovely way to lighten things up.*

# espresso-amaretto
## granitas

prep: 15 minutes   cool: 30 minutes   freeze: 6 hours   stand: 5 minutes
makes: 16 servings

½ cup water
¼ cup sugar
1½ cups strong brewed espresso, cooled
1 teaspoon amaretto or ¼ teaspoon almond extract

**1** In a medium saucepan combine water and sugar over medium heat. Cook and stir until sugar dissolves. Remove from heat. Cool about 30 minutes. Stir in espresso and amaretto. Pour into a 1-quart freezerproof container.

**2** Freeze, uncovered, for 2 hours, stirring and scraping frozen mixture from sides of container every 20 minutes. Cover and freeze, without stirring, about 4 hours or until firm.

**3** Let stand at room temperature for 5 to 10 minutes before serving. Using a metal spoon, scrape across the surface and spoon into chilled dessert dishes or cordial glasses.

nutrition facts per serving: 14 cal., 0 g total fat (0 g sat. fat), 0 mg chol., 3 mg sodium, 3 g carb., 0 g dietary fiber, 0 g protein.

*A ripe mango will smell sweet. Sniff near the stem: No scent means no flavor. A sour or alcoholic smell means the mango is past its prime.*

# mango and lime
# cream–filled spoons

start to finish: 20 minutes   makes: 12 servings

¾   cup sliced peeled
      mango (1 medium)
1   8-ounce carton
      mascarpone cheese
1   tablespoon powdered
      sugar
2   teaspoons finely
      shredded lime peel
1   tablespoon lime juice
¼   teaspoon salt
      Mango slivers or
      finely shredded lime
      peel (optional)

**1** In a food processor place mango slices. Cover and pulse until smooth. Add cheese, powdered sugar, the 2 teaspoons lime peel, the lime juice, and salt. Cover and pulse until smooth.

**2** Fill a decorating bag with mango mixture. Pipe into 12 soup spoons. If desired, garnish with mango slivers or additional lime peel.

nutrition facts per serving: 93 cal., 9 g total fat (5 g sat. fat), 24 mg chol., 59 mg sodium, 4 g carb., 0 g dietary fiber, 4 g protein.

*Perfect for any party, these petite cookie sandwiches give a big jolt of chocolate flavor.*

# milk chocolate
# cookie sandwiches

prep: 45 minutes  freeze: 30 minutes  bake: 9 minutes per batch
oven: 350°F  makes: 80 tiny cookie sandwiches

¾  cup all-purpose flour
¾  teaspoon baking
    powder
⅛  teaspoon salt
6  ounces milk chocolate
3  tablespoons butter,
    softened
½  cup sugar
1  egg
¾  teaspoon vanilla
1  recipe Milk Chocolate
    and Sour Cream
    Frosting

**1** In a medium bowl stir together flour, baking powder, and salt; set aside. In a small saucepan heat and stir milk chocolate over low heat until smooth. In a medium mixing bowl beat butter with electric mixer on medium to high speed for 30 seconds. Add sugar. Beat until combined, scraping sides of bowl occasionally. Beat in melted chocolate, egg, and vanilla until combined. Beat in flour mixture.

**2** Divide dough into 4 equal portions. Wrap each portion in plastic wrap. Freeze about 30 minutes or until easy to handle. (Or chill in the refrigerator for about 1 hour.)

**3** Preheat oven to 350°F. On waxed paper, shape one portion of dough at a time into a 10-inch-long log. Lift and smooth the waxed paper to help shape the logs. Using a sharp knife, cut logs crosswise into ¼-inch slices. Place slices 1 inch apart on ungreased cookie sheets. Bake for 9 to 10 minutes or until edges are set. Let stand for 2 minutes on cookie sheet. Carefully transfer to a wire rack; cool.

**4** Spread ½ teaspoon of frosting on each of the flat sides of half of the cookies. Top with remaining cookies, flat sides down. Serve the same day.

nutrition facts per cookie sandwich: 43 cal., 2 g total fat (1 g sat. fat), 6 mg chol., 15 mg sodium, 6 g carb., 0 g dietary fiber, 0 g protein.

milk chocolate and sour cream frosting: In a saucepan heat and stir 3 ounces chopped milk chocolate and 2 tablespoons butter over low heat until smooth. Cool for 5 minutes. Stir in ¼ cup dairy sour cream. Gradually stir in 1 to 1¼ cups powdered sugar to make a frosting of spreading consistency.

**make-ahead directions:** Layer unfilled cookies between waxed paper in an airtight container. Store at room temperature for up to 3 days or freeze for up to 3 months.

*Looking for a fast, fun dessert that will stand out at a party? Ready-made mini phyllo shells cut the preparation for these darling little tarts.*

# honey-nut tarts

start to finish: 15 minutes   makes: 15 tarts

⅓   cup chocolate-
    hazelnut spread
15   mini phyllo dough
    shells
½   cup salted mixed
    nuts
2   tablespoons honey

Spoon chocolate-hazelnut spread into the bottoms of tart shells, using 1 teaspoon spread for each shell. Top with salted mixed nuts and drizzle with honey.

nutrition facts per tart: 82 cal., 5 g total fat (0 g sat. fat), 0 mg chol., 30 mg sodium, 16 g carb., 0 g dietary fiber, 2 g protein.

# cream tartlets— three ways:

*Fill ready-made phyllo tart shells with your favorite creamed pudding and topper—a sublime treat for ending a party on a sweet note. Start with these easy ideas:*

orange: *Add grated orange peel to purchased vanilla pudding. Fill phyllo dough shells with pudding. Top with mandarin orange pieces, whipped cream, and orange peel.*

banana: *Place a banana slice in phyllo dough shells. Top with purchased vanilla pudding, whipped cream, and a maraschino cherry.*

coconut: *Fill ready-made phyllo dough shells with purchased vanilla pudding. Top with whipped cream and toasted coconut.*

*You'll need plenty of lemon peel because it is used in the bars and the glaze, so be sure to have lots of lemons on hand.*

# lemony glazed
# shortbread bars

prep: 40 minutes   bake: 40 minutes   oven: 300°F   makes: 32 bars

| | |
|---|---|
| 3 | cups all-purpose flour |
| ⅓ | cup cornstarch |
| 1¼ | cups powdered sugar |
| ¼ | cup finely shredded lemon peel (6 to 7 lemons) |
| 1½ | cups butter, softened |
| 1 | tablespoon lemon juice |
| ½ | teaspoon salt |
| ½ | teaspoon vanilla |
| 1 | recipe Lemony Glaze |

**1** Preheat oven to 300°F. Line a 13x9x2-inch baking pan with foil, extending foil over the edges of the pan; lightly grease foil. Set aside.

**2** In a medium bowl stir together flour and cornstarch. In a small bowl combine powdered sugar and lemon peel. Using your fingers or pressing against side of bowl with a wooden spoon, work lemon peel into powdered sugar until sugar is yellow and very fragrant.* Set aside.

**3** In a large mixing bowl combine butter, lemon juice, salt, and vanilla. Beat with an electric mixer on medium speed until combined. Gradually beat in sugar mixture. Stir in flour mixture.

**4** Using lightly floured fingers, press dough evenly into the prepared baking pan. Bake on the center rack of the oven for about 40 minutes or until center turns pale golden brown and edges start to brown.

**5** Remove from oven. Immediately spoon lemon glaze over the top and gently spread to evenly distribute. Cool in pan on a wire rack. Using the edges of the foil, lift the uncut block out of the pan. Cut into bars.

nutrition facts per bar: 181 cal., 9 g total fat (5 g sat. fat), 23 mg chol., 98 mg sodium, 25 g carb., 0 g dietary fiber, 0 g protein.

*note: Rubbing the lemon peel with the powdered sugar releases the lemon oil.

lemony glaze: In a medium bowl, combine 2½ cups powdered sugar, 2 teaspoons finely shredded lemon peel, 3 tablespoons lemon juice, 1 tablespoon light corn syrup, and ½ teaspoon vanilla. Whisk until smooth.

*Anyone with a burning passion for this little French number will adore the mini-size versions. Ooh la la!*

# tiny vanilla
# crème brûlées

prep: 35 minutes  bake: 25 minutes  cool: 30 minutes  chill: 4 hours
oven: 300°F  makes: 10 servings

1¾  cups whipping cream
½  cup sugar
¼  cup half-and-half or
    light cream
½  of a vanilla bean
6  egg yolks
¼  cup sugar

**1** Preheat oven to 300°F. In a medium heavy saucepan combine whipping cream, the ½ cup sugar, and the half-and-half. Split vanilla bean lengthwise; scrape seeds from bean. Add seeds and bean to saucepan. Cook and stir over medium heat just until mixture comes to boiling. Remove from heat. Cover and let stand for 15 to 20 minutes to infuse cream mixture with vanilla flavor. Strain, discarding vanilla bean.

**2** In a medium bowl whisk egg yolks until combined. Gradually whisk in warm cream mixture. Place 10 ungreased 2-ounce ramekins in a shallow roasting pan. Divide cream mixture evenly among ramekins, filling two-thirds full. Place roasting pan on oven rack. Pour hot water into the roasting pan to reach about ¾ inch up sides of ramekins.

**3** Bake for 25 to 30 minutes or until custards appear set in centers when gently shaken. Remove ramekins from water; cool on a wire rack for 30 minutes. Cover and chill for at least 4 hours.

**4** To serve, sprinkle the ¼ cup sugar evenly over tops of custards. Using a culinary blowtorch, heat until sugar melts.* Serve at once.

nutrition facts per serving: 244 cal., 19 g total fat (11 g sat. fat), 186 mg chol., 23 mg sodium, 17 g carb., 0 g dietary fiber, 3 g protein.

*note: If your ramekins are broiler-safe, you may melt the sugar under the broiler. Preheat broiler. Return the chilled custards to the roasting pan and surround with ice cubes and a little cold water. Broil about 5 inches from the heat about 2 minutes or until a bubbly brown crust forms.

*This winning combination of cool mint and decadent white crème de cacao will taste especially refreshing after hearty appetizers.*

# minty fresh
## whips

start to finish: 10 minutes   makes: 8 servings

½   cup whipping cream
¼   cup green crème de
     menthe
¼   cup crème de cacao
1   cup ice cubes

In a blender combine whipping cream, crème de menthe, and crème de cacao. Add ice cubes. Cover and blend until mixture is smooth. Pour into eight 2- to 3-ounce glasses. Serve immediately.

nutrition facts per serving: 108 cal., 6 g total fat (3 g sat. fat), 21 mg chol., 7 mg sodium, 8 g carb., 0 g dietary fiber, 3 g protein.

Frosty dessert drinks packed with panache and filled with flavor are perfect for an evening of entertaining.

*Who says you need a fork to enjoy tiramisu? Vodka, coffee liqueur, and coffee ice cream combine to make a frothy and delicious dessert drink.*

# tiramisu tippers

start to finish: 10 minutes  makes: 8 servings

½  cup coffee ice cream
2  tablespoons vodka
2  tablespoons coffee
    liqueur
1  tablespoon crème
    de cacao
½  cup ice cubes
    Chocolate-covered
    coffee beans,
    coarsely chopped
    (optional)

**1** In a blender combine ice cream, vodka, liqueur, and crème de cacao. Add ice cubes. Cover and blend until mixture is smooth.

**2** Pour mixture into eight espresso cups. If desired, top each with coarsely chopped coffee beans. Serve immediately.

nutrition facts per serving: 45 cal., 1 g total fat (1 g sat. fat), 3 mg chol., 6 mg sodium, 5 g carb., 0 g dietary fiber, 1 g protein.

dessert dazzlers

*Spiced rum, fresh banana, whipping cream, and caramel sauce make for a tantalizing spectrum of flavor.*

# bananas froster

start to finish: 10 minutes  makes: 8 servings

1  medium banana, halved
3  tablespoons crème de banana liqueur
3  tablespoons spiced rum
3  tablespoons whipping cream
2  tablespoons caramel ice cream topping
¾  cup ice cubes
   Freshly grated nutmeg (optional)

**1** Cut up half of the banana and place in a blender. Cut remaining half of banana diagonally into 8 slices; set aside. Add liqueur, rum, whipping cream, 1 tablespoon of the ice cream topping, and ice cubes to blender. Cover and blend until mixture is smooth.

**2** Drizzle remaining 1 tablespoon ice cream topping onto the insides of eight 2- to 3-ounce glasses. Pour banana mixture into glasses. If desired, sprinkle with freshly grated nutmeg. Garnish each glass with a reserved banana slice.

nutrition facts per serving: 73 cal., 2 g total fat (1 g sat. fat), 8 mg chol., 21 mg sodium, 9 g carb., 0 g dietary fiber, 0 g protein.

*What could be more irresistible than chocolate ice cream blended to perfection with Irish cream liqueur? A dash of dark crème de cacao makes it memorable.*

# chocolate
## dazzler

start to finish: 15 minutes  makes: 8 servings

2   ounces semisweet chocolate
⅓   cup chocolate sprinkles
1   cup chocolate ice cream
¼   cup Irish cream liqueur
2   tablespoons dark crème de cacao
2   tablespoons vodka
    Chocolate curls or grated chocolate

**1** In a heavy small saucepan heat chocolate over low heat until melted. Place sprinkles on a small plate. Dip rims of eight 1-ounce mini martini glasses or shot glasses in the melted chocolate and then dip in the sprinkles. Chill until serving time.

**2** In a blender combine ice cream, liqueur, crème de cacao, and vodka. Cover and blend until mixture is smooth.

**3** Pour into prepared glasses. Garnish with chocolate curls. Serve immediately.

nutrition facts per serving: 154 cal., 7 g total fat (3 g sat. fat), 10 mg chol., 51 mg sodium, 20 g carb., 1 g dietary fiber, 2 g protein.

*The cool flavor of peppermint gets a creamy twist that goes down easy, thanks to crème de cacao, light cream, and a smattering of peppermint candy.*

# peppermint
## frost

start to finish: 10 minutes  makes: 8 servings

1  lemon wedge
2  tablespoons finely crushed peppermint sticks
¼  cup white crème de cacao
3  tablespoons peppermint Schnapps
3  tablespoons half-and-half or light cream
2  tablespoons vodka
¾  cup ice cubes

**1** Rub rims of eight 1½- to 2-ounce shot glasses with the lemon wedge. Place peppermint on small plate. Dip rims of glasses in crushed peppermint candy; set aside.

**2** In a blender combine crème de cacao, Schnapps, half-and-half, and vodka. Add ice cubes. Cover and blend until mixture is smooth.

**3** Pour mixture into prepared glasses. Serve immediately.

nutrition facts per serving: 67 cal., 1 g total fat (0 g sat. fat), 2 mg chol., 4 mg sodium, 7 g carb., 0 g dietary fiber, 0 g protein.

For **wonderfully refreshing** dessert drinks, **chill glasses** in the freezer for an hour or so **before serving.**

*Get ready to glow after tasting this cheery concoction starring vanilla-tinged raspberry.*

# rosy cheeks

start to finish: 10 minutes  makes: 8 servings

½  cup whipping cream
¼  cup Chambord
3  tablespoons
     raspberry vodka
2  tablespoons vanilla
     vodka
½  cup ice cubes
8  fresh raspberries

**1** In a blender combine whipping cream, Chambord, raspberry vodka, and vanilla vodka. Add ice cubes. Cover and blend until mixture is smooth.

**2** Pour into eight 1½-to 2-ounce shot glasses. Garnish with raspberries. Serve immediately.

nutrition facts per serving: 98 cal., 6 g total fat (3 g sat. fat), 21 mg chol., 6 mg sodium, 3 g carb., 0 g dietary fiber, 0 g protein.

index

# metric information

*The charts on this page provide a guide for converting measurements from the U.S. customary system, which is used throughout this book, to the metric system.*

## Product Differences

Most of the ingredients called for in the recipes in this book are available in most countries. However, some are known by different names. Here are some common American ingredients and their possible counterparts:

- Sugar (white) is granulated, fine granulated, or castor sugar.
- Powdered sugar is icing sugar.
- All-purpose flour is enriched, bleached, or unbleached white household flour. When self-rising flour is used in place of all-purpose flour in a recipe that calls for leavening, omit the leavening agent (baking soda or baking powder) and salt.
- Light corn syrup is golden syrup.
- Cornstarch is cornflour.
- Baking soda is bicarbonate of soda.
- Vanilla or vanilla extract is vanilla essence.
- Green, red, or yellow sweet peppers are capsicums or bell peppers.
- Golden raisins are sultanas.

## Volume and Weight

The United States traditionally uses cup measures for liquid and solid ingredients. The chart below shows the approximate imperial and metric equivalents. If you are accustomed to weighing solid ingredients, the following approximate equivalents will be helpful.

- 1 cup butter, castor sugar, or rice = 8 ounces = ½ pound = 250 grams
- 1 cup flour = 4 ounces = ¼ pound = 125 grams
- 1 cup icing sugar = 5 ounces = 150 grams

Canadian and U.S. volume for a cup measure is 8 fluid ounces (237 ml), but the standard metric equivalent is 250 ml.

1 British imperial cup is 10 fluid ounces.

In Australia, 1 tablespoon equals 20 ml, and there are 4 teaspoons in the Australian tablespoon.

Spoon measures are used for smaller amounts of ingredients. Although the size of the tablespoon varies slightly in different countries, for practical purposes and for recipes in this book, a straight substitution is all that's necessary. Measurements made using cups or spoons always should be level unless stated otherwise.

## Common Weight Range Replacements

| Imperial / U.S. | Metric |
|---|---|
| ½ ounce | 15 g |
| 1 ounce | 25 g or 30 g |
| 4 ounces (¼ pound) | 115 g or 125 g |
| 8 ounces (½ pound) | 225 g or 250 g |
| 16 ounces (1 pound) | 450 g or 500 g |
| 1¼ pounds | 625 g |
| 1½ pounds | 750 g |
| 2 pounds or 2¼ pounds | 1,000 g or 1 Kg |

## Oven Temperature Equivalents

| Fahrenheit Setting | Celsius Setting* | Gas Setting |
|---|---|---|
| 300°F | 150°C | Gas Mark 2 (very low) |
| 325°F | 160°C | Gas Mark 3 (low) |
| 350°F | 180°C | Gas Mark 4 (moderate) |
| 375°F | 190°C | Gas Mark 5 (moderate) |
| 400°F | 200°C | Gas Mark 6 (hot) |
| 425°F | 220°C | Gas Mark 7 (hot) |
| 450°F | 230°C | Gas Mark 8 (very hot) |
| 475°F | 240°C | Gas Mark 9 (very hot) |
| 500°F | 260°C | Gas Mark 10 (extremely hot) |
| Broil | Broil | Grill |

*Electric and gas ovens may be calibrated using Celsius. However, for an electric oven, increase Celsius setting 10 to 20 degrees when cooking above 160°C. For convection or forced air ovens (gas or electric) lower the temperature setting 25°F/10°C when cooking at all heat levels.*

## Baking Pan Sizes

| Imperial / U.S. | Metric |
|---|---|
| 9×1½-inch round cake pan | 22- or 23×4-cm (1.5 L) |
| 9×1½-inch pie plate | 22- or 23×4-cm (1 L) |
| 8×8×2-inch square cake pan | 20×5-cm (2 L) |
| 9×9×2-inch square cake pan | 22- or 23×4.5-cm (2.5 L) |
| 11×7×1½-inch baking pan | 28×17×4-cm (2 L) |
| 2-quart rectangular baking pan | 30×19×4.5-cm (3 L) |
| 13×9×2-inch baking pan | 34×22×4.5-cm (3.5 L) |
| 15×10×1-inch jelly roll pan | 40×25×2-cm |
| 9×5×3-inch loaf pan | 23×13×8-cm (2 L) |
| 2-quart casserole | 2 L |

## U.S. / Standard Metric Equivalents

| | |
|---|---|
| ⅛ teaspoon = 0.5 ml | |
| ¼ teaspoon = 1 ml | |
| ½ teaspoon = 2 ml | |
| 1 teaspoon = 5 ml | |
| 1 tablespoon = 15 ml | |
| 2 tablespoons = 25 ml | |
| ¼ cup = 2 fluid ounces = 50 ml | |
| ⅓ cup = 3 fluid ounces = 75 ml | |
| ½ cup = 4 fluid ounces = 125 ml | |
| ⅔ cup = 5 fluid ounces = 150 ml | |
| ¾ cup = 6 fluid ounces = 175 ml | |
| 1 cup = 8 fluid ounces = 250 ml | |
| 2 cups = 1 pint = 500 ml | |
| 1 quart = 1 liter | |

# emergency substitutions

| If you don't have: | Substitute: |
| --- | --- |
| Bacon, 1 slice, crisp-cooked, crumbled | 1 tablespoon cooked bacon pieces |
| Baking powder, 1 teaspoon | ½ teaspoon cream of tartar plus ¼ teaspoon baking soda |
| Balsamic vinegar, 1 tablespoon | 1 tablespoon cider vinegar or red wine vinegar plus ½ teaspoon sugar |
| Breadcrumbs, fine dry, ¼ cup | ¾ cup soft breadcrumbs, or ¼ cup cracker crumbs, or ¼ cup cornflake crumbs |
| Broth, beef or chicken, 1 cup | 1 teaspoon or 1 cube instant beef or chicken bouillon plus 1 cup hot water |
| Butter, 1 cup | 1 cup shortening plus ¼ teaspoon salt, if desired |
| Buttermilk, 1 cup | 1 tablespoon lemon juice or vinegar plus enough milk to make 1 cup (let stand 5 minutes before using), or 1 cup plain yogurt |
| Chocolate, semisweet, 1 ounce | 3 tablespoons semisweet chocolate pieces, or 1 ounce unsweetened chocolate plus 1 tablespoon granulated sugar, or 1 tablespoon unsweetened cocoa powder plus 2 teaspoons sugar and 2 teaspoons shortening |
| Chocolate, sweet baking, 4 ounces | ¼ cup unsweetened cocoa powder plus ⅓ cup granulated sugar and 3 tablespoons shortening |
| Chocolate, unsweetened, 1 ounce | 3 tablespoons unsweetened cocoa powder plus 1 tablespoon cooking oil or shortening, melted |
| Cornstarch, 1 tablespoon (for thickening) | 2 tablespoons all-purpose flour |
| Corn syrup (light), 1 cup | 1 cup granulated sugar plus ¼ cup water |
| Egg, 1 whole | 2 egg whites, or 2 egg yolks, or ¼ cup refrigerated or frozen egg product, thawed |
| Flour, cake, 1 cup | 1 cup minus 2 tablespoons all-purpose flour |
| Flour, self-rising, 1 cup | 1 cup all-purpose flour plus 1 teaspoon baking powder, ½ teaspoon salt, and ¼ teaspoon baking soda |
| Garlic, 1 clove | ½ teaspoon bottled minced garlic, or ⅛ teaspoon garlic powder |
| Ginger, grated fresh, 1 teaspoon | ¼ teaspoon ground ginger |
| Half-and-half or light cream, 1 cup | 1 tablespoon melted butter or margarine plus enough whole milk to make 1 cup |
| Molasses, 1 cup | 1 cup honey |
| Mustard, dry, 1 teaspoon | 1 tablespoon prepared (in cooked mixtures) |
| Mustard, yellow, 1 tablespoon | ½ teaspoon dry mustard plus 2 teaspoons vinegar |
| Onion, chopped, ½ cup | 2 tablespoons dried minced onion, or ½ teaspoon onion powder |
| Sour cream, dairy, 1 cup | 1 cup plain yogurt |
| Sugar, granulated, 1 cup | 1 cup packed brown sugar, or 2 cups sifted powdered sugar |
| Sugar, brown, 1 cup packed | 1 cup granulated sugar plus 2 tablespoons molasses |
| Tomato juice, 1 cup | ½ cup tomato sauce plus ½ cup water |
| Tomato sauce, 2 cups | ¾ cup tomato paste plus 1 cup water |
| Vanilla bean, 1 whole | 2 teaspoons vanilla extract |
| Wine, red, 1 cup | 1 cup beef or chicken broth in savory recipes; cranberry juice in desserts |
| Wine, white, 1 cup | 1 cup chicken broth in savory recipes; apple juice or white grape juice in desserts |
| Yeast, active dry, 1 package | about 2¼ teaspoons active dry yeast |
| **Seasonings** | |
| Apple pie spice, 1 teaspoon | ½ teaspoon ground cinnamon plus ¼ teaspoon ground nutmeg, ⅛ teaspoon ground allspice, and dash ground cloves or ginger |
| Cajun seasoning, 1 tablespoon | ½ teaspoon white pepper, ½ teaspoon garlic powder, ½ teaspoon onion powder, ½ teaspoon ground red pepper, ½ teaspoon paprika, and ½ teaspoon black pepper |
| Herbs, snipped fresh, 1 tablespoon | ½ to 1 teaspoon dried herb, crushed, or ½ teaspoon ground herb |
| Poultry seasoning, 1 teaspoon | ¾ teaspoon dried sage, crushed, plus ¼ teaspoon dried thyme or marjoram, crushed |
| Pumpkin pie spice, 1 teaspoon | ½ teaspoon ground cinnamon plus ¼ teaspoon ground ginger, ¼ teaspoon ground allspice, and ⅛ teaspoon ground nutmeg |